KU-318-388

WARHAMMER

THE GAME OF FANTASY BATTLES

By Alessio Cavatore

PRODUCED BY GAMES WORKSHOP

British cataloguing-in-Publication Data. A catalogue record for this book is available from the British Library.

CONTENTS

BASIC RULES

ADVANCED RULES

THE WORLD OF WARHAMMER

The world of Warhammer is a land torn asunder by strife and conflict. From the high mountains to the deep jungles, armies march to the beat of drums and blowing horns, beneath a canopy of fluttering banners and gleaming standards. The Empire, greatest nation of Men, defends its borders against hordes of beasts and Northmen that worship the Dark Gods of Chaos. Below the peaks of the Worlds Edge Mountains, the stalwart Dwarfs defend their rocky homes from marauding bands of Orcs and Goblins, and the insidious undermining of the Skaven. Far away, on the fair island of Ulthuan, the High Elves dwell in near isolation, fighting a bitter centuries-long war against their twisted kin, the Dark Elves. To the south lie the sandy realms of the undying Tomb Kings who guard the riches of their tombs from plundering raiders.

BEGINNERS

For a complete novice, reading this book is not necessarily the easiest way to learn the game. If you can get to a Games Workshop store then the staff will be happy to give you an introductory game. Getting a friend who already knows the rules to teach you is another good idea. There are also sets specifically aimed at newcomers, such as 'Battle for Skull Pass', which contains a series of battles designed to teach the rules of Warhammer in easy-to-learn stages. It also has the big added bonus that it contains two complete armies.

If you are using this book to learn to play, then it can appear quite daunting. However, there are only two crucial steps:

First, you must, of course, get some models. You can start playing small games once you have three to four units assembled. Indeed, smaller battles are the best way to become acquainted with the rules – by concentrating on only a handful of units a player can get to know the game and some tactics without getting bogged down by trying to remember too much at once.

Similarly, you may want to get started with your models unpainted. You can paint your models later but this will take time, so it's best to learn how to play and fight a few battles first.

Secondly, you need to understand the basic rules of the game. This doesn't require reading the entire book, but rather skimming over the basic rules, which can be found on pages 2 to 46. Learning to move, shoot and fight with your basic troops is plenty to get started with, and the more advanced details – such as magic or war machines – can be learned later once you've mastered the essentials.

These are just some of the nations and armies that make up the Warhammer world. To play Warhammer is to enter this world and join the battle.

WHAT IS WARGAMING?

Warhammer is a miniatures wargame – but just what exactly does that mean? A miniatures wargame is a game in which players command armies of model soldiers and attempt to outmanoeuvre and outfight each other. Dice are used to work out the results as units of models – such as infantry, cavalry, monsters, and war machines – are moved into position to shoot, cast magic, or charge gloriously into hand-to-hand combat.

Wargames do not take place on a set playing surface like an ordinary board game, but instead any flat surface can be transformed into the battlefield. In the beginning, many players fight out their first conflicts across the kitchen table or upon a cleared space on the floor. A green cloth can represent a grassy battlefield and a few stacked books underneath for hills is a great start. More experienced or veteran players may have specially designed terrain boards or even a dedicated gaming table loaded with scenery.

The victor of a tabletop battle is the player who commands his army with the most strategy and skill. Superior tactics are the key to victory, while bold manoeuvres and luck will always lend a hand.

MORE THAN A GAME

Warhammer is a game but it can also be rightfully called a hobby. Most gamers dream of fighting a battle with gloriously painted figures on a sculpted landscape with forests and rolling hills, and so they make the effort to paint models and build terrain. Indeed, many devotees find these hobby-related activities to be the most rewarding aspects of Warhammer. Even a battle where everything goes against you is more enjoyable when it is fought over an awesome landscape with spectacularly painted models!

It takes a mix of skills, techniques and practice to become a master painter or expert terrain maker, but with a little patience and reasonable goals even your first efforts at painting or scenery making can be immensely satisfying.

DEGREES OF THE HOBBY

From humble beginnings, shown on the far right of the battlefield, you can build up your skills and knowledge until the left side of the battlefield is achievable.

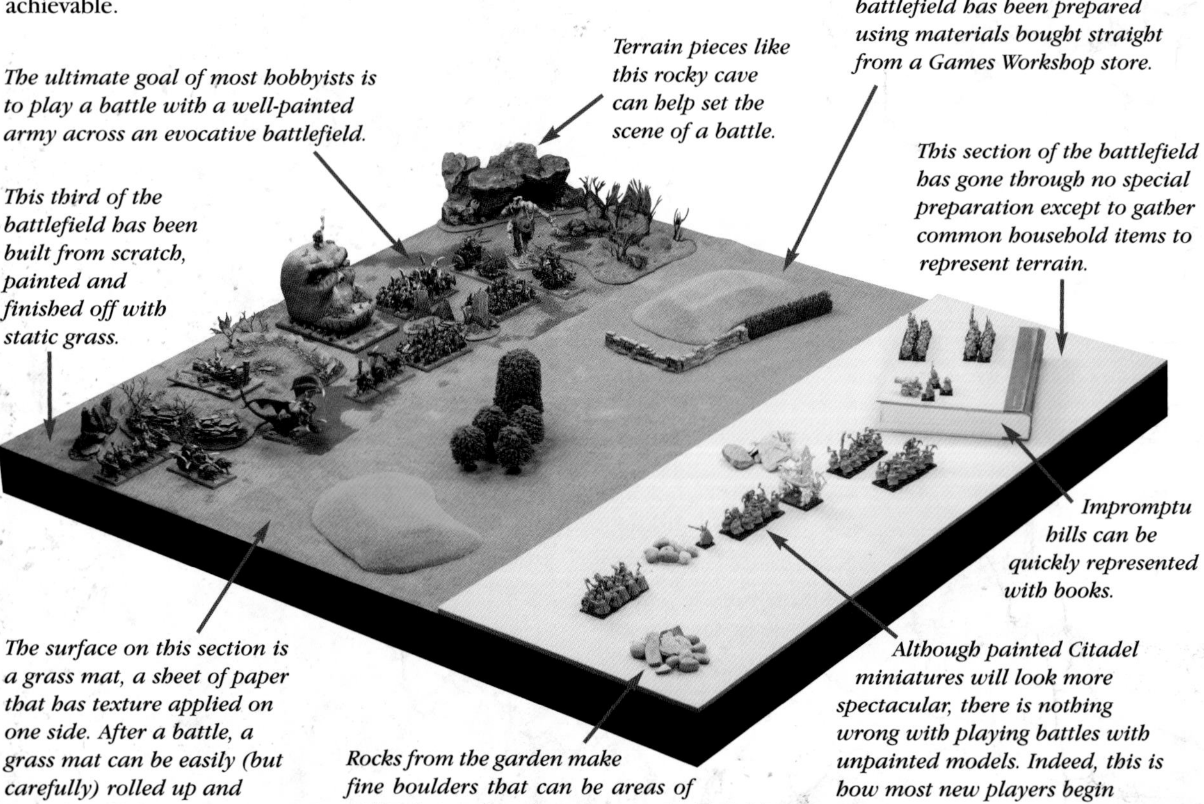

The ultimate goal of most hobbyists is to play a battle with a well-painted army across an evocative battlefield.
Terrain pieces like this rocky cave can help set the scene of a battle.
The middle third of this battlefield has been prepared using materials bought straight from a Games Workshop store.
This third of the battlefield has been built from scratch, painted and finished off with static grass.
This section of the battlefield has gone through no special preparation except to gather common household items to represent terrain.
Impromptu hills can be quickly represented with books.
The surface on this section is a grass mat, a sheet of paper that has texture applied on one side. After a battle, a grass mat can be easily (but carefully) rolled up and stored until the next game.
Rocks from the garden make fine boulders that can be areas of difficult terrain on a miniature battlefield.
Although painted Citadel miniatures will look more spectacular, there is nothing wrong with playing battles with unpainted models. Indeed, this is how most new players begin their wargaming career.

THIS BOOK

This book is divided into three main sections: the rules, the background of the Warhammer world, and an introduction to the hobby aspects of tabletop wargaming.

THE RULES

The rules start by explaining how to set up a game – both players will need an army of Citadel miniature warriors, plus a table with, preferably, some terrain laid out upon it.

The rules continue with the fundamental elements of moving, shooting and combat. This is followed with advanced rules that cover less common situations, and the abilities of specific types of model, such as war machines and terrifying monsters. The final part of the rules deals with magic – covering such things as wizards hurling fireballs, and arcane enchanted weaponry.

During a game you can consult the rulebook as much as you need. Very few players can remember all of the rules and for most of us, the rules section is a constant companion during our battles – often being referred to mid-turn to find out if such a move is possible or to double-check an action. Nevertheless, as you get more experienced, you'll find that you can often get by with just an occasional glance at the reference pages at the back of the book.

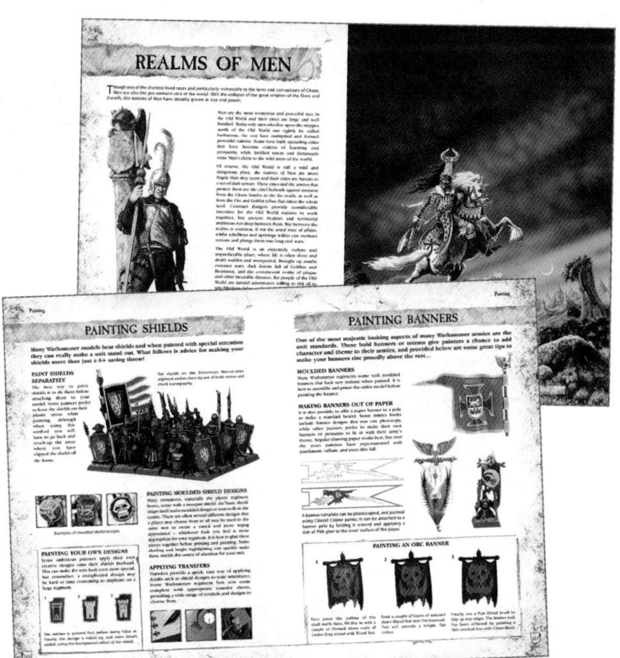

THE WARHAMMER WORLD

This section details the dangerous realm of conflict and war in which the game is set. It chronicles the history of the world – the coming of Chaos, the rise of the Undead, the Age of Man – and examines the armies that battle for supremacy over each other. The huge range of miniature warriors that are available for each army are showcased, so you can use this section to help choose which force to collect, as well as checking out the fiendish opponents you will be facing.

THE WARHAMMER HOBBY

The final third of the book puts everything that has come before into practice. It walks you through the essentials of collecting, assembling and painting your own army, as well as setting up a gaming table complete with terrain. You will find that these steps are not just a means to an end, but are actually highly enjoyable activities in their own right. The book ends with a look at the many exciting options that exist for expanding the rules of Warhammer, plus details of how to find further information and new opponents to battle against.

WWW.GAMES-WORKSHOP.COM

On the Games Workshop website you will find advice, tips and ideas on all aspects of the Warhammer hobby. There are rules clarifications and tactics articles, collecting and painting guides, and much more.

YOUR ARMY

 A GAME OF ARMIES

Warhammer battles are fought between armies, but what exactly is an army? The term 'army' is used throughout this book and refers to a number of 'units'. Units include regiments of infantry and/or cavalry. They also include war machines, monsters, and heroes – all of which are under the command of a single model – a General (or Warlord or King, depending on your chosen force). To find out more about each of the armies that you can play as in Warhammer (or battle against!) check out pages 142-202 of this book. For advice and tips on how to choose an army go to page 206.

An army can be almost any size – from a small warband of three to four units to a massive, sprawling horde. It is quite possible to play a game of Warhammer with an army that consists of every model you own, regardless of quantity or whether or not the miniatures are even from the same race. The rules for many common units are provided on pages 262-265, so you can get started straight away. Once you have collected more, there is a system of points values that allows players to fight evenly matched battles.

THE POINTS SYSTEM

To ensure that games are as fair as we can make them, every model is ascribed a points value which reflects its value in the game as closely as possible. This points system assigns a cost to each model relative to how well it can perform on the battlefield; a fire-breathing Dragon capable of devastating several enemy units will cost many times the points of a single Goblin warrior. This means that if you choose all the most powerful units, your army will be very small. Conversely, if you pick lots of weaker models, you will have the advantage of outnumbering your opponent. Whatever you choose, if the two sides add up to the same points total, then the game will be as fair as possible.

POINTS & TIME

In most battles, both sides choose armies to the same total points value. For example, 500 points a side gives a relatively small game that will last about an hour and can be played on a small battlefield with very little or no terrain. Larger battles (1,000 to 1,5000 points per side) will take a longer time to play. A 2,000 points per side battle will last about three hours and larger battles of 3,000 or more points could take an entire day or longer. There is

1 – *Boxed regiment of Chaos Warriors.*

2 – *The frames of plastic models from the regiment set.*

3 – *A fully assembled regiment.*

4 – *A fully painted regiment.*

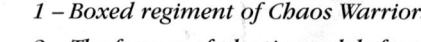

no limit to the size of a game, but if you plan on fighting a 10,000 points battle you will need a lot of models, time, and a large gaming surface!

THE ARMY LISTS

A list of basic characteristics and points values can be found in the back of this book (see Army Reference on page 266) but the full list of points values, troop types, magic items, and more can be found in the Warhammer Armies series of books. Each book covers one race and includes an army list that explains the troops the force is allowed, along with their points values. So, for example, there is one book that covers the Dwarfs, and others for the Empire, Dark Elves, Orcs & Goblins, and so forth.

An Army book also lists all the weapon options, upgrades, and defines any restrictions on particularly powerful heroes, monsters, war machines and elite troops. It would, after all, be plainly ridiculous for an army to consist entirely of fire-breathing Dragons, thundering cannons, or Giants, for example. An army chosen from a Warhammer army list will result in a reasonably balanced force that will make for an enjoyable game.

HOW TO CHOOSE AN ARMY

The army lists in each of the Army books are divided into four basic sections: Characters, Core troops, Special troops and Rare troops.

Characters represent individual heroic models – Heroes and Wizards – which are limited in number.

The most powerful are the Lords and Wizard Lords, while some armies also include priests, assassins and other individuals.

Core troops represent the most common warriors in the army. These usually form the bulk of the army and will often bear the brunt of the fighting. Every army has to include at least some Core units.

Special troops are the best of the army's warriors, as well as certain war machines or chariots. These are available in limited numbers.

Rare troops are scarce compared to ordinary warriors. This category includes uncommon monsters, unusual war machines and unique units of extraordinary troops.

The maximum number of characters, Special, and Rare units available varies with the size of the game being played, and some army lists may present additional differences.

For example, normally in a 2,000 points game, an army must include one character (the General) and a minimum of three Core units. There is no maximum to the number of Core units that can be added to the army, but the maximum number of characters is four (one of which can be a Lord), the maximum number of Special units is four and the maximum number of Rare units is two.

An example Hordes of Chaos army, chosen from the official Hordes of Chaos Warhammer Armies book.

THE BATTLEFIELD

Before opposing armies can clash, you will need to prepare an area for the game. The first concern is finding the playing surface that will actually become the battlefield where the armies of models will manoeuvre. This surface can be as simple as a cleared space on the floor or kitchen table, or as elaborate as a specially designed and modelled landscape.

The next concern is what, if any, terrain features there might be on the battlefield. 'Terrain feature' is a term used to describe individually modelled pieces of wargames scenery, such as a simple patch of forest, a hill or something more complex like a farmstead, border fort, or an ancient standing stone. These terrain features are designed to be placed on top of the gaming surface to create a varied battlefield.

Don't worry if initially you don't have much (or any) terrain as Warhammer can be played on a flat tabletop. Over time you can build up your scenery collection as terrain makes the gaming experience even more varied and interesting and a more

A building

A Standing Stone

A wood

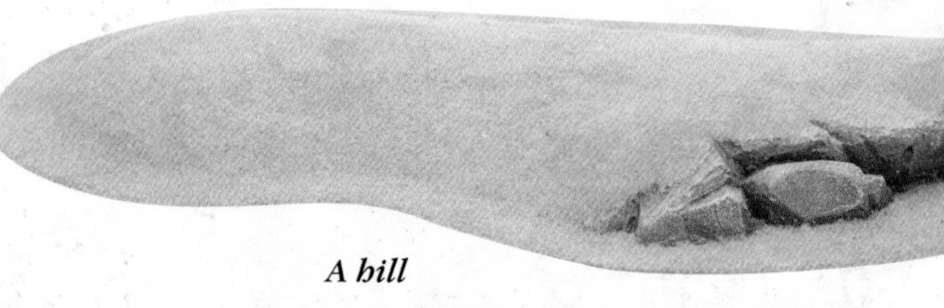

A hill

An obstacle

Terrain features are often modelled onto small bases, allowing flexible positioning on the battlefield and a greater range of layouts.

detailed battlefield certainly adds to the spectacular look of the hobby. How to make common terrain features, such as hills and woods, can be found later in the hobby section of this book.

For those who prefer to spend their time playing rather than in making terrain, Citadel has an ever-growing range of battle-ready features that can be purchased from any shop that stocks Warhammer games and miniatures.

TERRAIN FEATURES

The Warhammer world is a huge place and home to all manner of different environment. Trying to cover them all in this book would be quite impossible, but we have included a list of practical scenery as well as tips on how to make them later in the hobby section (see pages 234-241).

THE SIZES OF THINGS

First and foremost, the size of a gaming area will be limited by the amount of space you have available to you. Similarly, the amount and position of terrain is a personal choice, depending largely on your collection, so use the following recommendations as suggested guidelines and not as strict rulings.

Games of less than 1,000 points a side will work best played on an area of about 4' x 4'. At this size we'd suggest using two to four terrain features, such as hills, woods, or buildings. If players have modelled a particularly impressive terrain piece, they can use this as a special feature (for more about such special features see page 100).

Games of between 1,000 and 3,000 points work best played on an area of about 4' x 6'. At this size we'd suggest using four to six pieces of terrain, such as hills, woods, or buildings. Again, players can use a special feature if they have a suitable piece. Larger games require proportionally wider areas and higher numbers of terrain pieces, as you would expect.

The recommended sizes for terrain features will vary with the piece as obviously there can be tremendous variation in the size of hills, woods, swamps, and so on. For practical purposes it is recommended that a terrain feature cover an area of somewhere between 4" x 4" and 12" x 12". Some unusual terrain features may not fit within these broad boundaries, but these more distinctive pieces are not as universally useful as the other sizes.

A 4' x 4' table, with a building, a wood and a hedge.

A 6' x 4' table, with two woods and two hills.

WHAT ELSE YOU NEED

As well as this book, an army, an opponent and a battlefield, you will need the following additional items to play Warhammer:

PEN & PAPER

These will be needed to record your army list – detailing your regiments and their weapons, magic items and other information and make notes.

TAPE MEASURE

For measuring distances you will need a tape measure marked in inches, or a couple of plastic range rulers.

DICE

All dice rolls use a standard six-sided dice (usually shortened to D6). Sometimes you will be asked to modify the result of the dice roll. This is noted as D6 plus or minus a number, such as D6+1 or D6-2. Roll the dice and add or subtract the number indicated to get the final result. You may have to roll a certain number of dice in one go. For example, 2D6 means roll two dice and add the scores together.

You may also come across the term D3. As there is no such thing as a three-sided dice, use the following method for determining a score between 1 and 3. Roll a D6 and halve the score, rounding up: 1 or 2 equals 1, 3 or 4 equals 2 and 5 or 6 equals 3.

Sometimes in a game of Warhammer you will have to roll many dice to resolve mass shooting or a combat. To save time in these cases, it is best to roll all the dice required rather than one dice at a time.

RE-ROLLS

Sometimes the rules allow you a 're-roll' of the dice. This is exactly as it sounds – pick up the dice you wish to re-roll and roll them again. The second score counts, even if it is a worse result than the first, and no dice roll can be re-rolled more than once, regardless of the source of the re-roll.

Note that re-rolling a 2D6 roll means picking up both dice and re-rolling them both, not just one of the dice. For 3D6 this would be three dice, 4D6 would be four dice, and so on.

ARTILLERY DICE & SCATTER DICE

Warhammer uses two special dice: the artillery dice (marked 2, 4, 6, 8, 10 and MISFIRE), and the scatter dice (marked with arrows and HIT symbols). These dice are mostly used to represent the effects of various war machines, such as cannons and stone throwers.

Note that, except where clearly specified, the artillery and scatter dice cannot be re-rolled.

Special dice symbols are used to represent occurrences of luck or misfortune. From this point onwards these are referred to as HIT and MISFIRE. The corresponding symbols are shown below:

Misfire

Hit

TEMPLATES

Breath weapons of certain creatures such as Dragons, as well as the shots of certain war machines and a few magic spells, use templates to represent the area affected. There are three templates you need: a teardrop-shaped flame template and two round templates of 3" and 5" diameter respectively. At the back of the book we have included templates that you can photocopy for use in your games, but plastic transparent templates can also be purchased separately.

Leon Brachwurster's Mechanical Menagerie amazes the inhabitants of Wolfenburg.

PLAYING THE GAME

Presented here is a standard method for playing a battle, designed to produce a fair and exciting game.

1 SET UP TERRAIN

Before beginning the game, the pieces of terrain must be set up on the table. Begin by selecting the terrain pieces you're going to use (you need an amount appropriate to the size of the game being played, as suggested in The Battlefield section earlier). Each player rolls a D6 to determine who starts to place terrain (re-roll any ties) – the highest scoring player goes first. The player chooses one piece of terrain and places it anywhere on the table, but more than 12" away from the centre of the table. Then his opponent does the same, and the two players keep alternating like this until the terrain pieces run out (for the best quantity of terrain pieces, see The Battlefield section earlier), or either player declares that he will pass and stops deploying terrain. His opponent may then deploy one last piece of terrain and then the terrain set-up is finished. Note that both players must deploy at least one piece of terrain before they can pass.

A NOTE ON DIAGRAMS

Each diagram used in this rulebook is identified by two numbers. The first number indicates the page the diagram is on and the second number simply distinguishes between diagrams on the same page. For example, the first diagram on this very page is 2.1. If there was another diagram it would be called 2.2, a third would be 2.3, and so on.

2 SELECT SPELLS

After the terrain has been set up, it is time for both armies' Wizards to select their spells, as described in the Magic section (see page 107).

Once the Wizards have selected their spells, your armies are ready to be deployed on the battlefield!

3 DEPLOY FOR BATTLE

Armies cannot be deployed within 12" of the middle line of the battlefield, so that more than 24" of no man's land will stand between the armies at the beginning of the battle (as shown in Diagram 2.1). The areas outside this middle ground are called deployment zones. In a 4' deep table, the deployment zones are 12" deep, but if you're playing on a table of different size, you could end up having smaller or larger deployment areas. This is fine – the important thing is that the opposing armies must be separated by a distance of more than 24" at the start of the game.

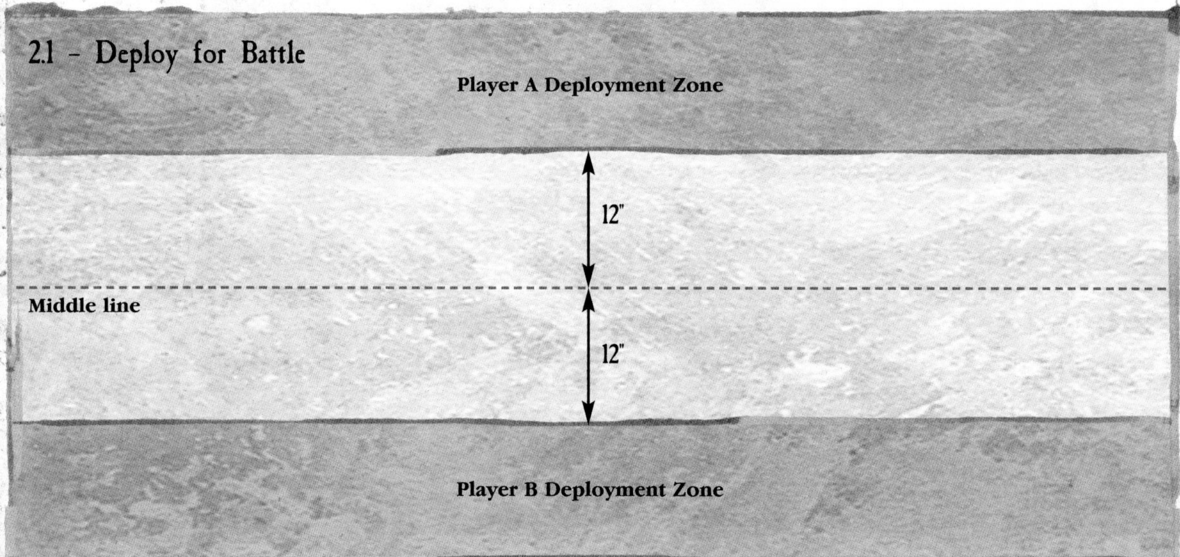

• Both players roll a dice once more, the player who scores highest must deploy one of his units in either deployment zone, thereby claiming that side of the table as his own.

At this stage, the players may need to move around the table so that they are now sitting behind their own side of the table.

• The other player then deploys one of his units in his own deployment zone.

• After that, taking it in turns, each player deploys one unit at a time in his own deployment zone.

• All the war machines in an army are deployed at the same time, though they can be deployed in different parts of the deployment zone.

• The characters in an army are all deployed simultaneously as the last unit the player deploys. Each of them may of course be deployed in a different part of the deployment zone and they may be deployed within units.

• Units with the Scouts special rule are not deployed with the rest of the army. Instead, they are placed on the table after all units in both armies have been deployed, as described in the rules for Scouts (see page 96).

4 WHO GOES FIRST?

After deployment is complete, it is time to determine which of the two armies is going to take the first turn. Both players roll a dice; the player who finished their deployment first (not including Scouts) may add +1 to their dice roll. The player who scores highest may choose whether to go first or second (if the modified result is a tie, the players must roll again).

5 PLAY THE GAME

The rules for playing the game are presented in the following pages of this rulebook (pages 4 to 122).

LENGTH OF GAME

A game of Warhammer lasts six game turns (both players get six turns) or until a player concedes defeat.

6 VICTORY!

At the end of game turn six, players use the victory points system to determine who is the winner of the battle. The complete rules to calculate victory points can be found on page 102, but for now all you need to know is that you have to try to wipe out the enemy army while minimising your own casualties. You also receive extra points for killing the enemy General, capturing standards and controlling large parts of the battlefield.

THE MOST IMPORTANT RULE!

Remember, you're playing to enjoy a challenging battle with friends, where having fun and keeping to the spirit of the game is more important than winning at any cost.

Warhammer is an involving game, with many different races, weapons, and endless possibilities. In a game of this size and level of complexity there are bound to be certain occasions where a particular situation lies outside the rules as they are written. Warhammer players should feel free to improvise where necessary, resolving such situations in a friendly and mutually agreed manner, and evolving the game far beyond the published rules if they wish.

When you come across a situation in a battle that is not covered fully by the rules, be prepared to interpret a rule or come up with a suitable house rule for yourselves.

When a situation of contention arises, players should agree on a fair and reasonable solution and get on with the game as quickly as possible. The most common way of resolving any disputes is for a player to roll a D6 to see whose interpretation applies in that instance. On the roll of 1-3 player A may decide, on a 4-6 player B may decide.

After the game has finished, sit down and discuss what happened with your opponent and see if you can both reach an agreement incase the same situation ever arises again (this is called a 'house rule').

Additional help and clarifications can be found on the Games Workshop website at:

http://www.games-workshop.com

CHARACTERISTICS

In Warhammer there are many different types of warriors, from lowly spearmen to lordly knights riding mighty chargers. There are many strange creatures too, some quite small like Goblins and others that are huge, such as fire-breathing Dragons. To represent these in the game, we have nine characteristics that describe the various aspects of their physical or mental make up. All characteristics are normally rated on a scale from 0 to 10.

MOVEMENT ALLOWANCE (M)

Often called Move, this shows the number of inches a creature can move on the tabletop under normal circumstances. Eg, a Man with a Move of 4 (M4) can move 4" when moving at full rate. A horse moves twice as fast and therefore has M8.

WEAPON SKILL (WS)

This defines how accomplished or skilled a warrior is with his weapons, or how determined and vicious a monster is. The higher the score, the more likely the fighter is to hit an opponent in close combat. An ordinary Man has WS3, whilst a battle-hardened leader might have WS4, WS5 or possibly even higher!

BALLISTIC SKILL (BS)

This shows how accurate a warrior is with ranged weapons such as bows or handguns. The higher this value is, the easier a creature finds it to hit with missile attacks. An ordinary Man has BS3, but a keen-eyed Elf has BS4. Some monsters have natural weapons that can be used at range (they might spit venom, for example) and their BS is used to determine whether they hit or not.

STRENGTH (S)

This shows how strong a creature is. An exceptionally puny creature might have a Strength characteristic of 1, while a mighty Giant has S6. Most Men have S3. Strength tells you how hard a creature can hit and thus how easily it can hurt an opponent it has struck.

TOUGHNESS (T)

This is a measure of a creature's ability to resist or withstand physical damage and pain, and reflects such factors as the resilience of a creature's flesh, hide or skin. The tougher a creature is, the better it can withstand an enemy's blows. A normal Man has T3, but a creature such as a Treeman with his tough wooden flesh has T6!

WOUNDS (W)

This shows how much damage a creature can take before it dies or is so badly hurt that it can't fight any more. Most Men and Man-sized creatures have a Wounds characteristic value of 1. Large monsters and mighty Heroes are often able to withstand several wounds, that would slay a smaller creature, and so have W2, W3, W4 or more.

INITIATIVE (I)

This indicates how fast a creature can react. Creatures with a low Initiative score (such as Orcs with I2) are slow and cumbersome, while creatures with a high Initiative score (eg, Elves with I5) are quicker and more agile. Humans have I3. In close combat, Initiative dictates the order in which creatures strike, since faster creatures will attack before slower ones.

ATTACKS (A)

This indicates the number of times a creature attacks during close combat. Most warriors and creatures have an Attacks value of 1, although some elite troops, monsters or heroes may be able to strike several times and have A2, A3 or more.

LEADERSHIP (Ld)

This indicates how courageous, steadfast, and self-controlled a model is. A creature with a low value is very unruly or cowardly! Humans have Ld7, which is average, whilst easily-scared Night Goblins have a Leadership value of only 5.

 CHARACTERISTICS OF 0

Some creatures have been given a value of '0' (sometimes shown as a dash: '–') for certain characteristics, which means that they have no ability whatsoever in that skill. This usually applies to creatures unable to use missile weapons, so they have BS0, but it might equally well apply to other characteristics too. For example, some creatures or war machines may have no Attacks (A0).

If any creature or object has a Weapon Skill of 0 then it is unable to defend itself in close combat, and any blows struck against it will automatically hit.

If at any time a model's Strength, Toughness or Wounds are reduced to 0 or less by magic or a special rule, it is slain and removed from play.

 PROFILES

Every model in Warhammer has a characteristic profile, which lists the value of its different characteristics. The examples below show the profiles for an Orc and a Man.

	M	WS	BS	S	T	W	I	A	Ld
Orc	4	3	3	3	4	1	2	1	7

	M	WS	BS	S	T	W	I	A	Ld
Man	4	3	3	3	3	1	3	1	7

As you can see, an Orc and a Man are similar in many respects. They both move at the same speed (4"), and they both have the same Weapon Skill and Ballistic Skill values, which means they are very evenly matched in combat.

Both have the same Strength value, so they can deliver blows with equal potency. When it comes to Toughness, however, the Orc wins over the Man – the Orc's value is 4 compared to 3. This is not a vast difference, but it does make the Orc better able to withstand blows and gives it the edge in any hand-to-hand fighting.

Both creatures have 1 Wound, which is the normal value for Man-sized creatures. The Orc loses out, however, when it comes to Initiative. This is not a terrible disadvantage, but it does mean that the Man will get to strike his blows before the Orc does when they get stuck into hand-to-hand fighting.

Both races have the same Leadership of 7, which is about average.

 SAVING THROWS

A creature's saving throw (often shortened to 'save') gives it a chance to avoid being harmed when struck or shot. Most creatures have a saving throw based on what kind of armour they are wearing, so their saving throw may be improved if they are equipped with better armour. The reptilian Lizardmen and other creatures that may have a thick skin or chitinous shell granting them extra protection receive a 'scaly skin' armour saving throw.

Armour saves are taken by rolling a D6 and trying to score equal to or higher than the armour save value. For example, if a creature has a 3+ armour save, it can normally avoid any wound it suffers by rolling 3 or more on a D6.

Some troops are protected by magic or are incredibly tough by nature. These creatures have what is known as a ward save, a special type of save that can protect them from almost any type of damage. We'll explain these saves in detail later on.

 CHARACTERISTIC TESTS

During a battle, a model might have to take a test on one of its characteristics. In order to pass the test, the model has to roll a D6 and score equal to or lower than the value of the characteristic involved. Note that if a 6 is rolled, then the model will automatically fail the test regardless of the characteristic's value and of any other modifier that might apply. If a model has to take a test for a characteristic that has a value of 0 on its profile, it will automatically fail the test.

 LEADERSHIP TESTS

Tests that are made against the Leadership characteristic of a model are done slightly differently to other tests. In the case of a Leadership test, roll 2D6. If the result is equal to or less than the model's Leadership value, the test has been passed.

If a unit includes models with different Leadership values, always use the one with the highest Leadership value.

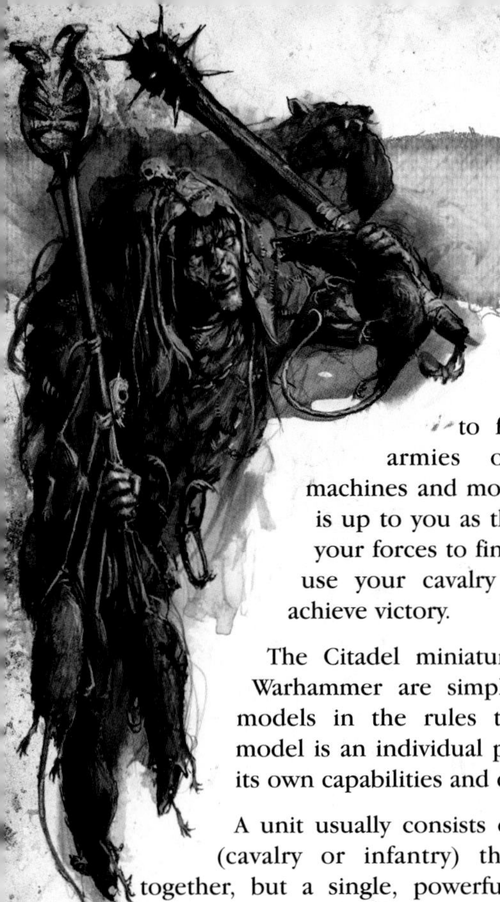

UNITS

Warhammer allows you to fight battles with armies of troops, war machines and monstrous beings. It is up to you as the commander of your forces to find the best way to use your cavalry and infantry to achieve victory.

The Citadel miniatures used to play Warhammer are simply referred to as models in the rules that follow. Each model is an individual playing piece with its own capabilities and characteristics.

A unit usually consists of several models (cavalry or infantry) that have banded together, but a single, powerful model such as a lone character, a chariot or a Dragon, a war machine and its crew, etc, are also considered to be a unit.

6.1 - Ranks & Files

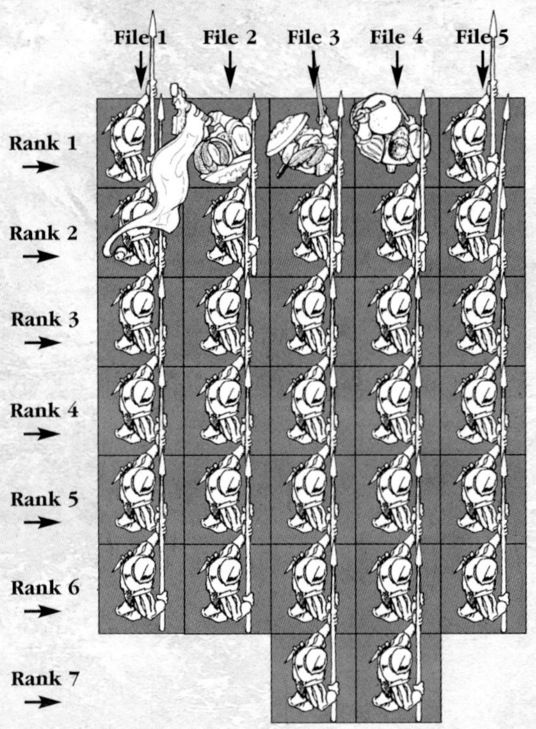

FORMING UP A UNIT

RANKS & FILES

Models in a unit of infantry or cavalry are arranged in a formation that consists of one, two, three or more horizontal lines, called ranks (See Diagram 6.1 – Ranks & Files). As far as possible, the unit always has the same number of models in each rank and, where not possible, it is always the rear rank that is left short (in which case it's referred to as an incomplete rank). The last rank is filled from the centre.

The vertical lines of models in a unit are called files, and that explains why sometimes the members of a unit are referred to as 'the rank-and-file troopers' (to distinguish them from characters that have joined the unit).

CHAMPIONS, BANNERS & MUSICIANS

Units of infantry and cavalry commonly include a standard bearer who carries the unit's banner and a musician such as a hornblower or drummer. It is also usual for units to be led by a champion; an experienced and able warrior.

The champion, standard bearer and musician, often referred to collectively as the unit's 'command group', are placed in the front rank of the unit whenever possible. When a unit turns to face its side or rear (see page 13), they are automatically rearranged in the new front rank.

As we shall see later, a unit can also be joined by a character, in which case these models are also arranged into the front rank alongside the champion, standard bearer and musician. Don't worry about this for now – the rules for characters are explained later.

UNIT TYPES

Units have different capabilities and are divided into several types (listed opposite). For example, when the rules refer to cavalry units, all troops that fall under the category of cavalry must follow those rules.

INFANTRY

Infantry includes all units of foot troops, be they Goblins, Men, Ogres, Trolls or any other of the myriad Warhammer races fighting on foot. Normally, infantry models are mounted on a 20mm, 25mm or 40mm wide square base. A typical infantry regiment can include 10, 20, 40 or even more models! Infantry forms the backbone of most Warhammer armies.

CAVALRY

The term cavalry refers to riders mounted on horse-sized creatures that have only 1 Wound in their profile, mounted on a 25mm by 50mm 'cavalry' base. It also refers to other four-legged creatures, such as warhounds, wolves, etc, that have 1 Wound on their profile and are mounted on a cavalry base. Cavalry units operate much in the same way as an infantry unit. A cavalry model is treated in all respects as a single model. Should the rider be slain, the entire model is removed from the battle. Cavalry models always use the rider's Leadership, Toughness and Wounds. The steed's Ld, T and W, as well as the rider's Movement, are never used.

WAR MACHINES

War machines are huge, lumbering engines of destruction, such as the Great Cannons of the Empire, Orc Rock Lobbers or the Repeater Bolt Thrower of the High Elves. Normally, war machines and their crew form a unit of three or more models.

CHARIOTS

A chariot is a wheeled war-vehicle drawn into battle by horses or other creatures and crewed by warriors armed to the teeth. Chariots are normally mounted on a 50mm by 100mm 'chariot' base. A chariot's crew and the creatures pulling it are an integral part of the chariot, and if this is destroyed they are killed. Powerful characters can also ride in chariots.

CHARACTERS

Characters are powerful individuals such as great heroes and sorcerous wizards. They can fight on foot as infantry, on a steed like a cavalry model, or ride in a chariot or on a monster. Some characters, like the mighty Daemon Princes of Chaos, are so large and powerful that they follow the rules for monsters!

MONSTERS

Creatures such as War Hydras, Giants, Griffons, Dragons or Great Eagles are called monsters. These normally move and fight individually and never join units. They are normally mounted on a 40mm or larger base. Sometimes monsters are used as mounts by powerful characters or they are goaded into battle by a group of beastmasters.

Empire Halberdiers

Chaos Marauder Horsemen

Dwarf Cannon & crew

Tomb Kings Chariot

Skaven Grey Seer

Dark Elf War Hydra & Beastmaster

 UNIT STRENGTH

Warhammer has several rules (such as outnumbering, fear, etc) where the unit with greater weight of numbers gains an advantage over its opponents. To measure this, each unit has a unit strength. In the case of most infantry units, you just need to count the number of models in the unit – for example, 15 Men on foot have a unit strength of 15 and clearly outnumber eight Elves on foot (unit strength 8).

Models such as cavalry, monsters, war machines, chariots, etc, are individually more powerful than a single man on foot. For example, each cavalry model counts as two infantry. To establish the unit strength of all your different units, you need to use the chart provided on page 71.

 FACING & ARC OF SIGHT

The direction of the front of the model's base is assumed to be its facing, the actual direction faced by the creature it represents. A model cannot charge or shoot at something it cannot see. To represent this, a target must lie within a 90° arc projected from the front of the model. Where models are on square bases, this can be imagined by projecting a line through the corners. This is the 'arc of sight' and determines which opponents the model can shoot at or charge (see Diagram 8.1).

 LINE OF SIGHT

In general (with the notable exception of the shooting phase), if one model in your unit can see at least one model from an enemy unit, that enemy is said to be 'in sight' of your unit.

A model's line of sight may be blocked if there is anything between him and his intended target that obscures his view. Thus, interposing models or scenery may block a model's line of sight to a target.

INTERPOSING SCENERY

Imagine a real battlefield with its contours, morning mists and haze of dust. Towering over our miniature battlefield we are unaware of all this, but the troops represented by our models would not be so lucky. Just as their real life counterparts cannot see through hills or hedges, we must assume that our models cannot see behind corresponding terrain features.

As it is impossible for us to say exactly what everyone's terrain looks like, it is not practical to be definitive about which kinds of terrain block line of sight. You must be prepared to use your own judgement within the following guidelines.

The easiest way of checking what a model can see is to get down over the table and take a model's eye view, but be reasonable about this, as in reality it would be much more difficult to see enemy troops than over a perfectly flat, mist-free gaming table.

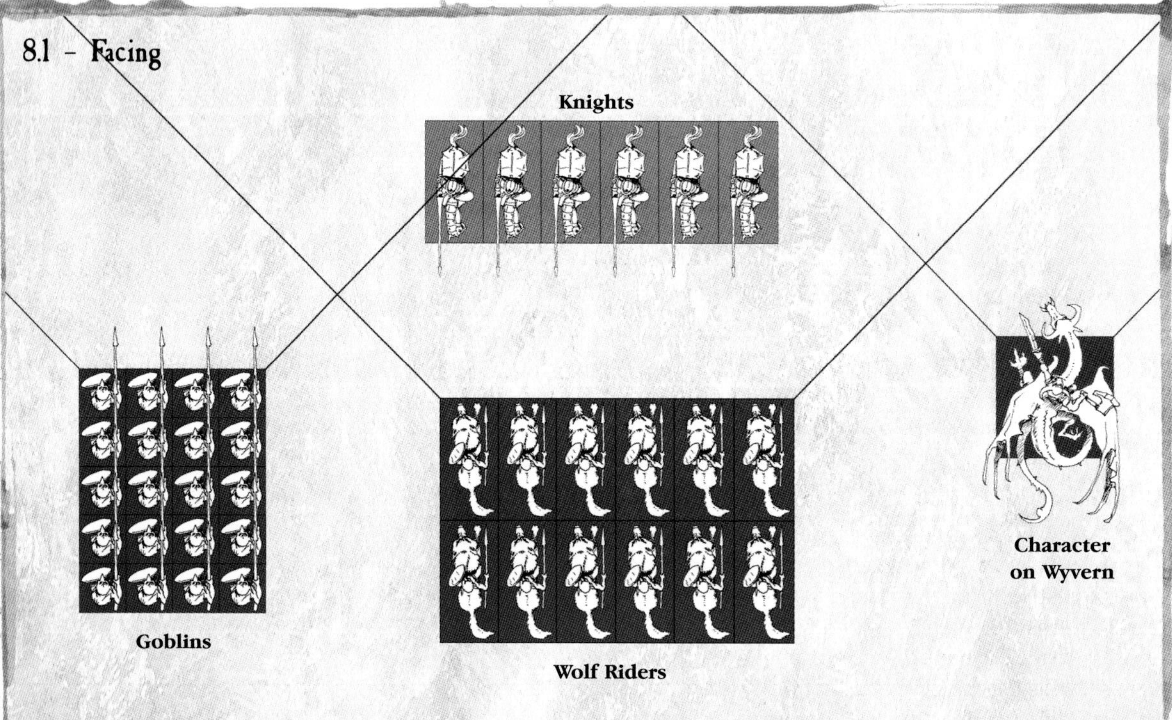

The unit of Goblins and the unit of Wolf Riders can both see the Knights, but the character on the Wyvern cannot see them as they are outside his arc of sight.

Woods
It is only possible to see through up to 2" of woodland. So, if a model inside a wood is within 2" of the edge, he can see out and he can also be seen. If it is further than 2" inside the wood, a model can neither be seen by models outside nor can it see them. If both the model and its target are inside the wood, then the line of sight is reduced to the farthest they can see – which is 2".

Normally in Warhammer, woods are represented by a few trees stuck on a base. It may happen that it is possible to see a model/unit on the other side of a wood because there is some space between the trees. For simplicity's sake, a degree of abstraction is required: players should always assume that the entire base of the wood is covered in trees as tall as the tallest tree on the base, and therefore the entire area marked by the wood's base blocks line of sight.

INTERPOSING MODELS
Troops, either friendly or unfriendly (ie, yours or the enemy's), block line of sight. Because of this, normally only models in the front rank of a unit are able to shoot, as those behind will not be able to see past their friends.

This does not apply if a target behind normal-sized models (such as Men or Dwarfs) is defined as a large target in its special rules. Large targets can draw a line of sight over interposing models that are not large targets themselves. Orcs or Goblins can't block line of sight to a Giant (large target), for example! This works the other way round as well, for example, a Dragon (large target) can be seen and shot at by enemy models over interposing friendly models that are not large targets, even by models in the back ranks of a unit of troops armed with missile weapons.

Note that this does not allow large targets to charge through any interposing models, which would object to being trampled by the huge creature.

HILLS & ELEVATED POSITIONS
Hills are tactically important positions, overlooking the entire battlefield and giving war machines and missile-armed troops an excellent opportunity to shoot at the enemy. Many battles have been won or lost depending on a General's ability to exploit the tactical use of hills.

Units on a hill can draw a line of sight from an elevated position and they can always shoot (and be shot at) over models that are not on a hill, in the same way as described for large targets. This means that models in the rear ranks of units on the flat may shoot against models standing on a hill.

When other pieces of terrain, such as woods, buildings or other hills block the line of sight of a unit on a hill, you should get down over the table and take a model's eye view to determine what the models on the hill can see. Therefore, most of the time your troops may be able to see over low obstacles that are on the ground below. It is difficult to give more precise guidelines about this matter as the terrain pieces in people's scenery collection vary greatly in size and shape. It is normally a good idea to discuss with your opponent how you are going to treat line of sight before starting the game.

MEASURING DISTANCES

Whenever you are measuring the distance between two models, use a tape measure, ruler or other similar tool to measure the distance between the bases of the models.

Whenever you are measuring the distance between two units, always identify the two closest models in those units and then measure the distance between their bases (see Diagram 9.1).

If a model does not have a base, as is the case with some war machines, tell your opponent which part of the model you are measuring distances from/to and stick to it for the entire game (popular choices are: the closest part of the model, the muzzle of cannons, the crossbar of stone throwers, etc,).

Note that when measuring distances for a charge, slightly different rules are used in order to take into account manoeuvring, difficult terrain, etc, as explained later.

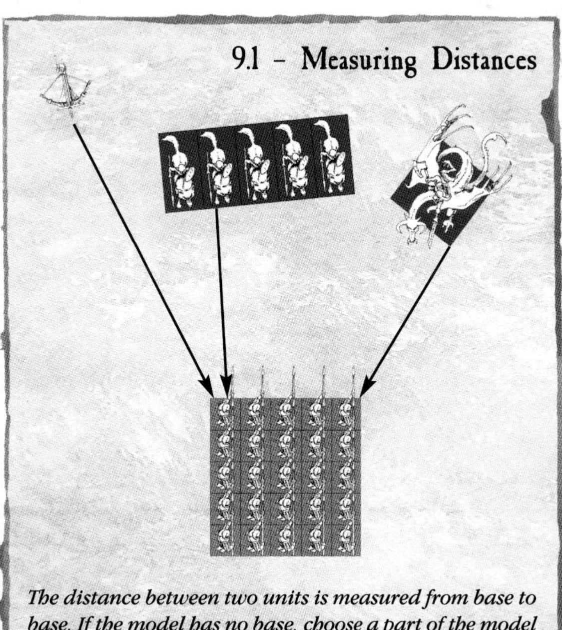

The distance between two units is measured from base to base. If the model has no base, choose a part of the model as a reference point (in this case the tip of the bolt).

THE TURN

Battles are fought between two opposing sides – two armies that will struggle for supremacy using all their armed might and cunning. The warring armies are commanded by kings and generals, wizards and heroes. Their model counterparts are commanded by you – the player.

In a real battle, lots of things happen at once and it is very difficult to tell exactly how the battle is progressing at any one moment. The fortunes of each side sway throughout the battle as one side charges and then the other, roaring with fury and bloodlust as they throw themselves upon the enemy. Mighty war engines lob their deadly cargoes towards their cowering foes and clouds of arrows darken the turbulent skies.

For simplicity's sake, in Warhammer we represent the howling maelstrom of action in turns, in a similar way to chess or draughts.

A game of Warhammer consists of six game turns. During each game turn, each player takes one complete player turn, so that by the end of the game both players will have played six player turns. For brevity's sake, the term 'player turn' is usually shortened to 'turn' throughout this rulebook and all other supplements for Warhammer. Players alternate taking turns until the battle is over.

Within the player turn, actions are performed in a fixed order – this is called the turn sequence. Each player turn is divided up into phases during which the player moves all his units, shoots with all his missile-armed units, resolves all close combat, and so on.

When it is your turn, it is up to you to keep track of where you are in the turn sequence. If you forget, your opponent should be able to remind you. The phases in a turn are always completed in the order given below, and all actions in that phase must be resolved before moving on to the next phase.

THE TURN - PHASES

1. START OF THE TURN PHASE

The rules often call upon a player to make tests or actions at the start of a turn. These are mostly Psychology tests (as discussed in the Psychology section), or special rules that apply to a specific race, such as the Animosity rule for Orcs & Goblins (described in the relevant Armies book).

2. MOVEMENT PHASE

During the movement phase you may move your models as defined in the rules for movement.

3. MAGIC PHASE

In the magic phase your Wizards may cast spells. The full rules for spellcasting and magic are described at the end of the rules section – they are quite advanced and not needed right from the start.

4. SHOOTING PHASE

During the shooting phase you may fire any missile weapons as described in the rules for shooting.

5. CLOSE COMBAT PHASE

During the close combat phase all troops in close combat fight. This is an exception to the normal turn sequence in that both sides fight, not just the side whose turn it is.

EXCEPTIONS

There are exceptions to the general turn sequence, when things are worked out as they occur rather than in any strict order and, regardless of whose turn it is, both players might have to do something at the same time. Occasionally the actions of one player will trigger the sudden appearance of a particular troop type, or may activate some special troop type or occurrence.

MOVEMENT

This section contains all the common rules for moving armies on the tabletop. The same rules govern almost all movement, including the movement of charging units and most compulsory moves. Any exceptions that apply to chargers and fleeing troops are discussed separately. Also, a few units move in a special way, flying creatures for example. These are exceptions to the usual rules which, for the sake of convenience, are discussed later.

Moving an army is an important and often decisive part of the Warhammer game. When opposing commanders are well matched, movement can be as challenging and satisfying as a good game of chess. However, unlike a chessboard, the tabletop is not divided into exact squares. Instead, movement is determined using a measuring tape or ruler.

The nature of the game, the varied terrain it is fought over and the stability of the models themselves means that it is impossible to be absolutely accurate about the movement of troops – the odd fraction of an inch will inevitably disappear as lines are neatened and models edged together. On the whole, this need not cause concern during play as it is better to keep the game flowing rather than worrying about unavoidable imprecision. It is recommended that where a move is especially important or an exact measurement is critical, it is good practice to agree what you are doing with your opponent before moving troops.

As with the turn sequence, the things that you can do within the movement phase are performed in a strict order. An overview of each part of the sequence is given below.

THE MOVEMENT PHASE

1. DECLARE CHARGES
If you want any of your troops to charge, you must declare this at the very start of the movement phase.

2. RALLY FLEEING TROOPS
If any of your troops are fleeing, you can attempt to rally them after declaring charges.

3. COMPULSORY MOVES
Move troops that are subject to a compulsory movement rule.

4. MOVE CHARGERS
Move charging troops and resolve other movement resulting from the charge.

5. REMAINING MOVES
Move the rest of your troops.

 MOVEMENT RATE

The normal Movement rate of a model (also referred to as its 'speed') is defined by its Movement allowance (M) characteristic value.

During their movement phase, units can move up to their Movement allowance in inches. For example, Men have a Movement characteristic of 4 and so may move up to 4". Elves, naturally faster and nimbler of foot, move up to 5".

Models do not have to move the full distance allowed, or can stay still if you prefer, but they cannot move further than their normal Move rate unless charging, marching, pursuing or fleeing (all of these types of move are discussed later).

Troops move and fight in a tight formation of one or more ranks. Such a formation is normally referred to with the coverall term 'unit', even though some races make use of more unusual terms such as regiment, squadron, mob, herd, etc.

When a unit moves around the battlefield it must maintain its formation, which means that models are not free to wander off on their own. The formation can move straight forward as a body perfectly easily, but if it wishes to change direction then it must make a manoeuvre.

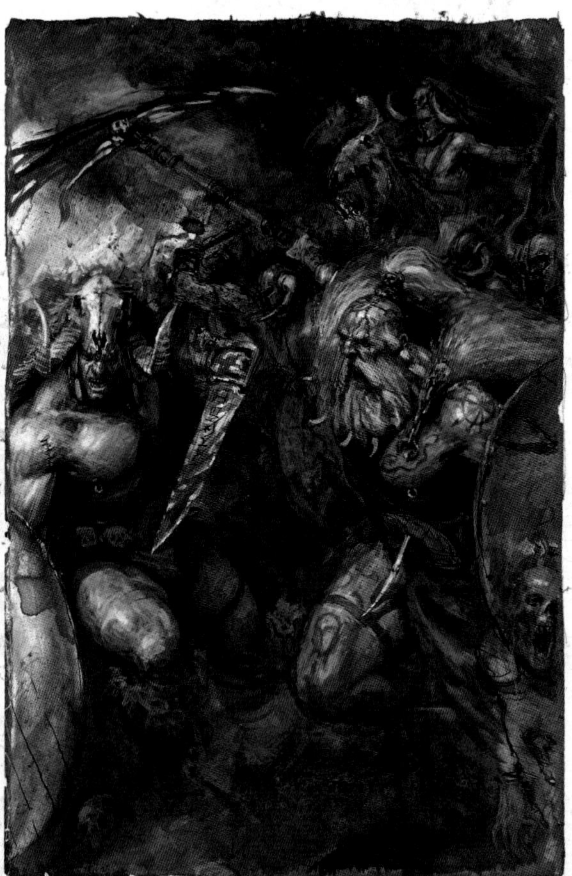

1" APART

Players will sometimes find that the movement of troops results in the tabletop becoming quite crowded, especially when several different units are engaged in close combat. It is obviously important to establish what units are actually fighting and which are close by but not engaged, perhaps merely passing by.

For this reason, opposing troops are kept at least 1" apart when they are not fighting. Models which would otherwise approach to within 1" of an enemy without engaging them are simply halted 1" away. Remember that in normal circumstances units may only engage in close combat by means of a charge. However, during charge moves a charging unit may approach within 1" of any enemy (not only the ones they are charging).

BARDING

Troops riding mounts with barding (horse armour) move more slowly because the weight of the armour impedes movement. A cavalry mount with barding suffers a -1" move penalty. For example, a Knight riding a horse can normally move 8". If the horse is wearing barding then the Knight moves 8"-1" (for the horse's barding), which equals a move of 7".

 MANOEUVRES

There are four specific types of manoeuvre that enable a unit to turn about or rearrange its ranks: wheel, turn, change formation and reform.

WHEEL

To wheel, the leading edge of the formation moves forward, pivoting round one of the front corners. The unit swings round like the spoke of a turning wheel and completes the manoeuvre facing a different direction (See Diagram 13.1).

When it wheels, the entire unit counts as having moved as far as the outside model. Once the wheel is complete, you may use any movement that the unit has remaining.

For example, a unit of Empire Spearmen might wheel 2" to the left and move 2" straight forward, for a total move of 4".

A unit can wheel several times during its move as long as it has enough movement to do so and is not charging. A unit that is charging is only able to wheel once, as described later.

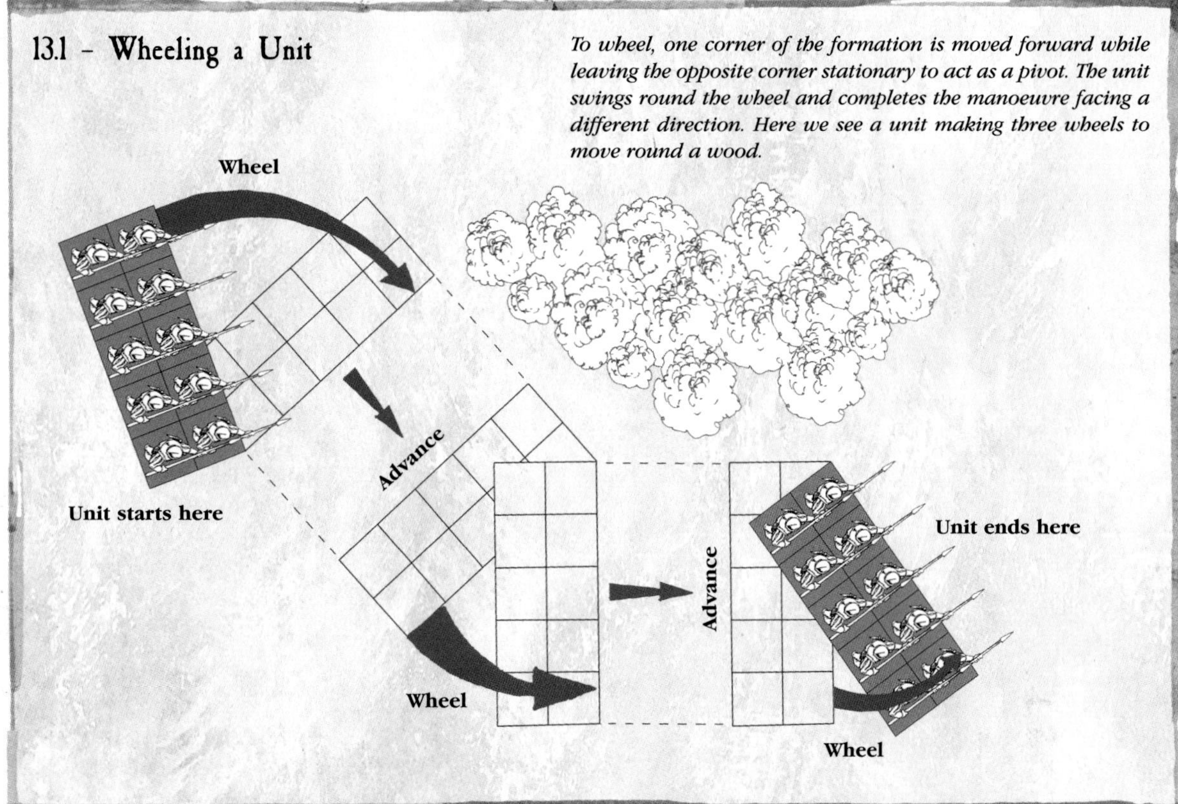

TURN

To execute a turn manoeuvre, all the models remain in place but are turned around through 90° or 180° to face their side or rear. To make a turn, a unit must surrender a quarter of its move.

For example, a unit with a Move of 4" must give up 1" in order to turn.

A unit is allowed to turn several times during its move unless it is charging or marching, in which case it cannot turn at all, but can only wheel.

When a unit is turned to face its side or rear, its champion is automatically rearranged into the front rank along with the standard bearer, musician and any other characters that are in the unit (See Diagram 13.2 – Turning). If there is not enough space in the front rank, such models are rearranged into the rear ranks.

When a unit is turned to face its side or rear, all models in the complete ranks are simply turned on the spot, while the models in the incomplete rank are moved to the rear of the unit in its new formation, as shown in Diagram 13.2.

The most common use of the turn manoeuvre is for a unit to turn around 90° or 180°, move half their normal move and then turn back to its original position. This effectively means that units can move backwards or sideways at half speed.

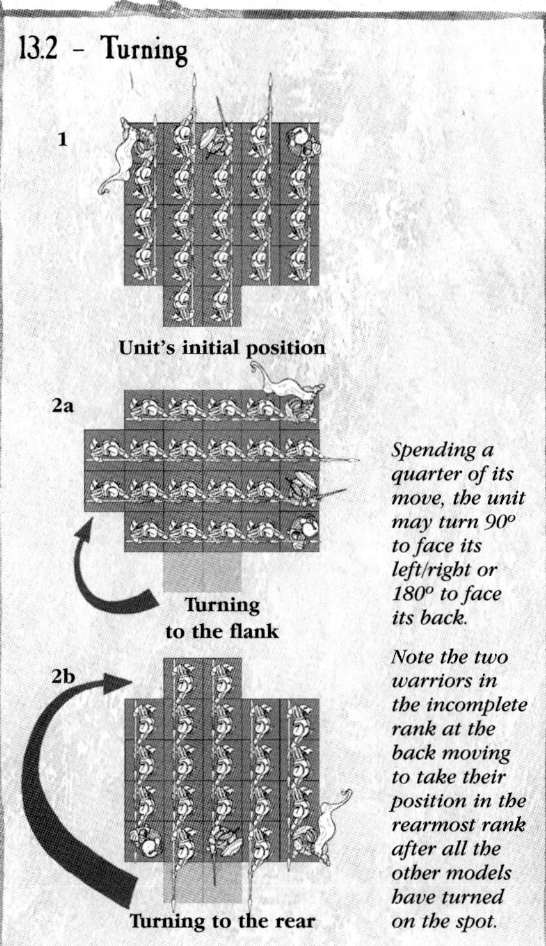

13.2 - Turning
1
Unit's initial position
2a
Turning to the flank
2b
Turning to the rear
Spending a quarter of its move, the unit may turn 90° to face its left/right or 180° to face its back.
Note the two warriors in the incomplete rank at the back moving to take their position in the rearmost rank after all the other models have turned on the spot.

CHANGE FORMATION

A unit of troops can also change its formation by moving models from/to its rear ranks to add or reduce the number of models in its front rank. For example, a unit that has five models in its front rank may add one model from its rear rank and have a front rank of six models. The models in the second and other ranks are then rearranged to match the number of models in the front rank.

A unit must surrender half of its move to add/deduct up to five models to/from its front rank. A unit may add/deduct up to ten models if it does not otherwise move at all. When redeploying models in this way it is important to remember that a unit always has the same number of models in each rank, except for the rear rank, which may contain the same or fewer models and is filled from the centre outwards (see Diagrams 14.1 and 14.2). The rear rank is still a rank whether it is full or contains only one model, although only ranks of five or more models are considered to be of any value in close combat, as described later.

REFORM

A unit of troops can change the direction in which it is facing and rearrange its formation all at once by means of a manoeuvre called reforming. The leader issues the order to adopt a new formation and the troops assume their new positions.

A unit of troops can reform during its movement phase as long as it is not in close combat, and is not subject to some compulsory moves. The player declares that the unit is reforming and regroups it into a new formation. Keeping the centre point of the unit the same, arrange the unit into a new formation of as many ranks as you please, facing whichever direction you wish, so long as none of the models in the unit move more than twice their Movement rate (ie, Men with Move 4 can move up to 8"). Characters, champions, standard bearers and musicians must still be placed in the front rank of the unit as normal.

A unit that reforms cannot move that turn because it takes the entire movement phase to reform. Also, reforming troops cannot shoot with missile weapons that turn because they are too busy assuming their new formation. Other actions, such as Wizards casting spells, are still allowed.

14.1 – Changing Formation: Reduce Front

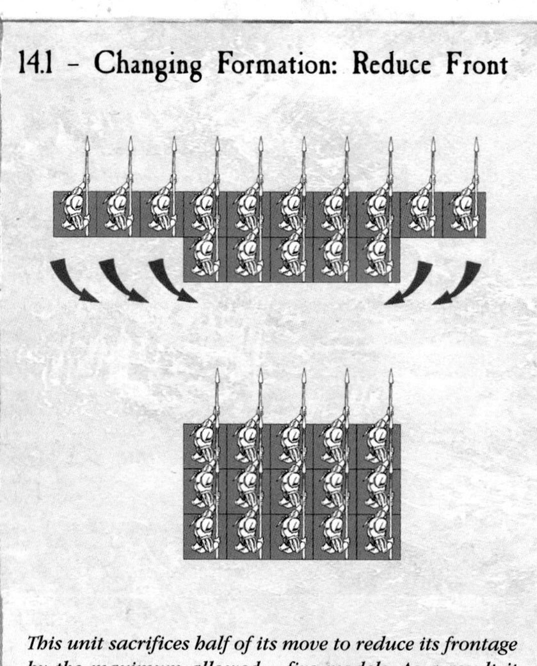

This unit sacrifices half of its move to reduce its frontage by the maximum allowed – five models. As a result it goes from ten wide to five wide and therefore gains an extra rank.

14.2 – Changing Formation: Increase Front

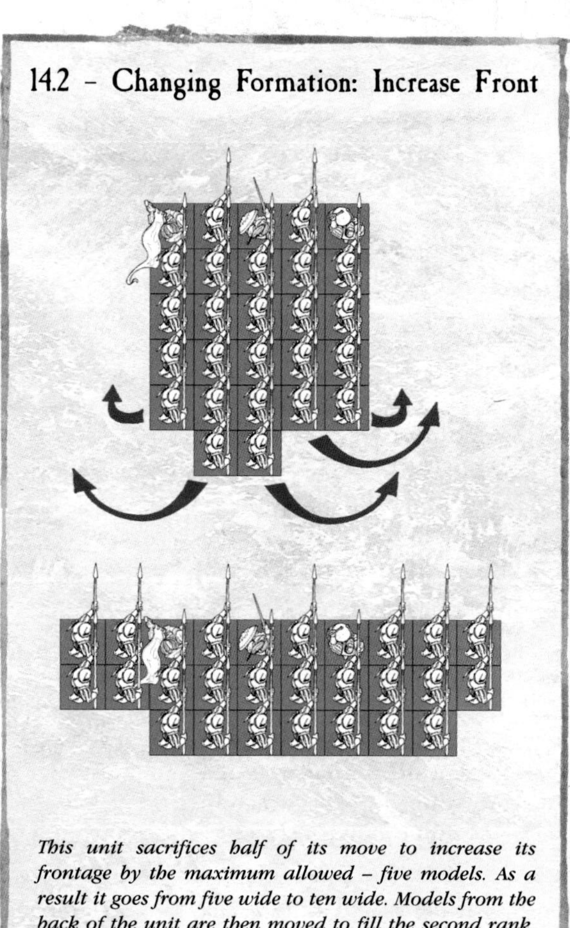

This unit sacrifices half of its move to increase its frontage by the maximum allowed – five models. As a result it goes from five wide to ten wide. Models from the back of the unit are then moved to fill the second rank, leaving only the third rank incomplete.

MARCHING

Marching at the double allows troops that are away from the main fighting to move more rapidly. This represents the swift movement of reserves to a critical area by means of a rapid march and helps to ensure that units do not get stranded away from the fighting. A unit that is on the march is not prepared for combat so marching is not suitable for a unit that is close to the enemy. In reality, no troops would approach the enemy without their weapons ready.

Marching troops move at twice their normal Movement rate, with weapons sheathed or shouldered. They are literally 'going at the double'.

Troops can march if there are no enemy models within 8" of them at the start of their move. If there are enemy models anywhere within 8" at the start of its move, the unit is too busy preparing to fight and so cannot march. Fleeing enemies are ignored as they present no immediate threat, and so they do not stop your units from marching. Note that the marching unit can move closer than 8" to an enemy as it moves.

A unit on the march cannot change formation or turn as this would disrupt its movement. It can wheel as normal, as you might imagine a column of troops would in order to follow a road, for example.

A marching unit cannot move through difficult or other obstructive terrain or cross obstacles. It must stop if it comes to these features. Units that ignore movement penalties from such terrain can march through it as normal.

A unit that has marched in the movement phase cannot shoot missile weapons during the shooting phase. Wizards with the unit can still cast spells.

INDIVIDUAL MODELS

Units that consist of models that move individually, such as large monsters with or without riders, can march move in the same way as units of troops.

MOVING OFF THE TABLE

Units can only move off the table when fleeing or pursuing, as described later.

Any other form of movement, whether voluntary or compulsory, treats the edge of the table as impassable terrain (unless differently specified in the special rules for a scenario, troop type, etc).

TERRAIN

Troops only move their full Movement rate over unobstructed ground. They will slow down if impeded by broken ground such as bushes or woods. Terrain is divided into four types to simulate this: open, difficult, very difficult and impassable terrain. As each player's gaming table and collection of scenery pieces is going to be very different, players should discuss before the battle begins which terrain features will be difficult, very difficult or impassable during the course of the battle.

OPEN TERRAIN

Open terrain is clear ground that doesn't impede movement at all. The battlefield is basically all open terrain unless otherwise agreed. This will normally include hills, as long as they are not too steep, as well as features such as roads and other firm surfaces.

DIFFICULT TERRAIN

Difficult terrain includes the following:

- Woods, orchards, growing crops & dense foliage.
- Brush, scrub and other clinging vegetation.
- Debris, wreckage, loose rocks and boulders.
- Areas of ruined buildings.
- Fords, streams and shallow water.
- Marshes, bogs and thick mud.
- Freshly ploughed, flooded and muddy fields.
- Sand dunes and areas of deep sand.
- Stairs, steps and ladders.
- Steep or treacherous slopes (this can include particular hills if both players agree before the game, otherwise hills are considered to be open terrain).

All distances count as double when moving through difficult terrain, so every inch moved across difficult ground counts as 2". For example, if your unit has Move 4 then it can only move 2" in a wood.

If troops move over open ground and difficult terrain during the same turn, then their movement over open ground is normal and movement over difficult ground counts as double the actual distance travelled. For example, a unit of Men (M4) moves 2" across open ground and then enters a wood. It now has 2" of its move left and this is difficult terrain, so it can only move a further 1" through the wood.

VERY DIFFICULT TERRAIN

Very difficult terrain includes areas that are even more arduous to move through, such as the following:

- Thick woods packed with briars and thorns.
- Sheer slopes.
- Fast flowing, but still fordable, rivers.

Distances travelled through very difficult terrain are quadrupled, so every inch counts as 4". Fractions are always rounded up to the nearest 1/2" to prevent unnecessary complication.

IMPASSABLE TERRAIN

Impassable terrain is terrain so difficult to move through that it cannot be crossed during the course of a battle and troops must go around it. It includes terrain features such as large monuments, rock spires, rivers, lakes, impenetrable swamps and sheer cliffs. Very small decorative elements of terrain, such as a signpost, a well or a chest should be completely ignored, just as if they were not there, and models can freely move through them.

OBSTACLES

Obstacles are things such as hedges, fences, walls and trenches that troops must clamber over to cross. Although obstacles may be similar in some respects to difficult ground, in that a hedge and a wood might both contain trees, there is an important difference. Obstacles are basically linear barriers, such as a wall, which troops must cross over before they can proceed. Difficult terrain describes an area of ground, such as a bog or marsh, that slows down a unit's overall speed.

It takes a model half of its move to cross an obstacle. So if a model has Move 4 it must surrender 2" to cross a hedge or a wall.

If a model has insufficient move left to cross an obstacle it has reached then it must halt in front of it and lose any remaining move. Where an entire unit of troops is attempting to cross an obstacle, the penalty continues to apply to the whole unit as long as any of the models are crossing.

Sometimes, the front of a unit may end up on one side of a linear obstacle and the back part on the other side. This is fine. Place the part of the unit that has crossed on one side of the obstacle and leave the part that has yet to cross on the other side.

As long as the ranks on both sides are in contact with the obstacle, this is perfectly acceptable. Once the troops have moved over the obstacle, the unit's ranks are returned to base contact. Remember that the unit suffers a half move penalty until all its troops have crossed the obstacle.

If a wall, hedge or fence has a gate in it then it is assumed to be open unless otherwise agreed, and troops may move through the gate without penalty.

If a unit's formation is divided by an obstacle then it may not manoeuvre by turning or wheeling, and it may not change its formation or reform. The unit must cross the obstacle before it can do any of these things. The unit may charge, but it must completely clear the obstacle before wheeling towards the enemy.

BUILDINGS

As buildings require a set of rather sophisticated (and therefore quite lengthy) rules, this book contains an entire section dedicated to them. This can be found on page 97.

Open terrain – a hill and a road

Difficult terrain – jungle and ruins

Difficult terrain – a steep slope and a stream

Difficult terrain – a wood and a field

Very difficult terrain – dense woodland, boulders and a river

Impassable terrain – a cliff and a deep pool

THE MOVEMENT PHASE

As we have seen before, the movement phase is divided in the following five sub-phases, which we will now analyse in more detail:

1. **Declare Charges**
2. **Rally Fleeing Troops**
3. **Compulsory Moves**
4. **Move Chargers**
5. **Remaining Moves**

1 DECLARE CHARGES

DECLARING CHARGES

At the start of your movement phase, the first thing you must do is declare which units will charge. Except in a few unusual circumstances explained later, you are never forced to charge. It is normally your decision which units, if any, will charge.

Charging is the only way that models are normally allowed to move into close combat. If you want to attack an enemy then you must charge him – you cannot simply move your model into close combat without declaring a charge first. All charges are declared at the start of your movement phase, in any order you wish.

To declare a charge, indicate which unit is charging and nominate one enemy unit that it is going to attack. For example, you might declare that your unit of Empire Knights is charging your opponent's unit of Goblins.

A unit may only declare a charge if at least one model in the unit can see at least one enemy model in the opposing unit, in other words, it has line of sight to the unit it wishes to charge. It is not necessary for every model to be able to see an enemy – the whole unit is able to charge the enemy so long as one model can do so. For more on line of sight see page 8.

Troops can only charge up to a predetermined distance – this is called a charge move and is normally double the Movement value of the unit in inches, as explained later. When you declare a charge you must do so without measuring the distance to the target, you must rely on your estimate of the distance to ensure that your troops can reach their target.

Before deciding to charge you must also take into account any terrain that might slow you down, as described later. Deciding whether to charge or not calls for a good judgement of distances!

18.1 – Stand & Shoot

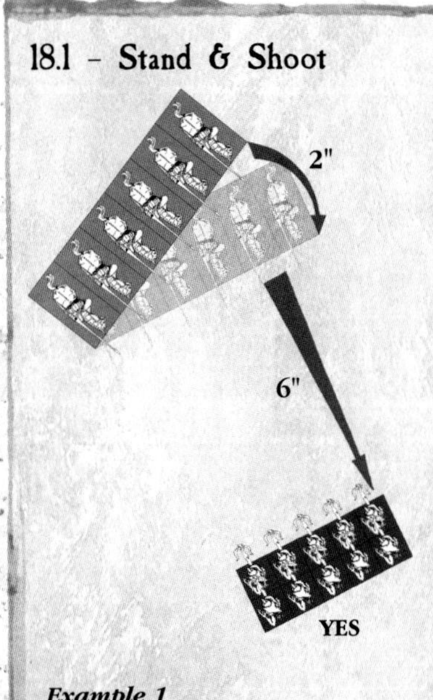

Example 1
The Knights have a charge move of 14". In this case, including the necessary wheel, they are 8" away, so the charged unit can stand & shoot.

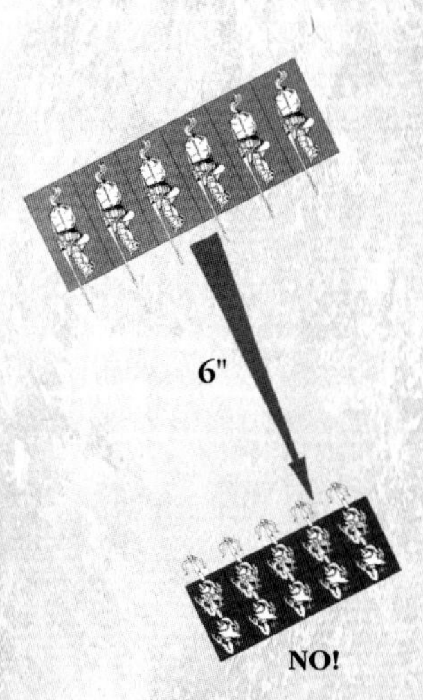

Example 2
The Knights have a charge move of 14". In this case, they are 6" away, so the charged unit cannot stand & shoot.

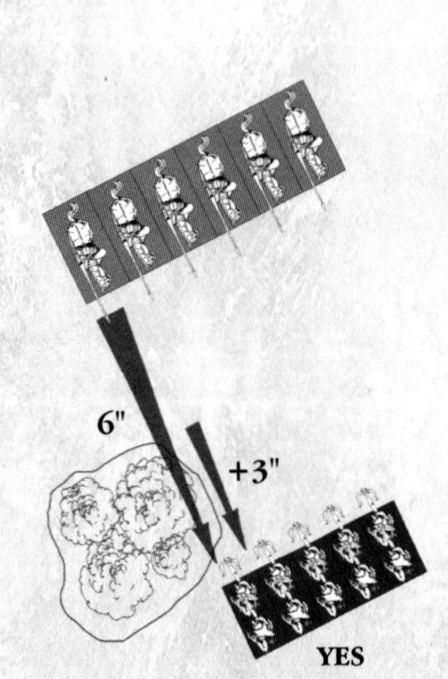

Example 3
The Knights have a charge move of 14". In this case, including the movement penalty for going through difficult terrain, they count as moving 9", so the charged unit can stand & shoot.

DECLARING CHARGE RESPONSES

After you declare your charges, but before you measure whether chargers are within range, your opponent declares how each charged unit will respond. Note that this is an exception to the turn sequence, as your opponent gets to move his troops, shoot, etc, during your turn.

A charged unit has three response options: stand & shoot, hold, or flee.

Units already engaged in close combat may only hold. Units already fleeing may only flee.

Stand & Shoot

If the charged unit has missile weapons and all of the units charging it are more than half their charge move away (taking into account wheeling and terrain penalties), troops can shoot at one of the charging units as they advance (see Diagram 18.1).

This shooting is worked out just before moving chargers, during the move chargers part of the movement phase – refer to the Shooting section for rules governing missile weapons (see page 25).

If the chargers start their charge beyond the maximum range of the shooting unit's missile weapons, their charge is interrupted and the shots are made at the maximum range of the weapons – the unit lets loose as soon as their enemies are within range of every firing model in the unit. If the volley fails to stop the enemy, the charge is then completed, while if the chargers Panic (see the Psychology section) they will flee from this position.

If the chargers are found to be too close to stand & shoot, treat the reaction as hold instead.

Hold

A unit can stand fast and receive the charge, representing individual troopers bracing themselves for the inevitable impact. This is the usual response of troops who do not have missile weapons or are too close to the enemy to use them.

Flee

Flee means just that – when your unit sees the enemy thundering down upon them, they turn tail and run! This is a rather desperate option as once troops begin to run they tend to carry on going, and may run away from the battlefield altogether, whether you want them to or not.

Units that have declared a flee reaction will flee in the compulsory moves part of the movement phase, (in the same order as the charges were declared).

Fleeing is done by first pivoting the units on the spot (around their centre) to face directly away from the charging enemy, and then moving them directly away from the charging enemy unit by 2D6" if their Movement characteristic is 6" or less, or by 3D6" if their Move is more than 6".

If a unit is fleeing from two or more different chargers, they will flee directly away from the enemy unit with the highest unit strength (roll a dice in the case of equal unit strengths).

2 RALLY FLEEING TROOPS

Having declared charges and charge responses, the player whose turn it is has the opportunity to rally each of his units that are currently fleeing, except for those that have begun to flee earlier during the same turn. Troops are normally forced to flee when they are defeated in close combat and that is why the rules for fleeing troops can be found in the Close Combat section of this book. They might also flee if they are frightened by terrifying monsters, or if they have suffered some other unusually traumatic experience. Fleeing troops are of no fighting value unless they can be rallied, which means they come to their senses and stop fleeing in readiness to fight once more.

In the 'rally fleeing troops' part of the movement phase, the player picks any one of his fleeing units and tests to rally it (as explained below). He then proceeds to the next fleeing unit and attempts to rally it, and so on, in any order he wishes.

To determine whether his fleeing units manage to rally, the player takes a Rally test, which is a normal Leadership test (see page 5). If the test is passed, the unit stops fleeing and has rallied. The unit must immediately execute a reform manoeuvre. If the fleeing troops fail their Rally test and continue to flee, they are moved next along with other compulsory moves, as described later.

If a fleeing unit has suffered a number of casualties it may be unable to rally – its warriors are too demoralised. If the number of models in a fleeing unit (including any characters that have joined the unit) is equal to or more than 25% of the unit's original numbers, the unit is still able to rally. If a fleeing unit (including any characters that have joined the unit) has less than 25% of its original numbers left, the unit cannot rally and will continue to flee until it leaves the table or is destroyed. Characters may never join/leave a fleeing unit.

For example, if a unit that was ten models strong, is reduced to two models and begins to flee, it cannot rally. If the same unit had been joined by a character before beginning to flee, it would now consist of three models and could still rally.

3 COMPULSORY MOVES

After the player whose turn it is has attempted to rally any units that are fleeing, it is time for him to make any compulsory moves that the rules require.

Generally speaking, a player can move his units however he wishes within the confines of the rules governing movement. However, sometimes troops go out of control for some reason, either because they are overcome by sheer terror, because they are compelled by magic, or because they are disorientated or confused. The player has no control over the movement of these troops and so these are referred to as compulsory moves.

The most common kind of compulsory move is fleeing. Fleeing troops initially flee away from whatever caused them to flee, and in subsequent turns towards the nearest table edge. They always move a randomly determined distance.

All compulsory movement is carried out before other movement takes place. This gives troops moving in this fashion the chance to get in the way, block lines of advance and do all sorts of other annoying things. Where both players have units subject to compulsory moves in the same phase (normally as a result of units fleeing from chargers), the player whose turn it is can decide in which order to resolve the compulsory moves.

4 MOVE CHARGERS

Once any compulsory moves are complete, including moving enemy units that have declared a flee reaction, it is time for the player whose turn it is to move any units that have declared a charge. Charges are resolved one at a time, in the order that they were declared. Remember to resolve any stand & shoot reaction that has been declared against the chargers at this stage, before measuring if the chargers have made it into contact with the intended target!

FLANK & REAR CHARGES

Sometimes you may find that your models are able to charge an enemy unit in the flank or rear. This is particularly good because an attack from an unexpected direction gives you an advantage in combat. A charging unit's position at the start of the movement phase determines whether it charges into the front, flank or rear of the enemy unit.

If the charging unit is in the target's frontal zone when the charge is declared then it charges into the front. As units generally begin the game facing each other, this is the most common situation that will arise. However, if the charging unit comes from the flank zone, it charges into the side; if in the rear zone, it charges into the rear. See Diagrams 20.1 & 20.2 – Front, Flank & Rear. Whether a charger is in the front, flank or rear of its intended target is determined before charges are declared.

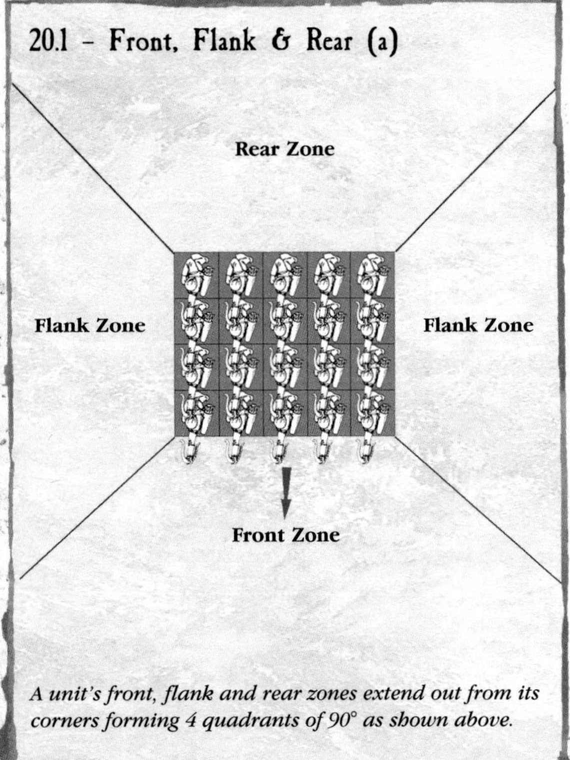

A unit's front, flank and rear zones extend out from its corners forming 4 quadrants of 90° as shown above.

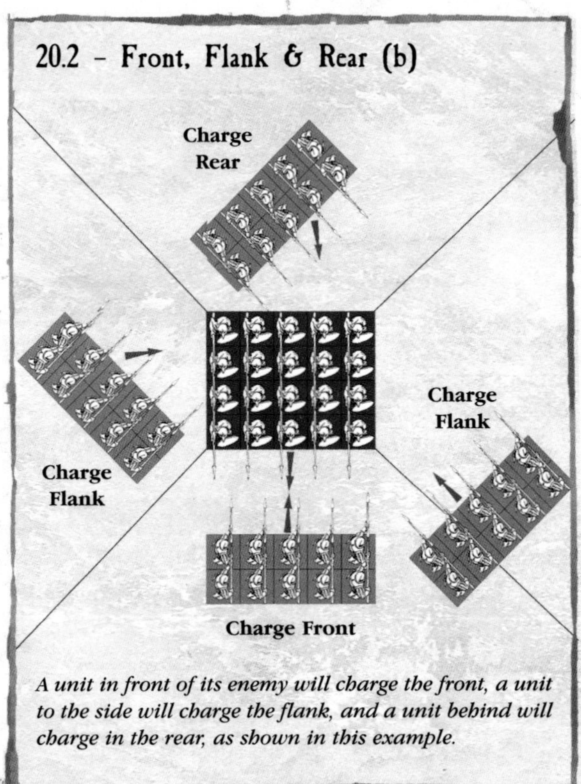

A unit in front of its enemy will charge the front, a unit to the side will charge the flank, and a unit behind will charge in the rear, as shown in this example.

If a charging unit straddles two zones, the unit is considered to be in the zone where the majority of its models are (as shown in Diagram 20.2). If the situation is so close you can't determine where a unit should charge, then roll a dice to decide.

CHARGING

Chargers move at double their normal Move rate, but must make the usual deductions for crossing terrain and obstacles. For example, mounted Knights have Move 7 and so can charge up to 14" in the open. If moving through difficult terrain or over an obstacle, such as a wood or a fence respectively, they move at half their speed, reducing their charge distance to 7". If the obstacle is defended by enemy troops, the charging unit does not need to cross the obstacle, but only to reach it, and therefore it will receive no penalty to its charge move (see defending obstacles in the close combat phase on page 35).

A unit may charge across an obstacle, but the unit's charge distance will be halved (for example, a unit with Movement 8 that is placed behind an obstacle can cross it and charge an enemy up to 8" away on the other side of the obstacle).

A FAILED CHARGE

If the enemy has fled out of reach, or if you have estimated your charge incorrectly, your troops might not be able to move far enough to reach their target. If this is the case, the charge has failed.

If a charge fails, the unit is moved at its normal Move rate rather than double speed. The unit is moved directly towards the intended target as if it were charging, but halts once it has covered its normal Move distance. This represents when troops have begun to charge before realising it is impossible to reach their enemy; consequently their movement peters out as they lose impetus and enthusiasm (See Diagram 21.1 – A Failed Charge).

A unit that fails its charge cannot shoot with missile weapons that turn, though Wizards may cast spells.

MANOEUVRING DURING A CHARGE

A charging unit cannot turn, change formation or reform – it may only wheel. This is because the troops are running or galloping once the charge has begun and are unable to execute delicate manoeuvres even if they were able to hear the orders of their leaders above the din.

When a unit charges an enemy, the player must endeavour to bring the maximum number of models from both sides into combat. This can sometimes be achieved by moving the chargers straight forward, but often it will be necessary to wheel slightly to face the enemy.

During a charge, a unit can wheel only once at any one point during its move. It can, and indeed must, wheel in order to maximise the number of models able to fight. Note that the unit does not have to complete its wheel if this would mean that it could not reach the enemy at all.

If chargers need to wheel towards their target, execute the wheel as already described, measuring the distance wheeled as you normally would. This distance counts as part of the total distance charged. For example, if a unit can charge 12", it might wheel 4" to bring models to face the enemy and then move up to 8" towards them.

Once a unit has completed any required wheel, it is moved straight forward towards the enemy and stops as soon as the two units touch.

ALIGNING THE COMBATANTS

Once the charging unit is in contact, it is automatically aligned against its enemy to form a battle line (See Diagram 22.1). This extra alignment move is free.

If it is impractical to align a unit properly because of interposing terrain, other models, or whatever, then it is acceptable to realign the charged unit as well (or instead) so that the battle lines remain neat. A confusing situation may arise when interposing terrain or models make it impossible to

21.1 – A Failed Charge

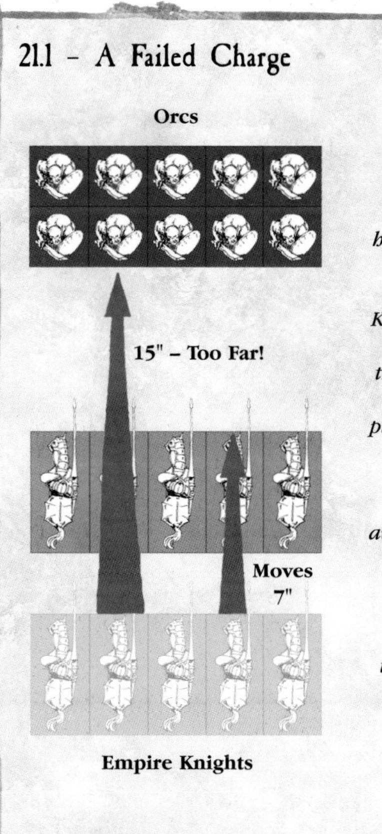

The Knights have declared a charge against the Orcs. The Knights' normal move is 7", so they can charge up to 14". The player measures the distance and finds the Orcs are 15" away – disaster! As the charge has failed, the unit must now move towards the Orcs as if it were charging, but must halt once it has covered its normal Move distance of 7".

align the whole unit, for example. Rather than clutter the rules with endless clarifications, we have included further examples on our website.

MOVING ENGAGED UNITS

Once opposing units are engaged in close combat they may not move away until one side or the other flees or is destroyed. Models already engaged in combat at the start of their turn cannot move, but must continue to fight in the close combat phase.

UNITS FLEEING FROM THE CHARGE

Occasionally, a flee charge reaction may cause complex situations to arise. The examples that follow cover the most common cases:

If a unit flees as it is charged, then it will move directly away from its chargers either 2D6" or 3D6" depending on whether its Movement rate is up to 6" or more than 6", as explained on page 19. It may be that fleeing troops move too far for the chargers to catch them, in which case the charge fails and the chargers must move their normal Move rate exactly as for any other failed charge (See Diagram 22.2).

Caught!

If fleeing troops do not move far enough away to avoid their attackers then they are in deep trouble! If the chargers have sufficient movement to catch them, the fleeing unit is destroyed (run into the ground or scattered beyond any hope of recovery) and immediately removed from the battle. The charging unit is moved its full charge distance, straight through the final position of the fleeing unit.

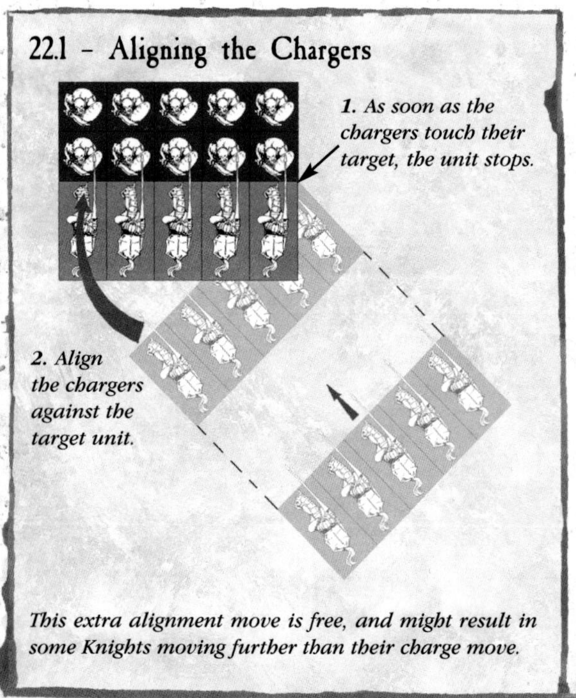

22.1 - Aligning the Chargers
1. As soon as the chargers touch their target, the unit stops.
2. Align the chargers against the target unit.

This extra alignment move is free, and might result in some Knights moving further than their charge move.

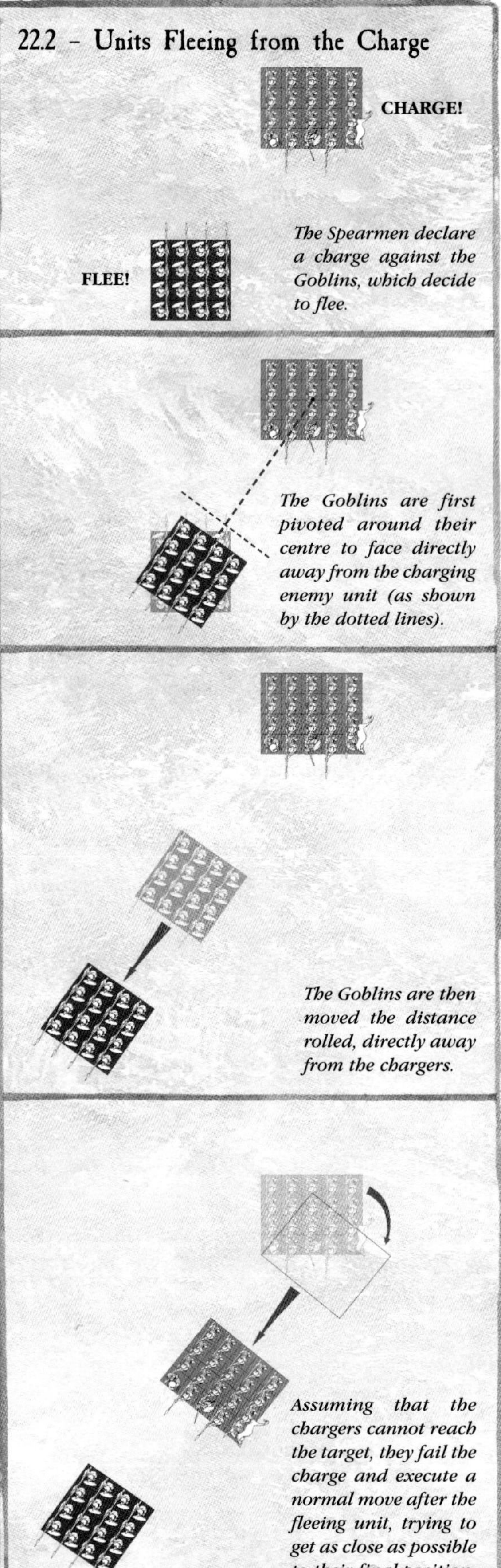

The Spearmen declare a charge against the Goblins, which decide to flee.

The Goblins are first pivoted around their centre to face directly away from the charging enemy unit (as shown by the dotted lines).

The Goblins are then moved the distance rolled, directly away from the chargers.

Assuming that the chargers cannot reach the target, they fail the charge and execute a normal move after the fleeing unit, trying to get as close as possible to their final position.

Enemy in the way

After a unit has fled from the charge, it can happen that the chargers, as they make their full charge move straight after the intended target (or right through them!), run into another enemy unit that is in the way of their move. Note that this may happen even if the original target is now so far away that the charge has failed.

If the charging unit runs into another enemy, they are allowed to immediately declare a new charge against the enemy unit now in their way.

The chargers do not have to do this, and can instead choose to stop their move 1" away from the enemy, as normal.

If the chargers decide not to stop their move, the player must now declare that his unit is charging against the new target, and the target must make a charge reaction as normal. If this second target flees as well, so that another unit lies in the way of the new move of the chargers, this procedure is repeated until the situation comes to either a successful charge or a failed charge.

MULTIPLE CHARGERS

When two or more friendly units are charging against a single enemy unit's front, flank or rear, they are moved in simultaneously and must try to bring as many models into the fight as possible.

If there is not enough space for all charging units to bring all of their models into combat, the units should try to bring into the combat an equal number of models and still fill the space available as much as possible (see Diagram 23.1).

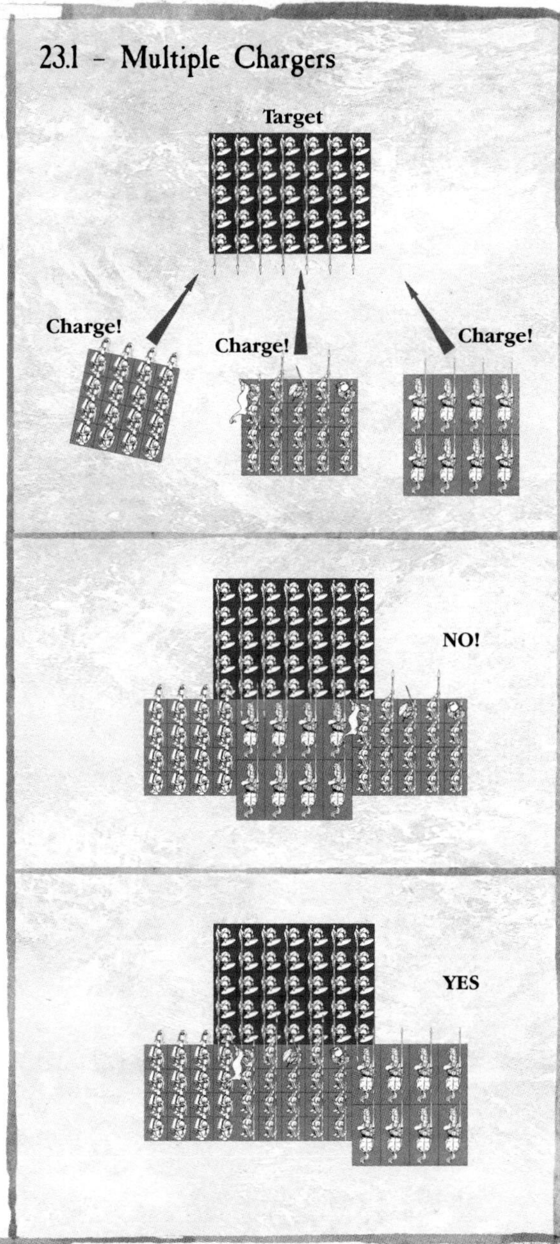

MULTIPLE TARGETS

It might happen that a unit cannot charge its intended target without simultaneously charging other enemy units. This is normally the case when charging a line of enemy units that are very close and flush to each other (see Diagram 24.1).

24.1 - Multiple Targets

A B C

CHARGE!

The Goblins could choose to charge unit A or C, in order to fight only two enemy units. Instead they decided to charge unit B, to engage all three units in the fight. Unit B decided to stand & shoot and the units of Spearmen decided to hold their ground.

In such awkward cases, a unit is allowed to charge all the enemy units involved, which can all declare their own charge reaction.

Note that the charging unit must still try to engage as many models as possible from the intended target and then, after this condition has been met, it must try to engage as many models as possible in the other units charged.

ODDBALL STUFF

A charge can sometimes trigger unexpected actions from the enemy (due to some spells, magic items, special rules, etc). It is up to the opponent to say that he has out of sequence movements or actions to perform at the appropriate moment.

5 REMAINING MOVES

Once compulsory moves and charges have been resolved, it is time to move the rest of your troops. Generally speaking, you do not have to move troops at all if you do not want to, or you can move them as short or as great a distance as you like, up to their permitted maximum Move distance.

THE MAGIC PHASE

After the movement phase is finished, the turn continues with the magic phase.

Magic belongs to the advanced rules, and the relevant section can be found on page 104. We shall now continue the core rules with the shooting phase.

SHOOTING

Though most often a battle will be decided with bloody close quarters fighting, hails of crossbow bolts and deadly cannonballs can soften up the enemy for the final charge, or perhaps even panic them from the field without a fight.

Once the movement and magic phases are over, it is time to work out shooting. Troops armed with bows, crossbows or other missile weapons may shoot at any enemy targets they can see. Unless otherwise specified, each model can only make one shooting attack in each shooting phase. You may also shoot with any war machines such as stone throwers, cannons, etc.

You always start shooting with any weapons that require you to guess the range of the shot (such as cannons and stone throwers for example). Guess all the ranges of these before measuring any of them. Next, resolve the results of these shots using the rules described in the War Machines section on page 84.

Once this first part is complete, continue on to the rest of your shooting. Nominate one of your units that you want to shoot and select one enemy unit you wish your unit to shoot at. Once you have declared your target, measure the range and resolve shooting using the rules described. Then proceed to the next unit that is shooting and continue as above until you have shot with everything able to do so, including any non-guess range war machines you may have.

THE SHOOTING PHASE

- Declare the ranges at which all guess-range weapons are firing.
- Resolve the firing of all guess-range weapons, in any order you wish.
- Resolve the firing of all units equipped with missile weapons that do not require you to guess the range, in any order you wish.
- The opposing player makes any Panic tests required (as explained in the Psychology section on page 48).

LINE OF SIGHT

The rules for determining a unit's line of sight are given on page 8, but in the case of shooting, each model firing needs to see its target (instead of using the entire unit's line of sight). It sometimes happens that some models in a firing unit will have line of sight to the target while other models in the unit will not (the target may be out of their arc of sight or obscured by terrain or other models). If this is the case, only those that have line of sight to the target can shoot and the rest automatically miss.

Remember that models and terrain block line of sight. This means that only models in the front rank of a unit are normally able to shoot, as those behind will not be able to see past their friends.

MISSILE FIRE FROM HILLS

Troops on a hill are considered to be in a good position to fire, so can fire with one additional rank compared to missile-armed troops on flat ground. For example, a unit of archers can shoot with its first two ranks when standing on a hill.

Troops on a hill can also draw their line of sight over models that are not on a hill. This works the other way around of course, making models on a hill visible to models that are not on a hill over intervening models, even over models in the same unit (see page 9 – Hills & Elevated Positions).

RANGE

All missile weapons have a maximum range that indicates the furthest distance they can shoot. If your declared target lies beyond this maximum range, your shots automatically miss. This is why you must pick targets before measuring the range.

For example, a unit of crossbowmen, whose weapons have a range of 30", declares that it is firing on the nearest Orc unit. When the distance is measured, it is found that the Orcs are 32" away. The hail of bolts therefore falls short of the Orcs.

It often happens that some models in a firing unit will be within range and other models in the unit will be out of range. If this is the case, only those that are in range can shoot and the remainder automatically miss.

These ranges are the maximum distances that the weapons can fire. Missiles lose power and accuracy long before they reach their maximum range, so ranges are divided into two types: short range and long range.

Targets within half the maximum range of the weapon are in short range.

Targets further than this (but still within maximum range!) are in long range.

For example, a short bow has a maximum range of 16". Targets within 8" are in short range. Targets that are more than 8" and within 16" are in long range. Targets more than 16" away are out of range.

As we shall see later, it is more difficult for a weapon to hit a target at long range.

SHOOTING & COMBAT

Units in hand-to-hand fighting are far too busy to use missile weapons and therefore may not shoot.

Units are not normally allowed to shoot against enemy units that are engaged in close combat – the risk of hitting their own comrades is far too high.

TEMPLATES AND ACCIDENTAL HITS

Some war machines (such as stone throwers) and other similar weapons, spells, etc, may miss their target, deviate and end up hitting units engaged in close combat. The shot has fallen in the thick of the fighting and both sides suffer the consequences. These weapons normally utilise a template to determine how many models are hit by a falling stone, and so on. Use the normal rules given on page 28 to determine which models are hit, even if they are on the same side of the firing unit.

ROLLING TO HIT

The chance of a shooter scoring a hit on his target depends on his Ballistic Skill, or BS. The higher the individual's BS, the greater his chance of hitting.

To determine whether you hit, you must roll a D6 for each model that is shooting. Note that the number of Attacks a model has will not affect the number of shots – each model can shoot only once unless the weapon he carries has a special rule that allows it to fire more rapidly.

Count how many models in your unit are shooting and roll that number of dice. It is easiest to roll all the dice at once, although you don't have to. If there are a lot of models shooting, you might need to roll several batches of dice. The following table shows the minimum score you will need to hit.

Ballistic Skill	1	2	3	4	5	6	7	8	9	10
To Hit score	6	5	4	3	2	1	0	-1	-2	-3

If you score equal to or greater than the number required, you have hit. If you score less, you have missed.

For example, you fire with five Empire Archers. Men have BS 3, so you need a score of at least 4 to hit. You roll five dice and score 1, 2, 2, 4, and 6 which equals two hits and three misses.

Of course, you cannot roll less than 1 on a D6, so troops with BS 6 or more will have a negative to hit score (see above). However, in Warhammer a To Hit roll of 1 on a D6 always fails, regardless of the dice modifiers and Ballistic Skill of the model.

COVER

Troops who are behind certain terrain features, such as hedges or walls, or inside a wood, can take advantage of cover. This makes them harder to hit because they can duck back out of the way, leaving arrows to splinter against a wall or tree. A unit is considered to be in cover if at least half of its models are in cover (or half of its body in the case of units consisting of single models).

If you find this hard to judge, you can just roll for it (see The Most Important Rule on page 3).

There are two sorts of cover: hard cover and soft cover. Their effects are explained in the To Hit modifiers chart.

Hard Cover

This offers real physical protection as well as partially concealing the target from view. The corner of a building, a large rock, walls and wooden palisades are all types of hard cover.

A model positioned at the corner of a building so that he is peeking round is protected by hard cover and models in trenches or pits are also in hard cover.

Soft Cover

Although it partially shields a target from view, soft cover provides scant protection against incoming missiles. You can hide behind a hedge, but a crossbow bolt or arrow has a chance of going straight through it. Hedges and crops provide soft cover and troops within woods automatically count as being in soft cover.

TO HIT MODIFIERS

Shooting isn't simply a matter of pointing your weapon at the target and letting fly. Factors other than your Ballistic Skill affect the chance of hitting, such as range and cover as already discussed. There are other factors too, some of which make it easier to hit and others that make it harder. Factors that make it easier are added to your dice roll. Factors that make it harder are subtracted from your dice roll.

These are called To Hit modifiers, and they are all cumulative. So if shooting at long range (-1) at a target behind soft cover (-1), the chance of hitting is reduced by -2.

+1 Shooting at a large target
A large target is anything that would be massively tall or that is especially bulky. Giants, Dragons and Greater Daemons are large targets, for example, while Men, Orcs, Elves, Ogres, Chariots, Cannons and the vast majority of troops are not. In every case, the creature's special rules in the relevant Army book will inform you whether it is a large target or not.

-1 Shooting while moving
If the shooting unit moved during the movement phase (or during the magic phase via the effect of a spell) then their chance of hitting is reduced. Even a simple turn or change of formation is enough to reduce their concentration and so counts as movement for this purpose.

-1 Target is behind soft cover
If the target is behind soft cover, then the chance of hitting it is reduced.

-2 Target is behind hard cover
If the target is behind hard cover, the chance of hitting it is drastically reduced.

-1 Shooting at long range
If the target lies at over half your maximum range, you are less likely to hit. Sometimes you will find some of the shooters are within short range and some are at long range. If this is the case, you must roll two batches of dice, one for each range.

-1 Stand & Shoot
If a unit is charged and elects to stand & shoot at its attacker, then their chance of hitting is reduced. While the enemy thunders towards them, their aim will be distracted and their shot hurried as they abandon their bows to take up their swords.

-1 Shooting at a single model or skirmishers
This penalty applies if the target is a single model with a unit strength of 1, or a unit of models with unit strength of 1 who are in skirmish formation. If the target model or unit is cavalry or larger (unit strength of 2 or more per model), this penalty does not apply. See the sections on Characters and Skirmishers for more details.

For example, ten Goblins are resolving a stand & shoot reaction against a unit of Elf cavalry at long range (the Elves start their charge 12" away). Because their BS is 3, the Goblins need 4s to hit, but since their targets are charging and at long range, they suffer a penalty of -2. Each Archer therefore needs to roll a 6 to hit. The player rolls ten dice and manages to get two 6s – two hits!

7+ TO HIT

If To Hit modifiers result in a required score of 7 or more when shooting, it is still possible to score a hit. As it is impossible to roll a 7 on a D6, you will first need to roll a 6 and then, for each shot scoring a 6, you will need to roll a further score as shown on the chart below. So, for example, in order to score an 8, you must roll a 6 followed by a 5 or more. If you require a score of 10 or more then it is impossible to hit the intended target.

7	6 followed by a 4, 5 or 6
8	6 followed by a 5 or 6
9	6 followed by a 6
10+	Impossible!

TEMPLATES

Some creatures, spells and war machines use templates (circular, teardrop-shaped, etc,) to determine what they hit. Normally, after the final position of the template has been determined following the rules of the war machine, creature or spell using it, all models whose bases are completely covered by the template are automatically affected (full hits), whilst models whose base is only partially covered by the template are affected on the roll of a 4+ (partial hits). Examples of this procedure are illustrated in Diagrams 93.1 and 95.1.

TO WOUND CHART

Weapon's Strength \ Target's Toughness	1	2	3	4	5	6	7	8	9	10
1	4	5	6	6	N	N	N	N	N	N
2	3	4	5	6	6	N	N	N	N	N
3	2	3	4	5	6	6	N	N	N	N
4	2	2	3	4	5	6	6	N	N	N
5	2	2	2	3	4	5	6	6	N	N
6	2	2	2	2	3	4	5	6	6	N
7	2	2	2	2	2	3	4	5	6	6
8	2	2	2	2	2	2	3	4	5	6
9	2	2	2	2	2	2	2	3	4	5
10	2	2	2	2	2	2	2	2	3	4

ROLLING TO WOUND

Not all hits will wound their target – some might merely graze it. Some creatures are so tough that arrows do not easily pierce their flesh, or are so resilient that they are able to ignore missiles sticking out of their body. Once you have hit your target, roll again to see if it has been wounded. To do this compare the weapon's Strength with the target's Toughness. The Strength values of common missile weapons are given later; the target's Toughness is included in its profile.

Roll a D6 for each hit scored and consult the To Wound chart above. Find the weapon's Strength and look down that column. Then scan along the row for the target's Toughness. The number is the minimum score on a D6 needed to score a wound. Where the value is 'N' this indicates that the target is too tough for you to hurt. 'N' stands for no effect – or no chance!

WEAPON STRENGTH

The following examples show the Strength of various missile weapons and are included here as examples. The section on Weapons (page 54) describes all missile and close combat weapons in more detail.

WEAPON	STRENGTH
Bow	3
Sling	3
Crossbow	4
Handgun	4

Continuing our earlier example: The Goblin player, having scored two hits on the Elves, consults the table. His Goblins' short bows are S3. The Elves are T3. He sees that he needs to roll 4s or more to wound an Elf. He rolls a 4 and a 2, wounding one Elf.

TAKING ARMOUR SAVES

Models that are wounded still have a chance to avoid damage if they are wearing armour or carrying shields, or if they are riding a horse or similar creature. These models have an armour saving roll.

Roll a D6 for each wound suffered by your troops. If you roll equal to or greater than the model's armour save, the wound has been deflected by its armour.

For example, a warrior carrying a shield and wearing light armour has an armour save of 5+, so he must roll a 5 or 6 to be saved by his armour.

ARMOUR SAVES

Armour worn	Armour save	Armour save if cavalry
None	None	6+
Shield or light armour	6+	5+
Shield & light armour or heavy armour only	5+	4+
Shield & heavy armour	4+	3+
Riders with shield & heavy armour, riding barded mounts	–	2+

Cavalry models that consist of a mount and a rider (but not those consisting of a single creature, like a wolf or a warhound) automatically have an armour save of 6 even if the rider is wearing no armour. This represents the extra protection afforded by the mount to the rider. If the rider is armoured, then his armour save will be 1 better than it would be if he were on foot, or 2 better if the mount is wearing armour (ie, barding) as well.

For example, a Man wearing light armour and carrying a shield has an armour save of 5+ on foot and 4+ when mounted.

Note that this bonus only applies to cavalry and not to models riding monsters. Rules for monsters and riders are discussed on page 58.

To continue our previous example, the Goblin player has scored 1 wound on the Elf troops. Since the Elves are mounted and wearing light armour, their armour saving throw is 5+. The Elf player rolls a 2 and so the Elf is slain. If he had scored a 5 or 6, the arrow would have bounced off and left the Elf unharmed.

ARMOUR SAVE MODIFIERS

Some weapons or creatures are so powerful that they can punch right through armour, so armour provides less protection against them. Such attacks confer modifiers that are subtracted from the foe's armour saving throw. This is shown by the table opposite.

For example, a crossbow bolt (S4) hits a warrior wearing light armour and shield. Normally, he would need to roll 5 or 6 to make his armour save and avoid taking the wound but, because of the crossbow's enormous hitting power, -1 is subtracted from his dice roll. Therefore, he must now roll a 6 to save.

ARMOUR SAVE MODIFIERS

Strength of hit	Reduce armour save by
3 or less	none
4	-1
5	-2
6	-3
7	-4
8	-5
9	-6
10	-7

MAXIMUM SAVE

Observant readers will have noticed that the best save on the armour saves chart is a 2+ on a D6 but it is possible to get a better save. Magic armour is one way to improve the wearer's armour save to 1+ or even less! However, a roll of 1 will always fail, so even a model with a 1+ or better armour save will suffer a wound if it rolls 1 when taking its armour save. The advantage of a 1+ save is that it offers better protection against weapons with save modifiers.

For example, a model with a 2+ armour save hit by a S4 attack (-1 save modifier) saves on a 3+, while a model with a 1+ armour save needs a 2+.

WARD SAVES

Some troop types and creatures are protected by more than mere physical armour. They may be shielded by magical charms, preserved by the gods, or perhaps are just astoundingly lucky.

Models with this sort of protection are referred to as having a ward save or ward. This type of save is quite different from an armour save and it is very important to understand the difference. Wards represent magical or divine protection that can save a warrior when armour would be of no use at all. Unlike an armour save, a ward save is never modified by Strength modifiers, etc. Even if a hit ignores all armour saves, a model with a ward may still try to make its ward save as normal.

Sometimes, a model has both an armour save and a ward save. In this case, the model must take the armour save first and, if it is failed, the model is allowed to try to make a ward save. No model can ever try to make more than one ward save against a wound it has suffered. If a model has two ward saves for any reason, use the better ward save. Note that, regardless of any modifier, a roll of 1 is always a failed save – nobody is invulnerable!

HITS INFLICTING MULTIPLE WOUNDS

Some war machines, spells or magic weapons are so destructive that if a model is hit and wounded by them, the victim doesn't lose only 1 wound, but a number of wounds equal to the roll of a D3, D6, etc, (as noted in the weapon's rules). In such cases, roll to hit and to wound as normal and then take any armour saves and ward saves that apply. Finally, for each such wound that is not saved, roll the appropriate dice and add their results together to determine how many wounds are caused. If the model has only 1 Wound on its profile, there is no need to do this, as models cannot suffer more wounds than they have on their profile. The victim dies instantly and any excess wounds are wasted.

 REMOVING CASUALTIES

Most troops can only sustain one wound before they fall casualty. Some models can take several before they become casualties, but they are the exception rather than the norm. The number of wounds a model can sustain before it dies is indicated by its Wounds value or 'W' on its profile.

CASUALTIES

Where troops have only a single Wound, casualties are removed as follows. If a unit of troops is hit and suffers wounds that it does not save, then, for each wound suffered, one model is removed as a 'kill'. Individual warriors are not necessarily dead, they may just be too badly wounded to fight on. For our purposes, the result is the same so we treat all casualties as if they were killed and remove them.

Although casualties would really fall amongst the front rank, for the purposes of game play remove models from the rear rank of the unit. This keeps the formation neat and represents rear rankers stepping forward to cover gaps in the line. If the unit is deployed in a single rank, then casualties are removed equally from both ends.

Suffering casualties may cause a Panic test as described in the Psychology section.

CAVALRY CASUALTIES

In the case of cavalry models, all shots are worked out against the rider. If the rider is slain, the mount is removed as well. This is a practical way of representing cavalry, as it dispenses with the need for dismounted riders and loose mounts. Some riders are dead, their horses bolting, and some mounts are killed, throwing their riders to the ground, but these things can be left to the imagination. Note that this only applies to ordinary cavalry and not to monstrous mounts (see page 59).

MULTIPLE WOUND CASUALTIES

If models have more than 1 Wound, casualties are removed as follows. A unit of Ogres suffers 5 wounds from arrow fire. Ogres are huge creatures and each model has 3 Wounds. The arrows would fall randomly among the unit, possibly wounding several creatures, but for our purposes we shall remove whole models where possible. So, 5 wounds equals one model dead (3 wounds) with 2 wounds left over. The wounds left over are not enough to remove another model, so the player must make a note that 2 wounds have been suffered by the unit. If the unit takes another wound from some other attack, then another Ogre model is removed. It is obviously important to keep a record of wounds taken by units such as this.

If a unit of creatures with more than 1 Wound on their profile is hit by a weapon that causes multiple wounds, determine how many wounds are caused on each model individually (remember that each model cannot suffer more wounds than it has on its profile). Add up all wounds caused on the unit and then remove the appropriate number of models, leaving any spare wounds on the unit.

For example, a cannonball from an Empire Great Cannon hurtles through a unit of Ogres, wounding three of them. The player rolls to determine the number of wounds, inflicting 2 wounds on the first Ogre, 2 on the second Ogre and 6 on a third Ogre (only count 3 wounds on the third Ogre, since that is the maximum a single Ogre can suffer). The unit has therefore suffered a total of 7 wounds (2+2+3), so the player removes two Ogres (3 wounds each) and records that the unit has suffered one additional wound (3+3+1).

FAST DICE ROLLING

Sometimes it is necessary to roll quite a few dice to resolve shooting – whole handfuls at once in fact! This doesn't take as long as you might imagine because all the dice are rolled together. The most practical way of going about this is to take as many dice as you have troops shooting and roll them all at once. So, if you're shooting with ten Archers, roll ten dice. Then pick out any dice that score a hit and re-roll them to wound. So, from ten dice rolled, four might typically score hits. These are re-rolled and may score 2 wounds, for example.

Dice that score wounds are picked out and handed over to your opponent to take his saving throws with. This same system applies when working out close combat.

CLOSE COMBAT

Once shooting has been resolved, it is time to deal with the brutal cut and thrust of close combat. Units engaged in combat cannot declare charges, move or shoot missile weapons – they must stand toe-to-toe with their enemy until one side is destroyed or forced to flee. Regardless of which player's turn it is, all models that are in contact with the enemy must fight. The close combat phase is therefore an exception to the normal turn sequence, in that both sides are taking part in the action.

During the close combat phase the player whose turn it is picks one of the fights and resolves it, following the procedure outlined in the chart below. Once that combat has been resolved, including any flee and pursuit moves, the player picks another fight and resolves it, continuing like this until all the engagements have been fought.

THE CLOSE COMBAT PHASE

- Pick any one of the combats on the table and resolve it, following the sequence given below.
- Pick another combat and resolve it.
- Continue like this until all combats are resolved.

HOW TO RESOLVE COMBATS

1. Fight Combat
Models in base contact with the enemy will fight, as explained in the rules that follow.

2. Combat Result
Work out which side has won the combat and by how much. If the fight is not a draw, the losing side will have lost by 1, 2 or more 'points'.

3. Break Test
Each unit on the losing side must take a Break test. Any units failing their Break test are deemed 'broken' and will run away.

4. Flee & Pursue
Units that have broken must flee away from their enemy. Units whose enemies have broken and fled that turn are allowed to pursue them and might possibly catch and destroy them.

5. Redress Ranks
Units are tidied up, ready to continue the battle.

1 FIGHT COMBATS

Work out each combat one at a time in the order chosen by the player whose turn it is – resolve each combat completely, including any flee and pursue moves, before moving on to the next combat.

A combat is often a fight between a single unit of troops from each side, but it is possible that several units, monsters and heroes may become involved in the same fight (see Diagram 33.1 – Examples of Combat). So long as fighting units are interconnected, they are participating in the same combat. The combat results for such a combat apply to all the units involved.

WHICH MODELS FIGHT?

Models can fight if they are in base contact with an enemy model when it is their chance to attack, even if the bases only touch at the corner. Even models attacked in the side or rear may fight (though the models are not actually turned to face their enemy).

If a model is touching more than one enemy, it can choose which one to attack when it is its turn to strike. If a model has more than 1 Attack, it can divide its Attacks as the player wishes so long as this is made clear before rolling to hit. For example, if faced with an enemy hero and an ordinary enemy warrior you might decide to attack the warrior because he is easier to kill, or you could take the outside chance of slaying the hero.

In the case of cavalry mounts that have their own Attacks, such as Warhorses and Giant Wolves, the rider's Attack and the mount's Attack are worked out separately and can be directed against different targets.

In any case, models in base contact with the enemy may not refuse to attack their enemies!

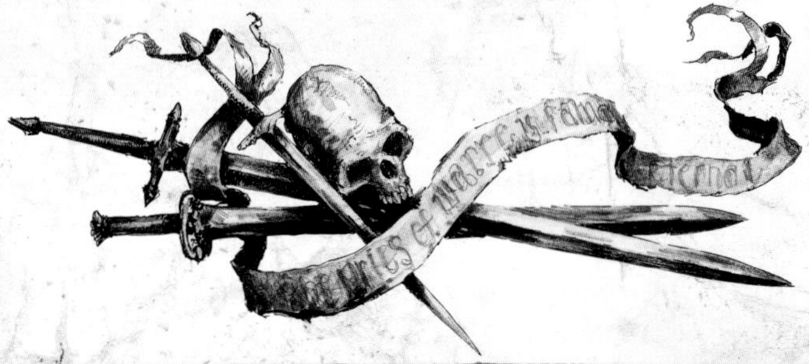

33.1 – Examples of Combat

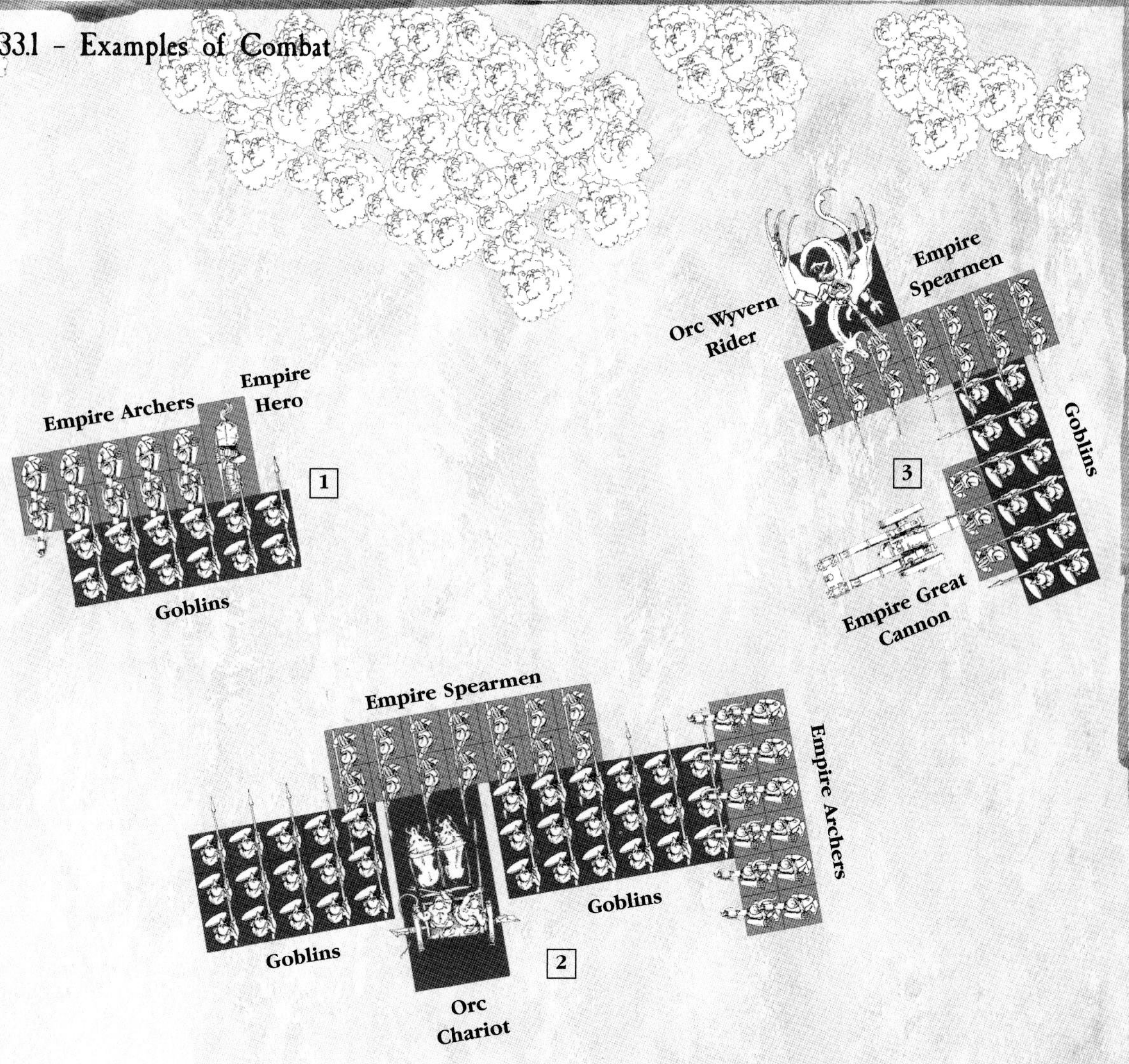

Empire Archers
Empire Hero
1
Goblins
Orc Wyvern Rider
Empire Spearmen
Goblins
3
Empire Great Cannon
Empire Spearmen
Empire Archers
Goblins
Goblins
2
Orc Chariot

On this part of the battlefield there are three separate combats:

1) An Empire unit and an Empire hero fighting against a unit of Goblins

2) A huge fight with two units of Empire troops against two units of Goblins and an Orc Chariot

3) A combat involving an Empire unit and the crew of a Great Cannon against a unit of Goblins and an Orc Wyvern Rider

33.2 – Which Models can Fight?

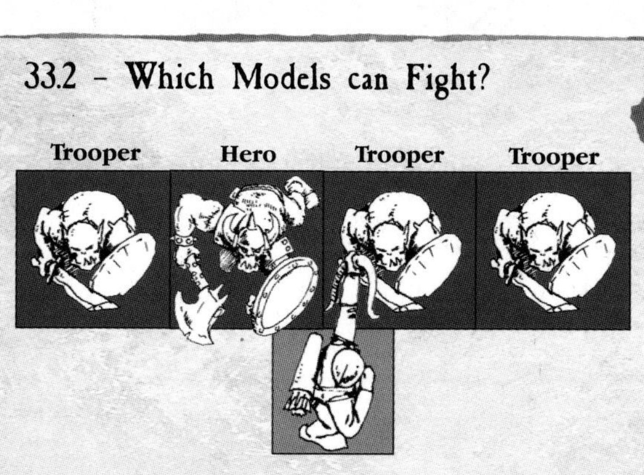

The attacking model may decide which enemy model to attack: the hero or the trooper.

33.3 – Corner-to-corner Fighting

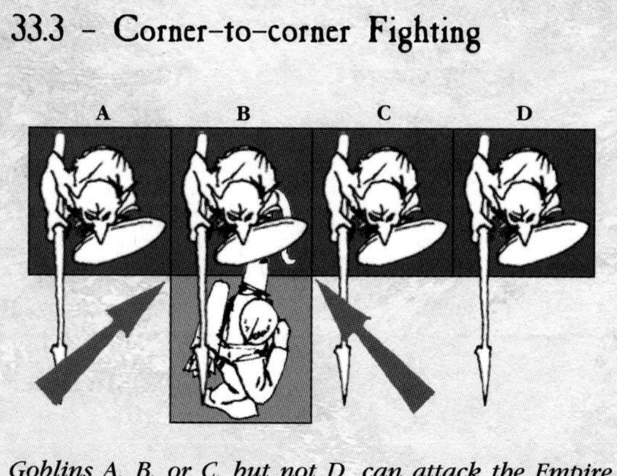

Goblins A, B, or C, but not D, can attack the Empire Archer.

 WHO STRIKES FIRST?

In the desperate hack and slash of close combat, the advantage goes to the best and fastest warriors, or to those who have gained the extra impetus of charging into combat that turn. To represent this, combatants strike blows in a strict order:

– Troops who have charged that turn automatically strike first.

– Otherwise, all blows are struck in strict order of Initiative (I). Combatants with a higher Initiative strike first, followed by those with a lower Initiative. This is important because if a model is slain before it has a chance to strike, it obviously cannot fight back. Striking first is a big advantage, which is why it is better to charge your enemy rather than allow him to charge you.

– If opposing troops would strike at the same time (eg, they have the same Initiative), then the side that won the combat in the previous turn may strike first.

– If this doesn't apply, you should roll a D6 to determine who goes first.

For example, a unit of Orc Boar Riders charges a unit of Elf Spearmen. The Elves have an Initiative of 5, while the Orcs only have Initiative 2. The Orcs strike first because they charged. Next turn, the Elves will go first because of their higher Initiative.

 HITTING THE ENEMY

To see whether any hits are scored, roll a D6 for each model fighting. If you have more than 1 Attack with your troops then roll a D6 for each Attack. For example, ten Elves have 1 Attack each so roll 10 dice, but four Ogres have 3 Attacks each so roll 12 dice!

The dice roll needed to score a hit on your enemy depends upon the relative Weapon Skills of the attacker and his foe. Compare the Weapon Skill of the attacker with the Weapon Skill of the model it is trying to hit and consult the To Hit chart to find the minimum D6 score needed to hit.

If you look at the chart, you will see that normally models hit an enemy on a 4+, but if the warrior's Weapon Skill is greater than that of his enemy, he will hit on a dice roll of 3+. In the rare case when an enemy's Weapon Skill is more than double that of the attacker, a 5+ is required for a successful hit. Sometimes modifiers apply to these rolls, but normally an unmodified roll of 6 always hits and an unmodified 1 always misses.

CAVALRY

When you are fighting against cavalry, all blows are struck against the rider using the rider's Weapon Skill and never against the mount. The mount fights using its own WS, Strength, Initiative and Attacks.

TO HIT CHART

Attacker's Weapon Skill \ Opponent's Weapon Skill	1	2	3	4	5	6	7	8	9	10
1	4	4	5	5	5	5	5	5	5	5
2	3	4	4	4	5	5	5	5	5	5
3	3	3	4	4	4	4	5	5	5	5
4	3	3	3	4	4	4	4	4	5	5
5	3	3	3	3	4	4	4	4	4	4
6	3	3	3	3	3	4	4	4	4	4
7	3	3	3	3	3	3	4	4	4	4
8	3	3	3	3	3	3	3	4	4	4
9	3	3	3	3	3	3	3	3	4	4
10	3	3	3	3	3	3	3	3	3	4

 WOUNDING THE ENEMY

Not all successful hits are going to harm your enemy – some may bounce off tough hide, while others may cause only superficial damage which doesn't prevent the creature fighting. Once you have hit your foe, you must roll again to see whether your hits inflict wounds.

This procedure is the same as is described for shooting. Consult the To Wound chart, cross-referencing the attacker's Strength with the defender's Toughness. Both values appear on the profiles of the creatures that are fighting. The chart indicates the minimum score required on a D6 to cause a wound.

Note that where the table shows an 'N' this indicates that the target is too tough to be hurt. N stands for 'No effect'.

WEAPONS' BONUSES

Unlike hits from shooting, the Strength value of the attacker is used to determine wounds rather than the Strength of the weapon itself. However, some weapons confer a bonus on the attacker's Strength. For example, Knights that are charging with lances receive a +2 bonus to their Strength. These bonuses are discussed together with other special rules in the section on Weapons (see page 54).

DEFENDED OBSTACLES

Troops lining up behind a wall, hedge or other obstacle can adopt a position to defend it. The front rank is moved right up against the obstacle to show this. Enemy wishing to attack the defenders can do so by charging them as normal. Attacking models don't have to physically cross the obstacle, indeed they are unable to do so while it is defended. Instead, the front rank is positioned on the opposite side to the defenders.

Models charging an enemy behind a defended obstacle do not get any of the bonuses normally associated with a charge and instead fight as if they were already engaged in the combat from a previous turn. This means they do not automatically strike first, but strike in Initiative order, do not get any Strength bonus from lances and other weapons that confer bonuses to the charger, no special rules that rely on them charging would work, and so on.

Flying models attacking enemy behind defended obstacles ignore the penalty.

TO WOUND CHART

Attacker's Strength \ Opponent's Toughness	1	2	3	4	5	6	7	8	9	10
1	4	5	6	6	N	N	N	N	N	N
2	3	4	5	6	6	N	N	N	N	N
3	2	3	4	5	6	6	N	N	N	N
4	2	2	3	4	5	6	6	N	N	N
5	2	2	2	3	4	5	6	6	N	N
6	2	2	2	2	3	4	5	6	6	N
7	2	2	2	2	2	3	4	5	6	6
8	2	2	2	2	2	2	3	4	5	6
9	2	2	2	2	2	2	2	3	4	5
10	2	2	2	2	2	2	2	2	3	4

TAKING SAVING THROWS

Combatants that are wounded have a chance to avoid suffering any damage if they are wearing armour, carrying shields or have a ward save. This is exactly the same as described for shooting, and the same rules apply.

CLOSE COMBAT & INCOMPLETE RANKS

Models in the incomplete rear rank must normally be kept as close to the centre as possible. If the unit is fighting to its flank, the models in the incomplete rank are moved in contact with the enemy and fight normally (See Diagram 36.1).

If the unit is fighting to its rear, some enemy models might end up not in base contact with the enemy because of the models in the incomplete rear rank (Diagram 36.2 shows an extreme case). In this situation, models can attack the models in the enemy unit, even if not physically in base-to-base contact. In reality, the chargers would not have stopped one step away from the enemy and would have moved in, finishing their charge.

36.1 - Incomplete Ranks in Combat

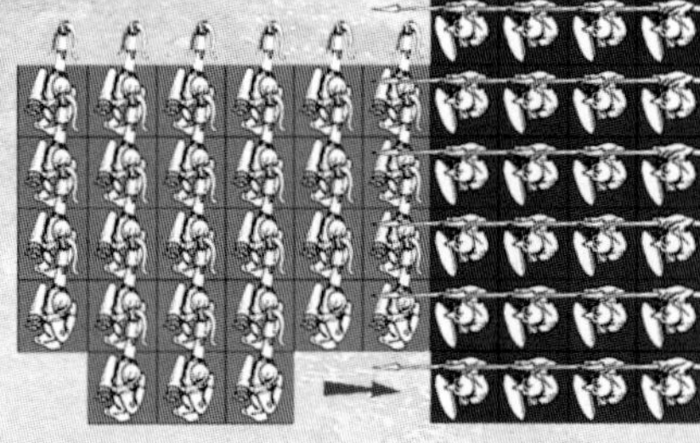

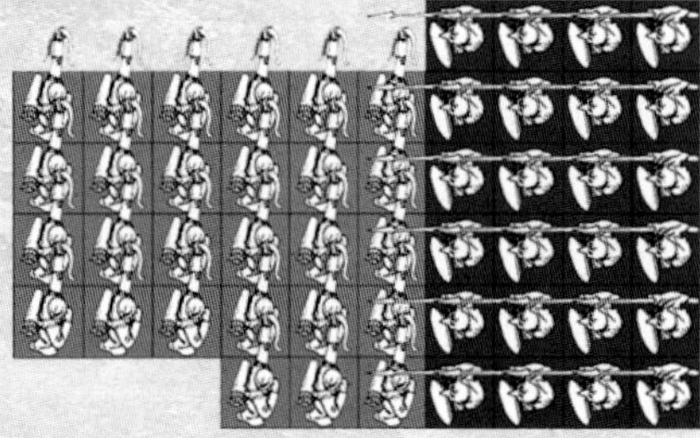

The models in the last incomplete rank are moved to be in contact with their enemies.

REMOVING CASUALTIES

Close combat casualties are removed in the same way as shooting casualties. Although casualties fall amongst the rank that is fighting, models in the rear ranks will step forward to fill any gaps that appear. Casualties will therefore be removed straight from a unit's rear rank.

It is a good idea not to immediately remove models that fall casualty but instead temporarily place them next to their unit. This is because when it comes to working out who has won the combat you will need to know how many casualties have been caused this turn. Also, models that are removed before they have had a chance to attack may not do so, and models that are stepping forward from rear ranks to replace them can't attack that turn. This means that any casualties inflicted will reduce the number of enemy left to fight back. You need to know how many models were killed that combat round to determine who cannot attack back.

EXCESS CASUALTIES

It can sometimes happen that a model causes more casualties than there are enemy models in base contact with it. When this happens, the excess casualties are removed as normal. This represents the attackers springing forward and following up their assault by striking over the fallen bodies of their foes. Such is the ferocity of their attack, and the surprise caused by their success, that the excess casualties are struck down where they stand and have no chance to attack back.

36.2 - Incomplete Ranks in Combat

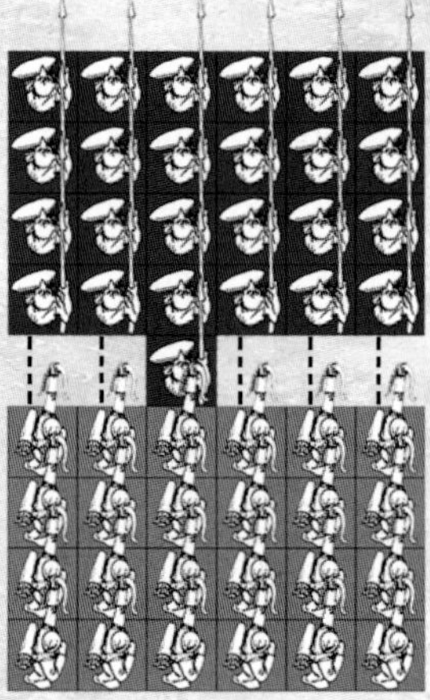

All of the Empire Archers and Goblins indicated by the arrows can fight. If casualties inflicted on the Goblins cause the units to be separated, move the Archers unit forward to mantain contact.

2 COMBAT RESULT

In the brutal hack and slash of close combat, it is rare for warriors to fight to the last man. Often combat is decided when the courage of one side fails.

Once all the models engaged in the combat have fought, you must determine which side has won. Of course, if one side has been completely wiped out in the fight, the other side is automatically the winner, regardless of the rules given below.

Each side scores a number of combat result points equal to the wounds caused in the combat. It does not matter which particular units inflicted the wounds, just add up all wounds caused by that side in the fight. Do not forget to add the wounds suffered by big creatures or characters that have not been removed as casualties. Do NOT count the wounds that were saved by an armour save or a ward save (in other words, only count unsaved wounds).

As well as points for wounds caused, a side can claim bonus points under certain circumstances – for example, if it has a standard bearer, if it is attacking the enemy in the flank, or if it is fighting from higher ground.

The combat result bonus chart on this page summarises all bonus points (which are described in more detail on the next page).

Each bonus point is added to the number of points for unsaved wounds inflicted to obtain a final combat result score for each side. So, for example, if both sides cause 3 wounds, the result is a draw, but if one side has a standard it adds +1 to its score, beating the enemy by 4 points to 3. These bonus points can make all the difference between winning and losing the combat (see Diagram 37.1).

The side with the highest total combat result score wins the combat. The other side has lost and must take a Break test, as described later. If both sides have the same total, the result is a Draw and the combat will continue in the next turn.

The higher the difference between the winner's combat result score and the loser's, the bigger and more decisive the victory. An 8 points against a 7 points victory, for example, is only a slight win because the difference in scores is only 1 point. An 8 points against a 2 points victory, however, is extremely decisive, as the difference in scores is a whopping 6 points. This difference in scores is important because it is used when working out whether a defeated enemy stands its ground or turns and flees.

COMBAT RESULT BONUS CHART

Situation	Bonus
Extra rank	+1 per rank after the first (maximum+3)
Outnumber enemy	+1
Battle standard	+1
Standard	+1
High ground	+1
Flank attack	+1
Rear attack	+2
Overkill	+1 per excess wound (maximum+5)

37.1 - Combat Result

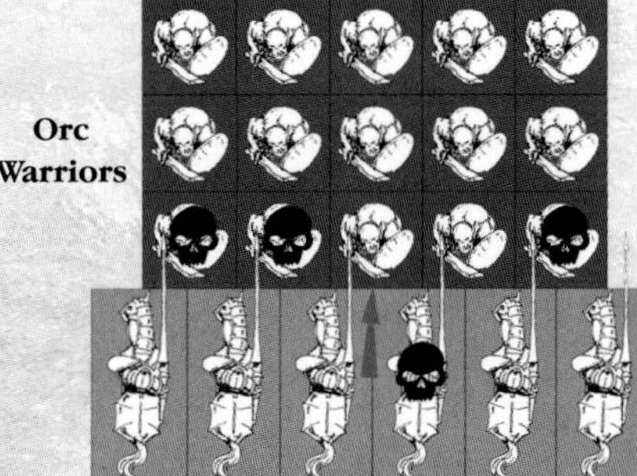

The Knights charge the Orcs and attack first, inflicting 3 casualties. The Orcs left alive fight back and kill a Knight.

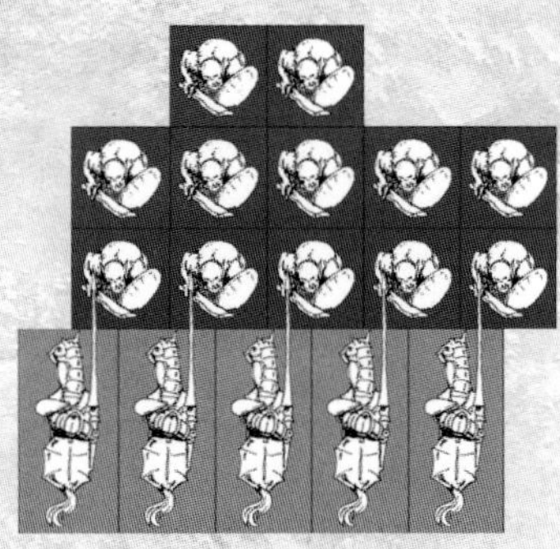

The Orcs score 1 point for Wounds, plus 2 bonus points for the extra ranks they had, plus 1 for outnumbering (they have a unit strength of 12 against 10 for the Knights), for a total score of 4. The Knights score 3 for the wounds caused.

The result is 3 to 4 in favour of the Orcs. The Knights have lost the combat and will have to take a Break test, as described later.

COMBAT RESULT BONUSES

The following is a description of all the combat result bonuses.

Note that normally all of these bonuses refer to the situation after all the models involved in the fight have finished attacking. The only exception is the extra rank bonus, which instead refers to the number of extra ranks the units had at the beginning of that turn of combat, before any casualties were caused.

Extra Rank

A massed formation of warriors trained to gather their full weight in an irresistible push is often enough to shatter the enemy's will to fight on.

If your unit's formation is at least five models wide, you may claim a bonus of +1 for each rank behind the first that the unit had at the start of that combat turn, up to a maximum of +3. The bonus can be claimed for an incomplete last rear rank, so long as it contains at least five models.

If you have several units fighting in a combat, count the bonus from the unit with the most ranks. Do not add up the bonuses from all the units fighting.

This bonus is lost if the unit is fighting to its flank or rear against an enemy unit with a unit strength of 5 or more. Note that this applies while the enemy unit in the flank/rear is in combat – if the enemy unit breaks and flees, or is reduced to a unit strength of less than 5, the unit regains its rank bonus at the beginning of the following turn.

Skirmishers and fast cavalry never gain a bonus for extra ranks (see pages 67 & 70).

Outnumber Enemy

When a group of warriors is facing uneven odds, it is considerably more likely to lose heart.

If the combined unit strength of all your units in the combat is greater than the combined unit strength of the enemy units, you receive a +1 bonus. See page 71 for the unit strength chart.

Standard

Having the colours of their city or nation flying at the front of a regiment is a great motivator.

If any of your units includes a standard bearer in its front rank, you may add a +1 bonus.

Note that if several units' standards are involved in the combat, you still only add +1, not +1 for each standard. Rules for standards are given on page 80.

Battle Standard

Having the personal banner of their General held high by a great hero is enough to encourage the warriors to even greater deeds of valour.

If the army's battle standard bearer is in the fight, you may add a +1 bonus (see page 82 for more details). Note that this bonus is on top of the bonus for a unit's standard, so a unit with a normal standard and the battle standard receives a +2 combat result bonus.

High Ground

Charging down a hill or mounting a stiff defence at the top of a rocky crag is a great advantage.

If you are fighting from a higher position than your enemy, for example, your troops are occupying the crest of a hill, then you may add a +1 bonus. In the case of a fight involving multiple units, the side that has the fighting rank in the highest position gets the bonus.

Flank Attack

Charging an enemy unit to its flank or rear is lethal, as the enemy warriors helplessly mill around in confusion trying to face the unexpected attack.

If you are fighting against an enemy unit's flank, you may add a +1 bonus so long as your unit has a unit strength of 5 or more after both sides have attacked. Note that you only count +1 even if both flanks of the enemy are engaged. The bonus is only applied once, regardless of how many flanking units are involved in the combat. If both sides have flanking units, the side with the most flanking units gets the bonus.

Rear Attack

The same rules for a flank attack also apply to units attacking the enemy in the rear, except that a rear attack gives you a +2 combat result bonus. This bonus and the bonus for a flank attack are cumulative, so if you are attacking in the side and rear you will receive a bonus of +3.

Overkill

Seeing the best fighter in the unit cut to pieces does not boost morale among his comrades.

If a character fighting in a challenge (see page 77) kills his opponent and scores more wounds than the enemy has, each excess wound scores a +1 overkill bonus towards the combat result, up to a maximum of +5. This bonus only applies in a challenge as described in the Characters section.

3 BREAK TESTS

The side that loses a combat must take a test to determine whether it stands and fights or breaks from the combat and runs away. This is called a Break test. You need to take a separate Break test for every unit involved in the combat on the losing side.

Depending on which units pass and which fail their test, some may break and flee whilst others stand their ground. Troops that are better led, braver, and more professional are more likely to stand firm, while wild, temperamental troops are far more likely to run for it.

Take the test as follows. Firstly, nominate the unit for which you are testing and then roll 2D6. Add the difference between the winner's combat result score and the loser's. If the total is greater than the unit's Leadership (Ld) value then the unit has broken and will flee.

For example, a unit of Elf Archers is fighting a unit of Goblins. The Goblins inflict 3 wounds on the Elves, and the Elves inflict 4 wounds on the Goblins. However, the Goblin player has four complete ranks in his formation, each rank beyond the first adding +1 to his score, and his troops outnumber the Elves, adding another +1. This gives him 3+3+1 = 7 points against the Elves' score of 4.

The Elves have therefore lost the combat, even though they have caused more casualties – the vast numbers of Goblins pressing from the back have overwhelmed them. The Elves must therefore take a Break test adding +3 to their dice score, because the difference between the scores is 3. Elves have a good Leadership value (8) but with the extra +3 modifier on the dice, the player will have to roll 5 or less to stand and fight. The player rolls 2D6 and scores 7. The +3 modifier brings his total to 10, which is greater than the unit's Leadership, so the Elves have broken and will flee.

INSANE COURAGE!

Occasionally, in the middle of a battle, the humblest regiment can be filled with steely courage and discipline and decide to stand their ground, no matter the odds! Such unpredictable occurrences are represented in the game by the Insane Courage rule. This simply means that if a unit rolls a double 1 for its Break test, it will always stand its ground, regardless of how badly they have lost the fight.

For example, a unit of Goblins is charged in the flank by a unit of Chosen Knights of Chaos. The combat is resolved and the Knights win the fight by 10 points. The Goblins' Leadership of 6 means that they would need to roll 6 or less with a +10 modifier to the dice, which is obviously impossible. There still is a point in rolling the dice for the Goblins though, because there is a remote chance of rolling a natural, unmodified, double 1, meaning that the Goblins would brave the onslaught and heroically (or foolishly!) stand their ground.

4 FLEE & PURSUE

Once you have completed all of the Break tests resulting from the combat, it is time for broken troops to flee and for victorious troops to surge forward, cutting down their retreating foes as their backs are turned.

We shall first consider the situation where all broken units are fleeing in the same direction, as it is the most common. The complex situation created by units fleeing in several different directions will be dealt with on page 44.

The sequence of actions for this most decisive moment of the battle is as follows:

FLEE/PURSUE SEQUENCE

- If any victorious unit does not wish to pursue, take a test to try to restrain them.
- Roll the dice to determine the flee distance of each fleeing unit.
- Roll the dice to determine the pursue distance of the pursuing unit.
- Remove each fleeing unit that has failed to outrun its pursuers.
- Move directly away from its pursuers each fleeing unit that has managed to outrun them.
- Move the pursuing units directly after the fleeing enemies.

DECLARE PURSUIT INTENTIONS

If a unit wins a combat and the enemies it is in contact with flee, then the victorious unit must normally pursue. Note that a unit will only pursue if all the enemies it is in contact with are fleeing – if one enemy unit breaks and flees while others fight on, the victorious troops cannot pursue.

Even if a unit can pursue, the controlling player may decide that he would prefer his unit not to pursue the fleeing enemies. Normally a unit must pursue if it is able to do so, but the player may attempt to halt the pursuit by making a test against the unit's Leadership (Ld). This represents the unit's leader calling to his troops to hold, while their natural inclination is to run after the enemy and destroy them. If the test is passed, the unit may remain stationary instead of pursuing.

A unit does not have to pursue if it is defending a wall, building, hedgerow or a comparable obstacle or fortification. As pursuit would force the unit to abandon its secure position there is obviously an incentive to stay put! In such cases, the player can automatically choose whether to pursue or not.

DETERMINE FLEE DISTANCE

It is difficult to say precisely how far fleeing troops will run because they are no longer fighting as a body but milling around in a frightened mob. To represent this, dice are rolled to establish how far the fleeing unit moves: if the unit normally moves 6" or less, roll 2D6; if the unit moves more than 6", roll 3D6. The result is the flee roll, which is the distance covered by the fleeing troops.

Determine the distance fled by each unit fleeing from the combat, but do not move the models yet. If there were many units involved in the same combat, it helps to leave the dice showing the flee distance next to each unit.

DETERMINE PURSUIT DISTANCE

Like fleeing, pursuit is a hectic and uncontrolled affair, so dice are rolled to determine how far the pursuing unit moves. After the fleeing distance of all fleeing units has been determined, but before the models are actually moved, the victorious units will determine their pursuit distance. To find out how far they pursue, roll 2D6 or 3D6 in exactly the same way as for fleeing troops. This is their pursuit roll.

REMOVE FLEEING UNITS CAUGHT

If a victorious unit's pursuit roll is equal to or greater than the flee roll scored by the fleeing enemy units, the fleeing units are completely destroyed where they stand. All the troops are cut down as they turn to run or are scattered beyond hope of regrouping.

MOVE SURVIVING FLEEING TROOPS

Fleeing units that rolled higher than any of their pursuers, or have not been pursued at all, have escaped. They immediately turn around (as per a turn manoeuvre), so that they face directly away from their enemy, and run as fast as they can. If they were engaged by several opponents, they must turn to face directly away from the enemy unit with the highest unit strength, as shown in Diagram 43.1 (roll a dice in case of equal unit strength).

Fleeing units abandon their formation and run from their enemy in a complete rout, blindly scrambling over the battlefield in their efforts to avoid destruction. Even though the fleeing troops move in a disorganised mob, for the purposes of moving the fleeing units it is convenient to keep them in formation. Pivot the unit on the spot to face the direction it is fleeing in and then move it the distance indicated by the dice roll.

Due to their disrupted formation, they ignore any penalty for obstacles and terrain (apart from impassable terrain, see below).

Move the fleeing unit directly away from its enemy, so that the closest part of the unit is 2D6" or 3D6" away and facing in the opposite direction.

Fleeing troops move straight through friendly units, fleeing enemy units, and all enemy units with a unit strength of less than 5. Fleeing units that would otherwise end up on top of such units are instead placed beyond them, as shown in Diagram 41.1. If this extra move means that the fleeing unit ends on top of another such unit, it is moved again through and beyond the new unit (as shown in Diagram 42.1 overleaf), continuing like this until clear of all such troops.

Fleeing troops that have to move through non-fleeing enemy units with a unit strength of 5 or more are immediately destroyed as soon as they move into contact with such enemies (see Diagram 41.2).

In a similar way, fleeing troops that have to move through impassable terrain are completely destroyed. We assume that they either died falling into treacherous waters or down a ravine, or are dispersed beyond any hope of rallying in a desperate attempt to negotiate the terrain blocking their escape.

The only exception to this is that units that break and flee from a multiple combat are allowed to move through any of the enemy units they were fighting (as in the case of a unit defeated by two enemies, one to its front and one to its rear), in the same way as described above.

41.1 - Fleeing Through Units

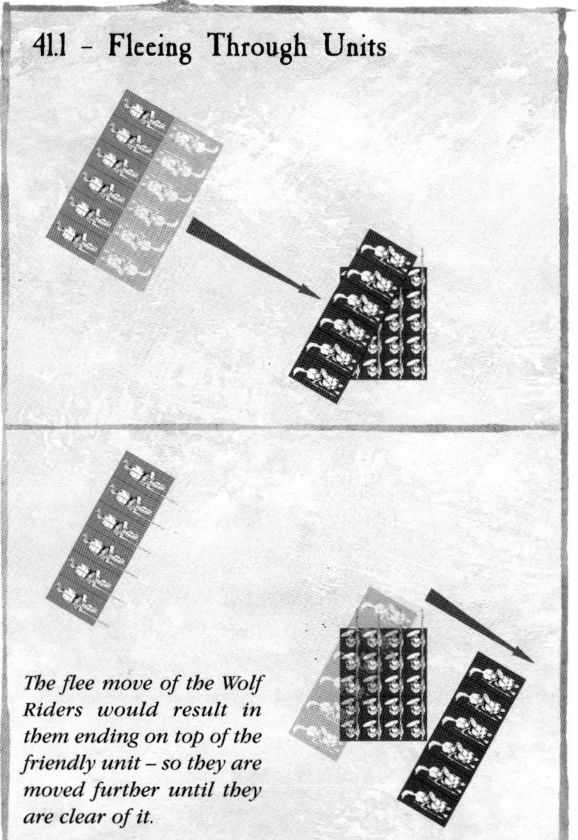

The flee move of the Wolf Riders would result in them ending on top of the friendly unit – so they are moved further until they are clear of it.

41.2 - Fleeing into Enemies/Impassable Terrain

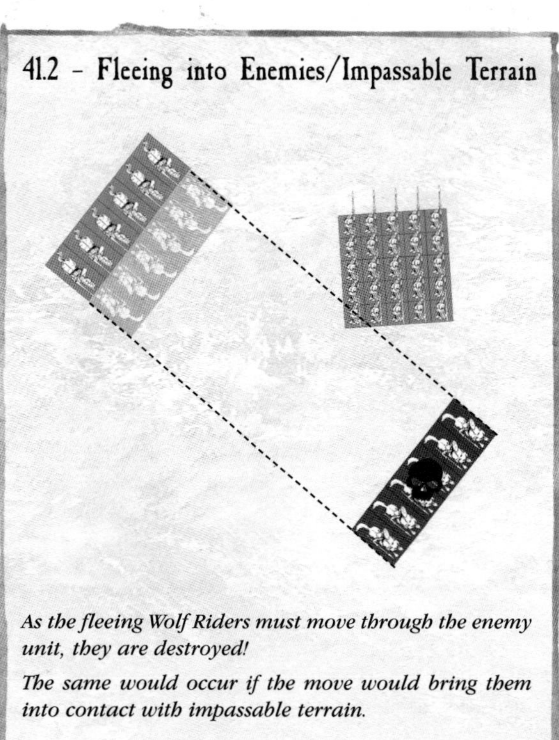

As the fleeing Wolf Riders must move through the enemy unit, they are destroyed!

The same would occur if the move would bring them into contact with impassable terrain.

42.1 – Fleeing Through Units 2

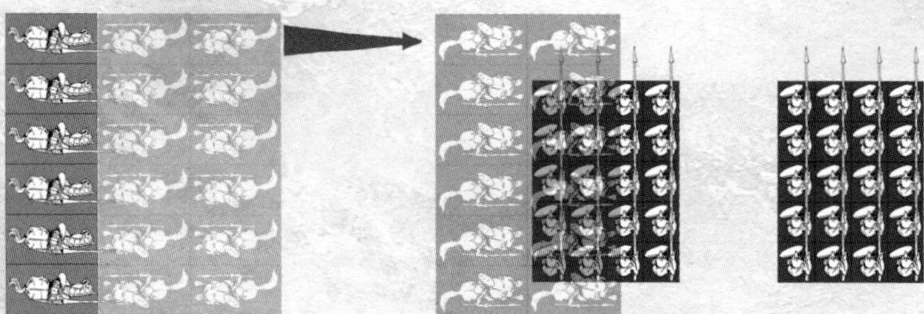

The flee move of the Wolf Riders would end on top of the first friendly unit, so they should be placed on the other side of the Goblins.

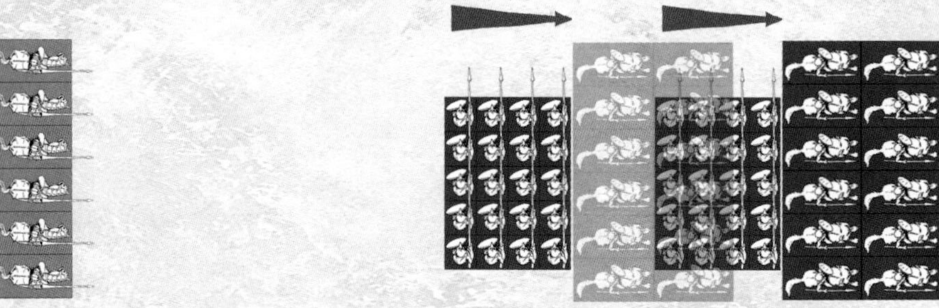

Because they would end up on top of the second friendly unit, the flee move of the Wolf Riders is continued until they are clear of both Goblin units, which will now have to take a Panic test (as described in the Psychology section).

MOVE PURSUING UNITS

Pursuing units pivot on the spot to face the chosen direction of pursuit and then move the full distance indicated by the dice (2D6" or 3D6", exactly like fleeing troops) in the same direction as the fleeing units they are pursuing (see Diagram 43.1).

Pursuers always move their full pursuit distance unless their pursuit takes them into contact with enemy (see Pursuit into Fresh Enemy, page 45), friendly units or impassable terrain, in which case they stop immediately. Pursuers ignore any penalties for obstacles and terrain (apart from impassable terrain) – their victory has given them the extra impetus to chase their fleeing enemies.

Note that units do not continue to pursue in subsequent turns; pursuit is a single bonus move that is made when a beaten enemy flees.

A unit can only pursue once per combat phase.

Occasionally, pursuing units can get in each other's way as they pursue. In such rare cases, move the pursuing units in order of decreasing unit strength.

OVERRUN!

If a unit charges into combat and, by the end of that turn's combat phase all its enemies have been wiped out, the unit may make a pursuit move, even with nobody left alive to pursue. This is an overrun move and represents the unit surging forwards, hungry to find more enemies to fight.

During this special pursuit move, victorious units move 2D6" or 3D6" directly forwards (as if they were pursuing a fleeing enemy to their front). Note that in this case the victorious unit does not have to pursue – the player may always elect to automatically restrain pursuit if there are no fleeing enemies to pursue.

PURSUIT OFF THE TABLE

A pursuing unit that moves into contact with the table edge moves off the table.

In its following movement phase (during remaining moves), the unit will be placed back as close as possible to the same point from which it left the table, in the same formation, facing directly towards the battlefield and with all of its rear rank touching the table edge.

The unit may not charge, as it has missed its opportunity to declare charges, but may move normally, and may not march, but can otherwise participate in the game as normal.

Even if it decides not to move, the unit counts as having moved for the purposes of shooting.

43.1 - Pursue!

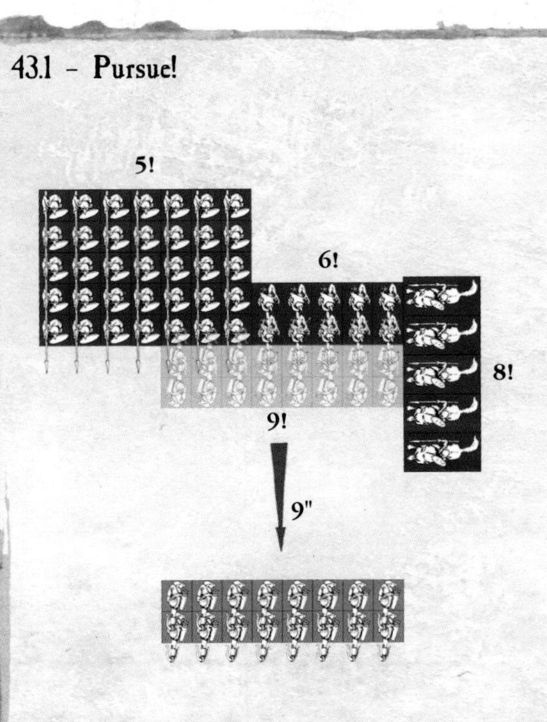

The fleeing unit has rolled a flee distance of 9", higher than the roll of any of the pursuers. The unit is therefore turned and moved directly backwards, as the enemy unit with the highest unit strength is fighting to its front.

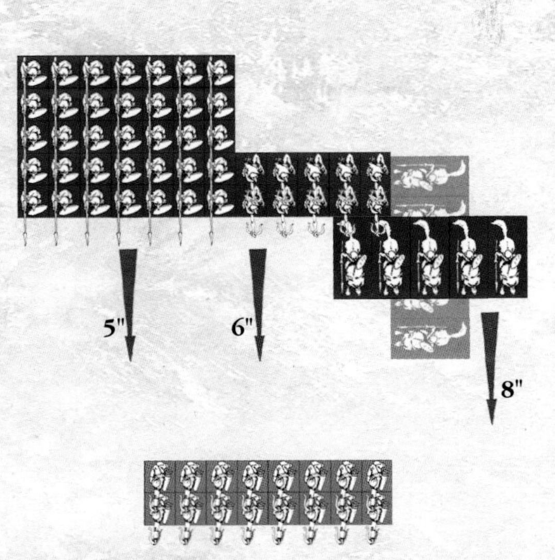

Both Goblin units on foot move straight forward after the fleeing enemies. The Wolf Riders pivot on the spot and move after the fleeing enemies. They might move enough to end in contact with the fleeing unit, because of the pivoting involved in their move. In this case they must stop 1" away from the fleeing unit. They cannot destroy the fleeing enemies because they have rolled less than their flee distance!

MULTIPLE FLEEING & PURSUING

It may happen that one or more victorious units have defeated several enemies that were engaging them from different sides, which is a rather complex situation.

For example, two enemy units are fleeing from the victor's front and another one is fleeing from the victor's right flank.

The sequence of actions in these cases is summarised below:

MULTIPLE FLEE/PURSUE SEQUENCE

- Declare in which direction each victorious unit is going to pursue and take tests to try to restrain pursuit of any victorious units that do not wish to pursue.
- Roll the dice to determine the flee distance of each fleeing unit.
- Roll the dice to determine the pursue distance of each pursuing unit.
- Remove fleeing units that have been caught by their pursuers.
- Move directly away from their pursuers all fleeing units that managed to escape.
- Move pursuing units directly after their fleeing enemies, in the directions declared.

A victorious unit that can pursue may choose to pursue any of the enemies that were engaged with it and are now fleeing away from it. All victorious units involved in the fight must first declare in which direction they are going to pursue – they can pursue the enemies fleeing from their front, from their right flank, from their left flank or from their rear.

After all flee and pursue rolls, compare the pursuit rolls of all pursuers with the flee rolls of all the enemy units they are pursuing. Destroy all fleeing units that have been caught.

To continue the example above, the winning unit declares it is pursuing the two enemies fleeing from its front. The enemy fleeing from the flank escapes automatically, as nobody is pursuing it. Then the pursuer will compare its pursuit roll with the flee roll of both units fleeing from its front and destroy those that have not scored higher. The pursuer is finally moved towards its front.

If the victor chose to pursue towards its flank or rear, the unit first pivots on the spot to face the direction it is going to move to and then moves straight forward (see Diagrams 43.1 and 44.1). Because of this pivoting, occasionally pursuers might move far enough to reach the unit they are pursuing, even if they rolled less than the fleeing unit (trust us, it might happen!). In such cases, stop the pursuing unit 1" behind the fleeing unit.

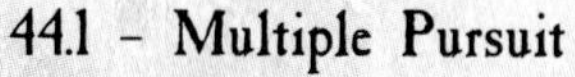

44.1 - Multiple Pursuit

In the unlikely event that the Spearmen win the combat and all their enemy units break and flee, the Spearmen must choose to pursue either the chariot on their left, the chariot on their right, or both units to their front.

PURSUIT INTO FRESH ENEMY

Normally, pursuers move the distance indicated by their dice roll and thereafter revert to the normal rules. So, in their following turn they may charge or move normally like any other unit.

It sometimes happens that pursuers move so far that they hit a fresh enemy unit. The pursuers are carried forward against the enemy unit as they chase their fleeing enemy. This is treated as if it were a new charge. If the fresh enemy causes Fear or Terror (see the Psychology section), the pursuers do not have to take a test to charge them – they are inspired by their victory and ready to fight any enemy, no matter how scary!

The unexpectedly attacked unit can only respond to the charge by holding or fleeing: any attempt to stand & shoot amidst the confusion of running bodies is deemed impossible. The charged unit must still make any necessary Psychology tests as normal (see the Psychology section).

If the newly charged unit flees, resolve their flee move before moving the pursuers, and if the pursuers catch them, the fleeing unit is immediately destroyed. The charger then completes its entire original charge move.

If the unit flees out of reach of the pursuers, simply move the pursuers the full pursuit distance towards the new target.

If the fresh enemy holds its ground, and since pursuit into fresh enemy is treated as a new charge, the pursuers must endeavour to bring as many charging models into combat as possible. This means that it is normally necessary to wheel in order to maximise the number of combatants.

If the unit that has been charged as a result of pursuit was engaged in combat with other enemy units from the beginning of that combat phase and its fight has not been resolved yet, the combat must be worked out immediately, and the pursuers get to fight another round of combat. The pursuers are charging and so get all the usual benefits and bonuses, except that if their side was to break or destroy the enemy again, they cannot pursue anymore, even if they normally are forced to because of Hatred/Frenzy, etc, (see the Psychology section). They are completely spent!

If the unit that has been charged as a result of pursuit was not engaged in combat with other enemy units from the beginning of this combat phase, or if it was engaged but that fight has already been resolved in this combat phase (and nobody has broken from combat), the combat is not resolved in this combat phase, but in the next (see Diagrams 45.1 and 45.2).

In the following combat phase the pursuers will still count as charging.

This may result in both sides having charging units in the same fight, in which case the charging units on both side will get the normal bonuses for charging and will strike before units that have not charged. If charging models are fighting other models that count as charging, solve their attacks in Initiative order (roll off if same Initiative).

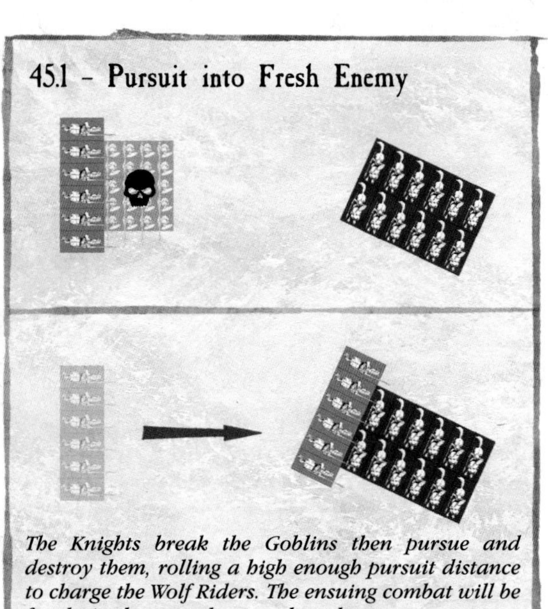

The Knights break the Goblins then pursue and destroy them, rolling a high enough pursuit distance to charge the Wolf Riders. The ensuing combat will be fought in the next close combat phase.

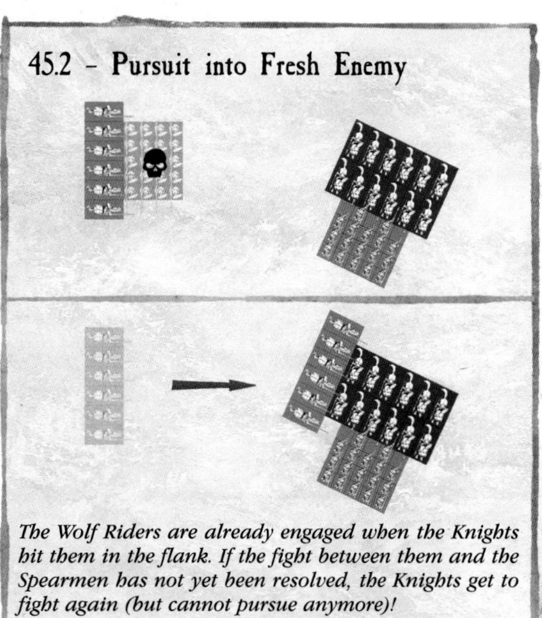

The Wolf Riders are already engaged when the Knights hit them in the flank. If the fight between them and the Spearmen has not yet been resolved, the Knights get to fight again (but cannot pursue anymore)!

SUBSEQUENT ACTIONS OF FLEEING TROOPS

If they are not destroyed and fail to rally (see the movement phase), fleeing units continue to move 2D6" or 3D6" during their subsequent movement phases. This is their flee roll. They must attempt to leave the battlefield as quickly as possible, which means that they will move straight towards the nearest table edge. Pivot the unit on the spot to face the direction it is fleeing in and then move it the distance indicated by the dice roll. This is a 'compulsory move' so fleeing troops are moved before other troops, once charges have been declared (see the Movement section). Due to their disorganised formation, they ignore penalties for obstacles and terrain (except for impassable terrain) and may move through friendly units (causing a Panic test), enemy units with a unit strength of less than 5, and fleeing enemy units.

A unit that is fleeing cannot fight, shoot or use magic, and is immune to all psychology.

If any model from a fleeing unit moves into contact with a non-fleeing enemy unit with a unit strength of 5 or more, impassable terrain or the edge of the table, the entire unit is destroyed. The troops have been scattered beyond recovery or have found places to hide themselves until the battle is over.

If an enemy unit successfully charges a unit that is already fleeing, the unit automatically declares and executes a flee reaction from the charge. The charge is then resolved as normal.

5 REDRESS THE RANKS

If the combat ends in a draw, or if at least one defeated unit passes its Break test, the fight will continue in the next close combat phase and the player will move to the next fight he wants to resolve during the present close combat phase. Before he does that though, it is best to tidy up the formations of the units involved in the previous fight. This will not always prove necessary, as much depends upon the casualties inflicted and the combat results.

Remember, a unit must always contain the same number of models in each rank as the first, except for its rear rank which may contain fewer. The process of redressing the ranks is intended to ensure that this remains true after combat, and also affords victors the chance to adjust their formation, as described below.

Casualties are usually removed from a unit's rear, as described earlier. Remember, a unit engaged in combat cannot move and so has no opportunity to change its formation in its movement phase.

If a character or champion in the unit is killed, this will leave a gap in the unit's front rank. Move a model forward from the rear rank to fill the gap, or, if the unit is fighting in a single rank, move a model from one end of the unit.

If a unit is engaged from its rear, or if a unit in a single line is engaged from the flanks, removing casualties could force some enemy units to lose contact with the unit. In these rare cases, move these units forward to keep in contact with the models they are killing (see Diagram 36.2).

In multiple combats it sometimes happens that at the end of a close combat phase some units are no longer engaged with any enemy unit (maybe because the unit they were engaged with has been completely destroyed). Such units are out of combat and can move normally from then on.

FREE MANOEUVRES

Units that have won the fight, but are still engaged in combat because their enemies did not break, can at this point execute one of the manoeuvres below.

These free manoeuvres can be executed only if the winning unit is engaged to just one of its sides (front, either flank or rear), and only in order to bring more models in base contact with the enemies. They cannot be executed if the winning unit is engaged on two or more sides or if the manoeuvre would result in reducing the number of models in base contact with the enemy!

- Winning units with enemies to their front can perform a free change formation manoeuvre to increase the number of models in their front rank by a maximum of five.

- Winning units with enemies to their flank/rear can perform a free turn manoeuvre to face their enemies (this allows characters, champions, standard bearers and musicians to move into contact with the enemy, see page 13).

END OF THE BASIC RULES

This is the end of the most basic rules you need to play Warhammer. We suggest that you play a few games with these rules first and, once you are familiar with them, you may add more detail to your games with the advanced rules, which can be found on the following pages.

Ten thousand flagellants dragging the automorial of Middenheim Delivered from the Darkness.

PSYCHOLOGY

It is an unfortunate fact that in the heat of battle troops often don't respond as you, their commander, might want them to. Faced with terrifying supernatural foes, their courage might fail, or they could simply be too dim to understand the orders they have been given. As the army commander, it is your duty to know about these things and take them into account. If you do not, then you may find that your best plans may not go exactly as you were expecting...

The Psychology rules are a set of special rules that represent these factors in the game. Some Psychology rules call upon the player to make occasional tests to determine whether his troops are affected by adverse psychology, such as Fear or Terror. Other Psychology rules, such as Frenzy and Hatred, always apply and do not require a Psychology test.

PSYCHOLOGY TESTS

Most Psychology tests are made in the same way, so we'll describe the procedure first before we look at the individual psychological factors.

When taking Psychology tests, roll 2D6 and compare the result to the Leadership value of the unit taking the test. If the result is less than or equal to the unit's Leadership score, the test is passed and all is well. If the result is greater than the unit's Leadership score, the test has been failed.

PSYCHOLOGY TESTS & BREAK TESTS

Players will immediately realise that a Psychology test is taken in a similar way as a Break test in close combat and uses the same characteristic, namely the Leadership value. However, a Break test is not a Psychology test. The two are quite separate. This is an important point to remember because some bonuses and special rules apply specifically to Break tests and others apply specifically to Psychology tests.

The most important rule to distinguish them is that units engaged in close combat and fleeing units never take Psychology tests (Panic, Fear, Terror and Stupidity). The reason for this is that troops that are busy fighting for their lives or already running madly for cover are less receptive and less prone to look around and be influenced by potentially upsetting events that happen around them, and their psychology is covered by the Break tests themselves.

USING RIDER'S LEADERSHIP

In the case of models such as cavalry, chariots and heroic individuals riding monsters, it is the rider's Leadership that is used and not that of the mount or monster. If a chariot has several crew members, use the Leadership of the crew member with the highest Leadership value.

USING SUPERIOR LEADERSHIP

Units use the best Leadership available for their tests, so if a unit of troops is joined by a character (or any other model with a better Ld), the unit uses the highest Leadership value available. Characters often have better Leadership values than ordinary troops, so a unit led by a superior character will be less prone to psychology effects. See the Characters section for rules concerning the interaction between characters and units of troops when they are subject to different Psychology rules.

TESTS AT THE START OF THE TURN

Some Psychology tests are taken at the start of the turn phase. For example, Terror tests caused by terrifying creatures within 6" and Stupidity tests are both taken at the start of the turn. Other tests, caused by special rules, spells, etc, are also taken at the start of the turn phase. When a player is called upon to take different tests at the start of the turn, then do them in the order they are listed here:

1) Terror

2) Stupidity

3) Other (caused by special rules, spells etc)

So, if a unit is obliged to take a Terror test and a Stupidity test, take the Terror test first, and only if this is passed will it be necessary to take the Stupidity test.

PANIC

This is the most common and most important psychological effect. Battles are often won or lost because an army panics and flees, even though it may not have been beaten in combat. Troops who are nearby when their friends are destroyed or run away can easily lose their nerve and flee themselves, causing other troops to lose heart until the whole army routs in blind panic.

A unit must take a Panic test in the following cases (which are described in more detail later):

1) It suffers 25% or more casualties.

2) A friendly unit within 6" is destroyed.

3) A friendly unit within 6" breaks from combat.

4) Fleeing friends move through the unit.

Note that you only need to take one Panic test per unit in each phase (start of the turn, movement, magic, shooting and close combat phase), even if there are multiple reasons to take Panic tests. Panic tests are often taken immediately when they are caused, and it is therefore a good idea to mark in some manner units that have taken a Panic test, as they will not have to test again as the phase continues. If a unit fails a Panic test, it must flee in the direction specified below.

After this first flee move, the unit will then try and leave the battlefield as soon as possible, so it will continue to flee towards the closest table edge until it leaves the battlefield or it rallies.

1) 25% Casualties

A unit must take a Panic test at the end of any phase (except the close combat phase) if it has lost 25% or more of the models it started the phase with.

For example, a unit of 20 models is shot at by an enemy unit and suffers four casualties – not enough for a Panic test. In the same phase, another enemy unit fires against them causing three more casualties. Seven out of twenty is above 25%, so the unit must take a Panic test at the end of the phase.

If the test is failed, the unit will flee directly away from the unit that has caused the most casualties (roll a dice in case of equal number of casualties).

War machines do not have to test if they lose one or more of their crew, and neither do ridden monsters or chariots if they lose their rider, or vice versa.

This test must also be taken if the unit suffers 25% casualties from random factors, such as miscasts, misfires, magical effects, unusual terrain or other special rules. This is intended as a 'catch-all' to cover units that suffer high casualties. A good example is casualties inflicted by whirling Goblin Fanatics, which cause casualties as they move. These Panic tests are taken immediately as the situation arises and not at the end of the phase, and may interrupt a unit's movement in the same way as a stand & shoot charge reaction.

If you cannot tell in which direction such strange situations would cause the panicking unit to run (as in the case of the casualties being caused by a member of the same unit exploding!), the survivors will flee towards the closest table edge.

This test must also be taken (immediately!) by a charging unit if its enemies stand & shoot and inflict 25% or more casualties. This may result in the charging unit panicking before it contacts its target (in which case it has been forced to flee from the hail of missiles unleashed by the defenders).

2) Unit destroyed within 6"

If a unit is completely destroyed (reached by a charger as it was fleeing, wiped out by missile fire, magic, close combat, or indeed any other occurrence), any friendly units within 6" of the destroyed unit must take a Panic test (you must measure this distance before removing the unit, of course). Units that had a unit strength of less than 5 at the beginning of the phase during which they were destroyed do not cause Panic.

If the test is failed, the unit will flee directly away from the point where the friendly unit has been destroyed.

3) Friends break from close combat within 6"

Test if a friendly unit with a unit strength of 5 or more within 6" has broken as a result of being defeated in close combat.

If the test is failed, the unit will flee directly away from the point where the friendly unit has broken.

4) Fleeing friendly models move through the unit

If a friendly unit with a unit strength of 5 or more moves through the unit as part of their flee move, the unit must take a Panic test.

If the test is failed, the unit will flee in the same direction as their fleeing friends, joining them in the mad rush to safety.

Exception: A unit that has declared a hold charge reaction and is panicked by fleeing friends running through its ranks before the enemy is moved into contact automatically changes its reaction to flee. This means they will flee away from the chargers instead of joining the friends that caused the Panic.

FEAR

Some creatures inspire fear as is indicated in their relevant Army book and these include large and disturbing monsters such as Trolls, as well as supernatural horrors such as Skeletons.

A unit must take a Fear test if it is faced by one of the following situations:

1) If charged by a Fear-causing enemy.

2) If a unit wishes to charge a Fear-causing enemy.

1) Charged by Fear-causing enemies

If a Fear-causing enemy unit declares a charge against it, a unit must take a test to see if it can overcome that fear and take the charge. First declare the unit's intended charge reaction, then test as soon as the Fear-causing unit is determined to be within charge range.

If the test is passed, the unit can react to the charge as normal.

If the unit fails its test and its unit strength is lower than the unit strength of the Fear-causing charging enemy unit, the unit must immediately change its charge reaction to 'flee'.

If the unit fails its test but its unit strength is equal to or higher than the unit strength of the Fear-causing charging enemy unit, it will fight on as normal but must roll 6s to score hits in the first turn of close combat against the Fear-causing enemy models (no modifiers or special rules apply – only by rolling an unmodified 6 can models score hits against these enemies).

If more than one Fear-causing unit is declaring charges against it, a unit must take each test separately.

2) Wishing to declare a charge against a Fear-causing enemy

If a unit wishes to declare a charge against an enemy that causes Fear, it must take a test to overcome its fear first. If the unit is unfortunate and the test is failed, it may not charge and must remain stationary in that movement phase, and for the rest of the turn is treated in the same way as a unit that has failed a charge.

If the test is passed, the unit may declare the charge as normal.

DEFEATED BY FEAR-CAUSING ENEMY

Units in close combat automatically fail their Break test if they are defeated by an enemy that they Fear and the combined unit strength of the units on the losing side is lower than the combined unit strength of all Fear-causing enemy units on the winning side.

Note that an act of Insane Courage will keep such units in the fight though, so it is worth rolling the dice in the hope of a double 1!

If the Fear-causing enemy units do not have a higher unit strength, Break tests are taken as normal. See the Close Combat section for details of combat results, Break tests and fleeing troops.

Note that this rule applies whether the defeated units have previously passed any Fear tests or not.

TERROR

Some monsters are so huge and threatening that they are even more scary than those causing Fear. Such creatures cause Terror.

Troops who are confronted by monsters or situations that cause Terror must test to see whether they overcome their terror. If they fail, they are completely terrified and reduced to gibbering wrecks. Troops only ever test for Terror once in a battle and then they are not affected again, even if the test is failed.

If a creature causes Terror, it automatically causes Fear as well, and all the rules described for Fear apply. However, you never have to take a Terror test and a Fear test from the same enemy or situation – just take a Terror test. If you pass the Terror test, you automatically pass the Fear test too. As any unit of troops only ever takes one Terror test in a battle, any subsequent encounters with terrifying monsters or situations will simply count as Fear.

A unit must take a Terror test if it is faced by one of the following situations:

1) If charged by a Terror-causing enemy.

2) If a unit wishes to charge a Terror-causing enemy.

3) If there is an enemy that causes Terror within 6" at the start of the unit's turn.

1) Charged by Terror-causing enemies

If a Terror-causing enemy unit declares a charge against it, a unit must take a test to see if can overcome the terror and take the charge. First declare the unit's intended charge reaction, then test as soon as the Terror-causing unit is determined to be within charge range.

If the test is passed, the unit can react to the charge as normal.

If the unit fails its test, it must immediately change its charge reaction to 'flee'.

If more than one Terror-causing unit is declaring charges against it, the unit takes a Terror test against the first unit that declared the charge and, if the test is passed, then treats the rest as Fear tests instead.

2) Wishing to declare a charge against a Terror-causing enemy

If a unit wishes to declare a charge against an enemy that causes Terror, it must take a test to overcome its terror first. If the unit is unfortunate and the test is failed, it may not charge and must flee in the compulsory movement part of its movement phase.

If the test is passed, the unit may declare the charge as normal.

3) Terror-causing enemies within 6" at the start of the turn

A unit must test at the start of its turn if there are one or more Terror-causing units within 6". If the test is failed, the unit will immediately flee directly away from the nearest Terror-causing creature.

FEAR & TERROR IMMUNITY

Obviously, a large monster is less likely to suffer from Fear or Terror itself. There is no way a huge Dragon is going to be scared of a Troll, for example.

A creature that causes Fear is not affected by enemies that cause Fear. Faced with an enemy that causes Terror, a Fear-causing monster only suffers Fear, not Terror.

A creature that causes Terror is not affected by Fear or Terror at all.

For example, a Troll causes Fear and a Dragon causes Terror. The Dragon is not at all worried by the Troll, but the Troll fears the Dragon.

This special immunity also applies to any rider of a Fear- or Terror-causing monster (or steed), so a Dragon rider wouldn't be afraid of a creature that would frighten him were he on foot.

Also, Fear tests or Terror tests are passed automatically if the Fear- or Terror-causing enemy is currently fleeing – their scariness is greatly hampered by them attempting to run away from the battlefield as fast as their legs can carry them...

STUPIDITY

Many large and powerful creatures are unfortunately rather stupid. Even some otherwise quite intelligent creatures act stupidly now and again because they are easily confused or distracted, or perhaps because they are under the effect of a spell. The Stupidity rules represent the sort of slow-wittedness or dumb behaviour that some especially thick beasts are prone to. Creatures that are Stupid are indicated as such in the Warhammer Armies books and include such models as Trolls and Cold Ones.

Stupid creatures that are not engaged in combat must make a test at the start of their turn to see whether they overcome their Stupidity. Make a test for each unit of Stupid troops. If they pass the test, all is well and good – the creatures behave reasonably intelligently and can move as normal. Nothing untoward has occurred beyond a bit of drooling and the odd spontaneous cackle.

If the test is failed, all is not well and the unit momentarily forgets what it is doing. The unit is moved directly forwards at half speed during the compulsory moves part of the movement phase (for example, Trolls with Movement 6 would move 3" forward). Skirmishing units will move at half speed in a direction determined by rolling the scatter dice.

This counts as compulsory movement and so occurs before other movement, but after charges have been declared (see the Movement section). Any enemy troops encountered are automatically charged. This is then treated as a normal charge, except that the charger will move only half its normal Move rate (3" in the example above), regardless of the outcome of the charge.

If there are friends in the way, the units blunder into each other and their ranks become confused, in which case both units are pinned in place for the rest of the movement phase and neither may move further.

Units that failed their Stupidity test cannot voluntarily declare charges, shoot and cannot cast spells for that turn.

These rules apply until the start of the creatures' following turn, when they must test once more to see whether they are affected by Stupidity. The effect of Stupidity also stops immediately if the creatures are engaged in close combat, as their fighting instincts overcome their Stupidity.

Other Psychology

Creatures affected by Stupidity are quite unaware of anything happening around them. Until they are no longer Stupid, these units are Immune to Psychology (see page 53).

Stupidity and riders

It sometimes happens that a cavalry rider or a monster rider will be riding a Stupid creature, for example, a Dark Elf riding a Cold One. If a rider's mount is Stupid, it will have to test for Stupidity at the start of his turn, but the rider's Leadership characteristic is used rather than that of the mount. If the test is failed, the rider is obliged to hang on and is unable to shoot and cast spells while the creature is Stupid.

FRENZY

Certain warriors can work themselves into a fighting frenzy, a whirlwind of destruction in which all concern for personal safety is ignored in favour of mindless violence. Many of these frenzied warriors are drugged or entranced, and have driven themselves into a psychotic frenzy with chanting, singing, yelling and screaming. These troops are described as Frenzied. In the case of mounted troops, Frenzy affects both riders and their steeds.

In the declare charges part of the movement phase, after the charges of all non-Frenzied troops have been declared (including relative charge reactions), measure to see if any enemies are within charge reach of any Frenzied troops (ie, within the unit's charge move and in their normal arc of sight). If so, the Frenzied unit must declare a charge against that enemy. The player has no choice in the matter; the unit will automatically make its charge move. If there are several eligible units within the charge reach of the Frenzied unit, the controlling player may decide which unit to charge.

Frenzied models fight with +1 extra Attack during close combat. Models that have 1 Attack on their profile therefore have 2, models with 2 Attacks have 3, and so on.

Frenzied models must pursue fleeing enemy whether the player wants them to or not. Unlike other troops, they may not attempt to hold back as they are far too crazed with battle lust. They even pursue if they are defending an obstacle. If they wipe out an enemy in the turn they have charged, they will always overrun.

Frenzied troops that are defeated in close combat, as determined by the combat results, immediately lose their Frenzy (this happens before taking their Break test). Their exuberant, crazed frenzy has been thoroughly beaten out of them and they continue to fight as ordinary warriors for the remainder of the battle.

Frenzied units are Immune to Psychology (see the next page) as long as they are Frenzied.

HATRED

Hatred is a powerful emotion and instances of hatred and rivalry are commonplace in the Warhammer world. There are grudges borne over centuries, racial animosity bordering on madness, and irreconcilable feuds that have left generations of dead in their wake. Some races hate other races with such bitter conviction that they will fight with astounding fury and this is specified in the troops' entry.

Troops fighting in close combat with a hated foe may re-roll any misses when they attack in the first turn of any close combat. This bonus only applies in the first turn of a combat and represents the unit venting its pent-up hatred on the foe. After the initial round of blood-mad hacking, they lose impetus and subsequently fight as normal for the rest of the combat.

Troops who Hate their enemy must always pursue them if they flee. They cannot attempt to avoid pursuit by testing against their Leadership as other troops can. They even pursue if they are defending an obstacle. If they wipe out a Hated enemy in the turn they have charged, they will always overrun.

IMMUNE TO PSYCHOLOGY

Some warriors and creatures in the Warhammer world are almost completely fearless, or are such grizzled veterans that situations that would make lesser troops panic have no effect on them. This will be specified in the unit's entry.

Troops that are Immune to Psychology (sometimes also called 'Immune to all Psychology') automatically pass all their Panic, Fear and Terror tests and are not automatically broken if defeated in combat by outnumbering Fear-causing enemies, but take the Break test as normal.

Troops that are Immune to Psychology may never flee as a charge reaction – they are far too proud and brave (or too dim-witted) to do this!

These troops have to take Break tests as normal.

STUBBORN

Some troops will fight on in close combat almost regardless of casualties. This can be because they consider themselves to be elite, have taken severe vows to hold their ground in combat or are simply too slow-witted to flee when defeated by superior troops! These troops are referred to as being Stubborn.

During a Break test, Stubborn units use the Leadership value on their profile. They always ignore Break test modifiers, regardless of how much they lost the combat by. This means, for example, that Stubborn troops with a Leadership value of 8 will only ever break on the roll of 9 or more when making a Break test.

UNBREAKABLE

Some creatures are utterly fearless and will never give up a battle, no matter how hopeless the situation might be. This could be because of the troops' extreme bravery, because of a magical effect or because the creatures fighting are not truly self-aware.

Unbreakable troops are Immune to Psychology (see above). In addition, if defeated in close combat (even by Fear-causing creatures that outnumber them), Unbreakable troops continue to fight on regardless of results. They automatically pass all Break tests, regardless of modifiers, can never flee and will literally die fighting under any circumstances.

Unbreakable Swarms

Units classed as Swarms in their special rules in the relevant Army book represent seething masses of small creatures, often summoned to the battlefield by way of magic. They are an unthinking mass, completely devoid of any self-awareness, and are consequently Unbreakable.

On the other hand, when swarms start to lose a fight, it's easy for their enemies to inflict lots of damage upon them (mostly by stomping all over the little critters!) – swarms that are defeated in combat immediately take a number of wounds equal to the difference they've lost the fight by. These additional wounds cannot be saved, not even by ward saves, nor can they be regenerated.

For example, a Rat Swarm loses a fight by 3 points. The unit immediately suffers a further 3 wounds.

Note that swarms who are subject to special combat result rules (like Undead and Daemonic swarms) do not have the Unbreakable rule, but use their army's own special rules instead ('Undead' and 'Daemonic Instability' in the examples above).

WEAPONS

In the grim and dangerous world of Warhammer, warriors employ many different types of weapons against a multitude of foes. From the fine swords of the Elves or the sharp axes of the Dwarfs to the spiked clubs used by less sophisticated creatures like the Ogres, every race has weaponry fitted to its preferred style of fighting.

WEAPONS AND UNITS

It is usual for all the models in a unit to carry the same weapons. So, a unit will be a unit of Spearmen, a unit of Halberdiers, a unit of Crossbowmen and so on. It is acceptable for a unit to include a minority of models that are differently armed for the sake of a varied and interesting appearance, but the whole unit still counts as being armed as the majority. Where models are varied in this way, it is important that the overall appearance of the unit is not misleading.

All troops and characters are assumed to carry hand weapons, such as swords, axes, clubs, maces and comparable weaponry. In addition, some troops carry another weapon such as a spear, lance or halberd. At the start of the first turn of a combat, each such unit can choose which of their weapons to use (the entire unit must use the same weapon, but characters can always choose separately). Whichever weapon they use must then be used for the entire combat. For example, troops armed with spears and shields may opt to fight with their swords if they want to benefit from the defensive bonus conferred by fighting with hand weapon and shield, but must then fight with swords for the duration of the combat, even if it lasts many turns, and cannot switch to their spears.

SPECIAL WEAPON RULES

Different types of weapons have advantages and disadvantages in different circumstances. Some are powerful but require both hands to use, some take a considerable time to load, and so on. These qualities are represented by the special weapon rules described here. Rules for individual types of weapon are listed later in this section.

STRENGTH BONUS

Some weapons give their wielders a Strength bonus in close combat or when shooting. This is clearly indicated in the weapon's profile. For example, a halberd has a +1 Strength bonus, so if used in close combat by a warrior with a Strength of 3, any hits caused are resolved with a Strength of 4. Note that this Strength bonus only applies when the warrior is using the weapon – his Strength characteristic remains unchanged for other purposes.

Some Strength bonuses only apply in the first turn of a combat. This reflects the fact that the weapons are especially cumbersome or exhausting to use. This restriction is indicated in the weapon's description.

Some Strength bonuses only apply if the user has charged that turn. These are weapons that rely upon the impact of the charge to pierce the foe. This restriction is indicated in the weapon's description.

REQUIRES TWO HANDS

Some weapons require two hands to use in close combat. These weapons usually have a long shaft and are heavy and cumbersome to use.

If a weapon requires two hands to use, it is not possible to simultaneously employ a shield or another weapon. If a shield is carried, it must be slung across the warrior's back or dropped behind him whilst he fights in close combat.

STRIKES LAST

Many weapons, such as the great sword favoured by some Empire troops or the great axes of the Dwarfs, are very heavy and require considerable training and stamina to wield. Such a weapon is described by the term 'strikes last'.

Troops armed with a weapon that strikes last will always strike last during close combat where they would otherwise strike in Initiative order. If fighting enemies who also suffer from the same penalty, they would use their respective Initiative to decide who is going to strike first. In the case of same Initiative, the troops that won the combat in the previous turn will strike first. If this does not apply, roll a dice to determine who goes first.

Note that troops that charge will still strike first in the initial turn of close combat, as charging troops always strike first rather than in Initiative order. For example, troops armed with great axes will strike first on the turn they charge and strike last thereafter.

FIGHT IN RANKS

Spears and similar weapons are well suited to fighting in deep formations. Weapons used for fighting in ranks enable troops in a second or subsequent rank to fight in close combat as well as the warriors in the first rank who are actually touching the enemy. For example, a unit of Spearmen can fight in two ranks – warriors in the second rank can stab past their comrades using their long spears.

If a unit is entitled to fight in this way then any model in a second or subsequent rank can fight if it is behind a model that is engaged in close combat to its front. Extra ranks cannot fight to their side or rear but only to their front. Where a weapon can fight in two or more ranks, this is indicated in the weapon's description, for example, 'spears fight in two ranks'.

In order to employ all of its additional ranks as described, a unit must not have moved in that turn. If a unit has moved, if it has charged for example, then it fights with one less rank than it otherwise would. For example, a unit of Spearmen can normally fight in two ranks, but will fight with only the front rank if they charge. The unit will be able to fight with the extra rank during subsequent rounds of close combat.

MULTIPLE SHOTS

Some missile weapons enable their users to shoot several times in each shooting phase – known as multiple shots. The number of times the weapon can fire is given as part of its description (eg, a Dark Elf repeater crossbow can fire two shots in each shooting phase so is noted as having 2 x multiple shots). These weapons can either fire once without penalty, or as many times as indicated in their rules with an additional -1 to hit penalty. All models equipped with such weapons in the unit must either fire multiple shots or single shots, the player cannot choose to fire single shots with some troopers and multiple with others.

Remember that a model's Attacks characteristic has no effect on the number of shots it fires. The Attacks characteristic refers to close combat attacks only.

THROWN WEAPON

Some warriors carry missile weapons that are designed to be thrown, such as javelins or throwing axes. These generally have a short range, but they can be very accurate. Thrown weapons do not suffer the usual to hit penalties for shooting at long range or for moving and shooting. Note that this doesn't entitle the warrior to throw his missile if he charges or marches, it is simply that the usual -1 to hit penalty for moving whilst shooting does not apply.

MOVE-OR-FIRE

Some missile weapons take a long time to load, such as crossbows and handguns. So, a model that is armed with a move-or-fire weapon may not fire his weapon if he has moved at all during that turn. It doesn't matter if the model was forced to move by some compulsory action or by magic. Any movement will prevent the model from shooting, even the simple act of turning round.

ARMOUR PIERCING

Certain weapons, most notably blackpowder weapons such as handguns, are even better at penetrating armour than their Strength value suggests. Therefore, the enemy armour save is reduced by an additional -1. For example, an armour piercing weapon that has Strength 4 would have a -2 armour save modifier rather than -1.

LIST OF WEAPONS

Listed on the following pages are some of the many and varied types of weapon used by warriors in the Warhammer world. The weapons that are covered here are those most commonly and universally used rather than a comprehensive list. Unusual weapons that are specific to individual races or armies are covered in the Army book for that particular race.

Sometimes the same weapon has two different entries, one referring to the use of that weapon made by infantry (and other models on foot), and the other referring to mounted models (cavalry and models riding monsters or chariots).

CLOSE COMBAT WEAPONS

Close combat weapons are just that... weapons used in close combat. Most warriors carry at least a hand weapon of some kind and many carry something more potent in addition. In close combat, warriors fight using their own Strength characteristic to resolve hits, but modified as indicated for the weapon they use.

HAND WEAPONS

Unless noted otherwise, all models are assumed to be carrying a hand weapon of some kind. The term 'hand weapon' is used to describe any weapon held in one hand and not otherwise covered by the rules. As such it includes swords, axes, clubs, maces, etc.

Hand weapons have the advantage that they can be used with a shield or another hand weapon, as described below. In both instances, these rules only apply to warriors fighting on foot and not to cavalry and warriors mounted on monsters or chariots.

Fighting with two hand weapons (infantry)
Some warriors carry two hand weapons, one in each hand, and can rain down even more blows on their enemy. This could include a sword in each hand, an axe and sword, or any combination of hand weapons.

If a warrior on foot fights with a hand weapon in each hand, he receives +1 extra Attack to account for his second weapon. Eg, if the warrior's Attack characteristic is 1, he fights with 2 Attacks, if his Attack characteristic is 2, he fights with 3 Attacks, and so on.

Fighting with hand weapon and shield (infantry)
Some warriors carry a hand weapon in one hand and a shield in the other, to easier deflect blows with either shield or hand weapon.

If a warrior on foot fights with a hand weapon and shield, he may increase his armour save by a further +1 in close combat against enemies fighting from his front. So, for example, if he has a shield, light armour and a sword, his armour save is increased from 5+ to 4+ when fighting in close combat.

This only applies in close combat, not against wounds suffered from shooting, magic, or other means.

Also, this only applies against opponents engaged to the model's front, not against foes fighting in the model's flank or rear.

GREAT WEAPONS (INFANTRY)

Great weapons are especially large and heavy weapons wielded with both hands. This includes great hammers, great axes, and such like. A blow from a great weapon can cut a foe in half and break apart the thickest armour.

Rules: +2 Strength bonus; requires two hands; strikes last.

GREAT WEAPONS (MOUNTED)

These are less effective when used by mounted models as freedom of movement is considerably reduced.

Rules: +1 Strength bonus; requires two hands; strikes last.

FLAILS

A cumbersome, heavy weapon used with both hands. It consists of heavy weights, often spiked, attached to a pole or handle by heavy chains. A flail drains the user's stamina quickly, but is very destructive.

Rules: +2 Strength bonus in first turn of combat; requires two hands.

MORNING STARS

A single-handed weapon that consists of one or more spiked balls on a chain. Like the larger flail it resembles, it is a tiring weapon so its advantage lies in the first round of combat.

Rules: +1 Strength bonus in first turn of combat.

HALBERDS

The halberd is a heavy bladed weapon mounted on a sturdy shaft. The steel blade has a point like a spear as well as a heavy cutting edge like an axe. It is held in both hands and used to chop as well as thrust.

Rules: +1 Strength bonus; requires two hands.

SPEARS (INFANTRY)

Spears are long shafts of wood with a sharp metal tip. Because stationary spearmen can fight in two ranks, spears are ideal defensive weapons for infantry.

Rules: Fight in two ranks.

SPEARS (MOUNTED)

All cavalry, monster riders and chariot riders armed with spears can use them to ride down enemy troops, spitting them as they gallop into their ranks.

Rules: +1 Strength bonus when charging.

LANCES (MOUNTED ONLY)

A lance is a heavier, longer version of the spear, used exclusively by mounted warriors.

Rules: +2 Strength bonus when charging.

PISTOL (HAND-TO-HAND)

Pistols are small weapons that employ a noxious and unreliable form of gunpowder to propel a small lead or stone bullet.

In close combat, the heavy butt of a pistol can be used as a club, counting exactly like a hand weapon.

If a model carries two (a 'brace') or more pistols it counts as being armed with two hand weapons in close combat.

Rules: Counts as a hand weapon.

MISSILE WEAPONS

Missile weapons are bows, crossbows and similar weapons whether simple or primitive like a javelin or more complex and advanced like handguns and pistols.

SHORTBOWS

Shortbows are small, short-ranged bows that are favoured by Goblins. Some cavalry also carry a shortbow because it is easier to shoot from horseback.

Maximum range: 16"; **Strength:** 3; **Rules:** none.

BOWS

The bow is used extensively in warfare. It is a compact, long-ranged weapon that is cheap to make and easy to maintain.

Maximum range: 24"; **Strength:** 3; **Rules:** none.

LONGBOWS

A longbow is a dangerous weapon – a skilled archer can hit an enemy from a great distance.

Maximum range: 30"; **Strength:** 3; **Rules:** none.

CROSSBOWS

A crossbow consists of a short strong bow stave mounted on a wooden or metal stock. It takes a long time to load and wind a crossbow, but each shot has tremendous range and power.

Maximum range: 30"; **Strength:** 4; **Rules:** Move-or-fire.

REPEATER CROSSBOWS

Used almost exclusively by the Dark Elves of Naggaroth, the repeater crossbow is a lighter, less powerful type of crossbow that has a magazine allowing bolts to drop into place ready for firing as the string is drawn. A repeater crossbow can fire a hail of shots in the time it takes to shoot one ordinary crossbow.

Maximum range: 24"; **Strength:** 3;

Rules: 2 x multiple shots.

SLINGS

Slings consist of a looped string of cloth or leather into which a stone is placed and then shot with surprising strength and accuracy.

Maximum range: 18"; **Strength:** 3;

Rules: 2 x multiple shots if enemy is within 9".

JAVELINS

The javelin is a light spear designed for throwing, and javelin-armed warriors often carry several to last them throughout the battle. The javelin is too flimsy to be used in hand-to-hand fighting. It is not a very common weapon as it has a short range, but the amphibious Skinks of Lustria use javelins extensively.

Maximum range: 8"; **Strength:** As user;

Rules: Thrown weapon.

THROWING STARS/KNIVES

Throwing stars and knives are small, easily concealed weapons and, consequently, they are favoured by assassins and lightly armed infiltrators. A perfectly balanced throwing knife is not suitable for close combat, but is deadly in the hands of a skilled thrower.

Maximum range: 6"; **Strength:** As user;

Rules: Thrown weapon.

THROWING AXES

Some warriors use heavy bladed throwing axes. These weapons are keenly balanced so they can be thrown accurately despite their weight. Even so, the strongest warrior cannot throw such a weapon very far, but if a throwing axe hits its target, the effect is devastating.

Maximum range: 6"; **Strength:** As user +1;

Rules: Thrown weapon.

HANDGUNS

A handgun is a simple firearm consisting of a metal barrel mounted on a wooden stock. The gunpowder charge is ignited by poking a length of burning cord, or match as it is called, into a small touch-hole. Some of the more advanced versions have levers and springs that hold the burning match and release the firing mechanism to fire the gun.

Handguns have a long range and hit very hard, making a mockery of even the thickest armour.

Maximum range: 24"; **Strength:** 4;

Rules: Move-or-fire, armour piercing.

PISTOLS (SHOOTING)

We have already described how a pistol can be used in close combat. In addition, a pistol can shoot up to a distance of 8".

Pistols do not suffer the usual to hit penalties for shooting at long range or for moving and shooting.

Pistols require very little time to fire and so can always be used to stand & shoot against a charging enemy, even if the enemy starts its charge within half of its charge distance, and then used as hand weapons in the ensuing close combat.

If a model carries two (a 'brace') or more pistols it counts as having 2 x multiple shots with its pistols.

Maximum range: 8"; **Strength:** 4;

Rules (single pistol): Armour piercing, always stand & shoot.

Rules (brace of pistols): Armour piercing, always stand & shoot, 2 x multiple shots.

MONSTERS

The Old World is a vast and untamed place where wild and monstrous creatures roam the dark forests and vast mountain ranges. There are many creatures roughly human in appearance, such as Orcs, Trolls, and Minotaurs, but there are also bigger and more bizarre monsters, such as Griffons, Dragons and Hydras.

It is with these monsters that this section of the rules is concerned. Monsters may be ridden to battle by mighty heroes and wizards. Many of these beasts must be hand reared by their master if they are ever to accept a rider, so the great leaders of the Old World pay vast sums to adventurers who collect eggs or hatchlings from the nests of Griffons and other winged monsters. This is a dangerous profession, and for many a fatal one, but it ensures that the Emperor's menagerie in Altdorf gains fresh creatures to rear on behalf of the nobles and wizard lords of the Empire.

Monsters are powerful elements of the army. Some monsters develop loyalty and devotion to their masters and will willingly fight for them, while others are placed under enchantments or simply driven forward towards the enemy in the hope that they will attack the right side.

THE MONSTER MODEL

Monsters always fight individually; they can never join other models to form a unit, except when they are ridden by a character.

Each monster is, in effect, a unit of one model and it has a front (used to determine its arc of sight as normal), flanks and rear as normal (see Diagram 59.2 – Monster's Front, Flank & Rear). Monsters follow all the rules for normal units, except for the differences described in this section.

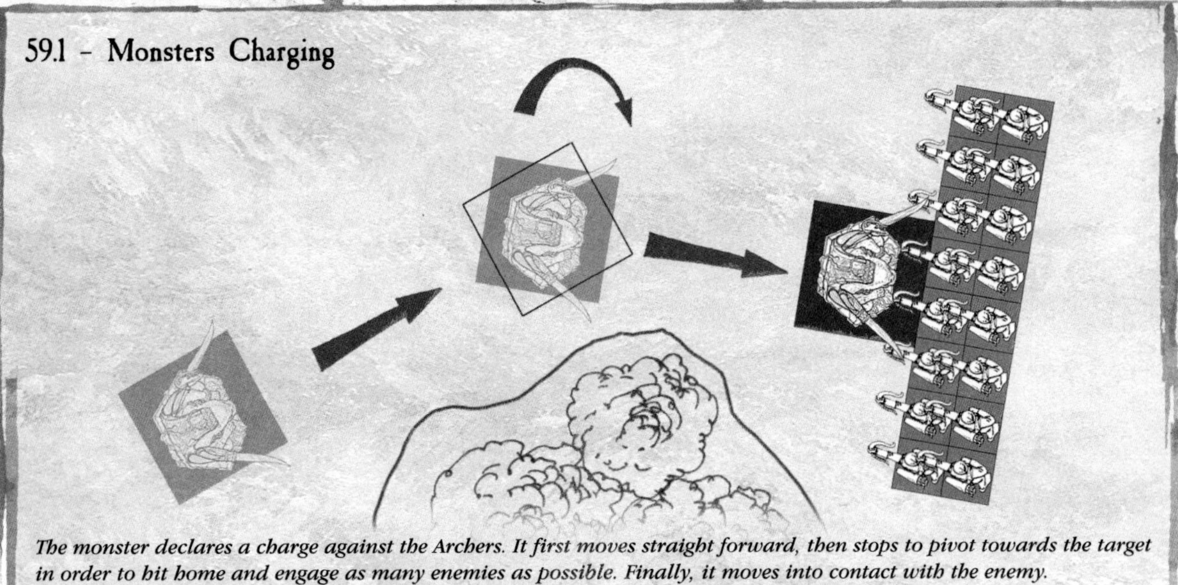

The monster declares a charge against the Archers. It first moves straight forward, then stops to pivot towards the target in order to hit home and engage as many enemies as possible. Finally, it moves into contact with the enemy.

MOVING MONSTERS

When moving a monster, simply measure the distance and move it. There is no need to turn or wheel, though the monster still has to have a line of sight to any enemy that it is going to charge. In effect, monsters can turn to face any direction (pivoting around the centre of the model) at any point during their move and as many times as they like without reduction to movement.

MANOEUVRING DURING A CHARGE

Like all units, monsters are more restricted in their movement during a charge. Monsters can pivot on the spot only once during a charge move if a straight move wouldn't hit the target or would not bring as many models as possible into combat, but are free to do this at any point during the move. This means they can either pivot and then charge in a straight line, or move directly forward, stop to pivot towards a different direction and then complete their move in a straight line (see Diagram 59.1 – Monsters Charging). Of course they must still abide by all normal rules governing charges, so they need to see their target at the beginning of the charge, cannot charge the flank of a unit if they start the charge in its front arc, must try to bring as many models as possible into the combat, and so on.

MONSTROUS MOUNTS

Monsters are often employed as mounts for characters. A monster and its rider or riders count as a single model in the same way as a cavalry model, although different rules apply.

Horses, wolves, war boars and other similar sized creatures that only have 1 Wound are covered by the rules already described for cavalry. This system is fine for these smaller creatures, but obviously wouldn't work for big monsters such as Dragons, which are far larger and much more difficult to kill than a horse or a wolf.

If a mount has 2 or more Wounds, it is classed as a monstrous mount and the following rules are used. These rules would therefore apply to a hero riding a Griffon, a Wizard mounted on a Wyvern, a Dragon and its lordly rider, and so on. No additional +1 is added to the rider's armour save, as the advantages of riding the monster are worked out in other ways instead.

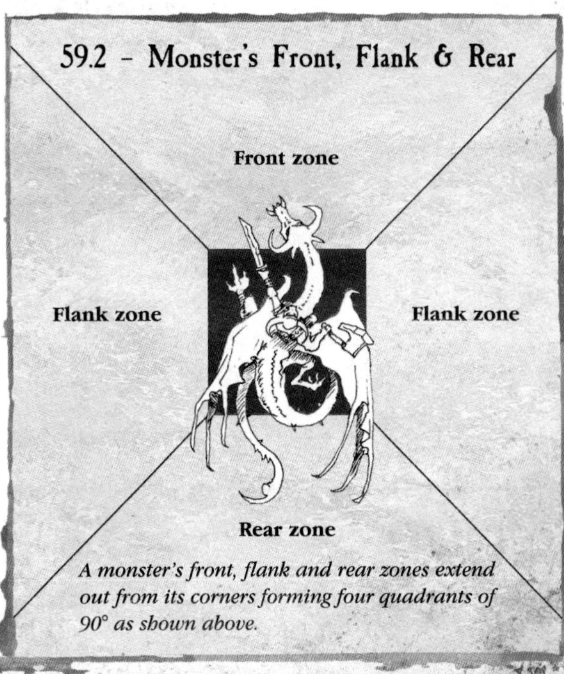

A monster's front, flank and rear zones extend out from its corners forming four quadrants of 90° as shown above.

SHOOTING AT MONSTROUS MOUNTS

As a single model, the monster and its rider are considered to be a single target. It is not possible to shoot specifically at either the rider or the mount.

When you shoot at a character riding a monster, the rules for shooting at characters apply, as explained in the section on Characters on page 74. However, if the monster is a large target, the enemy adds +1 to his To Hit score.

Once you have established how many hits have been scored, you must apportion them between the rider and the monster. For each hit scored roll a D6; on a roll of 1-4 the monster has been hit. On a 5 or 6 the rider has been hit. Roll to wound the monster or rider as normal.

Work out wounds separately on the rider and his mount. Take any saving throws due to the target as normal. Most monsters do not have an armour saving throw as they have no armour, but some have scaly skin that confers an equivalent save. Riders are permitted saves for their armour, but remember that they do not receive the additional +1 armour save as cavalry models do.

If a monster has two or more riders (a very unusual combination) then randomise any hits among the two riders. If models are glued in place (as is likely) it will be necessary to make a note of any casualties suffered.

If you use a weapon or spell that uses a template against a ridden monster, all the riders and the mount are automatically hit if the monster's base is entirely covered by the template, and all can be hit on a 4+ if the monster's base is only partially covered (roll separately for each). If the hole in the centre of the round template is on the monster's base, randomise if the rider or the mount is hit by the higher Strength hit as you would for a hit from normal shooting.

MONSTROUS MOUNTS IN COMBAT

In close combat, the enemy is faced with a deadly monster and, more often than not, a potent Hero as well. The monster will attack using its own characteristics, and the rider attacks separately using his characteristics. As the monster and rider are likely to have different Initiative values, they might strike their blows at different times. These attacks are worked out entirely normally, one batch for the rider and one batch for the monster, against any enemies in base contact with the monster.

When it comes to attacking back, enemies in base contact with the monster will be faced with two potential targets: the rider and the monster. The enemy can choose to direct his attacks against either the rider or the monster, and can distribute attacks between them in any way he likes. The opposing player must state how many attacks are against the monster and how many are against the rider before he rolls any dice, otherwise all attacks are assumed to be against the rider.

Attacks are worked out exactly as normal, and the score required to hit will depend upon the relative values of the monster or the rider's Weapon Skill, like all hand-to-hand fighting.

EXCESS WOUNDS

If a rider is slain and suffers more wounds than he has on his characteristic profile, excess wounds are discounted. They are not carried through onto the monster, nor onto a second rider if the monster has multiple riders. Similarly, any excess wounds inflicted on the monster are discounted; they are not carried over onto the rider.

SLAIN RIDERS OR MOUNTS

Wounds must be recorded separately for the rider and his mount. If the mount is slain, the rider may continue to fight on foot if you have a separate model to represent him. If the rider is slain, the monster might behave in an erratic fashion.

If the rider is slain, the monster must immediately take a monster reaction test: take a Leadership test on the monster's own Ld. If the test is passed, the monster fights on as normal. If the test is failed, roll a D6 and consult the monster reaction table below.

Regardless of the result of the test, a monstrous mount that has lost its rider must always use its own Leadership for any Leadership-based tests, even if it is within the army General's area of influence (see the Generals & Battle Standards section).

If a stand & shoot reaction kills the mount during a charge, the model is replaced by a foot version of the rider and the model does not move at all, as the rider frees himself from the monster's harness. If it kills the rider, take the test for the monster and then finish the beast's charge if possible.

MONSTER REACTION TABLE

D6	Reaction
1-2	**Uh?** Free of the will controlling it, the monster has now to think for itself and might find its presence on the battlefield extremely confusing. The monster fights on as normal, but is subject to Stupidity for the rest of the game.
3-4	**Whimper...** The monster stops moving immediately, remaining steadfastly where it is to guard the fallen body of its master. The monster will not move for the rest of the battle, except that it will always turn to face towards the closest enemy and use any breath or similar ranged weapon against the closest enemies within range if possible. If the monster is engaged in close combat it will fight, but it will not pursue fleeing enemy. From this point onwards, the monster is Unbreakable.
5-6	**Raaargh!** The monster is maddened by grief and rage at the death of its master, or simply reverts to its feral instincts. The monster fights on as normal, but is subject to Frenzy and Hatred of all enemies for the rest of the game (it can never lose its Frenzy, not even if defeated in combat) and will always charge the closest visible enemy.

CHARIOTS

Chariots are capable of charging into the midst of enemy units, cutting them down like wheat with their scythed wheels. Most chariots have at least two crew members with two creatures pulling the chariot – these creatures are normally horses, but many races of the Warhammer world utilise far more powerful and dangerous beasts. For example, Goblins capture and harness ferocious wolves to their chariots, while Orcs favour brutal, snorting warboars, and the chariots of the ruthless Dark Elves are pulled by deadly Cold Ones.

THE CHARIOT MODEL

A chariot, including its crew and the creatures pulling it, are considered to be a single model in the same way as a cavalry or monster model. Chariots normally move and fight individually in the same way as large monsters. Each chariot is, in effect, a unit of one model and it has a front (used to determine its arc of sight as normal), flanks and rear as normal. Chariots follow all the rules for normal units, except for the differences described in this section.

Chariots have separate characteristics for the chariot itself, the crew, and the creatures pulling it, but some characteristics are not included in the profile as they are never used.

EXAMPLES OF CHARIOTS

Goblin Wolf Chariot

	M	WS	BS	S	T	W	I	A	Ld
Chariot	–	–	–	5	4	3	–	–	–
Crew	–	2	3	3	–	–	2	1	6
Giant Wolves	9	3	–	3	–	–	3	1	–

Armour save: 5+

High Elf Tiranoc Chariot

	M	WS	BS	S	T	W	I	A	Ld
Chariot	–	–	–	5	4	4	–	–	–
Crew	–	5	4	3	–	–	5	1	8
Elven Steeds	9	3	–	3	–	–	4	1	–

Armour save: 5+

MOVING CHARIOTS

A chariot moves at the same speed as the creatures that are pulling it. Because they are massive, lumbering war machines, chariots can never march, although they do double their move when charging, in the same way as other models. When moving a chariot, simply measure the distance and move it. There is no need to turn or wheel, though the chariot still has to have a line of sight to any enemy that it is going to charge. In effect, chariots can turn to face any direction (pivoting around the centre of the model) at any point during their move and as many times as they like without reduction to movement.

MANOEUVRING DURING A CHARGE

Like all units, chariots are more restricted in their movement during a charge. Chariots, exactly like monsters, can pivot on the spot only once during a charge move if a straight move wouldn't hit the target or would not bring as many models as possible into combat, but are free to do this at any point during the move. This means they can either pivot and then charge in a straight line, or move directly forward, stop to pivot towards a different direction and then complete their move in a straight line (see the Monsters section for more details). Of course, they must still abide to all normal rules governing charges, so they need to see their target at the beginning of the charge, cannot charge the flank of a unit if they start the charge in its front arc, must try to bring as many models as possible into the combat, and so on.

OBSTACLES & TERRAIN

Chariots are not built to move over obstacles or difficult terrain, and they are likely to be damaged as their wheels strike rocks, their body becomes entangled in undergrowth, or they careen over a wall. If a chariot moves through any kind of difficult terrain or obstacle (except to cross a river at a bridge or a ford), the chariot sustains D6 S6 hits. Apply these hits immediately as the chariot touches the terrain/obstacle, treating them as hits from close combat (all the hits strike the chariot itself and not a character riding in it).

If the chariot is not destroyed, it can complete its move as normal and will not suffer such hits again if it crosses other obstacles or areas of difficult terrain during the same turn. If a unit of chariots moves through obstacles/difficult terrain, all models that move through the terrain will suffer D6 Strength 6 hits per model.

 CHARIOTS & SHOOTING

Chariot crew may also shoot any of their missile weapons in the shooting phase as normal.

When you want to fire against a chariot, treat it like any other unit. Roll to hit and to wound against the chariot in the same way as against troops. Any hits scored are targeted towards the chariot as a whole, unless any characters are riding in the chariot (see Characters & Chariots). Some chariots are large targets and you therefore get a +1 to hit bonus when shooting at them. If the chariot is a large target, this is clearly indicated in its army list entry.

Just like any other creature, a chariot can only suffer a certain number of wounds before it is destroyed. Roll to wound as normal, and take any saves that apply as explained below. A chariot has a pool of Wounds which represent the chariot itself, its crew and the creatures pulling it. When a chariot loses its last Wound, remove the whole model from the battlefield.

 CHARIOT ARMOUR SAVES

Most chariots have an armour save, just like troops, to take into account their heavy construction and the protection they offer to their crew. The army list entry clearly indicates the armour save value of each chariot.

 HIGH STRENGTH HITS

If a chariot is hit and wounded by an attack of Strength 7 or more, and fails any saving throw it might have, it loses all its remaining wounds and is removed – even the strongest chariot can be smashed apart if hit by a cannonball or by an extremely strong creature!

 IMPACT HITS

Most chariots are heavy and solid constructs, which cause considerable damage when crashing into the serried ranks of the enemy. In addition to this, the crew and steeds pulling the chariot may attack, making a chariot extremely dangerous in combat when it charges.

When a chariot charges a unit, it causes D6 hits with its own Strength. The number of hits is increased by +1 if the chariot is equipped with scythed wheels. These hits are inflicted at the very beginning of the combat, even before challenges are declared and before any model gets to attack. Any wounds caused by the charging chariot count towards combat resolution as normal. Remove any casualties as detailed in the Close Combat section. Like other casualties of close combat, models killed by impact hits do not get to fight.

The main danger from a chariot comes during its charge, so it is vitally important that it isn't outmanoeuvred and charged by the enemy. Chariots caught out in this way get no impact hits and are likely to be overwhelmed.

Impact hits against a unit of troops are distributed like shooting. See the section on characters on page 74 for details on how to distribute them among the models of a unit containing one or more characters.

Obviously, if a chariot charges against a character that is fighting on his own, all the impact hits will strike the character. If the character is riding another chariot or a monster, all the impact hits will strike his chariot or mount and never the character itself. Crew and creatures pulling the chariot are however free to attack the character as normal.

If a unit of chariots charges into combat, only chariot models that are in base contact with the enemy will cause impact hits.

PURSUIT CHARGES

It might occasionally happen that a chariot charges an enemy unit by pursuing into it, and then gets charged itself by some other enemy unit in the following turn. In this case, each enemy unit fighting to the front of a charging chariot will suffer D6 impact hits (+1 for scythes). Only units charging the flank or rear of a charging chariot do not suffer impact hits.

 CHARIOTS IN COMBAT

Enemies rolling to hit against the chariot compare their own Weapon Skill with the Weapon Skill of the crew or that of the creatures pulling it, whichever is highest. Roll to wound as normal and then record any wounds suffered.

CREW ATTACKS

All chariot crew (usually two, including the driver) may fight against enemy in contact with the chariot whether to its front, side or rear. They strike blows as normal, using their own Weapon Skill, Strength and Initiative.

CREATURE ATTACKS

The creatures pulling the chariot may fight if they have their own attacks. Due to restrictions of harness and reins, creatures can only attack enemies to the front of the chariot and not enemies in the flank/rear of the chariot. They strike blows as normal, using their own Weapon Skill, Strength, and Initiative.

CHARIOT UPGRADES

As indicated in the Warhammer Army books, some chariots can be upgraded as follows:

Upgrade	Effect
Extra crewman	+1 additional crew attack
Extra steed	+1 additional steed attack
Scythed wheels	+1 to impact hits

 FLEE AND PURSUIT

Chariots flee and pursue exactly like ordinary troops, with the exceptions listed here below.

Chariots take damage when fleeing/pursuing though difficult terrain or obstacles as described before.

If a chariot flees through a friendly unit, an enemy unit with a unit strength of less than 5 or a fleeing enemy unit, it will cause impact hits on it as it moves through. The chariot's flee move is executed as normal, and then the impact hits are resolved in the same way as missile fire against any unit it fled through.

If a chariot flees into contact with an enemy unit with a unit strength of 5 or more that is not fleeing, resolve the impact hits as described above and then remove the chariot.

 CHARIOT UNITS

Some armies, most notably the army of the Tomb Kings of Khemri, can group several chariots together into a unit. If chariots can be grouped into units, this is indicated in the army list, together with any special rules that apply to specific cases. These chariot units move like a unit of cavalry (except that they still cannot march!).

 CHARACTERS & CHARIOTS

Characters can ride chariots in much the same way they ride large monsters. When shooting at a chariot, the hits are randomised between the character and the chariot itself. Roll a D6. On a roll of 6, the attack hits the character. On a 1-5, it hits the chariot. Work out damage in the normal manner, except that the character either gains a +2 armour save bonus for riding the chariot or can use the armour save value of the chariot, whichever is the best.

In close combat, enemies can choose whether to attack either the chariot or the character riding it, in the same manner as combat against characters riding monsters.

If a chariot is destroyed, any characters in the chariot will continue to fight on foot. Such characters are immediately placed by the controlling player anywhere within 2" of the place where the chariot was. If the chariot was in close combat when it was destroyed, the controlling player places the character in base contact with the enemies that were in base contact with the chariot and the fight continues as normal.

SKIRMISHERS

A skirmishing unit is a small group of warriors fighting in loose or dispersed formation rather than formal ranks and files. In a normal battle, only specific troops are allowed to skirmish, as indicated in their Army book. Skirmishers follow all the rules for normal units, except for the differences described in this section.

FORMATION

A unit that can skirmish never moves in a rigid formation of ranks and files. Instead, it moves as a loose group or rough line. This enables skirmishers to move more quickly and to take advantage of minor folds in the ground, scrub, and other small features to shelter from shooting.

1" APART

Skirmishers are deployed on the battlefield in a formation consisting of a loose group. Models in a skirmishing unit are positioned up to 1" apart. The unit still blocks line of sight (see Diagram 65.1).

FACING

A skirmishing unit does not have a specific facing and can see all round (ie, it has an arc of sight of 360°), regardless of the actual facing of its models. This means that skirmishers can declare charges and shoot in any direction.

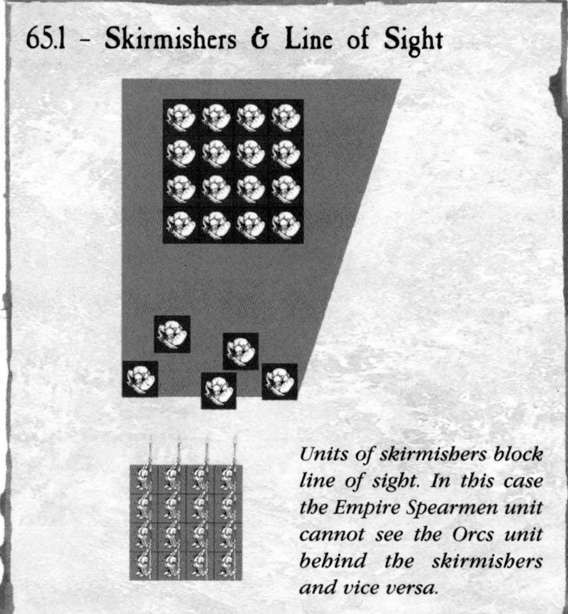

65.1 - Skirmishers & Line of Sight

Units of skirmishers block line of sight. In this case the Empire Spearmen unit cannot see the Orcs unit behind the skirmishers and vice versa.

MOVING

MANOEUVRES

Skirmishing models are moved in the same way as individual man-sized characters on foot. The unit does not turn, wheel, etc, and each model is free to move in any direction without penalty. Once movement is complete, the entire unit must form a loose group or line with models no more than 1" apart.

OBSTACLES & DIFFICULT TERRAIN

Skirmishers move around obstacles or over rough ground more easily than troops in formation. They suffer no movement penalties for crossing obstacles or for moving over difficult or very difficult ground and can even march through such terrain.

CHARGING

Like other units, skirmishers may charge an enemy that is visible to at least one of its models when charges are declared. To decide which side of the enemy is charged, follow the normal rules: the skirmishers will charge the enemy in the arc where most of the skirmishers are when the charge is declared. All models within charge reach are moved individually towards their foe and arranged into a fighting line.

When the maximum number of models has been brought into base-to-base contact with the side charged (including models fighting corner-to-corner), remaining skirmishers will begin to form up in ranks behind the first line of models in base contact with the enemy.

Any models unable to reach (because they don't have enough movement or because there is no space left in the fighting line) are placed in the rear ranks so that the unit forms up in what looks like a regular formation behind the models that have formed the fighting line (see diagrams overleaf).

If the skirmishing unit includes a banner, champion or musician, and any character that has joined the unit, such models are then moved to the fighting rank if there is enough space, swapping places with ordinary models.

66.1 - Skirmishers Charging (a)

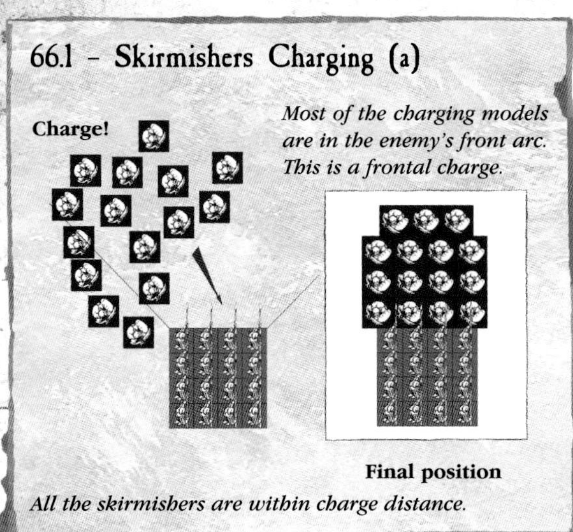

Most of the charging models are in the enemy's front arc. This is a frontal charge.

All the skirmishers are within charge distance.

66.2 - Skirmishers Charging (b)

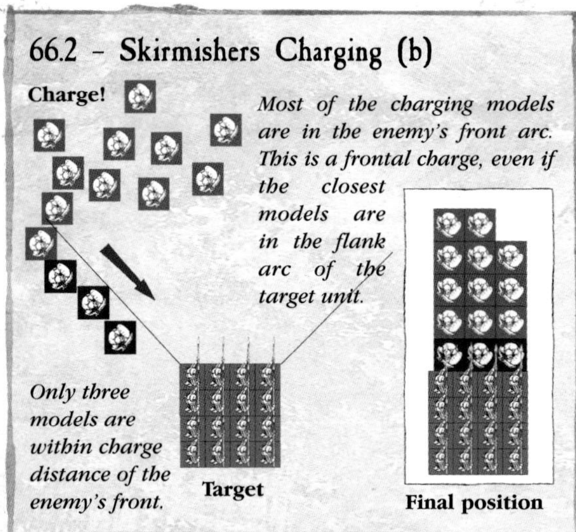

Most of the charging models are in the enemy's front arc. This is a frontal charge, even if the closest models are in the flank arc of the target unit.

Only three models are within charge distance of the enemy's front.

66.3 - Skirmishers Charging (c)

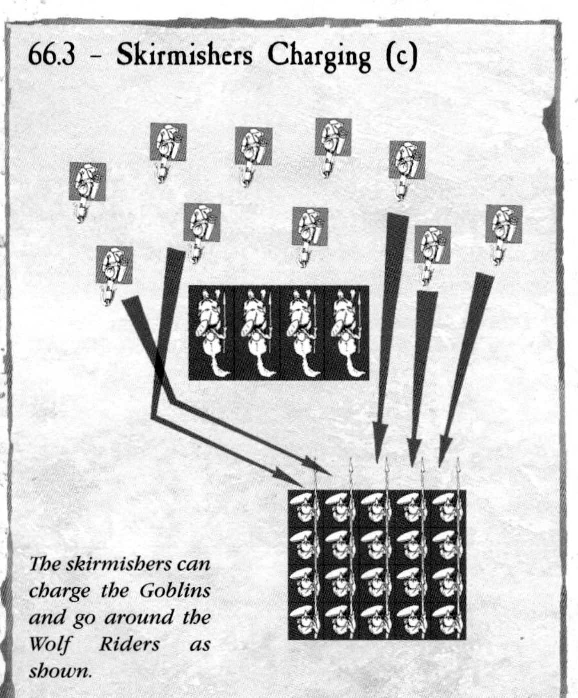

The skirmishers can charge the Goblins and go around the Wolf Riders as shown.

66.4 - Enemy Charging Skirmishers

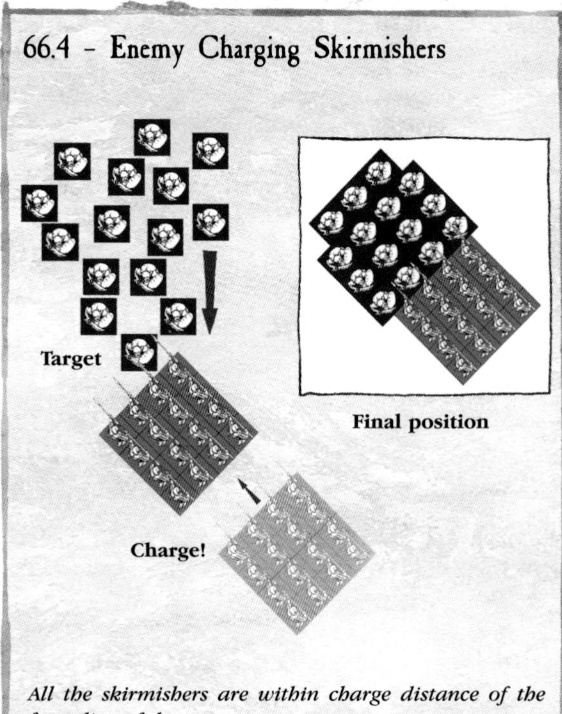

All the skirmishers are within charge distance of the front line of the enemy.

66.5 - Skirmishers Charging Skirmishers

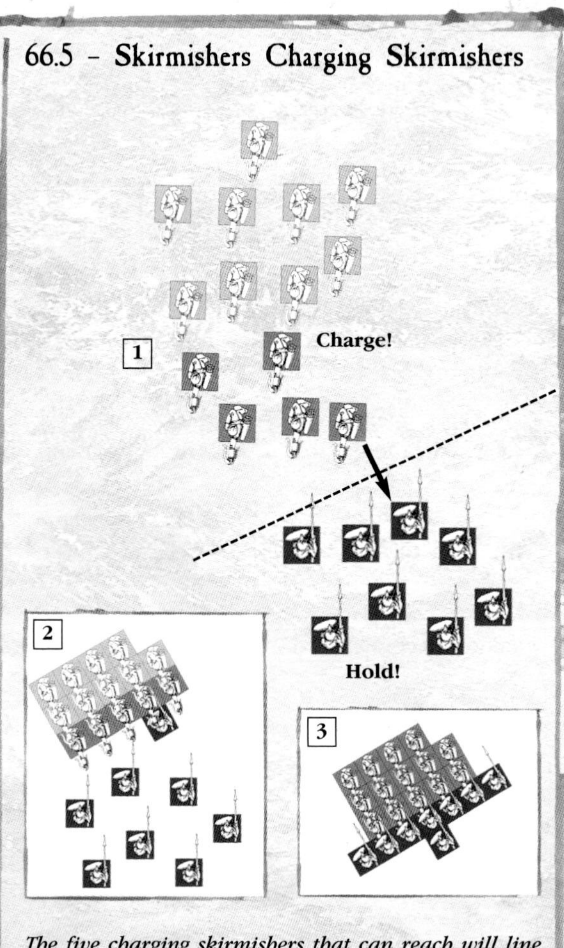

The five charging skirmishers that can reach will line up with the closest enemy skirmisher. Once this is done, the enemy skirmishers will form up as normal.

CHARGING AGAINST SKIRMISHERS

If the skirmishers are charged, the enemy is brought into base contact with the closest skirmisher as per a normal charge, except that the enemy is not aligned against the skirmishing model. The skirmishers form up as explained above, lining up alongside the enemy's front (their movement does not count as charging, of course). This is shown in Diagrams 66.1, 66.2 and 66.3.

SKIRMISHERS CHARGING OTHER SKIRMISHERS

When a skirmishing unit charges another skirmishing unit, take the model of the charging unit that is closest to the charged unit and move it into base contact with the closest model in the charged unit. Then, move all the charging models that can reach into a fighting line, lining them up with the first model moved, perpendicular to the line of charge. Other charging models that do not have enough movement to line up on the fighting line will form up behind it, as usual for skirmishers charging. Finally, the charged unit will form up as normal for a unit of skirmishers charged by an enemy unit (see Diagram 66.5 – Skirmishers Charging Skirmishers).

SHOOTING

Skirmishers can shoot in any direction, though individual models can be pivoted on the spot so that the unit looks more realistic (this does not count as movement).

Thanks to their special training and loose formation, models in a skirmishing unit do not block the line of sight of other members of their own unit (including characters that have joined the unit).

Enemies shooting against a unit of man-sized skirmishers suffer a -1 to hit penalty in the same way as if they were shooting at a single man-sized model (see the Shooting section).

CLOSE COMBAT

In close combat, skirmishers will remain in the ranked-up formation described above as long as the combat continues and will therefore have a front, flanks and rear as long as the fight continues, just like normal units. Skirmishers adopt their normal loose formation as soon as combat ends.

Skirmishers fight in a normal formation of ranks and files, but being extremely light troops, untrained in this form of combat, they lose most of the bonuses that apply to normal ranked-up units.

Skirmishers receive no combat bonus for the number of ranks in their own unit.

Skirmishers do not negate the rank bonus of enemy units when fighting them in the flank or rear.

If a skirmishing unit pursues the enemy and leaves the table, in the following turn place all models in the unit in base contact with the table edge, as close as possible to the point the unit left the table from, and then move normally, as described in the close combat phase (remember that they cannot march).

CHARACTERS

Roughly man-sized characters on foot can join a unit of skirmishers. No other characters can join skirmishing units.

MONSTERS & HANDLERS

Some rare units are made up of a monster that is goaded into battle by a small group of handlers or beastmasters.

These units normally move as skirmishers. When charging or being charged though, the handlers are completely ignored (as if they were not there) and the monster is the only model that matters. The monster's arc of sight and flank/rear are used to determine arc of sight for charges and the relative position of a charging enemy, as well as any charge distance, psychological reaction and so on.

The monster is also capable of negating the rank bonus of an enemy unit it has charged to the flank/rear if its unit strength is high enough.

Once the monster is in contact with the enemy, form the handlers up with the monster in the same way as you would for a unit of skirmishers. They will fight as normal in the ensuing fight.

When shooting at such units, the rules vary depending on the size of the monster and number of handlers. See the relevant Army book for details and other special rules that may apply to each unit.

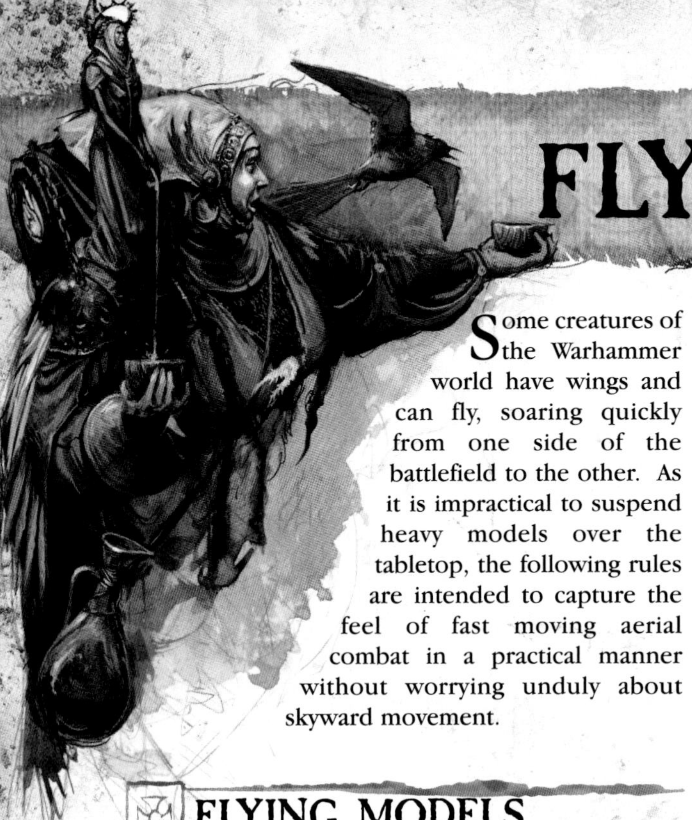

FLYERS

Some creatures of the Warhammer world have wings and can fly, soaring quickly from one side of the battlefield to the other. As it is impractical to suspend heavy models over the tabletop, the following rules are intended to capture the feel of fast moving aerial combat in a practical manner without worrying unduly about skyward movement.

FLYING MODELS

If a model is capable of flight it will have the special rule 'Fly' in its entry in the relevant Army book. For the sake of convenience these models are referred to as 'flyers'. Flyers follow all the rules for normal units, except for the differences described below.

There are two types of flyers: flying monsters and flying units. They share the same rules apart from a few exceptions for flying units, which are given later. All flying models are mounted on square bases like other troops in Warhammer. This is more convenient and makes it easier to resolve close combat between flyers and other units.

MOVING FLYERS

In Warhammer, flight is represented by a long swoop or glide of up to 20". The flyer starts off on the ground, takes off, flies to where it wishes to go, and then lands. Flyers, therefore, begin and end their movement on the ground.

Flyers never need to wheel or turn, but can always make their move in a direct line or stop to pivot at any point during their move. Of course, they still need to see any target they want to charge or shoot at and have a front, flanks and rear (used to determine their arc of sight as normal).

Flyers do not benefit from the extra Move distance conferred on ground moving models for charging or marching. The flying move is never doubled and flyers charge at normal speed.

Flyers suffer no movement penalties for flying over scenery or crossing obstacles. They may fly over other models, including enemy troops, without penalty. Flyers may not move, land in or take off from within a wood. If flyers wish to enter a wood, they must land outside it and walk inside using their ground movement in the next turn. Note that this applies to any terrain that both players consider would prohibit flying (it's a good idea for the players to discuss this before the game begins).

Flyers may not land on top of enemy formations – if they wish to attack an enemy they must charge them.

Most flyers are also capable of moving along the ground by walking or running. If a flyer has a Movement value, this represents its ground movement in the same way as any other model. When moving along the ground using its Movement characteristic the usual movement rules apply. A flyer may choose to fly or move along the ground, but cannot do both in the same move.

FLYING CHARGES

A flyer may charge an enemy within its 20" flight move. The charge must be declared in the normal way and the enemy has the usual response options. The flying move is not doubled like a ground charge is and so, even in the case of a failed charge, flyers will still move the full 20" towards the enemy. Note that a flyer must be able to see its intended target when charges are declared as normal, but can otherwise fly over models and scenery that would stop the charge of a normal model. The charging flyer moves straight towards the target, over any intervening terrain or models, and is placed in base contact with either the front, flanks or rear of the target depending on its initial position, exactly like any other charging unit.

Remember that flyers do not suffer from the normal penalties when attacking models that are defending an obstacle.

FLEEING & PURSUING

Flyers always choose to fly when fleeing, and so the distance flyers flee is based on their flying Move rather than their ground Move. The normal flee distance for flyers is therefore 3D6" in common with all models whose move is more than 6".

Flyers can flee over interposing terrain and units, but if their move ends inside impassable terrain (including woods) or non-fleeing enemies, they are destroyed as normal.

If flyers must flee along the ground due to some constraint that prevents them from flying, for example, if they are in the middle of a wood, then they flee 2D6" or 3D6" depending on their Movement characteristic, just like other troops.

Flyers can normally choose to pursue fleeing enemies either on the ground (using the normal pursue rules) or with a flying 3D6" move.

If they choose to use their flying move to pursue, they can ignore intervening terrain and units. During their pursuit, they can always choose to either fly over an intervening enemy unit or to charge it instead. They cannot end their pursuit move inside units or impassable terrain (including woods). If they would end their pursuit move in impassable terrain (like woods!) or over a friendly unit, they stop just before it. If they would end their pursuit move on an enemy unit, they must charge it.

UNITS OF FLYERS

Most flyers are single model units, like monsters or characters, but some units of troops can fly too, like Harpies and Carrion. Such units are clearly identified in their army lists. They follow all the normal rules for flyers given above, apart from the exceptions noted below.

Units of flyers operate as skirmishers (see page 65), except that obviously they cannot fly through woods or other terrain where flying movement is not allowed. If they decide to move on the ground using their Move value, then they move exactly like skirmishers, and ignore terrain penalties.

Models in a unit of flyers always have a unit strength of 1.

Characters can never join units of flyers, even if they ride flying creatures or are capable of flight themselves.

FLYING CAVALRY

Flying cavalry, as the name suggests, are units of cavalry mounted on flying steeds, like Bretonnian Pegasus Knights. They are treated as units of flyers, except that: they have a cavalry profile for use in combat, each model has a unit strength of 2 and the riders get a +1 armour save, as normal for cavalry. Also, if they decide to move on the ground using their Move value, they move as skirmishers, but they do not ignore difficult terrain penalties as the mounted warriors are much less agile than a skirmisher on foot.

FAST CAVALRY

Fast cavalry (sometimes called light cavalry) are riders of exceptional prowess, trained in lightning-fast manoeuvres and flank attacks. They are more lightly armed and armoured than knights, but make up for this with their flexibility. In battle, they act as scouts and outriders for the army, as well as harrying the flanks of enemy formations with missile weapons.

If a unit is fast cavalry, this is indicated in their entry in the relevant Army book. Fast cavalry units use regular formations and follow all the rules for normal cavalry units, except for the differences described in this section.

MOVEMENT

FREE REFORM

Unless it charges, a fast cavalry unit can reform as many times as you wish during its movement phase without incurring any penalties to its Move distance. See the rules for reforming on page 14. They can do this even whilst marching. Remember that no model in the fast cavalry unit can move more than double its maximum Move distance, despite reforming (see Diagram 70.1).

FEIGNED FLIGHT

Fast cavalry are extremely good at escaping from combat and regrouping. A unit of fast cavalry that chooses to flee as a charge reaction and subsequently rallies at the beginning of their next turn may reform as normal, but is then also free to move during the remaining moves part of the movement phase. The unit is also free to shoot as normal (but it always count as having moved). Note that if the flee move of the fast cavalry does not take them beyond the charge reach of their enemies, the unit is caught and destroyed as normal.

SHOOTING

SHOOTING & MOVING

Fast cavalry armed with missile weapons are expert at shooting from horseback (or wolfback!) and can therefore shoot even when marching or reforming. However, the normal -1 to hit penalty for moving still applies.

LINE OF SIGHT

A well-trained horseman can turn completely around in his saddle and shoot behind himself while moving forwards! In the shooting phase, fast cavalry models can fire all round, regardless of the direction in which the models are facing (this, of course, does not allow them to shoot through friendly models, which still block line of sight as normal). Note that for charging, stand & shoot reactions, etc, the model needs to be facing the enemy as normal.

COMBAT

RANK BONUS

Being light troops, fast cavalry receive no combat bonus for the number of ranks in their own unit.

CHARACTERS

Mounted character models may join fast cavalry units and move in the same manner as the unit, but do not benefit from any of the special shooting rules.

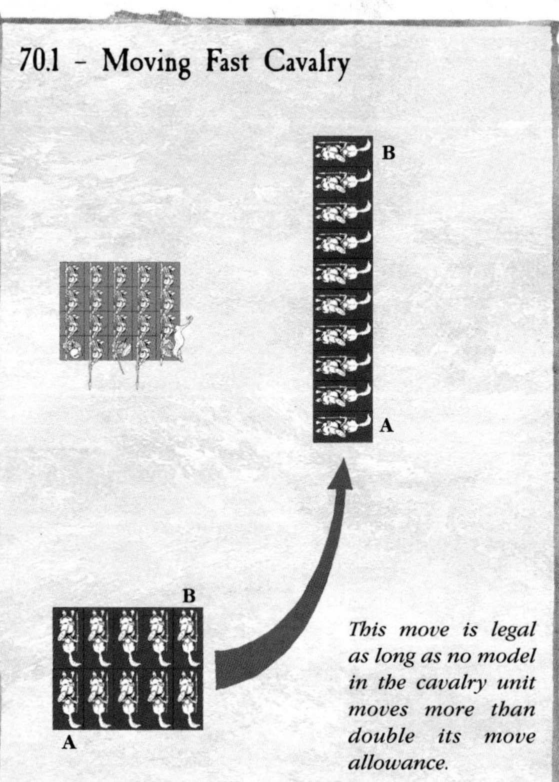

70.1 - Moving Fast Cavalry
B
A
B
A
This move is legal as long as no model in the cavalry unit moves more than double its move allowance.

UNIT STRENGTH

Warhammer has several rules (such as Fear) where a unit outnumbering its opponents gains an advantage. To establish the relative power of all these different creatures, you need to determine unit strength. In most cases this is worked out by simply counting the number of models in a unit. However, some huge creatures such as Trolls, chariots, etc, are more powerful than a man on foot! These creatures have a different unit strength, as described in the chart opposite.

For example, a chariot has a unit strength of 4, but if a character is riding in it, it will have a unit strength of 5 (4+1).

Some unique creatures may be an exception to the chart, but when this is the case, it will be clearly specified in that unit's special rules.

The chart gives you the unit strength value of each troop type. The unit strength listed is for each model in the unit. To work out the unit strength of a unit, count the number of models in the unit and multiply it by the appropriate number given. In the case of several models with different unit strengths in the same unit, simply add these together.

For example, a unit including three Rat Ogres (3 x 3=9) and three Skaven Packmasters (3 x 1=3) has a total unit strength of 12 (9+3).

UNIT STRENGTH CHART

Model Type	Unit Strength
Roughly Man-sized Square 20/25 mm base On foot	1
Up to & including Ogre-sized* Square 40/50 mm base On foot	3
Monster (larger than Ogre-sized)** Any base/no base	Starting Wounds
Cavalry*** 25 x 50 mm base	2
Chariots	4
Ridden monsters/chariots	Equal to monster/chariot +1
War machines	Equal to the number of crew remaining
Units of flyers	1
Flying cavalry	2

* Includes Swarms, Chaos Spawn, Dragon Ogres, etc.

** Includes Great Eagles, Stegadons, Giants, etc.

*** Includes Flesh Hounds, Dire Wolves, Chaos Hounds, etc.

CHARACTERS

The Warhammer world would not be what it is without the presence of potent individuals such as great lords, valiant heroes, mighty wizards or black-hearted necromancers. These add an entirely different aspect to the game, either as valuable leaders, or powerful warriors able to fight against vast numbers of lesser fighters. These individuals are known as 'characters'.

Some characters are tougher, meaner and more powerful than the average warrior. Others are faster than a typical member of their race, stronger and more skilled with weapons, or are natural leaders with the power to inspire. Some may have special powers, skills or abilities, such as the Dark Elf Assassins or Imperial Engineers.

In most cases they are known by different names appropriate to their nation or race. Orc characters, for example, are known by the 'Orcy' titles of Big Bosses and Warbosses, while the leaders of the Empire are known as Captains and Warrior Priests.

Of course, these types of valiant individuals cannot really represent every nuance of distinction between mighty warriors, bold leaders and cunning wizards, but it does enable us to fight with comparably powerful characters, whether they are goodly, honourable knights or are the most rotten-hearted perpetrators of evil.

Characters often have superior characteristic values compared to ordinary members of their race. For example:

	M	WS	BS	S	T	W	I	A	Ld
Man	4	3	3	3	3	1	3	1	7

	M	WS	BS	S	T	W	I	A	Ld
Captain	4	5	5	4	4	3	5	3	8

From this example, it is clear that characters are quite different from ordinary troops.

Characters such as Heroes and Lords, are represented by individual models, which fight as units in their own right. However, as we shall see, one of the most useful abilities of characters is to join other units in battle, so that they can bolster the battle line where needed.

WIZARDS

Some characters also have the ability to cast spells. In game terms, all such characters are called Wizards. The complete rules for Wizards, spellcasting, and magic items are covered by the Magic section of this book (page 104).

MOVEMENT

A character model is moved and fights as an individual piece, except that he may also join up with and fight alongside units of troops as described below.

Characters move and fight in different ways depending on their size (unit strength) and on the mount they are riding into battle:

Man-sized characters on foot (normally mounted on a square 20mm or 25mm wide base), have a unit strength of 1 and follow the movement rules for skirmishers, as described on page 65.

Characters that are larger than this (having a unit strength of more than 1), or that are mounted on a cavalry steed or a monster, follow the movement rules for monsters, as described on page 59.

Characters riding in a chariot follow the movement rules for chariots, as described on page 62.

CHARACTERS & UNITS

JOINING AND LEAVING UNITS

Characters normally move and fight on their own. In effect, a character counts as an individual unit comprising of only one model. However, during the course of a battle, a character is allowed to join a friendly unit of troops – infantry, cavalry, unit of chariots or a war machine's crew, but never a monster, single chariot, unit of flyers or another character! In this case, he becomes part of that unit until he decides to leave it.

Characters mounted on flying creatures cannot join units. Characters mounted on chariots can only join units of chariots.

To join a unit of troops, a character has only to move so that he is touching it. Once he has joined the unit, the model is automatically placed in its front rank. Note that a character will inevitably use up a proportion of his move to reach the unit he is joining. If the unit has not already moved, its further movement is limited to the fraction remaining to the character. Any movement lost represents the time spent waiting for the character.

If there is no room for the character in the front rank of the formation (because the standard bearer, musician and champion and/or other characters take up all the available positions, for example), one of these models must be placed in the second rank of the unit. As long as a character remains in the back ranks he cannot fight (even with a spear), or use magic or magic items. Also the unit cannot use his Leadership value for tests. If the character is engaged in close combat (via a flank or rear charge, for example) it functions normally.

Characters cannot normally join or leave units in close combat, although they may obviously join the fight by charging their enemies. Characters cannot join a fleeing unit.

Except in the circumstances noted below, a character that is part of a unit of troops can leave during the movement phase. A character is able to leave one unit of troops and join another in the same turn if you so wish, but he is unable to join and leave the same unit in the same turn.

A character may never leave or join a unit of troops while it is subject to a compulsory movement rule. For example, he cannot leave a unit that is fleeing, which has charged during the same phase, which has rallied that turn (because it cannot move) or which is engaged in close combat.

As mentioned above, if a character is with a unit when it declares a charge, he must charge with it. However, if the unit he is with does not declare a charge, a character may declare a separate charge of his own and therefore leaves the unit when he charges out of it.

Once close combat has begun, a character will not be able to leave a unit he has joined until the fighting is over and any compulsory movement, such as fleeing and pursuit, has been resolved.

The most important thing to remember when a character joins/leaves units as part of his move is that the character cannot use the fact he is joining/leaving units to extend his move beyond the distance he could have moved if he was simply moving on his own.

CHARACTERS MOVING WITH UNITS

If a character forms part of a unit of troops, the unit as a whole will dictate his maximum movement. He simply moves along like an ordinary member of the unit. If the character moves more slowly than his unit, the whole unit will have to slow down so that he can keep up with them. During a unit's normal move (ie, not during compulsory moves or charges), a character is free to change position in the front rank of the unit, swapping places with other models in the front rank of the unit. This allows the player to place his characters in the best position depending on the situation.

MOVING CHARACTERS WITHIN ENGAGED UNITS

It sometimes happens that a unit is engaged in combat and a character is positioned in the formation in such a way that he is unable to fight, perhaps because he is in the front rank and the formation has been charged in the flank, or because the enemy unit is smaller and the character is stranded beyond the fighting. In his next movement phase the player is allowed to move the character into a position where he can fight. Simply swap the character for an ordinary trooper model that is already fighting. This can mean that the character loses the chance to fight in the first turn of combat. Note that a character may not replace another character that is already engaged in close combat.

Although the above rule allows a character to move within a unit in order to fight an enemy, he cannot move once he is already fighting.

For example, he cannot move from the front to the rear if he is already fighting to the front, he must stay where he is and fight the enemy he is touching. Characters cannot move into a non-fighting rank to avoid fighting unless deliberately refusing a challenge, as described later. Once the combat is over, they are immediately returned to the unit's front rank.

SHOOTING

A character moving around on his own is treated as a unit consisting of one model. In this respect, a character is a viable target just like a regiment of infantry.

When deliberately shooting at a man-sized character model on foot, there is a -1 to hit penalty in the same way as firing against a unit of skirmishers, as described in the Shooting section.

CHARACTERS INSIDE UNITS

If a character is part of a unit that includes at least five rank-and-file models (ie, non-characters), he cannot be shot at. Any shots against the unit will hit ordinary troopers and not the character. If the unit contains less than five rank-and-file models when a ranged attack is targeted at it, then hits are allocated before rolling to wound. First, divide the number of hits evenly between all the members of the unit (including the characters). If after this there are still some hits left over, or if the number of hits suffered by the unit is smaller than the number of models in it, randomise which models are hit with a dice roll.

For example, if a unit composed of three rank-and-file models and two characters suffered seven hits, then each model would suffer a single hit, and you would allocate the remaining two hits randomly between the five models by rolling a dice for each hit (re-rolling any result of 6).

If a character model (including his mount) has a unit strength of 5 or more, then he can be picked out as a target regardless of the rules just given. Enemies may freely choose to either shoot at the character or the unit he has joined.

"LOOK OUT, SIR!"

Some ranged attacks, such as stone throwers and cannons, or the breath weapons of Dragons, for example, have unique targeting rules, which allow the player to deliberately aim his shot at a character inside a unit.

In the case of missile weapons that can be aimed in this way, there is a special "Look out, Sir!" rule that allows characters to avoid destruction thanks to a warning shouted by a comrade. This is intended to prevent characters becoming victims to these weapons in a manner that is definitely unheroic!

This rule applies to all war machines that work in a different way to ordinary shooting (ie, they don't fire against the unit as a whole, rolling to hit using their Ballistic Skill), and can therefore be aimed at characters who have joined a unit. It also applies to any other ranged attack that uses a template (like some spells and magic items).

If a character is part of a unit consisting of five or more rank-and-file models and is hit by such ranged attacks, roll a D6.

On the roll of a 1, the character fails to hear the warning and is hit. Work out damage as normal.

On a roll of 2 to 6, the character is alerted to the danger and avoids the missile. The character is not hit and the missile strikes another model – transfer the hit onto any rank-and-file model in the unit.

If a character model (including his mount) has a unit strength of 5 or more, then he cannot benefit from the "Look out, Sir!" rule.

CLOSE COMBAT

When a unit closes with its enemies in close combat, character models will inevitably find themselves confronted by enemy troops. As described in the Close Combat section, models can attack any enemy models whose base they are touching.

Troopers confronted by character models will usually have the option of attacking a character or ordinary enemies, as bases will usually overlap slightly when models move into combat. Where a player has a choice of attacking characters or ordinary troops, he must nominate which model(s) he is striking against before rolling to hit.

DIVIDING ATTACKS

Characters often come face-to-face with enemy characters, and the same choice applies to them as to other models – they may attack any enemy whose base they are touching. If a character has more than 1 Attack he can divide his attacks among characters and ordinary troops as described in the Close Combat section. A challenge is an important exception to this rule as described later.

EXCESS WOUNDS

As with combat between ordinary warriors, casualties inflicted by a character can extend beyond the models the character is touching. If a character has say, 4 Attacks and is facing two enemy troopers then his attacks are worked out against these. However, if the character scores sufficient wounds to slay three or four models, the enemy unit loses three or four troopers, not just two.

Don't be fooled by the fact that models are static and the battle lines rigid and straight. What is represented is the hectic swirl of real combat! Heroes are just the type to strike boldly left and right, stepping forward to cut down foes that step up to fill a gap.

If a model attacks an enemy character, or another individual model such as a unit's champion or a monster, then any excess wounds caused by those attacks are not carried over onto ordinary troopers fighting alongside. The attacker has chosen to concentrate his attacks on a single special foe and any wounds left over are wasted and do not count towards the result of the combat. The exception to this rule is during a challenge, as described next.

CHALLENGES

In each turn before working out any close combat, each side is allowed to issue challenges. The challenge represents one-on-one combat between powerful rivals, the final showdown between mighty adversaries in the midst of battle. The rules given below refer to characters, but a unit's champion can issue and accept challenges exactly like a character (see page 81).

ISSUING A CHALLENGE

One challenge can be issued in each combat that is being fought. For each combat, start with the player whose turn it is. The player may choose any one character from those in base contact wih the enemy to issue a challenge with.

The second player has the option of refusing or meeting the challenge. If he refuses, no challenge takes place and the refusing player must retire a character from the combat as described below. The challenger then fights normally in the following combat. If the challenge is accepted, the player selects one of his characters from those already fighting in the combat to take up the challenge.

If the player whose turn it is does not issue a challenge in that combat, his opponent may issue one himself, which may be accepted or declined in the same way.

Note that a challenge cannot be issued unless there is a character to fight – ordinary troopers or monsters cannot take up a challenge.

Also note that in order to participate in a challenge, either to issue it or to meet it, a character must be fighting in combat already. This means that the model must actually be positioned base-to-base against an enemy model. A character that is not already fighting, for example because he is in the front of a formation which has been attacked in the rear, cannot take part in a challenge.

REFUSING A CHALLENGE (BOO! HISS!)

If a challenge is refused, the declining player must retire one character nominated by his opponent (among those that could have accepted the challenge, of course!). The retiring character is moved to a position in the unit where he is not in base contact with any enemy and replaced with a rank-and-file trooper. If this is not possible, as there are no positions in the unit where the character can avoid being in base contact with an enemy, the challenge cannot be refused and must be met.

A character that has been retired after refusing a challenge may not fight or do anything else that turn and loses all of his advantages (see the rules for characters that are not in the front rank of a unit). The (so-called) hero has chosen to hide away behind his fellows rather than face the challenger one-on-one. The retired character is automatically returned to a fighting rank at the end of that close combat phase, ready to fight in the following turn. He is positioned in the same place as before.

Sometimes a single character, possibly mounted on a huge monster or a chariot, will attack a unit of troops. If the single character finds himself challenged, he cannot refuse as he has no formation to hide behind.

FIGHTING A CHALLENGE

Once a challenge is accepted, the character that accepted the challenge is moved in the ranks so that the two protagonists are opposite each other. If this is not possible, then the challenger is moved in the ranks to a position where he is in base contact with the character that accepted the challenge.

When combat is worked out, these two will fight together. No other models may attack them or their mount, even if their bases are touching.

Note that the striking order is not affected by the challenge – charging models still strike first and so on. Note also that occasionally the presence of two characters engaged in a challenge may stop other models from fighting at all if the only enemy model they are in base contact with is the character.

Once a challenge is underway no further challenges may be issued in that combat until one character is slain or flees from combat. The challenge might therefore last over several turns of combat.

If a character is riding a steed or a monster, the mount fights in the challenge as well as its rider.

If a character is riding in a chariot, the creatures pulling the chariot will fight in the challenge, but the other members of the chariot's crew (if any) cannot attack at all until the challenge is over. Any impact hits from the chariot are worked out against the unit rather than the character fighting in the challenge. Only if the enemy character was on his own when the chariot charged, are impact hits worked out against him.

If a character is killed in a challenge and its mount (monster or chariot) still had no chance to attack in that turn, work out their attacks as part of the challenge. The challenge is then over.

OVERKILL!

Excess wounds caused when attacking characters are normally discounted because all the effort of these attacks goes into fighting the character. As any excess wounds are not inflicted, they are not counted towards the combat result. However, any excess wounds scored when fighting a challenge do count towards the combat result (up to a maximum of +5), even though they are not actually inflicted. This is called the overkill rule.

For example, a Lord-level character and his dragon fight a champion in a challenge. They slay the champion before he has a chance to attack and cause seven wounds on him! Their combat result score is 1 (the original wound of the champion) plus 5 (the maximum overkill bonus) for a total of 6 combat result points. The last of the seven wounds is wasted.

This represents the situation where troops are watching their hero battling for his life against his adversary. All eyes are focused on the mighty clash and both sides are yelling encouragement. If the troops see their champion crushed to a bloody pulp before their eyes, they will inevitably get a bit upset and might decide to turn tail and run rather than stick around for a dose of the same.

In practical terms, the overkill rule means that it is an advantage to crush a challenged enemy as overwhelmingly as possible. It also means that players will benefit if they meet a challenge with as powerful a character as possible.

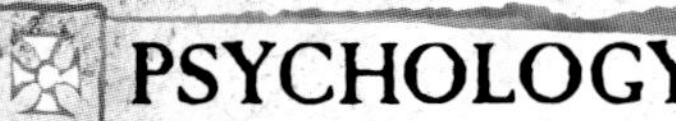

PSYCHOLOGY

CHARACTER'S LEADERSHIP

If a unit is led by one or more characters, it must use the highest available Leadership value for any Leadership-based tests it has to take (see page 48).

CHARACTERS & UNITS

While a character is with a unit of troops he is considered to be part of that unit in all respects. This means that if the unit flees, he must flee along with them at the same speed; if the unit pursues, he must pursue with them as well; if the unit declares a charge, he must charge as part of it.

Immune to Psychology

A character that is Immune to Psychology and joins a unit that is not Immune to Psychology loses his Immunity as long as he is with them. If the character leaves the unit by declaring a charge, he automatically regains his Immunity (including during that charge).

A character that is not Immune to Psychology and joins a unit that is, becomes Immune to Psychology for as long as he stays with the unit.

Frenzy/Hatred

If the unit is affected by Frenzy or forced to pursue because of Hatred, a non-Frenzied/Hating character must move along with the unit but does not benefit from any bonus unless he is affected by Frenzy/Hatred himself. In other words, a character does not go into a frenzy just because he is with a unit that can do so, although he has no choice but to accompany them when they charge.

A Frenzied character must declare a charge and leave a unit he is with if the unit is not declaring a charge that turn and there are enemies within charge reach of the character.

A Frenzied/Hating character that has joined a unit of non-Frenzied/Hating models causes the unit he is with to always fail their test to restrain pursuit.

Stupidity

If a unit is affected by Stupidity, any characters with the unit and any model within the Stupid unit that do not suffer from being Stupid themselves must move as the unit moves. Remember, a character cannot leave a unit when it turns Stupid, because such a unit is bound by a compulsory movement rule. We can imagine he is trying to goad the Stupid creatures into activity, or perhaps he is pinned down or hemmed in by the dribbling brutes and unable to move of his own volition. Such models may not shoot in the turn the unit is Stupid.

If a character subject to Stupidity fails this test while he is within a unit, the entire unit is affected by Stupidity, as the troopers mill about in confusion because of the stupid orders they are receiving.

Note that a Wizard subject to Stupidity cannot cast spells if he fails the test, but a Wizard that is not Stupid himself can cast spells even if the unit he is with is subject to Stupidity.

Fear/Terror

Sometimes an enemy unit of ordinary troops is led by a mighty character that causes Fear or Terror. Such units gain the same immunities as the character for as long as he is with them.

In the same way, if a character is liable to a Terror or Fear test that doesn't apply to the rest of the unit, he can ignore any tests. For example, if a character that is subject to Fear is in a unit of Fear-causing troops, such as Ogres, and is charged by enemies who cause Fear, he does not have to take a Fear test.

If an enemy wishes to charge a unit containing a Fear/Terror causing character, test for Fear/Terror only if a charge will result in the unit fighting the character in question.

In the case of Terror, a unit must also test if it is within 6" of a Terrifying character at the start of its turn, but not necessarily because it is within 6" of a unit that the Terrifying character is in. If the unit is charging a unit of enemy troops in the side or rear, so that the charging unit won't have to fight a Terror-causing model, then the unit does not have to test for Terror. This is common sense – if you don't have to confront the character, then no test is required.

Stubborn

Stubborn troops benefit from the superior Leadership of the army's General or a character that joined their unit for all Leadership-based tests, but in a Break test they always use their own unmodified Leadership if it's higher than the character's Leadership reduced by the Break test modifiers.

For example, a Stubborn unit has a Ld of 8 and is joined by (or within range of) the army's General, who has a Ld of 10. They can use the General's Ld 10 for Panic tests, Terror tests, etc. If they lose a combat by one point, they are still better off using the General's Ld – that would be modified to 9 by the Break test modifier – but if they had lost the fight by three or more points, they would use their Stubborn Ld 8 instead.

The same would be true of any non-Stubborn character joining a Stubborn unit.

If a character that is Stubborn himself joins a unit, then the unit can use the character's unmodified

Leadership for Break tests (effectively becoming Stubborn themselves if they are not already) as well as other Leadership tests.

Unbreakable

Characters who are not Unbreakable cannot join Unbreakable units and Unbreakable characters cannot join units that are not Unbreakable.

MOUNTS' PSYCHOLOGY

Fear/Terror. If a character is riding a creature causing Fear/Terror, then the entire combined model of rider and mount is assumed to cause Fear/Terror.

Stupidity. If either the rider or the steed suffer from Stupidity, test using the rider's Leadership – both are affected if the test is failed. If both the rider and the steed suffer from Stupidity, test only once for both.

Immunity to Psychology or Panic, Hatred, Frenzy, Stubborn, Unbreakable. If either the rider or the steed is subject to any of these rules, the whole combined model is. This means that all the parts of the model (a monstrous mount, or the crew and steeds pulling a chariot) are affected by these rules.

SPECIAL CHARACTERS

The Warhammer Army books include several different types of characters, be they Wizards or Heroes. However, we can easily imagine all kinds of wild individuals with different characteristic values from those given in the army lists. The characters described above are 'standard' types. They are typically representative of their race, and of the sort of Heroes and Wizards you can expect to find in a Warhammer army. Unique, named characters, those differing from the standard types, are referred to as 'special characters'.

Special characters are famous war leaders and mages, individuals renowned amongst their own kind and abhorred by their enemies. For example, they can be the mighty leaders of nations, such as the Emperor Karl Franz of the Empire; Goblin Warlords, such as Grom the Paunch of Misty Mountain; Malekith the Witch King of the Dark Elves, and many more besides. All of these special characters are quite different from the standard types. Some are better fighters than others, but some are better leaders, while many carry unique magical weapons or ride large monsters.

Numerous special characters are described in the Warhammer Armies books and other Warhammer supplements and, of course, players can make up their own if they wish. After all, who can resist the temptation to create a mighty leader of armies in their own image, to paint and perhaps even model him to suit their heroic vision, to name and invent a past for their character, and to deploy him in battle after battle!

The special characters models are normally equally exceptional, and players often field them in their army using the rules for a normal Hero or Lord character of their chosen army. This is perfectly fine, as long as you let your opponent know that the model is not the special character himself, but just a normal Lord or Hero that happens to look a lot like him!

COMMAND GROUPS

So far we have described units as consisting of identical rank-and-file troops. However, more often than not, warriors march to war under the leadership of a captain or some other officer, to the accompaniment of a drum or horn and beneath the fluttering standards of their cities and rulers. The regiments of the Empire march under flags bearing the coats of arms of their Electors and their Emperor. Bretonnians go to war bearing the glittering heraldic banners of their dukes and king. Orcs wave ragged banners covered in glyphs proclaiming the might and power of their chieftains.

Standards and drums also have a practical value: they are used to signal to the troops, direct their unit's movement and provide a highly visible point around which formation changes and manoeuvres can be made. The rules that follow represent the boost that the unit's 'command group' (its champion, standard bearer and musician) give to their comrades' fighting prowess. Remember that even if they have special rules, they are otherwise rank-and-file troopers in all respects.

POSITION WITHIN UNIT

The unit's champion, standard bearer, musician and any characters that have joined it, must be placed in the unit's front rank. If the unit's models turn to face the side or rear, the unit's champion, standard bearer, musician and any characters in the unit, are automatically rearranged into the new front rank.

If all such models cannot fit into the front rank, the player must place some of them into the second rank. Champions, standard bearers, musicians and any characters in the second rank cannot take part in close combat in any way unless they are directly engaged, via a flank charge for example. Also, some of the bonuses these models confer to the unit are lost, as described below.

STANDARDS

A unit of troops can often include a standard, which might take the form of a flag, banner, totemic idol or similar device. The standard is carried by a standard bearer, who can be bought as an upgrade to a normal model in the unit, as described in the relevant Warhammer Army book.

This model is assumed to be armed and armoured like the other models in the unit and fights in exactly the same way. Although the model might actually lack a shield or substitute a lance for a sword, such things are ignored and make no difference to the unit's overall fighting ability. The standard bearer also has to carry a banner as well as fight, but he is chosen from the strongest and most determined individuals in the unit, and this more than makes up for any disadvantage suffered because of the weight and inconvenience of his standard or any difference in his armour or weaponry.

The enemy cannot specifically attack standard bearers as he can character models. Standard bearers are not normally removed as casualties, as it is assumed that if the standard bearer is killed, another warrior will pick up the banner and take his place. Therefore, the player always removes an ordinary warrior in preference to a standard bearer, even if the ordinary warrior is not in base contact with the enemy.

COMBAT RESULT BONUS

If a unit includes a standard bearer, it will be more determined than ever to beat its foe. A unit that has a standard bearer in its front rank adds +1 to its combat result when deciding which side has won a close combat. See the Close Combat section for a complete description of how to work out which side has won a combat. In a multiple fight, this bonus is +1 if one or more units on your side have a standard, and not +1 per standard!

CAPTURING STANDARDS

If a unit is defeated in close combat and then subsequently breaks and flees, the enemy automatically captures its standard if they pursue. The standard is captured regardless of whether the pursuers catch and destroy the fleeing troops or not.

If victors do not pursue a broken enemy, the standard is lost in the tide of battle but it is not captured.

Standards are also captured if an enemy unit is completely destroyed in close combat, in which case there is no need to pursue.

In any case, when a unit breaks from combat, the standard bearer model is removed from the unit and, in the case of a unit that is not destroyed, it is replaced with an ordinary trooper model.

Note that standards are only lost if the unit is defeated and broken in close combat, not if the unit flees after it has failed a Psychology test.

Captured standards are placed behind the unit that captured them and carried about as trophies for the rest of the game. Trophies have no fighting value; they are merely used to indicate that the unit has captured its adversary's flag. The player's standard bearer model is surrendered for the duration of the game and his jubilant enemy places it behind his unit to proclaim his victory.

Captured trophies can be recaptured by defeating the unit that has them in close combat, thereby avenging their initial loss and restoring them to a proper place of honour, as well as capturing the enemy's own banner as a trophy. Any recaptured banners are immediately removed from the table, but at least will not end the battle in enemy hands!

Once the game is over, a player can claim extra victory points for enemy standards he has captured and still holds, as described in the victory points section (see page 102).

MUSICIANS

An army marches under its banners, but it does so to the beat of drums and the call of blaring horns.

A unit of troops can often include a single musician model, like a horn blower or a drummer, to accompany it into battle. He can be bought as an upgrade to a normal model in the unit, as described in the relevant Warhammer Armies books.

A musician model is placed in the front rank of its unit. His effect on the fighting ability of the unit is not as great as a standard bearer but is useful nonetheless.

Like standard bearers, musicians fight just like an ordinary member of their unit, even if the model itself has slight variances in armour or weaponry. Also, like standard bearers, the player does not remove musicians, but substitutes an ordinary model instead. However, unlike standard bearers, musicians are not removed automatically when a unit breaks and flees from combat. Their instruments are somewhat lighter and less cumbersome than a weighty standard. Musicians cannot be captured as trophies.

DRAWN COMBATS

If a unit of troops has a musician in its front rank, then an inspiring horn blast or rousing drumbeat can make all the difference between an evenly matched fight and a victory.

If a close combat is drawn, but one side has one or more musicians in its front rank and the other doesn't, the side with the musicians wins the combat by 1 point. If both or neither sides have musicians in the front rank, the result is still a draw.

RALLYING BONUS

If a fleeing unit includes a musician, it will gain a +1 Leadership bonus in any attempt to rally, up to a maximum of Leadership 10.

CHAMPIONS

A unit of troops can often include a single champion. He can be bought as an upgrade to a normal model in the unit as described in the relevant Warhammer Armies books. Champions are extremely skilled or tough, and comrades look up to them and take pride in their prowess. Champions of units have various names depending on the army they fight for – Orc champions are called Bosses, while Empire champions are called Sergeants or Marksmen, for example. No matter their name, champions always follow the same rules.

The champion is always armed and equipped in the same way as the rest of his unit, unless otherwise noted (even if the model is sometimes different in order to stand out). The champion is normally placed in the front rank along with characters and the unit's standard bearer and musician.

Unlike standard bearers and musicians, enemy models can direct attacks against champions and kill them – if a champion is removed as a casualty he is not replaced by another model (see page 76). If the unit suffers enough wounds to kill every model in it, the champion is removed together with his comrades, being after all a rank-and-file model.

Although they normally have slightly better characteristics than normal troopers, champions are not characters but members of their regiment and always fight as part of it, moving, attacking, fleeing and pursuing alongside the unit as a whole. If the unit has any special rules that apply to it, such as being Stubborn or subject to Frenzy, then these also apply to the champion. Unlike characters, a champion can never leave his unit or join another one.

Even though they are rank & file models rather than characters, champions are subject to the following rules that govern characters (see the Characters section on pages 72-79 for details).

- Champions can move within their unit in exactly the same way as characters (but may never leave their unit).
- Champions can accept and issue challenges (and, of course, refuse them!).
- Champions are treated as characters when their unit is hit by ranged attacks (eg, they benefit from the "Look out, Sir!" rule, etc).

GENERALS & BATTLE STANDARDS

 THE GENERAL

Every army has a heroic character to command it. The General model is in command of the whole army and represents you personally. We refer to this character as the General, although this is only to distinguish him from other heroes. He might be an Orc chieftain, a Bretonnian Duke, etc. Some armies are commanded by the ruler of their entire nation. For example, the Emperor of the Empire and King of Bretonnia are mighty warriors who are ever-ready to ride out at the head of their forces.

The character with the highest Leadership value is the General of your army.

If several characters have the same (and highest) Ld value, choose one to be the General at the start of the battle and announce it to your opponent. The General is an important character, because he can inspire others to fight on where they might otherwise turn and flee.

GENERAL'S LEADERSHIP

All friendly units within 12" of the General model always use the General's Leadership value instead of their own when making any Leadership-based test (unless their own Leadership is higher, of course). This normally means that a unit near the General uses his superior Leadership when testing for Break tests in close combat, when attempting to rally, for Psychology tests such as Fear and Panic, and for any other Leadership-based test. This rule ceases to apply while the General is fleeing, so it is normally a good idea to start rallying your fleeing units beginning with the General, so that the other units attempting to rally can benefit from his Leadership (assuming he rallies, that is!).

 THE BATTLE STANDARD

Armies may include a special standard bearer carrying either the General's personal banner or the battle standard of the army itself. This battle standard bearer does not have to move along with the General but it is most useful when he is close by.

An army's battle standard is usually carried by a character model who cannot normally be the General model itself. The battle standard cannot be passed to another model if its bearer is slain.

If the battle standard bearer is slain or breaks and flees from combat (either on his own or as part of a unit), the battle standard is lost and may be captured as described later.

COMBAT BONUS

A battle standard bearer can join a unit of troops in the same way as any other character. If he is in the front rank of a unit that is fighting in close combat, or if he is anyway fighting the enemy (he could have moved to fight enemies engaging his unit from the rear, for example), his side receives an extra +1 combat bonus when working out combat results.

A unit can benefit from both its unit standard bearer and the battle standard bearer bonuses, therefore receiving a +2 combat result bonus.

RE-ROLL BREAK TESTS

All friendly units within 12" of the battle standard automatically re-roll failed Break tests. This rule ceases to apply while the battle standard is fleeing or if he is hiding at the back of a unit instead of fighting. Remember that you are only allowed to re-roll the dice once.

Note that the controlling player may not choose whether or not a unit is going to use the battle standard re-roll, but must always use it if the first test is failed.

If the General is within 12" of the unit as well, then it will also benefit from being able to use his Leadership value. These two factors combined, the General's Leadership and the opportunity to re-roll a failed Break test, mean that units near to the General and the battle standard will tend to hold their ground a lot more resolutely.

Note that a battle standard allows a unit to re-roll a failed Break test – and only a Break test. It does not entitle a unit to retake any other Leadership test, such as a Psychology test or a Rally test.

CAPTURING THE BATTLE STANDARD

This follows the rules for capturing standards (see page 80), with the following exceptions.

If the battle standard bearer is fighting on his own, the enemy may capture the battle standard by either killing the bearer in close combat or by breaking him and pursuing. The standard is then captured and held as a trophy exactly like unit banners.

If the battle standard bearer has joined a unit and the unit breaks from combat and flees, he will flee with the unit and lose the standard. In this case, the enemy may capture the battle standard (together with the unit's standard if it has one) by pursuing, as normal. If this happens, replace the bearer model with one that does not have the banner or otherwise mark the model to represent that it does not carry the banner any more.

If the battle standard bearer has joined a unit and he is slain in close combat and his unit breaks and flees in the very same turn, the battle standard can be captured as described above.

If the battle standard bearer has joined a unit and is slain in close combat, but his unit does not break in the same turn, the battle standard is simply removed as a casualty and cannot be captured.

WAR MACHINES

War machines are an important part of many armies in the Warhammer world. Amongst the most spectacular of these engines of destruction are the mighty cannons of the Empire and the Dwarfs, but their manufacture is difficult and the secrets of gun casting and black-powder manufacture are carefully guarded. Other races build gigantic stone throwers that lob boulders high into the air to come crashing down upon enemy formations or behind city walls. Bolt throwers are giant crossbows that can send a spear-sized bolt clean through several ranks of enemy, skewering each in turn. These are all relatively common war machines that can be found in several armies, and thus their rules are included here. Many other weird and unique war machines are described in the Warhammer Armies books, like the infamous Skaven Warp-lightning Cannon and the wacky Goblin Doom Diver. Their rules are included in the appropriate book.

MODELS

A war machine comprises the machine plus a crew, which usually consists of two to four crewmen. The crew are based separately, unlike the model of a chariot or a ridden monster, where the crew or riders are likely to be physically glued to the chariot or mount. This is necessary because a war machine's crew can be forced to flee from their machine. These models must be kept within 1" of their machine to count as crewing it.

MOVEMENT

The machine's crew can move their machine, perhaps to gain a better position to fire. The machine and its crew are moved like a unit of skirmishers (see page 65), except that they cannot charge enemy units (not even if Frenzied!), can never march and pay normal penalties for moving through difficult ground.

The Movement rate is the speed at which the machine can move with its full crew and it is the same as the crew's – if any crew members are slain, then its speed is reduced proportionally. For example, if the machine is normally moved at normal speed by a crew of three, it will lose a third of its movement for each model below three that is moving the machine.

CHARACTERS

A character model may join a war machine's crew in the same way as he might join a unit of troops, by moving to within 1" of the machine itself. The war machine benefits from the associated character's Leadership value in the same way that a unit of troops would. However, only crew can operate a machine, a character cannot (unless specified in their special rules).

On the positive side, this means that characters are never hurt should the machine misfire. Characters are sensible or experienced enough to keep sufficient distance between themselves and the dangerous mechanism to be safe.

Characters are free to fire their own missile weapons at a different target from the one that the machine is being fired at.

SHOOTING

In the shooting phase, a player may freely pivot a war machine to face any direction he likes before shooting. Apart from this, a war machine may not be fired in a turn when the machine itself, or even just its crew, have moved.

Normally, the controlling player must be able to draw a line of sight to the target from the machine itself.

Each type of war machine is fired differently, as described in its own set of rules. For now it is enough to know that some war machines are fired like normal missile weapons and so make use of the crew's Ballistic Skill, but other machines require you to guess the distance between the machine and its target and make use of the artillery dice and the scatter dice. The scatter dice is the dice marked with arrows on four sides and the HIT symbol on two sides. The artillery dice is marked 2, 4, 6, 8, 10 and MISFIRE.

Remember to always start the shooting phase by guessing the range for all war machines that require you to do so.

SHOOTING AGAINST WAR MACHINES

When shooting at a war machine, shots are worked out against the entire unit, and any hits scored are randomised between the crew and war machine.

A war machine is treated exactly as any normal unit with regards to modifiers to hit. A war machine and its crew don't count as skirmishing, and so don't benefit from the -1 to hit penalty. Some war machines may be classed as large targets (this will be noted in the war machine's specific rules).

Once hits have been established, randomise where they strike by rolling a D6. If the result is 1-4, roll to 'wound' the machine. If the result is a 5 or 6, roll to wound against the crew. Once all crew are slain or have fled, or once the machine is destroyed, further hits do not need to be randomised but will strike the machine or a crewman, as appropriate.

Remember that war machine crew do not take Panic tests for casualties suffered from ranged attacks, such as missile fire and spells.

HITS FROM TEMPLATES

Any shots from stone throwers, or weapons and spells that use a template, are worked out as normal. Once the template has been placed, any models whose bases are fully covered are hit and models whose bases are partially covered are hit on a 4+.

HITS ON CREW/CHARACTERS

Usually a machine's crew members are identical, so it is not necessary to determine which is hit, but if a machine includes a character, he may be hit by shots directed at the machine. In this case, randomise any crew hits to determine whether the character is hit. For example where there are two crew and a character roll a D6: 1-2=crewman A, 3-4=crewman B, 5-6=character.

LOSS OF CREW

Normally a war machine requires a full crew to work it properly – to carry ammunition, push the machine round to bear on its target, and so on.

If members of the crew are slain, this will affect the movement rate of the machine as described above, but will not slow its rate of fire until there is only one crewman left. The last crewman left will then be unable to cope – the machine can be fired normally one last time, but from then on it will have to miss a whole turn (for the remaining crewman to reload it) before it can shoot again. This is in addition to any penalty imposed by a misfire result. Obviously, the machine requires at least one crewman to work, so the machine will become useless should all of its crew be slain.

Some war machines, such as the bolt throwers made by the Elves, are smaller and much easier to operate than the larger, more cumbersome ones. If a war machine has a crew of only two models from the beginning of the game (as specified in their entry in the appropriate Army book), they can be operated by a single crewman. If one of the crewmen of this machine is slain, the remaining one can therefore keep firing without slowing down the machine's rate of fire.

CHARGE RESPONSES

If charged, a war machine's crew can either hold or flee but cannot stand & shoot with their war machine as the artillery piece is too slow and cumbersome to allow this.

The crew and attached characters can, of course, stand & shoot with their own missile weapons (such as bows, pistols etc), if they have any.

HOLD

In close combat, the crew will defend their machines. The crew and any characters that might have joined the crew are lined up in front of their war machine, perpendicular to the direction of the charge, so that they are interposed between the machine and the chargers (see Diagram 84.1).

FLEE

If a machine's crew flees from a charge, the chargers must stop when they reach the machine and will normally destroy it in the close combat phase, as described later. The machine itself does not flee as such, but is abandoned by its crew and any associated characters and will be automatically destroyed in the ensuing combat.

FLEEING CREW

Once separated from their war machines, crewmen become a normal fleeing unit. For the purposes of rallying, the original number of crewmen is the original size of the unit (this will usually be three).

If they rally, they are treated like a skirmishing unit until they re-crew a friendly war machine.

84.1 - Crew in Combat

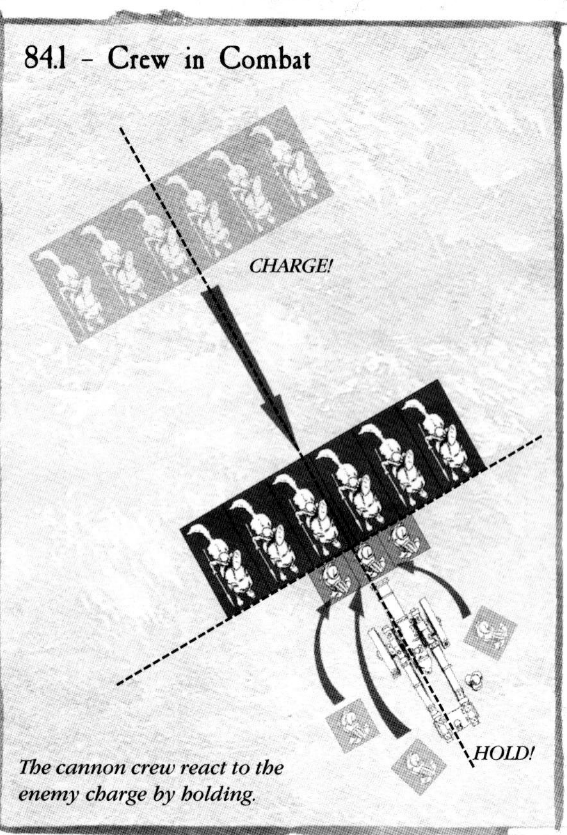

The cannon crew react to the enemy charge by holding.

CLOSE COMBAT

During the close combat phase, enemy models fight the crew and attached characters as normal. The machine itself does not fight back. A war machine that is attacked in close combat is assumed to have a WS of 0 and is therefore hit automatically. Resolve the combat as normal. If the machine has no crew left to defend it at the end of a combat (because the crew fled from the charge, have broken from combat or are wiped out), the enemy automatically destroys the machine, and is immediately free to pursue the broken crew or overrun as normal.

A war machine's crew can automatically choose not to pursue enemy breaking from combat if they are still crewing their war machine (unless under the effects of Frenzy or Hatred). If they choose to pursue, they will abandon their machine and pursue as normal.

ABANDONED MACHINES

An abandoned machine can be re-crewed by any other friendly war machine crew if their own machine has been destroyed or if they have abandoned their machine. The entire crew may deliberately abandon a war machine, perhaps in order to crew another.

CANNONS

Cannons are dangerous, if sometimes unpredictable, weapons whose manufacture is limited to Human and Dwarf experts. When they work, cannons can shatter the most determined enemy, pouring deadly shot into his massed formations, levelling his cities and toppling huge monsters. However, cannons often go wrong. Weaknesses in the casting methods can leave minute cracks or other deficiencies, which cause them to explode when fired, or black-powder can fail to ignite or may explode prematurely. Despite the occasional spectacular accident, cannons are extremely potent weapons that have been instrumental in winning many battles.

FIRING A CANNON

Pivot the cannon on the spot so that it is pointing in the direction of the model it is going to fire against. Declare which enemy model is going to be the target (remember, the target has to be visible from the machine itself) and then declare how far the cannon is going to shoot, up to its maximum range (eg, 24", 30", 32", etc). Do this without measuring the distance to that target, so try to guess the range as accurately as possible.

Once you have made your guess, roll the artillery dice and, assuming you haven't rolled a misfire, add the score of the dice to the distance that has been declared. The cannonball travels the distance that the player has nominated plus the score of the artillery dice from the cannon itself towards the target, and will either land short, pass straight over, or hit depending on how accurately the player guessed the range and what effect the dice roll has.

Remember the dice will always add at least 2" to an estimate, and can add up to 10", so you should guess a few inches short of the target.

Once it is established where the cannonball hits, place a small coin or other marker directly over the spot. Hopefully, the cannonball will not stop where it hits the ground, but will bounce straight forward and cut a line through any targets in the way. To determine how far the cannonball bounces, roll the artillery dice again and mark the spot where the cannonball comes to land. If the cannonball bounces into impassable terrain that in reality would stand in the way of the shot, such as a sheer cliff (as opposed to a lake), it stops immediately, but other than this, nothing can stop a cannonball!

If you roll a misfire on either rolls of the artillery dice, something has gone wrong, see the rules for misfires given overleaf.

Any models between the points where the ball first strikes the ground and where it eventually comes to land are hit by the bouncing cannonball.

For example, a cannon is fired at a unit of Goblins. The player makes his guess and declares that he is aiming 12" directly towards the middle of the Goblin unit. Having made his guess the player then rolls the artillery dice and scores a 4, which equals 4". This makes a total of 16". He measures 16" towards the Goblins and places a marker where the ball hits. If he has guessed well, this will be just in front of them. The ball now bounces forward the score of the second artillery dice roll. This time an 8 is rolled and the ball bounces 8" straight through the Goblin unit, hitting all the models in the way.

This is completely straightforward in the case of skirmishing units and war machines and their crew, in which case any model touched by the line drawn by the bouncing ball is hit. However, when a cannonball hurtles through a ranked-up unit, only one model per rank can be hit. Of course if the cannonball is coming from the flank of the unit, the unit's files will count as ranks. The diagrams overleaf show how this works.

If a cannonball hits a model that has several parts, like a character riding on a monster or chariot, resolve which part of the model is hit just like shooting with bows. For example, in the case of a cannon hit on a character riding a chariot, roll a dice: on a 1-5 the chariot is hit, and on a 6 the character is hit.

DAMAGE

Any model struck by a cannonball takes a Strength 10 hit. Roll to wound as normal. No armour saving throw is permitted for wounds caused by cannons. If a cannonball hits you, no amount of armour is going to do you any good. Ward saves can be taken as normal. Unsaved wounds cause not 1 wound but D3 or D6 wounds, depending on the size of the cannon. As most models have only 1 Wound anyway, it will not be necessary to roll this extra dice, but it is important when it comes to rolling for Heroes, big monsters and other models that can take several wounds.

GRAPESHOT

Instead of firing a normal shot, cannon crew can opt to fire grapeshot, loading the gun with rusty nails, handgun bullets and other small, sharp projectiles, effectively creating a huge blunderbuss!

To do this, pivot the cannon so that it is pointing towards the target and then roll the artillery dice.

If the result is a misfire, the cannon does not fire and the player must roll on the misfire chart.

If the result is a number, place the flame template so that the small end is touching the muzzle of the cannon. Models whose bases are fully covered by the template are hit automatically, while those whose bases are only partially covered are hit on a roll of 4+ on a D6. Models hit suffer a hit with a Strength equal to the number rolled on the artillery dice, with an additional -1 armour save modifier (this is the 'armour piercing' weapon rule). Unsaved wounds cause D3 wounds on the target.

CANNON MISFIRE CHART

D6	Result
1	**DESTROYED!** The cannon explodes with a mighty crack. Shards of metal and wood fly in all directions leaving a hole in the ground and a cloud of black smoke. The cannon is destroyed and its crew slain or injured. Remove the cannon and its crew.
2-3	**MALFUNCTION.** The powder fails to ignite and the cannon does not fire. The crew must remove the ball and powder before the cannon can shoot again – which takes another turn. The cannon therefore cannot fire either this turn or the next turn. It is a good idea to turn the cannon round to indicate this.
4-6	**MAY NOT SHOOT.** A minor fault prevents the cannon from firing this turn, perhaps the fuse is not set properly or maybe the crewmen mishandled the loading procedure. The cannon is unharmed and may shoot as normal next turn.

MISFIRES

The artillery dice is usually rolled twice when a cannon is fired, so there are two chances of rolling a misfire result. However, the two results will be different. If a misfire result is rolled on the first dice, the cannon has literally misfired and may explode. If a misfire is rolled on the second roll, the 'bounce' roll, the cannon is unharmed, the misfire result merely indicates that the cannonball has stuck in the ground where it hits and travels no further. If the shot lands on top of a model then that particular model is hit as normal, but there is no further bounce damage.

If a misfire is rolled as the cannon is shot, roll a dice and consult the misfire chart.

PROFILES

Cannons are hand forged by master craftsmen, and each is different with little standardisation in the way of calibres or length. In gaming terms, however, most cannons can be grouped into two categories: great cannons or normal cannons.

The difference between the two types is range and damage. Bigger cannons carry a larger charge and so have a longer range and cause more damage.

	Range	Strength	Damage	Special
Cannon	48"	10	D3	No armour save
Great Cannon*	60"	10	D6	No armour save
Grapeshot	Template	Artillery dice	D3	Armour piercing

Cannons have a profile with a Toughness value and number of Wounds that they can sustain before they are destroyed. As with other details these may vary, but the typical cannons have the value shown here:

Movement	Toughness	Wounds
As crew	7	3

CANNON SUMMARY

1) Align the cannon on the target and declare the distance you are aiming.

2) Roll the artillery dice and add the score to the distance aimed. The cannonball travels forward this distance before striking the ground.

3) If you roll a misfire refer to the misfire chart. Otherwise, mark the point where the cannonball strikes the ground and roll the artillery dice to establish the bounce distance. All models in the path of the bounce are hit.

4) If you roll a misfire for the bounce roll, the ball sticks in the ground and does not bounce.

5) Work out the effect of hits normally. Models have no armour saving throw for a cannon hit.

89.1 - Cannons (a)

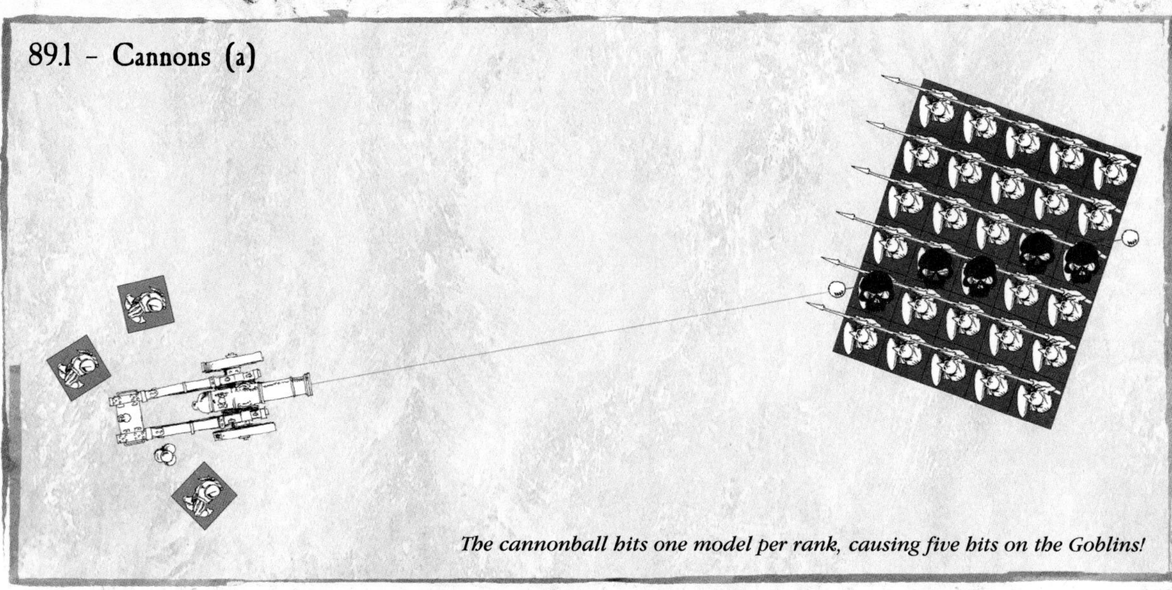

The cannonball hits one model per rank, causing five hits on the Goblins!

89.2 - Cannons (b)

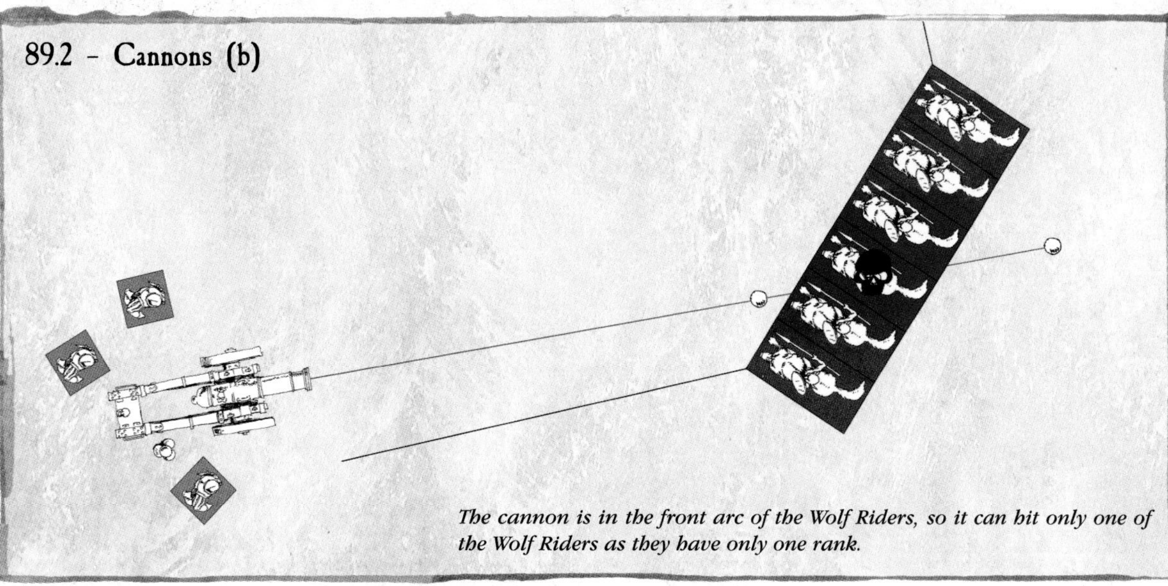

The cannon is in the front arc of the Wolf Riders, so it can hit only one of the Wolf Riders as they have only one rank.

89.3 - Cannons (c)

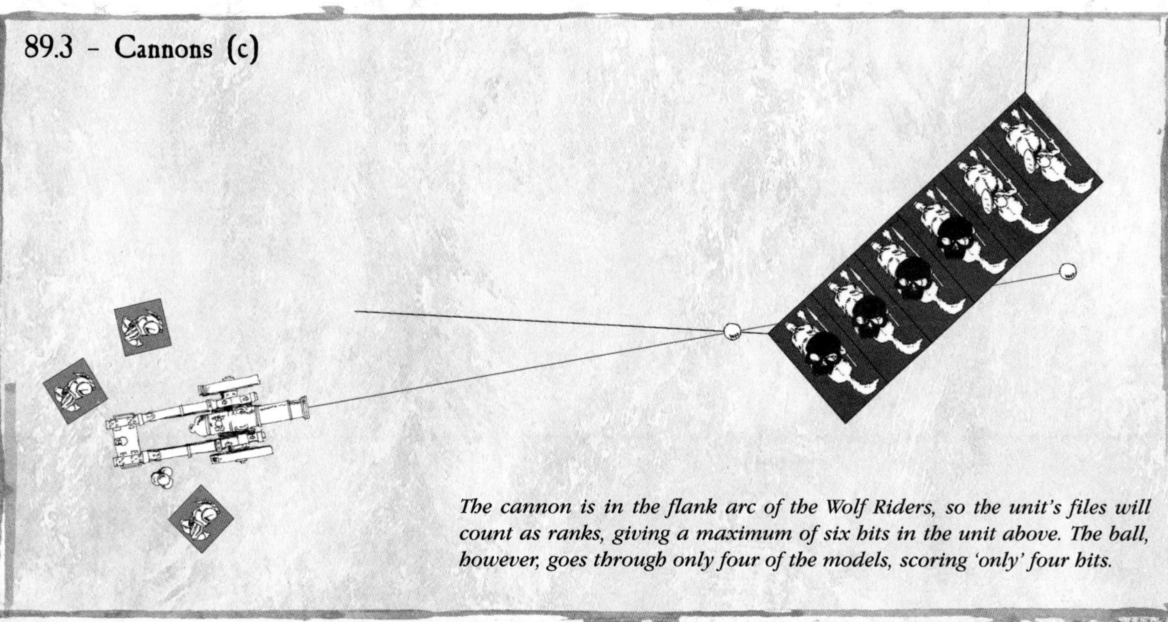

The cannon is in the flank arc of the Wolf Riders, so the unit's files will count as ranks, giving a maximum of six hits in the unit above. The ball, however, goes through only four of the models, scoring 'only' four hits.

BOLT THROWERS

Bolt throwers are huge crossbows that shoot a spear-sized missile. They are so large that they are mounted on their own stand, often with wheels so they can be pivoted easily. A crew of two or more is required to wind back the powerful torsion arms and position the huge bolt ready for firing.

FIRING A BOLT THROWER

Bolt throwers are fired in the shooting phase along with other missile weapons. First select a target unit following the normal rules for shooting, drawing line of sight from the machine itself. Now pivot the bolt thrower on the spot so that it points towards its intended target. To determine whether the bolt is on target, roll to hit using the crew's BS in the same way as bow shots, crossbows, and other missile weapons. The usual modifiers apply, except no penalty is imposed for turning the machine, as it is designed to be used in this way. See the Shooting section for details.

If the shot misses, the bolt hits the ground or sails into the air and comes down harmlessly somewhere else. If a hit is scored, work out damage as described below.

If the target is a unit of five or more ranked-up models, the bolt will always strike a regular trooper in the unit's first rank (as opposed to a champion or character in the unit) if the bolt thrower is in the unit's front arc, or the last rank if the machine is in the unit's rear arc. If the bolt thrower is in the flank of the target unit, the unit's files will count as ranks. The diagrams opposite show how this works.

If the rank hit by the bolt is made entirely of characters (including champions) or if the total of rank-and-file models in the unit is less than five, it will be necessary to randomise which model in the rank is hit.

DAMAGE

A bolt thrower is a powerful weapon that can hurl its bolt through several ranks of troops, piercing each warrior in turn. If it hits, resolve damage against the target using the bolt thrower's full Strength of 6. If the first model hit is slain, the bolt hits the trooper directly behind in the next rank: resolve damage on the second model using a Strength of 5. If the second trooper is slain, the model directly behind in the next rank is hit: resolve damage using a Strength of 4. Continue to work out damage as the bolt pierces and slays a model in each rank, deducting 1 from the Strength for each rank pierced.

Stop rolling once the bolt fails to slay a model or it has gone through all of the ranks in the unit.

Armour saves are not allowed against hits from a bolt thrower because the missiles are so fast and deadly that any armour is pierced along with its wearer. Ward saves may be taken as normal. An unsaved wound causes not 1 but D3 wounds, which means that even large monsters can be slain by a hit from a bolt thrower.

PROFILES

The bolt thrower hurls a metal-tipped heavy spear that causes considerable damage. The chart below shows its details.

	Range	Strength	Damage	Special
Bolt Thrower	48"	6 (-1 per rank)	D3	No armour save

Bolt throwers are made from solid wood and iron. They have a profile like a creature, with a Toughness value and a number of Wounds that they can sustain before they are destroyed.

Movement	Toughness	Wounds
As crew	7	3

BOLT THROWER SUMMARY

1) Align the bolt thrower on target and roll to hit, using the crew's BS.

2) Resolve damage at Strength 6. No armour save is allowed against a hit from a bolt thrower.

3) If the target is slain roll for damage against the second rank at Strength 5.

4) Continue rolling for damage until you fail to slay the target or run out of ranks.

5) Deduct 1 from the Strength for each model already slain.

91.1 - Bolt Throwers (a)

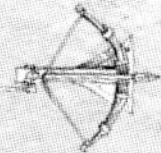

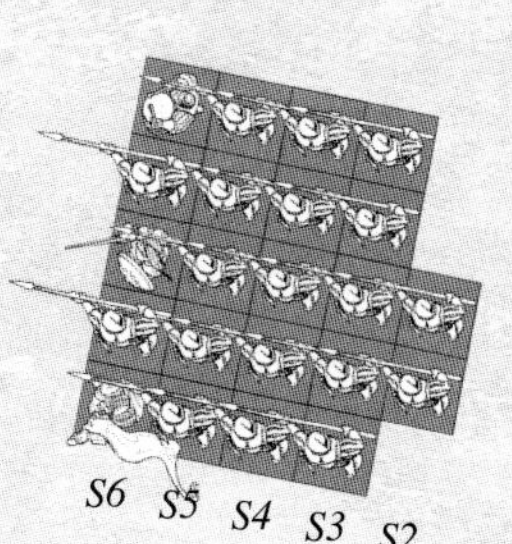

Up to five Spearmen can be killed by the shot of this bolt thrower. The Strength that each rank is hit at is shown next to it.

91.2 - Bolt Throwers (b)

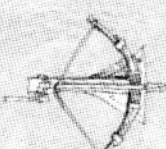

S6
S5

As the bolt thrower is in their front arc, up to two Knights can be killed by its shot.

91.3 - Bolt Throwers (c)

S1
S2
S3
S4
S5
S6

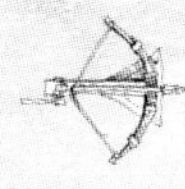

As the bolt thrower is in their flank arc, up to six Knights can be killed by its shot.

91.4 - Bolt Throwers (d)

The bolt thrower can see the Knights, so the unit is a valid target. As the bolt thrower is in their flank arc, up to six Knights can be killed by its shot, regardless of the fact that the bolt thrower cannot actually see their flank – obviously a well-aimed arced shot!

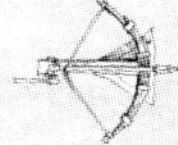

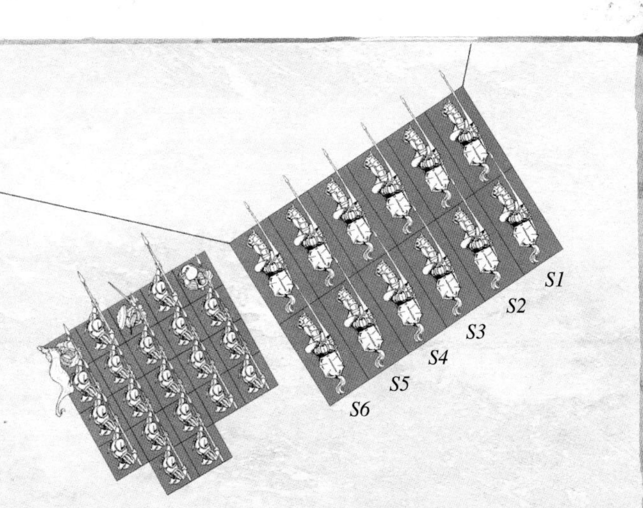

STONE THROWERS

These are powerful and destructive weapons that lob large rocks into the air, sending them crashing through enemy ranks. Many races in Warhammer use these devices. Not all are built in the same way: some use a massive counterweight to catapult their missile into the air while others use torsion power like a giant crossbow. The bigger the engine, the larger the rock it can throw and the more damage it can do. The very largest stone throwers can hurl a projectile big enough to flatten the most powerful of monsters or knock down city walls!

FIRING A STONE THROWER

To work out hits from a stone thrower you will need the small 3" round template. The stone is not as big as the template, of course, (that would require a very large engine indeed) but it shatters on impact, sending shards of sharp stone over a wide area.

Pivot the stone thrower on the spot so it is pointing in the direction of the model it is going to fire against. Declare which enemy model is going to be the target (remember, the target has to be visible from the machine itself). Then declare how far the rock is to be fired – this can be any number of inches between a minimum of 12" and the maximum range of the stone thrower (normally 60"). Do this without measuring the distance to that target, so try to guess the range as accurately as possible. Once you have made your guess, measure that distance from the stone thrower itself along the line between the machine and the intended target, and then place the centre of the template directly over the spot where you have guessed.

For example, a stone thrower is firing at a unit of Bretonnian Knights. The player makes his guess and declares that the stone thrower is firing 28" directly towards the unit's champion. He then measures 28" towards the target. If he has made a good guess the template will lie over its intended target. If not, there's still a chance the stone may hit something.

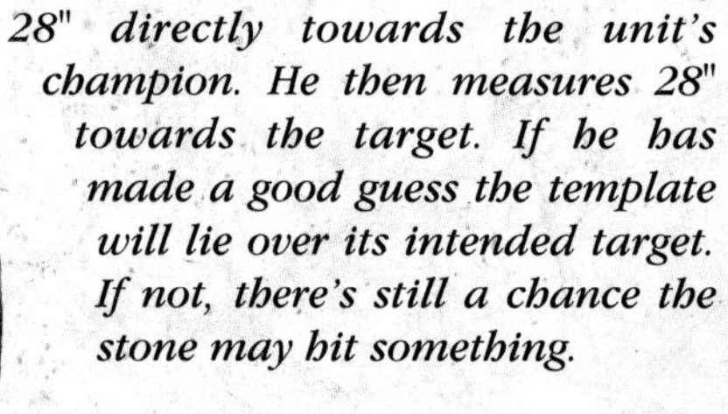

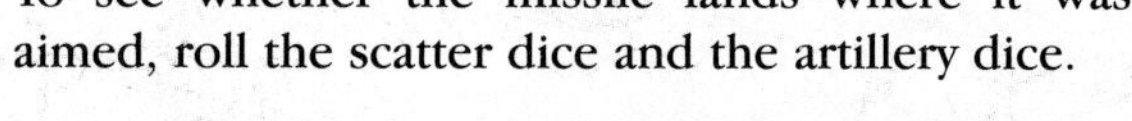

To see whether the missile lands where it was aimed, roll the scatter dice and the artillery dice.

If a misfire has been rolled on the artillery dice, something has gone wrong – roll a D6 and consult the misfire chart. A misfire roll automatically cancels out the whole shot regardless of the scatter dice result.

If a number is rolled on the artillery dice, this is the distance in inches the missile veers off target as shown by the arrow on the scatter dice. Move the template the distance indicated in the direction shown by the arrow.

If a hit is rolled on the scatter dice, the missile lands exactly where it was aimed and the numbers on the artillery dice are ignored, a number simply indicates that the shot has not misfired.

If an arrow is rolled on the scatter dice, the missile veers off in the direction shown by the arrow.

For example, the player guesses bang on and the template is placed directly in the middle of the chosen target. He then rolls both special dice. The scatter dice shows a hit! It has landed right on target. The artillery dice score is 4 – the number indicates that nothing is amiss – a fine hit!

STONE THROWER MISFIRE CHART

D6	Result
1	**DESTROYED!** The engine cannot stand the strain placed upon it and breaks under the tension as it is fired. Bits of wood and metal fly all around, the stone tumbles to the ground splintering the engine and throwing debris into the air. The engine is destroyed and its crew slain or injured. Remove the engine and its crew.
2-3	**DISABLED.** The normal smooth running of the machine and its crew is disrupted by some accident or freak occurrence. A rope snaps and lashes about wildly, a crewman sets the machine up wrongly so that it pulls itself apart, or maybe a careless operator has become entangled in the mechanism. The engine does not shoot this turn and cannot fire next turn either while the damage is repaired. To help you remember, it is a good idea to turn the machine round to face away from the enemy. In addition, one of the crew is slain – caught by a snapping rope, entangled in the machinery, or thrown high into the air in place of the stone!
4-6	**MAY NOT SHOOT.** A minor fault prevents the machine shooting this turn. A crewman drops the stone as he lifts it into position, maybe a ratchet jams or a rope loosens. The machine is unharmed and may shoot as normal next turn.

93.1 - Number of Models Hit

SPLAT! The model at the exact centre point of the template is hit at double Strength. Four models are hit at normal Strength. Sixteen more can be hit on a 4+.

Once it is established where the stone lands, damage can be worked out. Any model that lies completely under the template is hit automatically, while each model whose base lies partially under the template is hit on a 4+. See Diagram 93.1 for details.

You will have to use your judgement and common sense to decide exactly which models lie under the template – sometimes it is not easy to judge precisely.

DAMAGE

Once it has been worked out which models are struck, work out damage in the usual way. Roll for each target to see whether it has suffered damage. Stone throwers normally have a Strength of 4 or more. Refer to the To Wound chart for details.

No armour saving throw is permitted against wounds from a stone thrower. When a big rock lands on you, you are squashed regardless of what armour you may be wearing! Ward saves may be taken as normal. Unsaved wounds from a stone thrower cause D6 wounds, but as most creatures have only 1 Wound, it is not necessary to take this dice roll. It is, however, useful when attacking characters, monsters, etc.

Any single model that lies directly under the centre of the template suffers one automatic hit at twice the stone thrower's usual Strength (even if its base is not completely covered by the template!) – the stone lands directly on top of that model. This means that a stone thrower can easily wound even a very tough monster or character.

PROFILE

Most stone throwers use the following profile:

	Range	Strength	Damage	Special
Stone Thrower	12"-60"	4(8)	D6	No armour save

Stone throwers have a profile like a creature, with a Toughness value and a number of Wounds that they can sustain before they are destroyed.

As with other details, these might vary in specific cases, but a typical engine has the values shown here.

Movement	Toughness	Wounds
As crew	7	3

STONE THROWER SUMMARY

1) Declare target and guess range.

2) Position the 3" template and roll scatter and artillery dice.

3) If the artillery dice is a misfire, refer to the misfire chart, otherwise…

a) If the scatter dice is a hit, the stone strikes home.

b) If the scatter dice is an arrow, the stone lands in the direction shown, 2", 4", 6", 8" or 10" away from the aiming point as shown on the artillery dice.

4) All models completely under the template are hit automatically, those partially under are hit on a 4+.

5) Work out wounds as normal. Models are allowed no armour saving throw from a stone thrower.

OTHER WAR MACHINES

Stone throwers, bolt throwers and cannons are common to several armies, but in addition there are many strange war machines that are available only to specific armies. These are described in the Warhammer Armies books together with the special rules that apply to them. Examples include Dwarf Flame Cannons that spout a sheet of flames, undead catapults firing screaming skulls, and the deadly Helblaster Volley Guns of the Empire.

Some of these unique war machines are so different that they have entirely new rules, but others are similar to the machines described above in that they consist of a weapon and its crew. In general, the same rules apply to these crews as to the crews of stone throwers, cannons and bolt throwers. Exceptions to these procedures, together with the special rules for the weapons, are described in the appropriate Warhammer Armies books.

SPECIAL RULES

Many troops in the Warhammer game have unique and unusual abilities and skills. In the game, these abilities and skills are represented by special rules. Any creature may have one or more special rules and, unless otherwise mentioned, the effects from special rules are cumulative.

The following list is by no means exhaustive, but it does detail the most common special rules (more can be found in the Warhammer Armies books).

ALWAYS STRIKES FIRST

Some warriors are equipped with magic weapons or are under the effects of spells allowing them to strike with supernatural speed.

Models with this special rule always strike first in close combat, even before models that have charged that turn and regardless of Initiative. If fighting another model with the same special rule, use the models' Initiative to determine who strikes first (roll a dice in case of same Initiative).

BREATH WEAPON

Fiery Dragons and the dreaded Hydras of the Chaos Wastes, as well as some even more bizarre creatures, have the ability to breathe fire, noxious gas, lightning or even stranger substances.

A model with a breath weapon may use it in the shooting phase, even if it has marched. Use the flame template, placing the broad end over your intended target as you wish and the narrow end next to the creature's mouth(s). Note that the monster must be able to see all its potential targets. Any model that lies completely under the template is hit automatically, while models whose bases lie partially under the template are hit on a 4+. The Strength and any special effects of the breath weapon will be detailed in the creature's rules. Characters under the template are eligible for "Look out, Sir!" rolls if they are in a unit, as normal.

Breath weapons may not be used as a stand & shoot charge reaction, and neither can they be used when engaged in close combat (and, of course, cannot be targeted at units that are engaged in combat).

95.1 - Breath Weapons

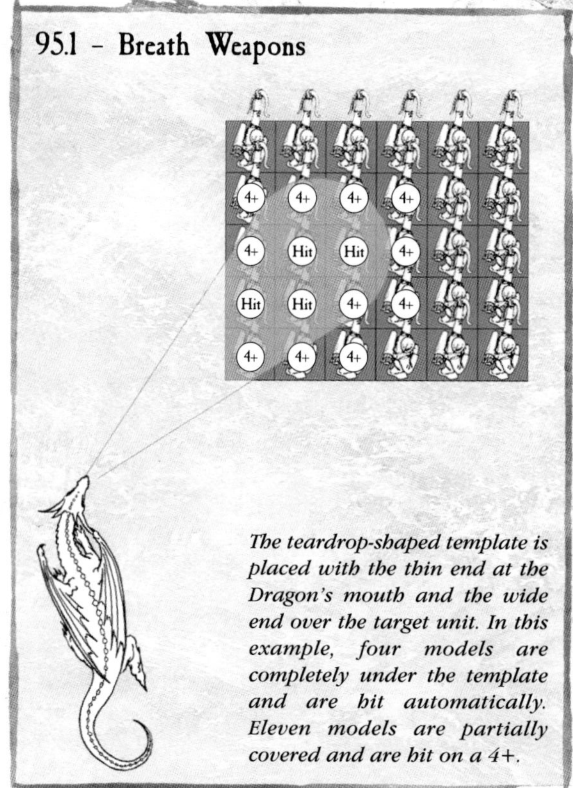

The teardrop-shaped template is placed with the thin end at the Dragon's mouth and the wide end over the target unit. In this example, four models are completely under the template and are hit automatically. Eleven models are partially covered and are hit on a 4+.

FLAMING ATTACKS

Some war machines, like the Warpfire Thrower of the Skaven, and a few arcane creatures, such as the dreaded Flamers of Tzeentch, use fire as a deadly form of attack. Their attacks will cause double wounds against creatures that are flammable. The flesh of a regenerating creature cannot regenerate if it has been burnt. Wounds suffered from a flaming attack cannot be regenerated.

FLAMMABLE

Some creatures, such as Mummies and Treemen, burn easily and so have this special rule in their profile. A flammable creature hit by a flaming attack will take double wounds, so every wound suffered by a flammable creature will be doubled to 2 wounds. As normal, take any saves before multiplying the wounds.

KILLING BLOW

Some warriors have honed the craft of killing into an art. Tales are told of master swordsmen who can decapitate a man with one stroke of their blade.

If a model with the killing blow special rule rolls a 6 when rolling to wound in close combat, he automatically slays his opponent. No armour saves or regeneration saves are allowed against this wound, though ward saves can be taken as normal.

This attack is only effective against models with a unit strength of 2 or less. It can be used against characters mounted on chariots and characters mounted on monsters, as long as the riders themselves have a unit strength of 2 or less and only hits directed against the rider and not the mount/chariot will use the killing blow rule.

Rarely some models may have the ability of using the killing blow rule with ranged attacks (such as spells or missile weapons). When this is the case, it will be clearly specified in their special rules in the relevant Army book's entry.

MAGIC RESISTANCE (1-3)

Some units have a natural resistance to magic, or they are protected from hostile magic by magical artefacts they possess. The number in the brackets indicates the maximum number of extra dice that may be rolled when trying to dispel each spell that affects the magically resistant model. These can either be used on their own against any spell targeted against the unit, or in combination with dispel dice from Wizards or other sources. For details of dispelling see the Magic section.

If a character with magic resistance joins a unit, the resistance affects the entire unit. In the same way, if a character that is not magic resistant joins a unit that is, the character will be protected by the unit's magic resistance, even if he is the only model affected by the spell.

Magic resistance is never cumulative, so if a magic resistant character joins a magic resistant unit, or a different magic resistance is bestowed on the unit by a spell or similar, never add the different magic resistances together, but use the best available.

POISONED ATTACKS

Some warriors of the Warhammer world use lethal toxins to envenom their weaponry. The Dark Elf Adepts of Khaine and the Skinks of the steaming jungles of Lustria are among the most infamous. Also remember that substances that are innocuous for some races may be lethal to others, as the pure water blessed by powerful priests is to the Undead.

A warrior with poisoned attacks will wound his target automatically if he scores a 6 when rolling to hit in either the shooting or close combat phases, or sometimes both (see the model's entry in its Army book for more details). The dice itself must score a 6 – a lower number increased by modifiers to a 6 does not count. Armour saves are taken as normal, modified by the Strength of the attack.

If the poisoned attack needs a 7+ to hit (in the case of ranged poisoned weapons), the rule has no effect. If you do score a hit, roll to wound normally.

War machines (but not their crew) are immune to poison. A few other troop types can be immune to poison as well, but if this is the case, it will be clearly defined in their Army book entry. Chariot models, because they include many elements that would be vulnerable to poison (crews, steeds), are not immune to poison.

REGENERATION

Some creatures, such as Trolls, are able to regenerate damage – their flesh immediately healing from the most serious of wounds.

This rule confers a special regeneration save to the model which works exactly like a 4+ ward save (see page 30), with the following exceptions:

- Wounds suffered from a flaming attack cannot be regenerated – no regeneration save is allowed against such attacks.

- Regeneration saves are not ward saves, and can therefore be taken after armour saves and ward saves have been failed!

For example, a Von Carstein Vampire Count has a an armour save of 5+ (due to his barded steed). He is also wearing the infamous Carstein Ring, which gives him a ward save of 4+ and the Regeneration special rule. If the Vampire is wounded by a crossbow shot (-1 armour save modifier), he will take his modified armour save of 6+ first. If this is failed, he will then take his Ward save of 4+, and if this is failed too, he will take a regeneration save of 4+ (as the crossbow is not a flaming attack). He's really hard to kill!

SCALY SKIN

Some creatures, the reptilian Lizardmen in particular, have tough scaly skin, which acts exactly like armour. This save is variable – Lizardmen Saurus warriors, for example, have a scaly skin save of 6+, while mighty Dragons could have a save of 3+ or more! The effectiveness of the scaly skin can be combined with armour, so a model with a 5+ scaly skin save and a shield would have a 4+ save. Note that scaly skin is an armour save to all intents and purposes, and may be modified by high Strength, etc.

SCOUTS

These troops are skilled at sneaking forwards to scout out the enemy before the main force arrives. By making the best use of cover, advancing at night, or with other troops providing a diversion, they are able to deploy ahead of the rest of the army.

Scouts are set up after both armies have been deployed. They can be set up anywhere on the table, more than 10" away from the enemy and must be out of the sight of any enemy troops and in or behind interposing terrain (not out in the open!). If they are deployed in the controlling player's deployment zone, they can be in full view of the enemy.

If both armies contain scouts, each player should roll a D6, with the player scoring the highest deploying one of his scout units before the enemy. The unit is deployed exactly as described above. After that, the players alternate deploying one of their units of scouts at a time until all scouts are deployed.

BUILDINGS

A watchtower, roadside inn or temple can become a focal point of a battle. Buildings offer substantial protection to those inside, and are a good vantage point for troops with bows, handguns and other ranged weapons. Warriors firmly ensconced in a building can only be driven out by a determined assault.

Players should identify at the start of the game all pieces of terrain for which they are going to make use of the buildings rules given here. This is important, as during the game these rules may give a clear advantage to some infantry units. Players may agree to treat some buildings as impassable (very small ones, or those with a strange shape, for example...) and use these rules for other, more normal, ones.

MOVEMENT

Buildings are impassable to all models except for infantry, and only one unit may occupy a building at a time. The maximum unit strength of a unit that can occupy a building is 30 – units larger than this may not enter a building.

If an infantry unit moves into contact with a building, it may enter it, though it cannot do this in the same turn that it marches or reforms. Place a representative model from the unit in, on or next to the building to remind you that the unit is inside (standard bearers are the best at this!), and place the rest of the unit aside from the battlefield.

To leave the building, use the same rules as a unit that re-enters the table after pursuing off the table – simply place the unit back on the table in the same formation it was in when it entered the building and with its rear rank in contact with any point of the building, and then make a normal move (remember, they cannot charge or march).

Once it enters a building, the unit is assumed to disperse as individual soldiers take up positions at windows and doorways, and spread through its storeys. As such, a unit in a building has no ranks, no flanks and no rear.

In almost all respects, it is best to think of the unit now occupying the space that is represented by the building model – its walls are the edges of the unit.

All distances relevant to the unit (for Psychology effects, spells, missile fire, etc) are measured to and from the building itself.

Note that characters that count as infantry may leave or join a unit that is occupying a building (and vice versa) by simply entering or leaving the building as described above. The characters and the unit still count as a single unit occupying the building, as normal for characters joining units (their combined unit strength must still not exceed 30!).

SHOOTING

SHOOTING INTO BUILDINGS

A unit in a building can be targeted by any enemy that can see the building itself. In other words, if an enemy can see the building, it can see the unit inside it. For ordinary shooting, missile fire is worked out as normal – the unit inside counts as being skirmishers in hard cover, for a massive -3 to hit (skirmishers don't get their normal -1 modifier on top of this). Remember that the unit has no ranks as such and so attacks that can affect multiple ranks, such as bolt throwers, will only hit one model.

Against cannons, stone throwers and other attacks that do not roll to hit or that use templates, if any part of the building is touched or crossed by the attack, the unit will take D6 hits. If such an attack inflicts hits at different Strength values, like a stone thrower, then all hits are worked out at the lower Strength.

SHOOTING FROM BUILDINGS

If a building has a single storey, the unit occupying it has a line of sight in all directions, drawn from a height equal to the models themselves. A number of models up to a unit strength of 5 may shoot.

If the building has more than one storey, then another group of models up to a unit strength of 5 may shoot per extra storey, and these extra models may also trace line of sight over other models just as if they were on a hill.

Players should agree at the beginning of the game the number of storeys for each building.

The range is measured from the edge of the building and all the normal shooting rules apply.

ASSAULTING BUILDINGS

The only way to take a building after it has been occupied by an enemy unit is by the bloody tactic of storming in with one of your infantry units. This is called an assault.

Each occupied building may be assaulted by a single infantry unit during each movement phase. The assaulting unit must declare a charge against the unit in the building. There can be no multiple assault charges against a building, as the assaulting unit is imagined to surround the building and try to break their way through windows, doors and other openings. If multiple units that must charge enemies in range (such as Frenzied units) are in charge reach of an enemy-occupied building, only one must charge and the controlling player may decide which one will do so.

Assault charges are resolved just as if the building were the target unit. If the unit's charge move allows it to get into contact with the building, it is successful, otherwise the charge is failed as normal.

A unit in a building may hold, flee or stand & shoot as normal, and is subject to the rules for shooting and fleeing from buildings (given later). If the unit flees the building in response to the charge and the assaulting unit has enough movement to reach the building, they will immediately occupy it.

Note that a charge during the movement or magic phase is the only way to initiate an assault. Other situations that would normally trigger a charge (such as a pursuit into fresh enemies during the combat phase) cannot initiate an assault and units must stop 1" away from the building.

An infantry unit inside a building may not declare charges, even if it would normally be forced to do so because of Frenzy or some other similar rule.

If an assaulting unit is engaged in combat with any other enemy unit (by a counter-charge or some other special rule or odd special circumstance), it will not fight the assault, but it will fight the enemies outside the building instead. The unit in the building takes no part in the fight whatsoever and, if the assaulting unit is still in contact with the building after the normal fight, the assault automatically fails (as described below).

FIGHTING AN ASSAULT

As models are not physically in base contact when fighting in a building, a little abstraction is required when working out combat.

It is hard to maintain the impetus of a charge in a confined area, and so models charging a unit inside a building lose all charging bonuses (including striking first, Strength bonuses for weapons, and so on).

For both the attacking and the defending unit, a number of models up to a unit strength of 10 may fight. For example, if a unit of twenty Goblins was assaulting or defending a building, ten models could fight. If the unit consisted of eight Ogres, up to three models could fight, as Ogres have a unit strength of 3 per model.

If characters, champions, or other models that can normally be singled out if they are in base contact, are involved in the fight, up to a unit strength of 5 of the enemy models fighting may choose to attack them (as often such heroes will be in the thick of fighting at doorways or on stairwells).

A single challenge may be issued and accepted as normal (within the unit strength 10 of models fighting and not in addition to this).

For special attacks and items that affect models in base contact, a model fighting in a building is assumed to be in base contact with one enemy model nominated by the controlling player – unless fighting in a challenge, of course, in which case they are in contact with the model they are fighting!

COMBAT RESOLUTION

In the crush of a building, brute force or skill at arms counts more than any other factor. As such, only wounds inflicted by each side are counted for combat resolution, no other points are scored (note that musicians still have their normal effect in case of a draw on combat resolution scores).

If the result is a complete draw or the assaulting unit loses the fight, the assaulting unit has failed to storm the building and the combat ends immediately. No Break test is taken, the assaulting unit is simply moved back 1" (still facing the building), and is not engaged in combat anymore.

If the defending unit loses the fight, it must take a Break test as normal. If the test is passed, the assault is failed and the attackers moved back, as above.

If the defenders break and flee, or are wiped out, the assault has succeeded. The assaulting unit cannot pursue the fleeing enemies, but it occupies the building instead, if it fits inside (this counts as pursuing for the purpose of capturing banners).

BUILDINGS & FLEEING

A unit that flees from inside a building is placed outside directly opposite the assaulting unit and it then makes its fleeing move as normal – the building does not slow them in any way. Fleeing units otherwise treat all buildings as impassable terrain.

BUILDINGS & MAGIC

Buildings do not offer any additional protection against magic missiles, spells that affect the entire unit, that target individual models, etc. Spells that use templates though will follow the rules given above for templates, hitting D6 models instead.

Wizards inside a building may cast spells as normal following the rules for line of sight and range given for units shooting from a building.

SPECIAL FEATURES

As mentioned in the section for setting up the battlefield, there is a class of terrain called special features. This category includes several different items of scenery that can benefit the army in possession of them, and the struggle for control of a special feature may play a prominent role in the battle.

Such is the nature of special features that we recommend you only use one on the table. You can of course use more, but be prepared for the battle to be dominated by the fight for possession of these important terrain pieces.

A special feature is placed like any other piece of terrain. Each of the special features described contains examples of how that feature might be represented on the battlefield. A single piece of terrain might be representative of several special features so players should agree what sort of special feature a piece of scenery is before they begin placing terrain. If you really can't decide what something should be treated as, simply count it as a historic landmark.

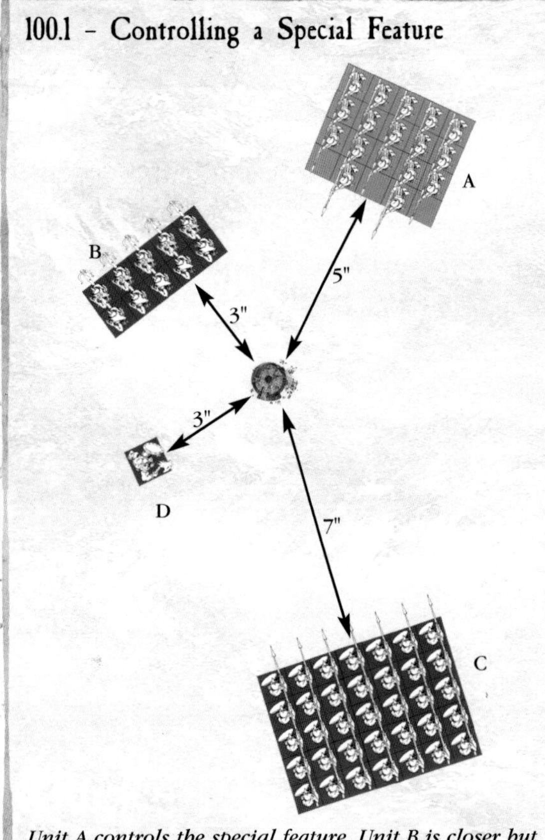

Unit A controls the special feature. Unit B is closer but fleeing, while unit D is closer but at less than unit strength 5. Unit C is further away from the special feature and so cannot control it.

CONTROL OF A FEATURE

Usually, the benefits of a special feature only go to the army or unit that currently controls it. Control is calculated at the start of every phase, and it is possible for possession of the special feature to change during the course of a player's turn. To control a special feature, a unit of unit strength 5 or more must be within 12" of the special feature and closer than any enemy units that can control it. Units that are fleeing may not control a special feature.

Unless the players agree differently when setting it up, the special feature is treated as impassable terrain and blocks line of sight as normal.

SPECIAL FEATURES

HISTORIC LANDMARK

This is the broadest of all special features and could be represented by almost anything: a statue of a famous leader, a wayside shrine, a notable rock formation, a hag tree or maybe a gibbet. The landmark denotes a site of strategic significance or cultural importance and to protect or capture it will give great heart to the opposing armies.

The army that controls the historic landmark at the end of the battle gains an additional 100 victory points.

ARCANE MONOLITH

All across the Warhammer world are areas where magical energy spilling from the north pools and gathers. Over the years, many races have attempted to tap into this mystical power source or tried to disperse its baleful energies. Examples of arcane monoliths include Elven waystones, Beastmen herdstones and Chaos altars.

The army that controls an arcane monolith gains an extra power dice in its magic phase and an extra dispel dice in the enemy's magic phase. These are added to the pool of dice available to all Wizards.

ACROPOLIS OF HEROES

The battle is being fought over a much older battleground, where the forebears of the armies once clashed. Perhaps the remnants of the battlefield can be still seen where a famous last stand was made, or maybe the victorious army raised up a monument to its general. The acropolis of heroes can be represented by a small patch of tumbled down columns, a group of Dwarfen oath stones, a cairn of skulls and so forth.

The unit controlling the acropolis of heroes always counts as outnumbering its enemies, regardless of the actual unit strengths involved in the fight.

ANCIENT IDOL

All races create great edifices in praise of their gods, from the crude idols of Gork and Mork built from the dung of greenskins, to the magically flaming shrines the High Elves build in their worship of Asuryan. To defend or despoil these important symbols is a strong incentive for any army to fight a battle.

An ancient idol allows the controlling army to re-roll failed Leadership tests to rally fleeing units.

FELL RUINS

A dark aura surrounds these tumbled down stones, and coiling mists hang around their edges. This might be a forbidding forest dell, a rune-etched trilithon, an open mass grave or the ruins of a Garden of Morr.

If the unit controlling the fell ruins causes Fear/Terror, all enemy units deduct 1 from their Leadership when taking Fear/Terror tests caused by the unit. If the unit does not cause Fear/Terror, it adds 1 to its Leadership when taking any Fear/Terror tests.

MONUMENT OF GLORY

Many of the nations and races of the world celebrate their victories and conquests by erecting monuments to their leaders and gods. A monument of glory might be a gilded statue of a god of war, a monolith declaring the triumphs of a Chaos champion, or perhaps the rotten and vermin-gnawed remains of the losers!

The unit that controls the monument of glory Hates all enemies.

OTHER SPECIAL FEATURES

These rules are just a sample of the types of special features you could use in your game, and will cover most of the terrain pieces found in someone's collection. However, players can devise their own special features for particularly spectacular scenery pieces, perhaps just to try out something different or to recreate a specific battle from Warhammer history. There are also different types of special features for specific battles or types of games in White Dwarf magazine, on our website and in our growing series of Warhammer books.

VICTORY!

Warhammer uses victory points to determine who has won the battle. victory points (sometimes shortened to VPs) are a way of measuring how much damage has been done to the enemy army, as well as giving a value to other factors such as a better tactical position and morale-boosting endeavours like capturing enemy banners.

At game end (normally after both players had six turns), the victor is determined as follows.

First both players add up all their victory points, following the rules given on this page, obtaining a total victory points score for each player. Then they cross-reference the difference between the players' scores and the size of the battle on the Victory chart opposite to determine the magnitude of the result.

ENEMY UNITS DESTROYED

You receive a number of VPs equal to the points value of each enemy unit destroyed, units that are fleeing or have fled the table count as destroyed.

For example, a unit with a points value of 400 is worth 400 VPs.

Each character is counted as a separate unit for this purpose, and characters mounted on monsters are also counted separately from their mount.

For example, a hero on a Dragon is slain, but the Dragon is still alive, so the enemy scores the VPs for the hero only.

If the players are not using points values for their armies, maybe because they simply decided to use their entire collection of models, each unit is worth 100 VPs.

A NOTE ON WAR MACHINES

In games where victory points are awarded for fleeing or destroyed units, a war machine is considered to be destroyed for the purposes of calculating victory points if either the machine has been destroyed or a crew is not in a position to operate the machine at the end of the game (whether they have fled, been killed or moved away). Casualties inflicted on the crew and wounds inflicted on the machine never score any victory points until the machine or crew are destroyed, so it is not possible to score half the points of a war machine, as it will always be all-or-nothing.

ENEMY UNITS AT HALF STRENGTH

You also score VPs equal to half the unit's points value (round up) for each enemy unit reduced to half its original starting number of models or less. Models that fight on their own and not in units (such as characters, chariots and monsters) are worth half their points value in VPs if reduced to half their starting number of Wounds or less. Do not count this if VPs have already been scored for the unit being destroyed.

For example, a unit costing 325 points is worth 163 VPs if reduced to half strength. Also, a character costing 133 points and starting the game with 2 Wounds on its profile is worth 67 VPs if it has suffered a wound at the end of the game.

CAPTURED TABLE QUARTERS

Divide the table into four quarters. Each table quarter that contains at least one of your units and no enemy units is worth 100 VPs (units with a unit strength of less than 5 and fleeing units do not count for either side). Note that a unit can only capture a single quarter, so if a unit is positioned across two different quarters, it will capture the quarter where the majority of its models are (roll a dice if you cannot decide).

ENEMY GENERAL SLAIN

If the enemy General is slain, fleeing or has fled the table, you score an extra 100 VPs, in addition to VPs scored for the General being a destroyed unit.

CAPTURED UNITS' STANDARDS

Each enemy unit's standard captured at the end of the battle is worth 100 VPs. Note that the unit that has captured the standard must survive and not be fleeing at the end of the battle.

CAPTURED BATTLE STANDARD

The enemy battle standard captured at the end of the battle is worth 100 VPs. Note that the unit that has captured the standard must survive and not be fleeing at the end of the battle.

OTHER VICTORY POINTS

Occasionally there will be other factors determining how many victory points are scored. For example, the players may be using a historic landmark special feature, or some of the troops involved in the fight may have some special rules modifying their value in victory points, and so on.

VICTORY CHART

SCORES' DIFFERENCE (points)	SIZE OF GAME (points per side)					
	Up to 999	1,000 to 1,499	1,500 to 1,999	2,000 to 2,999	3,000 to 3,999	4,000+
0-74	**D**	**D**	**D**	**D**	**D**	**D**
75-149	**MV**	**D**	**D**	**D**	**D**	**D**
150-224	**SV**	**MV**	**D**	**D**	**D**	**D**
225-299	**SV**	**MV**	**MV**	**D**	**D**	**D**
300-449	**M**	**SV**	**MV**	**MV**	**D**	**D**
450-599	**M**	**SV**	**SV**	**MV**	**MV**	**D**
600-749	**M**	**M**	**SV**	**SV**	**MV**	**MV**
750-899	**M**	**M**	**SV**	**SV**	**MV**	**MV**
900-1,199	**M**	**M**	**M**	**SV**	**SV**	**MV**
1,200-1,499	**M**	**M**	**M**	**M**	**SV**	**SV**
1,500-1,799	**M**	**M**	**M**	**M**	**SV**	**SV**
1,800-2,099	**M**	**M**	**M**	**M**	**M**	**SV**
2,100-2,499	**M**	**M**	**M**	**M**	**M**	**SV**
2,500+	**M**	**M**	**M**	**M**	**M**	**M**

D=Draw
MV = Marginal Victory
SV = Solid Victory
M = Massacre!

If a player concedes, the opponent automatically scores a 'Massacre!' Of course, players are free to negotiate more honourable surrendering terms if they feel so inclined...

MAGIC

This section introduces such things as mighty wizards, magical spells and sorcerous items into the Warhammer game. In the Warhammer world, magic is a very real force – a force to be both feared and respected.

Only beings that possess awesome mental and physical power can even hope to bend the powers of magic to their will. Lesser persons would be consumed in an instant – their minds torn apart by unfettered energies and their souls dragged to the darkest underworld by cackling daemons. Even the most accomplished of sorcerers walk a narrow path at the edge of sanity, between ultimate power and eternal damnation.

In the Warhammer world, all magic is derived from the same source – the fickle Winds of Magic. From the Realm of Chaos in the north, this magical gale spills across the world bringing with it the power for great good or evil.

The potency of the Winds of Magic vary from time to time, waxing and waning as the rent in reality in the north expands and contracts. Wizards must therefore learn to use best what power they can, tapping into the winds to channel its energies into their spells, or disrupting its flow to dispel the incantations of others, Thus, magic is not a sure strategy for any general, for though it can sweep aside whole armies when it is strong, it can just as easily slip through the grip of a caster with no effect.

WIZARDS

In the Warhammer game, we commonly refer to a model able to cast spells as a Wizard. Some races use different terms, such as Sorcerer, Mage, Shaman or Seer, but all of these and others are considered to be types of Wizard. Their use in the game is covered by the rules described on the following pages.

WIZARD LEVELS

In the Warhammer game we divide Wizards into four degrees of ability called levels.

Level 1: Wizards of the first level are those of basic ability, although their skills are still highly valued by army generals.

Level 2: Wizards of the second level are experienced spellcasters whose powers are significantly greater than mere first level Wizards.

Level 3: Wizards of the third level are great sorcerers of a kind rarely seen on the battlefield except in times of dire need.

Level 4: Wizards of the fourth level are the mightiest of all Wizards, the very equal of kings amongst the realms of sorcery.

The higher a Wizard's level, the greater his ability to draw magical power from the Winds of Magic.

Each Wizard begins the game with one pre-generated spell for each magic level he has. We'll explain how to generate spells later. For now it is sufficient to know that first level Wizards have one spell, second level Wizards have two, and so on.

SPELLS

In the player's magic phase, his Wizards can cast spells. These can be terribly destructive, or powerfully protective, or might confer special abilities on the caster or other models. A comprehensive list of spells is given later.

Some races have their own unique types of spell that they can use instead of those in this book. These are not described here as there are a great many, and they are only of specific interest to a player who owns that particular army. They are therefore included in the Warhammer Army book for each race.

MAGIC ITEMS

A magic item is an artefact or device imbued with magical power. Such items are not common in the Warhammer world and their extraordinary value and arcane nature means that they often take the form of treasured heirlooms belonging to noble houses or powerful magical covens. The kings and lords of the Old World possess many such devices, but rightly fear to use them except in the most dire of circumstances.

We have provided a short list of magic items in this book. These are items of a relatively general type, the kind of artefacts that can be made and duplicated by an accomplished artificer of magic. However, most magic items are unique and their nature is strongly bound to the race that created them. You will find many more magic items specific to each race described in the Warhammer Army books.

MAGIC PHASE SEQUENCE

1. Generate Power Dice & Dispel Dice

The player whose turn it is assigns specific power dice to his Wizards and accumulates dice in his pool of power dice. The opponent accumulates dice in his pool of dispel dice.

2. Cast

One of that player's Wizards casts a spell using the power dice.

3. Dispel

The opposing player may attempt to counter the spells using his dispel dice.

4. Spell Fails or Spell Succeeds

Apply the effect of the spell if it succeeds.

5. Repeat Steps 2 to 4

Provided that he has more spells to cast and more power dice remain, a Wizard can cast another spell. The opponent can attempt to dispel again with any remaining dispel dice.

6. Dispel Spells in Play

Once the player has finished casting his spells, he may use any remaining power dice to try to dispel spells in play (not the ones cast in that magic phase).

Finally, the opposing player may use any remaining dispel dice to try to dispel any spells in play (not the ones cast in that magic phase).

POWER & DISPEL DICE

POWER DICE

These are expended throughout the magic phase when rolling to cast spells.

There are two types of power dice, those that belong to each Wizard and those that are in a common pool of power dice and can be shared by all the Wizards in the army.

At the start of the magic phase, the player's Wizards draw magical energy from the winds of magic, each in proportion with their level of mastery. The player whose turn it is gives one dice to each first level Wizard, two dice to each second level Wizard, three dice to each third level Wizard and four dice to each fourth level Wizard in his army. Fleeing models and those that are not on the table do not generate any power dice.

These dice belong to the Wizard they are given to and no other Wizard can use them. It is a good idea to place the dice next to the models they belong to, whilst the dice in the common pool are placed in front of the player where they can be seen, or alternatively placed into a cup, a box or some other convenient place where they will not get mixed up with other dice used in that magic phase. Alternatively, the players may wish to use different coloured dice to represent groups of power dice belonging to different Wizards.

After doing this, the player makes up his pool of power dice (sometimes also referred to as the 'pile' of power dice). This pool consists of two power dice, plus any power dice that are added to it by magic items or other special rules.

The dice in the pool do not belong to any specific Wizard and can be tapped into and used by any of the Wizards in the player's army.

Power Dice Pool

	Number of Power Dice
Basic	2
Extra dice from magic items and special rules	+variable

DISPEL DICE

The dispel dice are expended throughout the magic phase when attempting to dispel spells that have been cast by the opposing player.

At the same time as the player whose turn it is gets his power dice, his opponent makes a pool of dispel dice. This pool consists of two dispel dice plus one further dice for each first or second level Wizard or Dwarf Runesmith in his army, and two dice for each third or fourth level Wizard or Dwarf Runelord in his army.

With an army of Dwarfs, an innately magic-resistant race, the player may add two more dice and, as with power dice, magic items and special rules can add dice to the dispel pool.

Differently from power dice, all dispel dice are collected into the dispel pool and can freely be used by any of the Wizards in the army to dispel enemy spells – they can be used even if there are no Wizards in the army. As with power dice, the dice forming the dispel pool should be placed in front of the player where they can be seen, or alternatively placed into a cup, a box or some other convenient place where they will not get mixed up with other dice used in that magic phase.

Fleeing models, and those that are not on the table, do not generate dispel dice.

Dispel Dice Pool

	Number of Dispel Dice
Basic	2
Dwarfs	+2
Each first level Wizard, second level Wizard and Runesmith	+1
Each third level Wizard, fourth level Wizard and Runelord	+2
Extra dice from magic items and special rules	+variable

CASTING SPELLS

Once the players have gathered the appropriate number of power and dispel dice, the player whose turn it is can begin to cast spells.

In a player's magic phase, each of his Wizards on the battlefield can attempt to cast each of his spells only once.

Spell casting is determined by rolling dice, and the number of dice available to roll limits the number of spells that can be attempted.

Fleeing Wizards and those not on the table cannot attempt to cast spells. Note that Wizards who have rallied in the movement phase can act as normal in the magic phase.

To cast a spell, a Wizard nominates one of his spells to cast and declares the target of the spell.

Wizards cannot cast spells at units engaged in close combat, unless the spell only affects the caster himself or the spell's description specifies otherwise.

Then the player declares how many power dice the Wizard is going to use to try to cast the spell. These dice can be taken from the Wizard's own reserve of dice and from the pool of power dice, in any combination. The maximum number of power dice a Wizard can use to cast a spell is one more than the Wizard's level, as shown in the chart.

Maximum Casting Dice Chart

Wizard Level	Maximum Number of Dice
Level 1	2
Level 2	3
Level 3	4
Level 4	5

The dice are rolled and their results added together to get a casting result. For example, if one dice scores 4 the result is 4, if two dice score 4 and 6 the result is 10, if three dice score 3, 5 and 6 the result is 14.

Each spell has an associated casting value, which varies from a minimum of 3 to a maximum of 15, depending on how difficult a spell is to cast. Spells with higher casting values are more powerful and more dangerous to cast. If the casting result equals or exceeds the spell's casting value, the spell is cast (though it may still be dispelled and neutralised by enemy Wizards). If the result is less than the spell's casting value, it is not cast.

In either case, all dice rolled are expended. As can be appreciated, the chances of casting a spell can be increased by rolling more dice, but doing so will reduce the number remaining and hence the chances of casting further spells.

MINIMUM 3 TO CAST

No matter how powerful a Wizard might be, he cannot cast a spell where the total of the dice result is less than 3. A result of 1 or 2 is always considered a failure, despite any modifiers. This is true regardless of any bonuses that might apply in any form, whether from a magic item or some other source.

SPELLCASTING & RE-ROLLS

If a Wizard is allowed to re-roll a failed casting attempt, he must re-roll all the dice he rolled and accept the second result, as normal with re-rolls.

IRRESISTIBLE FORCE & MISCAST

So far we have seen that spells are cast by rolling a result equal to or more than the required casting score. In addition, there are two special rules that apply to Wizards when they cast spells: these are irresistible force and miscasts.

Irresistible Force

When rolling to cast a spell, any result of two or more unmodified 6s means that the spell has been cast with irresistible force. The spell is cast successfully and the enemy cannot attempt to stop it working by dispelling it, as described below. It cannot be resisted!

Miscast!

If a player rolls two or more 1s when rolling power dice to cast a spell, this is a very bad thing. Note that a miscast spell does not normally succeed, regardless of the actual casting result rolled by the Wizard.

The Wizard, and by extension the player, is about to find out what kind of terrible consequences occur when foolish creatures dabble in things best left alone. The player must roll 2D6 and consult the miscast table opposite.

Obviously the chance of rolling a miscast or irresistible force is increased by rolling more dice. Such is the nature of magical power! If a spell is miscast and is cast with irresistible force at the same time (eg, from five dice the player rolls two 1s and two 6s) then the spell counts as a miscast. Miscasts take precedence in this case.

With miscast and irresistible force, it is the actual dice scores that are considered, irrespective of bonuses and before any re-rolls from magic items are taken. Unless otherwise specified, a re-roll cannot cause a spell to be cast with irresistible force, nor can it prevent a miscast.

DISPELLING

If a spell is cast, the opposing player can make one attempt to dispel it. The player takes as many dispel dice as he wishes from the army's dispel pool, rolls them and adds their results, obtaining a dispel result. He then compares the dispel result with the casting result rolled by the caster's power dice.

If the dispel result is equal to or higher than the caster's score, the spell is dispelled – it is not cast and has no effect.

If the dispel result is lower than the caster's casting result, the spell is said to have been ***cast successfully***. Measure the range to the target and resolve the effects of the spell if in range.

For example, if the caster used four dice and got a result of 20, the dispelling player must score 20 or more on his dispel dice to dispel the spell.

Note that even an army that does not include any Wizards can still attempt to dispel an enemy spell, representing its natural magical resistance.

As dispel dice are rolled, they are expended just like power dice, reducing the player's ability to dispel further spells.

MISCAST TABLE

2D6	Result
2	The fibre of reality itself is torn apart as a passage to the Realm of Chaos opens. A gigantic taloned hand emerges from the gate, seizes the screaming Wizard and drags him through the rift, disappearing with a chuckle in a flare of multi-coloured light. The Wizard is annihilated and immediately removed as a casualty, regardless of any protective magic item or special rule he might have. Models in base contact, friend or foe (including the Wizard's monster or chariot mount) suffer one Strength 10 hit (no armour saves allowed) as their flesh mutates and their soul is sucked away.
3-4	The Wizard's body is wracked by a discharge of pure magical energy, warping and burning everything in his close proximity. The Wizard and all models in base contact with him (including his monstrous mount or chariot) suffer a Strength 6 hit, with no armour saves allowed.
5-6	The magical energies backlash as the Wizard loses his concentration. The opposing player may immediately cast any one of his own spells. No casting roll is required – the spell is automatically cast – but it can be dispelled by the player whose turn it is as normal (by using power dice in the same way as dispel dice). He needs to beat the basic casting value of the spell to dispel it.
7	The Wizard struggles to keep the magical energies in check. The caster suffers one Strength 2 hit (no armour saves allowed), loses all his remaining power dice and cannot do anything else during this magic phase.
8-9	A massive vortex of power drains away the sorcerous energy. The caster suffers one Strength 4 hit (no armour saves allowed). In addition, all spells currently in play on the entire battlefield are automatically dispelled and the magic phase ends. All power and dispel dice stored in magic items are also lost.
10-11	The caster's mind is ravaged by the attention of a hideous Daemon. The caster suffers one Strength 8 hit (no armour saves allowed) and loses a Wizard level (the spell lost must be the one he just attempted to cast). If the caster reaches Level 0, he stops counting as a Wizard and therefore will not be able to use any arcane magic items he is carrying (see the Magic Items section) and will generate no power/dispel dice.
12	The caster mispronounces one of the secret words of power binding the power of the spell, triggering an anomaly. The spell he attempted to cast is successful and counts as having been cast with irresistible force, but after this the caster forgets how to cast the spell and will not be able to cast it again during this battle.

Some magic items may allow a Wizard a second dispel attempt, or a re-roll, but these are exceptions and in normal circumstances only one attempt can be made to dispel a spell. In addition, the result can be increased further by the use of magic items. Any number of magic items can be combined to boost the score, but the player must declare that he is using any magic items before he makes the dispel dice roll. It is not permitted to roll the dice and then decide to use a magic item retrospectively. Many of these magic items can only be used a limited number of times, so it is important to be clear about whether you are using them or not, before rolling the dice.

DOUBLE 1S & 6S

Trying to control massive magical energy to dissipate an enemy spell is extremely taxing and difficult, and can easily go wrong. Therefore, just as with casting spells, if two or more of the dispel dice come up as 1s, the attempt to dispel a spell automatically fails. Regardless of how many bonuses you might have accrued from magic items, etc, a roll of two or more 1s is always a failure.

If a player rolls two or more 6s when dispelling a spell, the dispel succeeds automatically. Note that an automatic fail takes precedence over an automatic success when dispelling a spell. For example, the player rolls five dice for a dispel attempt and gets two 1s, a 4 and two 6s. Even if the total of the dice is enough to beat the casting result and the player has rolled two 6s, the two 1s take precedence, and the spell is cast successfully.

IRRESISTIBLE FORCE

As we have already mentioned, if two or more 6s are rolled when casting a spell, the spell is considered to have been cast with (adopt deep booming voice now) irresistible force! A spell cast with irresistible force is irresistible, just like it says... you cannot dispel the spell and no dispel roll can be attempted (not even Dispel Scrolls can stop it!).

SPELLS COMMENTARY

Remember that characters on their own, large monsters, war machines, etc, are classed as units as well, so spells that target units can be cast on these targets. Characters in units cannot be targeted separately unless otherwise noted.

When any spell inflicts a number of hits or wounds on a target unit, these are distributed in the same way as hits from normal shooting, unless differently specified in the spell's description.

MAGIC MISSILES

Many spells are described as magic missiles – for example, *Fireball*. In this case, the Wizard conjures a ball of flame and hurls it at a target. All magical missiles are thrown or projected in this fashion.

A magic missile can only be cast at a target if it would be a viable target according to the rules for shooting. For example, the Wizard must be able to see the target, and characters can only be picked out from a unit they have joined in the same circumstances as with normal missile fire, as described under 'shooting at characters'. Unless otherwise noted, magic missiles hit their targets automatically.

Unless otherwise specified, a Wizard cannot cast these spells if he, or the unit he is with, is engaged in close combat.

SPELLS WITH TEMPLATES

Certain spells utilise one of the templates provided with the game.

When using templates, any models whose base is completely under the template are considered to be affected by the spell. Models whose bases are partially covered are hit on a dice roll of 4+. Characters do get their "Look out, Sir!" roll against spells that use templates.

'REMAINS IN PLAY' SPELLS

Most spells are cast instantly and their effect is worked out at once. For example, a magic missile spell is cast, it strikes a target and damage is resolved. In this case, the spell has no further effect in the game during the same magic phase, and the spell cannot be cast again in that magic phase, as normal.

Some spells last for longer than this and they are clearly marked as 'remains in play' in their description. Once cast, one of these spells lasts until it is dispelled, until the Wizard chooses to end it (which he can do at any time), attempts to cast another spell, leaves the table or is slain. Obviously, these spells cannot be cast again by the same Wizard while in play.

If a character under the effects of a spell that remains in play joins a unit, the spell does not affect the unit.

If a character joins a unit that is under the effects of a spell that remains in play, the spell will affect the character as well as long as he is with the unit.

If a character and a unit are under the effects of a spell that remains in play, and then the character leaves the unit, the caster must decide which one will be affected from then onwards – character or unit.

Note that there may be exceptions to the above rules, and they will be specified in the spell description or other special rules.

SPELLS LASTING ONE OR MORE TURNS

Some spells do not remain in play, but they have effects that are not immediate and last one (or more) turns. Once they are in play, the effects of these spells cannot be dispelled, unless the spell description specifies otherwise. Wizards are free to cast other spells and even if they are killed or flee the table, the effects last for their normal duration.

DISPEL SPELLS IN PLAY

After a player has finished casting his spells, he is allowed to dispel any spells that remain in play (unless they were cast in that magic phase), using as dispel dice any power dice not used to cast spells. These dice can always be added together, regardless of which Wizard they belong to. Note that the player only needs to beat the casting value of the spell in question – he does not have to beat the original casting score. Spells originally cast with irresistible force can be dispelled as normal in subsequent turns if they remain in play.

Finally, his opponent is allowed to dispel any spells that remain in play (unless they were cast in that magic phase) if he has any dispel dice left, as described above.

Magic Resistant units that are under the effects of a spell that remains in play from a previous turn may at this stage attempt to dispel it using the dice given by their resistance, with or without the addition of any dice from the player's other available dice.

CANCELLING SPELLS

It is quite possible for the effect of one spell to contradict the effect of another. For example, a unit has a spell cast upon it by a Wizard that prevents it from moving, and it might subsequently have a spell cast upon it by another Wizard that obliges it to move. In these cases, the most recent spell automatically dispels the previous spell.

THE LORES OF MAGIC

This rulebook includes eight different kinds of magical lore, each of which is represented by six spells making a total of 48 individual spells. Each lore is based upon one of the eight magical traditions of the High Elves whose learning far exceeds that of any other race in the Warhammer world. The Men of the Empire learned their sorcery from High Elf mages and so use the same system as their basis of study – though their knowledge is by no means as great.

The sorcery of the other races of the Warhammer world is also based upon one or more of the eight kinds of magic but often includes spells unique to a particular race. The Warhammer Armies books contain further spell lists for specific armies where appropriate.

THE EIGHT LORES

The names of the Eight Lores of Magic are not the only names by which they are known, by any means, but these terms serve our purposes perfectly well. The eight different lores of magic in Warhammer are: Fire, Metal, Shadow, Beasts, Heavens, Light, Life, and Death.

SELECTING SPELLS

Wizards usually know only one magical lore.

The Warhammer Army books describe exactly which kinds of lore are used by the different Warhammer races and provide further race specific spells in most cases. Those given here are used primarily by the Wizards of the Empire and by Elves, but form the basis for the magic of other races too.

Wizards normally have one spell for each magic level. Wizards of the first level have one spell, Wizards of the second level have two spells, third level Wizards have three spells and Wizards of the fourth level have four spells.

The standard procedure for selecting spells is for each player to randomly generate spells for each of his Wizards before both sides deploy their troops.

Players must declare which Lore of Magic each of their Wizards is using before generating any spells.

If both sides are using Wizards, roll a dice to see who generates his spells first. Start generating spells for the Wizard with the highest level first. If two Wizards in the same army are using the same Lore of Magic, they may gain duplicates of spells, but no single Wizard can have the same spell twice.

Two Wizards on opposing sides may use the same spell lists, thus both sides may have the same spells.

The spells in the lists are numbered from one to six. To randomly generate spells for a Wizard, roll a D6 per level of the Wizard and consult the chosen Lore of Magic (these are found on the following pages of this section). If you roll the same spell twice for the same Wizard, roll again until you obtain a different result. This is normally done openly and players will therefore be aware of which spells their opponent has generated. A Wizard can always substitute one of his spells with the first spell that is on the list. For example, a Wizard of the second level who chooses to use Fire magic and rolls a 4 and a 5 (getting *Fiery Blast* and the *Conflagration of Doom* spell) could substitute either of these spells with the *Fireball* spell.

LORE OF FIRE

Aqshy, the Fire Wind, is utilised by pyromancers to summon magical flames and create whirling fireballs. These Wizards are of fiery temperament and quick to anger. In the Empire, the Lore of Fire is studied by the Bright College. All spells in this list are flaming attacks (see the section on special rules on page 94).

1 FIREBALL
Cast on 5+

The wizard conjures a flaming missile from his hands and hurls it towards the enemy where it explodes and showers the foe with magical fire.

This is a magic missile with a range of 24". If successfully cast, the Fireball hits its target and causes D6 Strength 4 hits.

2 FLAMING SWORD OF RHUIN
Cast on 5+, remains in play

A glowing blade materialises in the caster's hand, rippling with magical flames and the concentrated power of fire magic. Fast as quicksilver, the blade strikes with great power and accuracy and there are few who can survive the searing wounds it inflicts.

This spell is cast on the Wizard himself. A magical flaming blade materialises in the Wizard's grasp. This counts as a magic weapon. The Wizard gains +1 additional Attack to his profile for the duration of the spell. All the Wizard's attacks will hit on a basic score of 2+ and he adds +3 to his Strength whilst using the Sword of Rhuin. Whilst he has the Flaming Sword, the Wizard must use it as his sole weapon – he cannot combine it with other weapons.

3 THE BURNING HEAD
Cast on 8+

The wizard unleashes a terrifying vision that laughs insanely as it burns a trail of destruction across the battlefield.

A spectral flaming skull shoots 18" from the caster in a straight direct path (any direction chosen by the controlling player). Each model that lies in the direct path of the Burning Head suffers a Strength 4 hit (this is resolved much in the same way as a bouncing cannonball). Any unit suffering one or more unsaved wounds from the Burning Head must take a Panic test.

4 FIERY BLAST
Cast on 8+

The wizard hurls an incandescent gout of magical flames towards the enemy.

The Fiery Blast is an especially dangerous magic missile – it is more powerful version of the Fireball, being both more powerful and harder to cast. The Fiery Blast has a range of up to 24". If successfully cast, the Fiery Blast hits its target and causes 2D6 Strength 4 hits.

5 CONFLAGRATION OF DOOM
Cast on 11+

This volatile conjuration allows a wizard to engulf whole units of enemy warriors in a blazing inferno.

This can be cast on one enemy unit anywhere on the table, as long as it is visible to the caster. If successfully cast, the target bursts into flames taking D6 Strength 4 hits. The target can take additional hits depending on how long the fire burns. To represent this, both players immediately roll a D6. If the casting player's dice score is lower than or equal to his opponent's, the flames go out and nothing else happens, but if he rolls higher, add the dice roll to the number of hits caused. Both players then roll a further D6 and repeat the process until the casting player rolls equal to or less than his opponent. Once the casting player fails to roll higher, no further hits are caused. Roll to wound as normal for all extra hits caused in this way.

6 WALL OF FIRE
Remains in play — Cast on 12+

The wizard raises a blazing wall of fire in front of an enemy regiment.

This spell has a range of 24". Each model (including characters) in the unit's front rank suffers one automatic Strength 4 hit.

As long as the spell is in play, if the target unit moves for any reason, every model in the unit suffers a further Strength 4 hit, and then the spell is automatically dispelled.

If cast on units with a 360° line of sight, such as skirmishers, the Wall of Fire does not form and the spell has the same effect as a Fireball.

LORE OF METAL

The Gold Order of the Imperial Colleges of Magic study the alchemical arts and the Lore of Metal. Transmutation of base elements, the animation of mechanical creatures and the study of sorcerous elixirs are all made possible by the Wind of Chamon.

1 RULE OF BURNING IRON

Cast on 5+

Drawing power from the Winds of Magic, the alchemist commands the armour of his target to recall the fiery heat of its forging. Armour plates sear bare flesh and mail shirts become a burning yoke around the neck of the wearer.

Burning Iron has a range of up to 24". If successfully cast, the spell hits a single model (chosen by the caster, no targeting restrictions apply except that the Wizard needs line of sight to the target) and causes one Strength 1 hit if the target has no armour save, one Strength 2 hit if the target has an armour save of 6, one Strength 3 hit if the target has an armour save of 5+, one Strength 4 hit if the target has an armour save of 4+, one Strength 5 hit if the target has an armour save of 3+, one Strength 6 hit if the target has an armour save of 2+ or one Strength 7 hit if the target has an armour save of 1+ or better.

No armour saves are allowed against wounds caused by this spell. This is a flaming attack.

2 COMMANDMENT OF BRASS

Cast on 6+

Uttering secret words of command, the caster causes the war engines of his enemy to falter as nails break and bend, barrels are distorted and the very wheels of the machine are warped by his authority.

This spell has a range of 24" and can be cast on any enemy war machine or chariot. If successfully cast, the machine cannot move or shoot until the end of its own following turn. If forced to flee for whatever reason, the spell is broken and the unit flees.

3 TRANSMUTATION OF LEAD

Cast on 7+

As the wizard beckons the Winds of Magic to do his bidding, the weapons of his enemy turn into leaden weights in their hands, their armour becoming more of a burden than a protection.

This spell can be cast on any enemy unit that is within 24", and which is engaged in close combat. If successfully cast, the enemy's armour, weapons and other equipment are transmuted to lead for the duration of the ensuing close combat phase. The affected unit suffers a -1 to hit and to wound penalty in close combat, and their armour saves suffer a -1 penalty during that turn's close combat phase.

4 DISTILLATION OF MOLTEN SILVER

Cast on 8+

Holding a small silver coin aloft, the alchemist channels the power of the Winds of Magic into it, sending ribbons of molten silver splashing and burning across the oncoming foe.

The Distillation of Molten Silver is a magic missile with a range of up to 24". If successfully cast, a squall of molten silver hits the target and causes 2D6 Strength 4 hits. This is a flaming attack.

5 LAW OF GOLD

Cast on 8+

With a mighty effort the wizard forces the weapons of the enemy to deny their magical bindings, rendering them useless for a time, sometimes forever.

This spell can be cast on any enemy unit that is within 24" of the caster. The opposing player must nominate one magic item carried by any model in the unit. The caster rolls a D6: on the roll of 1-3 the item cannot be used until the end of the enemy's next turn, on a 4-6 the item cannot be used for the rest of game. The Law of Gold has no effect on a unit that does not include any models with magic items.

6 THE SPIRIT OF THE FORGE

Cast on 12+

Unleashing the full fury of the forge, the alchemist causes the armour of his foes to scald and burn, and ranks of warriors writhe in fiery agony as their protection becomes their death.

This spell can be cast on one enemy unit that is within 24" and visible to the caster. If successfully cast, the enemy's armour starts to heat up until it is searing their flesh. The effects of this spell are exactly the same as the Rule of Burning Iron described above, except 2D6 models in the target unit will be affected (randomise hits like shooting).

LORE OF SHADOW

Those that deal with the Lore of Shadow are often distrusted, suspicious figures. They are illusionists that use the Wind of Ulgu to create glamours and nightmarish terrors. Of all the Colleges of Magic, it is the Grey Order that perhaps are feared the most by common men.

1 STEED OF SHADOWS

Cast on 5+

Tendrils of night entwine the sorcerer before coalescing into a coal-black drake, that carries the wizard away on wings of night.

This spell may be cast upon the Wizard himself or any single friendly character within 12" of him, no line of sight is required. The spell can only be cast on a model with a unit strength of 1 (it won't work on a mounted model or a model riding in a chariot, for example), even if engaged in close combat.

If successfully cast, the model can make a normal flight move of up to 20", which may be a charge (the charged unit gets its normal charge reactions). The model can even fly out of close combat if desired, but in this case it cannot charge.

2 CREEPING DEATH

Cast on 6+

As the wizard stretches out his hand, the shadow beneath it comes alive with dark, wriggling things that spread out toward the target, becoming a nightmarish torrent that washes over them, ripping and tearing.

Creeping Death is a magic missile with a range of up to 24". If successfully cast, the Creeping Death hits its targets and causes 3D6 Strength 1 hits. No armour saves are allowed against wounds caused by the Creeping Death.

3 CROWN OF TAIDRON

Cast on 8+

The wizard summons up an aura of ectoplasmic tendrils that writhe over his head. These lash at anything around the caster, suffocating their victims in an embrace of choking death.

If successfully cast, all units within 12" of the caster are affected, friend and foe alike, even if engaged in close combat (excluding the caster himself!). Each unit takes D6 Strength 4 hits, distributed exactly like shooting.

4 SHADES OF DEATH

Cast on 9+, remains in play

The wizard changes the appearance of his comrades so that all enemies will see the decaying bodies of their long-dead brothers and friends walking against them.

This spell can be targeted on any single friendly unit within 12" of the Wizard, even if the unit is engaged in close combat. The unit now causes Fear. If the unit already causes Fear, it now causes Terror instead.

5 UNSEEN LURKER

Cast on 11+

The allies of the wizard are shrouded by mystical fog that hides them from view and allows them to travel unseen in the realm of mists.

This spell can be cast on a friendly unit within 12". The unit can immediately make a move in the same way as a normal move made in the movement phase. The unit can charge an enemy if opportunity permits, and the same rules apply as for a normal charge made during the movement phase.

6 PIT OF SHADES

Cast on 12+

The earth opens beneath the feet of the enemy and the terrified warriors fall screaming into a bottomless pit filled with shadow and the incessant wailing of 'Those who dwell below'.

The Pit of Shades can be cast on any one unengaged enemy unit within 24" and visible to the caster. If successfully cast, the ground falls away beneath the unit's feet.

Take the small round template and place it over a single enemy unit. All models in the target unit completely under the template are automatically hit and those partially covered by it are hit on a 4+ on a D6. Models hit must immediately take an Initiative test to avoid falling into the pit. If the test is passed, the model is not affected, but models failing this test are swallowed up by the ground and removed as casualties, regardless of any magical protection or special rules they may have. After this, the ground seals up and closes the pit, leaving no trace.

LORE OF BEASTS

Ghur is the name wizards give to the Lore of Beasts, practiced by the Amber College of the Empire. It allows the wielder to commune with and control the wild creatures of the world, and even to take on their powers and appearances.

1 THE BEAR'S ANGER
Cast on 4+, remains in play

Calling upon the power of Ursos the Bear, the wizard channels the ferocity and strength of the great beast and infuses it into the recipient.

This spell may be cast upon the Wizard himself or any single friendly character within 12" of him, no line of sight is required. The spell can only be cast on a model with a unit strength of 1 (it won't work on a mounted model or a model riding in a chariot, for example), even if engaged in close combat.

The target becomes as wild and powerful as a mighty bear. He adds +3 Attacks, +2 Strength, and +1 Toughness to his characteristics. He cannot wield a weapon nor use a shield whilst using this spell.

2 THE OXEN STANDS
Cast on 5+

Calling upon the power of Buccos the Oxen, the wizard placates fear and inspires renewed courage into the hearts of the fleeing warriors.

This spell can be cast on any friendly fleeing unit on the tabletop. If successful, the unit rallies immediately, regardless of how many models are left in it.

3 THE CROW'S FEAST
Cast on 7+

Calling upon the power of Corvos the Crow, the wizard unleashes a storm of avenging spirit-ravens against his enemies.

Corvos the Crow's Feast is a magic missile with a range of up to 24". If successfully cast, the spell causes 2D6 Strength 3 hits.

4 THE BEAST COWERS
Cast on 7+

Calling upon the power of Kinos the Beast, the wizard grasps the will of the enemy war beasts, overruling their training and sapping their will to fight.

This spell can be cast on an enemy cavalry unit, swarm, chariot or a single ridden or unridden monster anywhere on the battlefield, even if the target is engaged in combat.

If successfully cast, any creatures in the unit (but not their riders) will cower and therefore may not attack in that turn's close combat phase. In addition, they will stubbornly refuse to move until the end of their next movement phase other than to flee, in which case they will be more than happy to oblige.

5 THE HUNTER'S SPEAR
Cast on 8+

Calling upon the power of Venor the Hunter, the wizard conjures a pure manifestation of amber-hued magic in the shape of a mighty hunting spear.

The Hunter's Spear is a magic missile with a range of up to 24". If successfully cast, the spear inflicts a Strength 6 hit, with no armour saves allowed.

The spear then goes through the ranks of the target in the same way as a missile from a bolt thrower (see the War Machines section, pages 90-91, for more details).

6 THE WOLF HUNTS
Cast on 9+

Calling upon the power of Lupens the Wolf, the wizard bolsters the energies of the creatures in his army, sending them rushing forward howling with battle-lust.

This spell can be cast on a friendly cavalry unit, swarm, chariot or a single ridden or unridden monster that is within 24" of the caster.

If the spell is cast successfully, the unit moves 2D6" towards an enemy unit that it can see. If no enemy are visible then it will not move. If the distance is sufficient to reach the enemy, the unit is deemed to have declared a charge and all the normal charging rules apply, except that if the charge is failed, the unit still moves the full distance rolled.

LORE OF HEAVENS

In the cities of Men, the Lore of the Heavens is called astromancy. The Winds of Azyr bring with them prophecy and foresight, and through its power the Celestial Wizards of the Imperial Colleges can glean the future from the stars and moons.

1 PORTENT OF FAR
Cast on 5+

Divining auspicious signs, the wizard guides the minds of his fellow warriors, allowing them to predict the actions of their foes.

This spell can be cast on a friendly unit within 12", even if engaged in close combat.

If successfully cast, all subsequent dice rolls of a 1 made either to hit or to wound by that unit can be re-rolled that turn. Re-rolled scores of 1 stand – you can never re-roll a re-rolled dice.

2 SECOND SIGN OF AMUL
Cast on 5+

The wizard conjures up an astrological prophecy, looking into the future along the Winds of Magic. With this knowledge, he forewarns his comrades of the enemy's intent.

This spell gives the player a chance of re-rolling dice during the remainder of his own turn. These re-rolls may be used for rolls to hit, rolls to wound, armour saves and ward saves.

If successfully cast, roll a D3 to determine the number of re-rolls the player can make. Any re-rolls not used by the end of the caster's turn are wasted.

3 CELESTIAL SHIELD
Cast on 7+, remains in play

The wizard manipulates the magic of the air to raise a scintillating blue shield capable of deflecting even the most powerful of projectiles.

This spell can be cast on a friendly unit that is visible to the caster and within 24". The unit has a 4+ ward save against all normal and magic missiles.

4 FORKED LIGHTNING
Cast on 6+

Roiling clouds of energy gather over the wizard as he chants incessantly, until arcs of lightning streak down from the skies, blasting the foe.

This spell can be cast on any enemy unit in sight of the caster. If successfully cast, the unit is struck by lightning causing D6 Strength 4 hits.

5 URANON'S THUNDER BOLT
Cast on 9+

With a crack of thunder that shakes the ground, the wizard calls down an almighty ball of lightning from the dark clouds above the battlefield.

This spell can be cast on any enemy unit in sight of the caster. If successfully cast, the unit is struck by a thunderbolt causing D6 Strength 4 hits with no armour save possible.

6 THE COMET OF CASANDORA
Cast on 12+, remains in play

Reaching out across the Winds of Magic into the highest heavens, the wizard draws in a wandering meteorite and hurls it towards the battlefield.

This spell can be cast upon any fixed point on the tabletop. If successfully cast, place a suitable marker over the exact spot affected – a small coin is ideal for this.

For as long as the spell lasts, the player rolls a D6 at the start of each player's turn (ie, at the start of his turn and at the start of his opponent's turn). On a score of 1-3 nothing happens, but place another marker on the first. On the score of a 4-6 the spot is struck by the comet. All units from either side that are within D6" multiplied by the number of markers already placed are struck by the comet. Each unit struck by the comet takes 2D6 Strength 4 hits. For example, if there are two markers in place and the D6 roll is a 4, all units within 4 x 2 = 8" are struck. A successful dispel neutralises the spell completely and all counters are removed.

LORE OF LIGHT

Suffusing all things, the Wind of Hysh is a fickle energy, but those that can trap and direct it are gifted with great powers. The Light Wizards study the magic of the sun, and can use its life-giving energies to heal, or harness its destructive might to blind and sear their foes.

1 BURNING GAZE
Cast on 5+

The pure white light of the sun streams from the wizard's eyes in incandescent beams that burn and slay anything that comes under his forbidding gaze.

Burning Gaze is a magic missile with a range of up to 24". If successfully cast, the spell causes D6 Strength 4 hits. Undead and Daemons take D6 Strength 6 hits instead.

Burning Gaze is a flaming attack.

2 PHA'S ILLUMINATION
Cast on 5+, remains in play

With a single word of power, the wizard projects the light in his soul, igniting the air around him and imbuing the hammer blows of his fists with the power of solar flares.

This spell may be cast upon the Wizard himself or any single friendly character within 12" of him, no line of sight is required. The spell can only be cast on a model with a unit strength of 1 (it won't work on a mounted model or a model riding in a chariot, for example), even if engaged in close combat.

Regardless of his characteristics, he has 3 Attacks and Strength 5 whilst this spell lasts. He cannot wield a weapon whilst using this spell. Magic weapons used to attack him count as mundane weapons of the same type whilst the spell lasts.

3 HEALING ENERGY
Cast on 5+

Clasping his hands to his chest, the wizard glows brightly as he lets the healing light of the sun flow through his veins. The spellcaster can re-knit even the most grievous wounds simply by speaking the true name of a wounded ally.

This spell can be cast upon the Wizard himself or upon any friendly model anywhere on the tabletop, even if engaged in close combat. No line of sight is required.

If successfully cast, the model regains 1 Wound suffered during the game. In the case of a ridden monster/chariot, choose either the monster or the rider. This spell has no effect on Undead, Daemons, war machines and chariots.

4 DAZZLING BRIGHTNESS
Cast on 6+

Reaching out with a ritual gesture, myriad tendrils of light flow from the wizard's ringed fingers. These serpentine threads earth themselves in the eye sockets of enemy warriors, leaving them dazzled and vulnerable to attack.

This spell can be cast on any enemy unit that is engaged in close combat and that is within 18" of the caster, no line of sight is required. If successfully cast, the target unit is dazzled and its WS characteristic is reduced to 1 for the duration of that turn's close combat phase.

5 GUARDIAN LIGHT
Cast on 8+, remains in play

As he utters an ancient incantation, a golden hemisphere of light ebbs from the wizard, and in appearance he becomes a miniature sun. All around him feel the warmth of true courage like the summer sun upon their skin.

This spell affects all friendly units that are within 12" of the caster. No line of sight is required. If successfully cast, all these units are now immune to psychology, and fleeing units rally immediately, regardless of how many models are left in them.

6 CLEANSING FLARE
Cast on 10+

With a deafening shout, the spellcaster summons shards of pure light from the heart of the sun itself. These rain from the skies into the ranks of the enemy like arrows from heaven.

If successfully cast, all enemy units within 12" of the caster are affected, even if engaged in close combat. Each unit takes D6 Strength 5 hits, distributed exactly like shooting. Undead and Daemons take D6 Strength 6 hits instead.

LORE OF LIFE

The Jade College of the Empire is learned in all things natural, from the language of plants, to the secrets of the rocks. With the power of the Wind of Ghyran, these Elementalists can bind these sources of power and change them to their will.

1 MISTRESS OF THE MARSH

Cast on 4+

The wielder of the Lore of Life knows the secret words of power that can bring the waterways of the world gushing forth.

This spell can be cast upon an enemy unit, even if engaged in combat, that is within 12" of the caster or within 12" of a river, stream, bog, or any other water feature on the tabletop that has been identified as such before the game. If successfully cast, the ground beneath the unit is temporarily turned to swamp and the unit moves at half speed until the end of its own following turn. If forced to flee/pursue, for whatever reason, the unit flees/pursues at half speed (roll dice as normal based on the unit's normal Move value and then halve the result). This spell has no effect on flyers or ethereal creatures.

2 MASTER OF THE WOOD

Cast on 6+

For many, the shadows of the forest offer nought but terror, as roots and branches reach out to rend the intruder limb from limb.

This spell can be cast upon an enemy unit that is within 12" of the caster or within 12" of a wood, copse or any other wooded feature on the tabletop that has been identified as such before the game. The target must also be visible to the caster. If successfully cast, the unit is battered by the branches of trees if within a wood, or lashed at by roots that erupt from the ground if there is no wood nearby, inflicting D6 Strength 4 hits on the target (D6 Strength 5 hits if it is partially or wholly within the wood).

3 GIFT OF LIFE

Cast on 7+

Tapping the primal energy that flows through all living things, the wizard draws to him a small portion – enough to heal his injuries, but never so much that the balance of life is undone.

This spell can be cast upon the Wizard himself or upon any friendly model within 12", even if the target is engaged in close combat. No line of sight is required.

If successfully cast, the model regains all its lost Wounds. In the case of a ridden monster, choose either the monster or the rider as the target of the spell. This spell has no effect on Undead models, Daemons, war machines and chariots.

4 THE HOWLER WIND

Cast on 7+, remains in play

The fury of the skies unbound is a force that few can hold at bay – woe to the object of its wrath!

This spell can be cast upon the Wizard himself. If successfully cast, no shooting with Strength 4 or less can be targeted at units within 12" of the Wizard – even if some models in the unit are more than 12" away. War machines are never affected by this spell. This doesn't prevent units from firing through or out of the affected area at targets beyond.

5 THE RAIN LORD

Cast on 8+

The spirits of air and water unite as the wizard calls upon them to unleash their combined anger against his foes.

This spell can be cast on an enemy unit visible to the caster and within 24". If successfully cast, the target unit is drenched in rain and counts as soaked for the rest of the game.

All soaked models suffer a further -1 modifier on their shooting to hit rolls, increased to -2 if the model's weapon has the armour piercing rule. If the unit does not fire using BS (a cannon, for example), then it may only fire if the player can first roll a 4+ on a D6 each turn. There is no additional effect for being soaked more than once.

6 MASTER OF STONE

Cast on 8+

Stone bears the power of slow-colliding continents. Accumulated over aeons, this energy is unleashed with devastating effect.

This spell can be cast upon an enemy unit that is within 12" of the caster or of a hill, rocky outcrop, ruins or any area that has been identified as high ground, rocky or ruinous before the game. The target must also be visible to the caster. If successfully cast, shards of stone erupt from the ground and fly against the unit, inflicting D6 Strength 5 hits on the unit (D6 Strength 6 hits if the unit is partially or wholly within the feature).

LORE OF DEATH

Though reviled by most, the necromancer plays an important role in the world, for through his power the spirits of the dead can be contacted, while the power of Death itself lies in his hands. The grim Amethyst Wizards use the chilling Wind of Shyish to aid the counsels of the Emperor and support his armies.

1 DARK HAND OF DEATH
Cast on 5+

The wizard creates a shadowy avatar of himself, and sets it loose upon the foe to freeze blood, marrow and heart.

This is a magic missile with a range of up to 24". If successfully cast, the spell hits its target and causes D6 Strength 4 hits.

2 STEAL SOUL
Cast on 8+

Binding the balance of life and death into his service the wizard reaches out to a chosen foe, tearing their mind and body asunder.

This spell can be cast on any enemy model within 12" (with no targeting restrictions whatsoever). The enemy model loses 1 Wound. No armour save is allowed. In addition, the casting Wizard gains 1 Wound for the duration of the battle. This spell can be used to increase the caster's Wounds characteristic beyond its normal maximum level, and can be used several times to increase the caster's Wounds even further.

3 WIND OF DEATH
Cast on 8+

The caster gathers unto him a cloud of black and icy shards, each one a vengeful fragment of a stolen destiny, and hurls them with crushing force towards his enemies, relentlessly stripping flesh from bone.

This is a magic missile with a range of 24". If successfully cast, the spell hits its target and causes 2D6 Strength 4 hits.

4 WALKING DEATH
Cast on 9+, remains in play

An invisible aura of dread surrounds the warriors chosen by the wizard.

This spell can be targeted on any single friendly unit within 12" of the Wizard, even if the unit is engaged in close combat. The unit now causes Fear. If the unit already causes Fear, it now causes Terror instead.

5 DOOM & DARKNESS!
Cast on 9+

Vittor de Avertila's greatest work, this spell compels the spirits of the departed to assail the caster's foes, choking the sky with darkness and sapping their resolve with an icy touch.

This spell can be cast upon one enemy unit that is within 24" of the caster, even if engaged in combat. If successfully cast, the unit is shrouded by a black cloud of despair.

For the duration of the turn, the affected unit will suffer a -3 penalty to any Leadership-based test it is required to take. At the start of its following turn, the unit must take and pass a Leadership test (at -3), otherwise it remains affected for the duration of that turn as well. After this, the spell's effects end. Units that are Immune to Psychology are not affected by this spell.

6 DRAIN LIFE
Cast on 10+

Calling forth the oldest and most powerful of magics, the Death Wizard directs the forces of entropy against all who oppose him, tearing their souls from their bodies and casting them into the void.

If cast successfully, each enemy unit within 12" of the Wizard is affected, even if engaged in close combat.

Each unit takes D6 Strength 3 hits. No armour saves are allowed against a Drain Life spell. These hits are distributed exactly like hits from shooting.

MAGIC ITEMS

The world of Warhammer is rich in magical artefacts and holy relics of great power. Mighty soul-drinking swords, impenetrable suits of amour encrusted with runic powers, ancient tomes of sorcerous knowledge and lost rings of power – many a war has been fought for the sole possession of such treasure.

The Warhammer Armies books describe in detail the many different kinds of magic items that each army can use. Here we shall examine the magic items that are commonly used by all races. In cases of contradiction, the special rule of a magic item takes precedence over normal game rules.

Magic items can be carried by characters and, in some cases, by the standard bearer or champion of a unit of troops. This is indicated in the army list for each army in the appropriate Warhammer Army book. A character can only have one magic item of each type (weapon, armour, etc), unless otherwise indicated.

No specific magic item can be carried by more than one model in the army (eg, there cannot be two models equipped with a Sword of Striking in the same army). Scrolls are an exception to this – several scrolls of the same type can be carried by the same Wizard or by different Wizards if you wish.

Fleeing models cannot use any magic items that are one use only, bound items and similar magic items that require a decision on when to activate their powers. Only magic items whose effects are permanent still work for fleeing models.

 TYPES OF MAGIC ITEM

For the sake of convenience, we distinguish between the types of magic item in the following way:

MAGIC WEAPONS

By which we mean most commonly swords, but also: axes, maces, spears, bows, crossbows, etc.

A character that has a magic close combat weapon cannot use any other close combat weapons, although it can carry a shield as normal. No character can carry more than one magic weapon. Magic weapons always ignore any special rules that apply to an ordinary weapon of the same type unless otherwise specified in the description of the weapon.

MAGIC ARMOUR

If a character wears magical armour, he cannot also wear ordinary armour and, needless to say, he can only wear one set of armour. Magical shields and helms are also counted as magical armour, so you cannot have a suit of magical armour and carry a magical shield or helm unless specifically stated in the description of the magic item.

If a model has a magic shield he is allowed to wear a suit of normal armour. If a model is wearing a magic helm he is allowed to wear a suit of normal armour and carry a normal shield. If the model is wearing a suit of magic armour he is allowed to carry a normal shield.

A character that is not allowed to wear ordinary armour cannot be given magic armour/helms (unless differently specified in the Army book). A character that is not allowed to carry ordinary shields cannot be given magic shields (unless differently specified in the Army book). This includes many kinds of Wizard whose natural magical harmony would be seriously affected by armour.

TALISMANS

Talismans, charms, amulets and wards are tokens of magical protection. A character cannot have more than one talisman.

ARCANE ITEMS

Arcane items are items that enhance a Wizard's magical powers in some fashion. Only a Wizard can carry an arcane item and no character can carry more than one.

Scrolls

Scrolls are a type of arcane item that contain powerful enchantments that enable Wizards to manipulate the power of magic. They are useful aids to spellcasting and to resisting an enemy's spell. Unlike other arcane items, there is no limit on the number of scrolls a Wizard can carry, other than the total points value of magic items he is permitted. Wizards can have one arcane item as well as carry several scrolls (of the same or of different type).

Once a scroll is read, it crumbles to dust or its writing fades to nothing. Each scroll can therefore only be used once during the whole battle.

ENCHANTED ITEMS

Many magic items are unique or belong to limited categories, such as rings, amulets, magic boots, etc. These items are enchanted items. No general restrictions apply to these (specific exceptions may), except that a character cannot have more than one enchanted item.

BANNERS

Magical banners can only be carried by standard bearers as indicated in the army lists in the Warhammer Army book for each army. The only character permitted to carry a magic standard is the army's battle standard bearer, and he can carry only one magical banner. Occasionally, some units are allowed to carry magic banners as well, as detailed in their army list entry.

BOUND SPELLS

Some magic items contain bound spells – spells that are wrought into their very fabric and can be unleashed by their wielder during the magic phase. Possessing a bound spell item does not make a character a Wizard.

The spell held in a magic item is cast in the player's magic phase just like other spells (for example, it cannot be cast by fleeing models) and can be countered in the same way as ordinary spells.

Bound spells are cast automatically – no power dice are needed. A spell from a bound spell item can be cast once per magic phase. Each bound spell item has a power level included in its description. An opponent must score equal to or greater than this power level to dispel the spell, or he can use Dispel Scrolls as normal. Magic items that dispel and destroy spells work as normal against spells cast from a bound spell.

A character cannot have more than one bound spell.

COMMON MAGIC ITEMS

The following magic items are considered to be common items – which is to say that they are common to all armies in the Warhammer world and not that they are commonplace in any sense. Even the least potent magic item is a dangerous device, steeped in the fickle powers of sorcery, and is extremely rare. Complete lists of magic items available to each of the different armies are included in the Warhammer Army book for each race.

SWORD OF STRIKING

Magic Weapon – A Sword of Striking is possessed of a keen intelligence that guides its blade to the target. The sword confers to the character wielding it a bonus of +1 when rolling to hit. For example, where a 3 is normally required to score a hit, the character will hit on a 2. However, a dice roll of 1 is always a miss regardless of bonuses.

SWORD OF BATTLE

Magic Weapon – A Sword of Battle is forged with potent magic that enables its wielder to employ it with dazzling speed and deadly effect. The blade confers +1 Attack on the character wielding it.

SWORD OF MIGHT

Magic Weapon – A Sword of Might is wrought with enchantments that bind within its fabric a great and magical strength. The blade confers upon the character who fights with it +1 Strength when rolling to wound.

BITING BLADE

Magic Weapon – The Biting Blade is forged with bitter curses that work against the armour of its foes. The blade confers an additional -1 armour save modifier on any blows stuck, so a blow struck at Strength 3 or less will have a -1 armour save, a Strength 4 hit has a -2 armour save, Strength 5 has a -3 armour save and so on.

ENCHANTED SHIELD

Magic Armour – The Enchanted Shield protects its user with powerful magic. The shield confers an armour save of 5+ rather than a mundane shield's armour save of 6+. This can be combined with other mundane armour – for example, light armour + Enchanted Shield = armour save 4+, heavy armour + Enchanted Shield + mounted = armour save 2+.

TALISMAN OF PROTECTION

Talisman – The Talisman of Protection is a protective charm. This confers a ward save of 6+ upon its wearer.

STAFF OF SORCERY

Arcane Item – A Wizard who has this benefits from the arcane power stored within it. Whenever he dispels a spell, his dispel result is increased by 1.

DISPEL SCROLL — One use only

Arcane Item – A Dispel Scroll is inscribed with a powerful anti-magical invocation. When it is read out by a Wizard, the effect is to drain away magical power and weaken a spell that has been cast. As soon as a spell has been cast, any Wizard who has a Dispel Scroll can read it instead of attempting to dispel the spell by using dispel dice. This automatically dispels the enemy spell; no dice roll is required.

Note that even a Dispel Scroll will not help if the spell has been cast with irresistible force. Note also that Dispel Scrolls cannot be used to dispel spells that remain in play other than at the moment they are cast.

POWER STONE — One use only

Arcane Item – A Power Stone is imbued with a powerful magical invocation. When it is activated by a Wizard before he rolls any dice to cast a spell, the effect is to enhance the efficacy of the spell. Two dice are added to the casting roll (they can be the only two dice used to cast the spell). Note that using a Power Stone will allow a Wizard to use more power dice than he is normally permitted. For example, a second level Wizard may activate a Power Stone and thus use five power dice to cast a spell (3 basic + 2 from the Power Stone). A Power Stone can only be used once – after one use its power is exhausted.

In a similar way to scrolls, Power Stones are not unique items, but they are prepared by a Wizard prior to battle. It is therefore possible for several Wizards to carry Power Stones, and for a Wizard to carry more than one, in addition to one other arcane item. However, only one Power Stone can be used to cast a spell.

WAR BANNER

Magic Banner – The War Banner carries powerful enchantments that fill all those who fight beneath it with heroic courage and determination. A unit that has a War Banner adds a further +1 to its combat resolution when working out which side has won the combat.

The thaumodivinator of the Colleges of Magic on the eve of the Altdorf Mage Riots of 2217.

THE WARHAMMER WORLD

In this section we look at the races of the Warhammer world and chart the history of their battles. Later you will find a guide to the various armies that you can field in your Warhammer games. A lot more information about the races – their origins, how and where they live and fight, their warriors and great heroes – can be found in the Warhammer Armies range.

THE OLD ONES

In the very earliest times, many thousands of years before the present day, the ancient and highly advanced race known only as the Old Ones crossed the stars from their distant worlds and settled upon the Warhammer world. They constructed a stellar gate that allowed them to cross over into an alternate realm and traverse the great depths of space. None can say for sure why these godlike beings chose to do this, and what was their ultimate purpose. It may have been that they wished to create a world that could sustain itself without them, or perhaps they saw something of the disaster that was to befall their civilisation and the races of the Warhammer world were an attempt to prevent this. We shall never know; all that is sure is that their great plans never came to fruition.

First the Old Ones used their powers to move the world closer to its sun, warming the climate to one more suitable to them. They then reshaped the continents into forms more to their liking. At this point the Warhammer world was already populated by many beasts and creatures of little or no sentience. Alongside these animals dwelt the Dragons. Intelligent and articulate, the Dragons had dealings with the Old Ones, learning a little of their magical lore. Many of their kind avoided the Old Ones, and hid in the dark places of the world beneath the seas and mountains, the Dragons' once-cold world now too warm, forcing them to slumber for centuries.

THE FIRST RACES

The Old Ones began to introduce new races to the world. The first, the Slann, were highly adept at using the energies harnessed by the Old Ones, and to them were entrusted many of the tasks required to raise the cities of their people, to adjust the flow of the oceans and carve the mountains from the bare rock. The Old Ones then introduced the Lizardmen to aid the Slann in their works. Reptilian warriors guarded their lands while immense beasts of burden lumbered through the primordial jungles, and workers laboured at erecting their mighty cities, all overseen by an army of Lizardmen scribes, artisans and other functionaries.

Next came the Elves, imbued with a natural affinity for the energy wielded by the Old Ones – the energy that Men call magic. The isle of Ulthuan was raised from the bed of the ocean for the Elves to live upon, and here they studied magic under the tutelage of the Old Ones and the Slann. As the Elves learned how to tap into magical energy, it became clear that they were not as resistant to the effects of magic as the Old Ones had hoped, and so were corruptible.

With this in mind, the Old Ones introduced the race of Dwarfs. They were the balance to the Elves – sturdy, dependable and, above all, resistant to magical energy. They were taught the ways of craftsmanship, and became excellent artisans. Unfortunately, the Dwarfs were also prone to their own kind of corruption, and the very qualities that were supposed to be virtues had the possibility of being exaggerated into stubbornness, avarice and insularity.

THE YOUNG RACES

At some point, the Orcs arrived. Quite probably their insidious spores were unwittingly introduced to the world by the star vessels of the Old Ones, although possibly they drifted through the voids of space and came to the world by their own means. Either way, in the hidden wilderness, the greenskins spread to become a constant thorn in the side of the other races.

Mankind was the next race to be introduced. Man has neither the physical, mental or magical prowess of the Dwarfs or Elves, so it seems odd that the Old Ones created them. Perhaps Man wasn't complete, for when the disaster came, they were still primitive, living in caves with barely a language or society to speak of.

Finally, the Old Ones created the Halflings and the Ogres just before their fall; two somewhat desperate last-ditch attempts to create a magically-resistant race. Halflings were physically and mentally resistant to magic but at the expense of being inbred, stunted and, to be quite frank, pretty vulgar. The large and tough physique of the Ogres was compromised by their dim-witted, clumsy and belligerent demeanour.

THE RISE OF THE DWARFS

While the Elves dwelt in relative contentment on the island of Ulthuan, learning from the Old Ones, the Dwarfs travelled northwards across the world, along the mountains where they had been raised. The ancestors of the Dwarfs delved deeply into the rocks, and mined the minerals and ores beneath the world, for their love was always of the places under the earth rather than the open sky.

Their craftsmanship grew with their empire, until their weapons and devices were unmatched except by the artifices of the Old Ones themselves. The Dwarfs settled in the Worlds Edge Mountains, where grand underground cities were linked by subterranean highways lit with magical lanterns and decorated with silver and gold.

While the Elves perfected their magic, the Dwarfs used the knowledge of the Old Ones to create their rune lore. They bound weapons with great strength, forged unbreakable armour and devised all manner of charms that pleased them greatly. Their love of wealth grew, but at this time the Dwarfs were content in their delvings and the works of their artificers, blissfully unaware of the strife to come.

THE COMING OF CHAOS

The races were not to know peace, as they were beset by great catastrophe. For reasons that will never be fathomed, the gate of the Old Ones collapsed. Perhaps the destruction of the gate was caused by the Old Ones themselves, to forestall an invasion from the nightmare realm that lay beyond; maybe it was attacked by the incorporeal creatures that dwelt within the formless dimension beyond the gate. In a detonation of raw power that lit the sky and shook oceans and mountains, the disaster imploded the poles so that they are now raging gateways into the raw ether. A ball of pure chaos matter called warpstone was thrown into an erratic orbit around the world and to this day showers down particles and lumps of tainted rock.

Whether the Old Ones fled before or after the disaster, or were destroyed by it, is not recorded. All that is known is that the Old Ones never again walked the face of the Warhammer world, though many of the Slann prophecies say that the Old Ones will return when the time is right.

When the gate collapsed, the world was immersed in magical energy and Chaos was born. As the skies burned and the earth quaked, all the primal fears and dreams of the Warhammer races came to the fore, and dark gods were born in the magical conflagration. Given life by the emotions of mortals, the Chaos gods became aware of the realm of Elves, Men and Dwarfs and they came to covet it.

It was during this catastrophe that the first true creatures of Chaos began to appear. Hippogryphs, Chymaeras, Manticores, Griffons and their like stalked the lands, descended from normal creatures warped by the magical energies now poisoning the Warhammer world. The Beastmen came too; depraved Men that had reverted to their bestial subconscious, their bodies warped to reflect their animalistic desires, and beasts that had mutated to walk on their hind legs in the form of Men. In the marshes in the north of what would become the nation of Tilea, intelligent, misshapen rat-things began burrowing and plotting, digging beneath the world in secret, unseen and unknown.

With the birth of the Chaos gods came the first Great Incursion. A host of immaterial daemonic creatures of Chaos, larger than any to have walked the world since, erupted from the shattered gate in the north. The world was awash with vast waves of magical energy and the Daemonic creatures of the Chaos Gods could walk abroad at will. The daemonic armies swept over the lands and eventually came to the Elven isle of Ulthuan. Here the fate of the world would be decided. If the Elves fell, then Chaos would consume the Warhammer world. If they prevailed, then that fate would be staved off, for a time at least.

THE ELVES' SACRIFICE

The Elves survived, thanks to Aenarion and the Elven Mages. Aenarion was the first Phoenix King of Ulthuan, known in legends as the Defender. It was the great Elven warrior that drew the ancient Sword of Khaine from its resting place on the Blighted Isle, and with its power slew a host of Daemons. Yet, by wielding the cursed Sword of Khaine, forged for the god of war himself, the taint of Chaos burnt in Aenarion's blood and the Curse of Aenarion would dog his descendants to the present day.

An endless tide of nightmare creatures assailed the realm of the Elves, and though Aenarion and his army prevailed in battle after battle, it was clear to the wisest of the Elves that they were doomed to lose the war – even the mighty hosts of Ulthuan could not fight for eternity. So it was that as Aenarion's host, aided by flights of Dragon Riders, defended the Isle of the Dead against a mighty daemonic army, the Elven prince Caledor and his fellow mages put into motion a great ritual.

The Elves risked everything, erecting a circle of mystical stones that created a magical vortex through their realm that threatened to sink the island. This vortex drew in the raging winds of magic that now tore across the world. Without magic to sustain them, the Daemons' grip in the mortal realm became unstable and their hosts were crushed by Aenarion, though the Phoenix King himself was mortally wounded in the battle. Ever since, Ulthuan has constantly teetered upon the brink of destruction, threatened by the vast energies the lodestones must dissipate. It is true when the Elves say the world is not as magical as it once was, for much magical power is taken into the stones on Ulthuan, and the magical artefacts and sorceries of the distant past can never be recreated.

With the first incursion thwarted, the Elves set out to explore this changed world, and they met with the Dwarfs. Trade between the Dwarfs and Elves flourished, while the primitive ancestors of Man spread across the globe, unwittingly protected by these two great civilisations. Perhaps a great alliance may have, in time, given rise to a world able to stand against Chaos. It was not to be.

THE TIME OF THE SUNDERING

Born to Morathi, Aenarion's second wife, Prince Malekith of Nagarythe was the greatest of Elves. He was an unparalleled general and his armies crushed the brutish hordes of Chaos across the world. In his dealings with the Dwarfs, he was fair and patient, and became a personal friend of the Dwarf High King Snorri Whitebeard. Between the two of them, they forged an alliance that would see the dark creatures of the world pushed back to mountain caves and the dark depths of the forests.

Yet in his heart, there was a taint in Malekith that simply bided its time. Jealous of the other Elven princes, Malekith was filled with unnatural lust and ambition, and desired the Phoenix Throne for himself. When Prince Bel-Shanaar was chosen to become Phoenix King ahead of Malekith, this desire flared into murderous intent, and eventually Malekith accused Bel-Shanaar of worshipping the gods of Chaos. When the Phoenix King was found dead by poisoning, none at the time doubted Malekith's claim that Bel-Shanaar had taken his own life rather than be punished for his corruption.

With no rival, Malekith took the throne for himself. To prove that he was blessed by the gods, the Elven prince walked through the sacred Flames of Asuryan, just as his father had done. The flames rejected him and he was hideously burnt and scarred – to this day his body is wracked with the pain. Malekith's treachery had been revealed and his supporters and opponents took up arms.

The time of the Sundering came, when Elf fought Elf and the lands of Ulthuan were ravaged by powerful sorcery. Their souls poisoned, the followers of Malekith became twisted and focussed on a single purpose – revenge against their kin. Nowhere is this more embodied than in the Witch King Malekith himself.

In his arrogance, Malekith believed the forces of Chaos could be controlled and mastered, just like everything else, and saw it as the Elves' destiny to rule the world as the rightful successors to the Old Ones. Though eventually driven out across the sea to the bleak land of Naggaroth, Malekith and his Dark Elves had unwittingly destroyed any hope the world may have had of resisting Chaos.

But it was not just this that sealed the world's fate. Though the Dwarfs and Elves had forged an alliance with one another, they were the two dominant powers of the world, and therefore ultimately rivals. Not only this, their character and cultures were wholly different to each other.

It was spiteful acts of treachery by the Dark Elves against the Dwarfs that tumbled the two greatest empires the world had seen since the Old Ones. Dark Elf raiders ambushed Dwarf trade convoys, and the Dwarfs accused the Elves of breaking their oaths of friendship. The High Elves in their arrogance shaved the beards of the Dwarf ambassadors and threw them out of court. The stubbornness of the Dwarfs and their natural dislike for the Elves dragged them into a confrontation from which they could not back down.

The War of the Beard – or War of Vengeance as the Dwarfs prefer it to be known – lasted for hundreds of years and devastated both races. This age-long war was directly responsible for both Elves and Dwarfs retreating from the wider world to their own realms. Although this allowed Men to prosper in their stead, it also allowed the wild things to take control once again – the walking dead, the Orcs and Goblins, the Trolls and creatures of Chaos.

For centuries the world was an extremely dangerous place, even more perilous than now, and Mankind was beset by unnumbered foes while the Elves and Dwarfs were content to look to their own woes.

The Glittering Host

THE RISE OF THE UNDEAD

At this time a new civilisation was arising, a realm that at its peak would stretch far across the Badlands and into what would become the Old World and rival any later empire of Men. The desert tribes of the Southlands began to build large settlements in the desert, perhaps dimly remembering the ancient cities of the Old Ones in the jungles to the south. This realm they would come to call Nehekhara.

While Orcs and Beastmen laid claim to the forests of the north, the Men of the south prospered and grew in number. Over centuries, the kingdoms of Nehekhara rose out of the blistering sands, and their rulers traded and warred with each other in their struggle for dominion. Some five thousand years before the present day, one city rose to pre-eminence; Khemri, kingdom of the great Priest King Settra.

Settra was an unparalleled general, and was driven by such an extreme vanity that he would brook no threat to his reign. Even as his heralds spread Settra's demands to the other Priest Kings, the lord of Khemri led his army to victory upon victory against his foes. One by one the other cities allied themselves to Khemri or were conquered by Settra.

However, there was one foe that Settra could not defeat: death. He commanded his priests to seek ways to prolong his life, so that his glories would never fade, and they devised long rituals to preserve their lord in life. However, they could not stay the hand of death itself, and so when Settra was upon his deathbed they conducted a great ceremony they claimed would preserve his body and allow him to return to an immortal life after a thousand years of sleeping.

For the next five hundred years the fortunes of Khemri and Nehekhara waxed and waned, as alliances came and went, and the cities fought amongst themselves. Following Settra's example, the rulers of Nehekhara became increasingly obsessed with death and avoiding its cold grip. Soon the greater part of their society and endeavour was bent towards raising great pyramids and gravehouses to keep their bodies while they awaited their return to life. Families and bodyguards died alongside the Priest Kings and were buried with them to serve them after death. Beside each city rose a great necropolis, larger than the buildings of the living, their dead inhabitants outnumbering those still alive.

NAGASH

Some five centuries after the reign of Settra a new power arose in Nehekhara. The brother of the Priest King of Khemri, Nagash was unequalled in his knowledge of the mortuary rites, but for him preserving the dead for reawakening was not enough. His obsession with mortality far outstripped even the desires for eternal life of Settra and his every fibre was set to unlocking the secrets of immortality.

Though his own studies were extensive, it was the chance capture of a group of Dark Elves shipwrecked upon the Nehekharan coast that was to lead Nagash to unravelling the secrets of Dark Magic, and in turn he used this knowledge to create the foul art known as Necromancy.

Nagash distilled an elixir of life using the blood of his subjects, and with this he sustained his existence. Granted unnatural longevity, Nagash usurped his brother with the aid of disciples lured to his cause by the promise of immortality. The renegade priest then ordered the construction of a mighty black pyramid, to trap the fitful Winds of Magic and swell his power.

As Nagash and his minions ruled over the people of Khemri like bloodthirsty gods, the other Priest Kings grew wary of his power and united against Nagash. Led by the Priest King Lahmizzar, the Priest Kings' armies attacked Khemri, forcing the Great Necromancer to seek shelter in his Black Pyramid. His disciples were caught and executed, though Nagash himself was never found. Believing Nagash to have been thwarted, the leaders of the alliance once more fell to bickering amongst themselves, and the memory of Nagash began to fade.

BIRTH OF THE VAMPIRES

However, Nagash's evil could not be so easily conquered. Against all agreement, the Queen of the city of Lahmia, Neferata, took some of Nagash's diabolical texts from his tomb chamber and returned to her city with them. She tried to recreate Nagash's elixir of life, and in part it worked. However, she thirsted for the blood of Men, and only by feeding on her subjects could she sustain herself. Her court was also corrupted by the curse of vampirism, and just as Nagash had stirred the other Priest Kings to action, so too did the tales of the blood rites of Lahmia.

While the Vampire rulers of Lahmia endeavoured to remain secret, the unquiet soul of Nagash wandered the desert and the wastes. Formless and half-mad, he came across the Sour Sea, and the great mountain of Cripple Peak upon its shore. Here he found large quantities of warpstone, raw magic given solid form, and with this was able to increase his necromantic powers. Using skeletal slaves raised from the dead of ancient battlefields, he dug the great labyrinthine fortress of Nagashizzar. Nagash fought long with the Skaven, who had also been drawn to the area by the warpstone, but eventually he made a pact with the Chaos ratmen.

By now, the Vampires of Lahmia had become aware of the return of Nagash and sent heralds and emissaries to parley with him. It was soon clear that they were in his thrall, unwitting slaves to his necromantic arts, and they had no choice but to ally themselves to the Great Necromancer's cause. With their aid, Nagash waged war against the Priest Kings, as the Vampires sought to rule over the people that had once bowed to them and had now cast them out.

THE WARS OF THE DEAD

Never again wanting to be slaves of Nagash, the cities of Nehekhara united against the Undead invasion. For over a decade Nagash and the Vampires fought against the armies of Nehekhara. The greatest Priest King since Settra, Alcadizaar the Conqueror defeated the army of the dead and scattered it into the desert. Nagash would not be thwarted and unleashed a plague across the lands, swelling his armies with the thousands that died. Alcadizaar was defeated by this new host and captured, then dragged in chains to Nagashizzar.

Nagash then embarked upon his Great Awakening and, after consuming vast quantities of warpstone, he unleashed the mightiest necromantic spell ever to have darkened the world. All across Nehekhara, the living withered and died while the dead stirred in their tombs.

The Skaven of Cripple Peak realised their alliance with Nagash was over and devised a cunning scheme to rid themselves of their enemy. They forged the Fellblade, a weapon of almost pure warpstone, and freed Alcadizaar from his cell. Placing the baneful weapon in the Priest King's grasp, they led him to Nagash. The Priest King hacked off Nagash's hand and ended the Great Awakening before it could be completed. The two clashed, Alcadizaar aided by the sorceries of the Skaven, and eventually Nagash's body was destroyed. Alcadizaar fought his way out of Nagashizzar, his body and mind burning with the Chaos-tainted magic of the Fellblade, and eventually fell into the Blind River and drowned.

Although he had not completed the Great Ritual, Nagash's spell had changed the world forever. The Priest Kings and their armies, entombed beneath the sands, had been returned to some semblance of life. They rose from their crypts and waged war upon each other, as they had in life. That was until the rising of Settra the Imperishable, mightiest and most ancient of their number. As he had done many centuries before, Settra cowed the other cities to his rule, vowing eternal vengeance against Nagash for bringing him back to life too early. Instead of a shining body of immortal gold, Settra found himself as a withered corpse, writhing with dark magic and clothed in tattered mortuary rags.

With Nagash defeated, the first Vampires fled the armies of the Tomb Kings. Some went into the north where the tribes of Men were emerging from their caves and building settlements of huts, others into the east and south. Nagash was to return, for even the energies of the Fellblade could not wholly destroy him. Seeking domination of the living, he waged war upon the fledgling Empire of Sigmar. But that is another story, for calamitous events were to once again alter the course of the world.

THE WOES OF THE DWARFS

No more than six decades after the defeat of the Elves and their retreat from the Old World, the Dwarf empire was struck by catastrophe. The Worlds Edge Mountains rumbled and shook as massive earthquakes rent the land and volcanoes belched forth great rivers of lava. The Dwarf strongholds were shaken, many halls collapsed and the underground highway that linked the holds, the Undgrin Ankor, was breached in many places and rendered impassable.

Suddenly isolated from each other, and reeling from the devastation of the cataclysmic upheavals, the Dwarf holds were vulnerable. In particular, the Orcs and Goblins that had been flourishing since the end of the War of the Beard filled the mountains in countless hordes, assailing the strongholds of the Dwarfs.

The first hold to fall was Karak Ungor in the far north, invaded by Night Goblins. Thousands upon thousands of greenskins overwhelmed the beleaguered defenders over months of bitter fighting, and eventually the Dwarfs were forced from their tunnels and halls into the wilderness. Karak Ungor became the abode of Goblins, Skaven and other dark creatures and has ever after been known as Red Eye Mountain.

In the years to follow, many mines and holds were overrun, the seemingly impregnable Dwarf cities now laid open to attack by Orcs, Ogres, Trolls and other creatures. The Silver Road Wars erupted around Mount Silverspear as the Dwarfs defended their city against the warriors of the Orc warlord Urk Grimfang. The fall of Mount Silverspear, renamed Mount Grimfang by its conqueror, signalled the end of the Dwarfs' realm in the eastern reaches of the Worlds Edge Mountains, and thousands of refugees fled to the remaining holds.

THE GOBLIN WARS

The move westward brought only a brief respite as the remaining holds were attacked and besieged in a series of battles that lasted nearly a thousand years. These battles are known to the Dwarfs as the Goblin Wars, though Skaven, Beastmen and other fell things were also responsible for many Dwarf deaths. Skaven tunnels were found beneath the halls and mines of Karak Eight Peaks, and for the next two hundred years the Dwarfs fought a losing battle against the subterranean invaders. The Dwarfs were crushed when Goblins attacked and the Skaven unleashed deadly poisoned wind gas.

Karak Azgal fell soon after, despite successfully repulsing several Orc and Goblin attacks. The victorious greenskins swept onwards and overran Karak Drazh. Karak Azul and the capital Karaz-a-Karak both felt the wrath of the greenskins, although both were eventually held.

With much of their empire in ruins, and the surviving Dwarf holds a pale shadow of their former glories, the Dwarfs sought alliances with the growing tribes of Men now living in the forests west of the Worlds Edge Mountains. One relationship in particular was to change the fate of Men and Dwarfs for the next two and a half thousand years.

THE AGE OF MAN

For hundreds of years, Man had continued to evolve and spread through the world, to distant Cathay and Ind, across the steppes and Chaos Wastes of the far north and to the lands between the Great Ocean and Worlds Edge Mountains, which they would come to call the Old World. At the start of the age of Man, with a few exceptions such as Nehekhara, Mankind was a tribal society. Small, scattered groups lived in log dwellings and caves, hunting in the hills and forests, defending themselves as best they could against the vicious Beastmen and Goblins that dwelt beside them in the wild places of the world.

But that was to change with the coming of Sigmar, greatest warrior and leader of Men; a Man that would found the Empire and leave a legacy that has lasted to the present day. A child of the Unberogen tribe, Sigmar was remarkable from an early age, and by the time he was fifteen he was already an accomplished hunter and warrior. It was perhaps fate that brought him to the rescue of a small column of Dwarfs captured by Orcs as they travelled to the Grey Mountains.

Amongst the Dwarfs was none other than their High King, Kurgan Ironbeard. The grateful ruler of the Dwarfs gifted Sigmar with a mighty rune hammer, known as Ghal Maraz, the skull-splitter. It was to become Sigmar's symbol, wielded in countless battles as the young Man set about crushing the enemies that had preyed upon his people for so long.

Sigmar understood the threat posed by the greenskins and the northern tribes aligned to the power of Chaos, and set about ordering the world in the way he saw best fit to combat these threats. Sigmar's creed was to shape the Empire to this day, for it was a dream of unity under a strong leader.

Through diplomacy and war, Sigmar forged a confederation amongst the tribes of the lands that would become the Empire. The lands west of the Worlds Edge Mountains and north of the Grey Mountains were now under Sigmar's control, and although Beastmen and Forest Goblins still remained in the darkest, most remote places, their threat to the future of Men had been ended.

However, one last battle still remained; in Black Fire Pass, Sigmar and his tribal allies stood alongside Kurgan Ironbeard and a host of Dwarfs, facing a near-endless horde of greenskins marauding north from the Badlands. Despite vicious fighting and their horrendous losses, the army of Men and Dwarfs prevailed and the power of the Orcs in the west was broken.

SIGMAR'S EMPIRE

After the victory at Black Fire Pass, the Empire of Sigmar knew great prosperity and relative peace for many decades. For their part in the battle, King Kurgan set the great Runesmith Alaric the Mad to forge twelve magical swords for Sigmar's chieftains, and in the times to come these Runefangs became the symbols of their power. For fifty more years, Sigmar reigned, and remained strong and healthy even aged eighty. Though his strength was undimmed and his wisdom greater than ever, Sigmar gave up his rule, passing the fledgling Empire to the control of the chieftains that formed his confederation.

To avoid bitter infighting over the rulership of the Empire, the chieftains chose to elect one from amongst their number to take the position of Emperor. Sigmar passed on Ghal Maraz as a badge of office and travelled into the east, some say to see his friend Kurgan Ironbeard, others to fight on against the greenskins in the Dark Lands beyond the Worlds Edge Mountains.

For many centuries the Empire grew, its settlements expanding into towns and mighty cities. The descendants of the tribal chieftains continued to elect one amongst their number to reign over the Empire and lead their people, and they took to themselves the titles of Elector Counts. With aid from the Dwarfs, the Empire's craftsmanship and construction advanced rapidly, and the alliance between the two peoples flourished. In time, the people of the Empire began to worship Sigmar as a god and a great church spread across the lands to honour him.

However, peace was not to last. Corrupted with vanity and ambition, the Electors fought amongst themselves. The enemies of the Empire grew, in hidden places in the forests and in the dark beneath the world. Plagues devastated the Empire, and armies of rat-like Skaven erupted from underground warrens to enslave entire towns. The armies of the Counts were laid low by the contagions secretly spread by the Skaven.

With the Empire tearing itself apart, the Skaven were unopposed until the Count of Middenland, Mandred, assembled a great army and fought back. Driven from the ruins of the Empire's farms and villages, the Skaven were forced back into their subterranean world. Rallying behind their new leader, the Counts elected Mandred as the new Emperor and for a few years the decline was stalled. The Skaven were to make a spiteful yet devastating last blow in the war, when assassins sent by the Council of Thirteen slew Mandred and the electoral system was again thrown into a turmoil of infighting, betrayal and murder.

THE THREE EMPERORS

Over the following centuries the Empire tore itself apart with politics and civil war as the Counts fought amongst themselves for power. Sigmar's legacy was left in shreds as armies of Men marched against their fellows in pursuit of power and wealth for their increasingly selfish nobles. As more claimants to the Imperial throne emerged, the system of elections was totally swept aside. For many centuries there was sporadic civil war, and this period is known as the Time of the Three Emperors due to the rival claims to the throne.

The Empire was constantly beset by foes in these divided times. They were ill-prepared to face such enemies, the Counts unable or unwilling to call upon their comrades for aid. The first great war came with the invasion of Gorbad Ironclaw, a mighty Orc warlord that led his horde through Black Fire Pass and rampaged across the south of the Empire. The lands of Solland were burnt and plundered and the Count slain, his Runefang taken as loot by Gorbad. Wissenland and the city of Nuln were overrun and Gorbad's horde poured into the Reikland and besieged the great walls of Altdorf. There was no quick victory for Gorbad at Altdorf, despite the death of the Reikland Count during the fighting, and eventually the fractious nature of the greenskins took hold as the infighting warbands went their own way.

Another three hundred years of civil war and anarchy were to pass before the next menace arose, so threatening that many of the Counts put aside their differences for the first time in a thousand years in order to thwart its rise. From the cursed lands of Sylvania, a place infamous across the Old World for its grim woods and unquiet graveyards, a new contender for the throne declared himself: Count Vlad von Carstein.

Vlad was no mortal foe, for he was the first of the Vampire Counts. It is not known whether he was one of the first Vampires, under a new guise, or one of their infernal descendants. His armies of Undead ravaged the Empire for forty years during the Wars of the Vampire Counts, as Vlad attacked Ostermark and Stirland. Vlad was eventually slain at another great battle around Altdorf. The High Priest of Sigmar, the Grand Theogonist Wilhelm III, threw himself from the battlements of the city, dragging Vlad onto the stakes at the bottom of the wall.

The threat of the Vampires did not die with Vlad, as his unholy progeny multiplied and continued to attack the Empire for decades to come. In the midst of this fighting, another great event was to stir the Counts to selfish action.

A mighty comet smashed into the city of Mordheim, capital of Ostermark. Showering the ruined settlement with shards of warpstone, the comet left Mordheim pulsing with Chaotic energy. Not realising the corruption they risked in claiming such power, all manner of interested parties began to send armies and mercenaries to Mordheim to claim the warpstone for themselves. Eventually the city was cleansed by knights and witch hunters commanded by the Grand Theogonist, and the ruins of the city obliterated. It is still an area of ill reputation, where the taint of Chaos lies heavily on the land.

THE GREAT WAR

Over the ages, the Old World has known many wars and endured innumerable perils. The fragile kingdoms of Men have met and defeated each threat, though every new danger that emerges seems greater than the last, and every battle is won at an ever-increasing cost. Of all these wars one alone is known as the Great War – the Great War against Chaos.

In the far north, the Realm of Chaos swelled with power. The dark shadow of Chaos spilled southwards, engulfing the wastelands and absorbing them. Before this irresistible tide the minions of Chaos advanced, and as the shadow moved south so the forces of Chaos grew.

Monsters from the Northern Wastes were joined by bands of Chaos Warriors from the borders of the Troll Country. In the deep forests of the Empire, Beastmen assembled and readied themselves for war. In the winter of 2302 Kislevite forces attempted to hold several bridges across the Lynsk, but were overwhelmed by the Chaos horde.

During the fighting, several champions earned dire reputations, but of all the warlords there was one whose name was to cause dread to the foes of Chaos – Asavar Kul. Though the horde was so large that no single Man could be said to rule the mass of Chaos creatures, Kul's deeds and presence brought the banners of many lesser champions under his command. A chieftain from the savage Kurgan people, Kul was a fearless warrior, canny leader and vicious devotee of the Chaos gods, and wherever he led his army, terror and death were his companions.

The northern Kislevite city of Praag was the first stronghold to feel the wrath of Kul and his allies. Warped beasts, daemonic creatures and frenzied warriors assailed the walls of the city for many days. Though their dead were piled high, the Chaos forces launched assault after assault on Praag until the defenders could fight no more and the city was sacked. So powerful were the Chaos sorceries unleashed during the final attack that Praag was forever tainted by its mark. It is now an ill-regarded place, full of ghostly voices, shifting walls and plagued by the walking dead.

Moving south, the Chaos horde headed towards the capital, Kislev. Meanwhile, the Tzar of Kislev had sent word to the Empire for aid. Most of these messengers went unheeded, as the Electors ignored the danger of the Chaos horde and instead were consumed by their own petty ambitions. In the city of Nuln, however, a young man named Magnus preached a rallying call to the sons of Sigmar and began to amass a sizeable army. With passionate speeches and a rousing call to arms, Magnus appealed to all Men of the Empire to join his army and fight in defence of Sigmar's realm. Soon even the Elector Counts took notice of the force in Nuln, and with none of them wishing to be outmanoeuvred by their competitors they each sent a contingent of their own troops to bolster the army.

In the Worlds Edge Mountains, in the hold of Karaz-a-Karak, the Dwarf High King also recognised the threat posed by the Chaos horde and he marched forth at the head of a host of Dwarfen warriors intent on assisting the city of Kislev. The High King arrived to great cheers of welcome. Though his force was comparatively small, the presence of his stout Dwarf warriors did much to relieve the panic that had begun to grip the city.

As Magnus' army marched northwards, the Chaos horde fell upon Kislev. A bitter siege engulfed the defenders as Kul and the other champions sought to breach the defences. Greater Daemons rampaged along the walls only to be stopped by the sturdy Thanes of the Dwarf High King, while monstrous siege engines rained down rocks, bolts and magical fire at the walls themselves.

It was then that the Elves arrived. For many generations no High Elf host had set foot upon the lands of the Old World. Now, in its time of greatest need, the Old World was to be bolstered by the arrival of the most unexpected allies. Teclis, greatest of the Loremasters of Ulthuan, led an army to Kislev, their white ships arriving on the shores of the Sea of Claws. A glittering army disembarked, ready for battle. A part of the Elven host joined Magnus' force as it advanced from the citadel of Middenheim, while the rest made straight for Kislev.

The Battle at the Gates of Kislev was the largest in the history of the Old World. Men, Daemons, Elves, Beastmen, Dwarfs and Chaos Warriors all fought in a struggle that lasted for days. Asavar Kul and other mighty champions of the Dark Gods cut a bloody swathe through the allied host, but victory was not to be theirs.

Magnus had sent an army of knights drawn from many different Orders to relieve Praag, but they had arrived too late. Pursuing the remnants of the Chaos army from the north, joined by Kislevite survivors of the war, they came to Kislev and fell upon the rear of Kul's force in a single bone-splintering charge. The defenders of the city sallied forth to add their numbers and, attacked on three fronts, the Chaos army was utterly broken.

Legend claims that Kul himself was slain by Magnus, though this seems unlikely – Magnus was far more a leader than a warrior and would have been little match for the near-immortal servant of Chaos. However, Kul was slain in the battle though his body was never recovered, and the horde was scattered. For many years after, lone warbands continued to plague Kislev and the Empire, as they do to this day.

EMPEROR KARL FRANZ

Following the Battle at the Gates of Kislev, the power of Chaos ebbed away. The Daemons melted back into the Realm of Chaos. Darkness withdrew from the land once more. The twisted ruins of Praag were levelled and the city rebuilt, though ever afterwards it has remained a haunted city.

Magnus the Pious, as he was known from then on, had united the Empire and was elected as Emperor. Purges were made against the Beastmen in the forests and Ostland and Ostermark were freed from their grip. The forces of Chaos were eventually pushed back to the Troll Country and beyond and relative peace ensued.

The true impact of the Great War is subtle, for it saw the Elves returning to the Old World and the coming of Teclis, who led the founding of the Colleges of Magic. A new understanding between the Elves of Ulthuan and the Empire grew, and the Empire now stood between the Dwarfs and Elves, learning from both, perhaps some day ready to take its part in the final war against Chaos.

Since the Great War, the Empire has resurfaced as a great power in the world, united once more behind a single Emperor. Magnus was the first of the so-called Griffon Emperors – after the griffon statues of his home city of Nuln – but in time the seat of power passed to the Counts of Reikland, and the rulership moved to the ancient palace buildings of Altdorf on the River Reik.

Through several generations the Princes of Altdorf have reigned over the Empire, and in 2502 Prince Karl Franz of Altdorf, Count of Reikland, became Emperor. In over two decades of ruling the Empire, he has proven to be a strong and courageous leader. Although still beset by many foes, Karl Franz strives daily to maintain the legacy left to him by Sigmar and Magnus, and is widely reputed as the greatest statesmen in the history of the Old World. Through various means, he continues to unite the provinces and rulers of the Empire and to forge alliances beyond its borders.

It is well that he has done so for the threat of Chaos remains ever present, as seen during the tumultuous events of the Storm of Chaos when the warlord Archaon led a devastating attack on the city of Middenheim. Orcs and Goblins grow in numbers once more, while the Skaven dig and scheme beneath the cities of the Empire. The dead still do not rest easily in their graves and the Vampires still hunt in the shadows. The world is dangerous, and only by the strength of its armies does the Empire remain.

Emperor Boris's extravagant tomb barque arrives at Marienburg.

Chaos Wasteland
The Land of Chill
Ghrond
Iron Mountains
Naggarond
Har Ganeth
Karond Kar
Sea of Chill
Sea of Chaos
Albion
The Old World
L'Anguille
Bordeleaux
Bilbali
Magritta
Hag Graef
Hex Gate
Sea of Malice
The Monoliths
Black Forest
Naggaroth
Red Desert
Doom Gate
Clar Karond
Blackspine Mountains
Plain of Spiders
Sewer Gate
Witch Gate
Vaul's Anvil
Doom Glades
The Great Ocean
Blighted Isle
The Shifting Isles
Anlec
Tor Achare
Forests of Avelorn
The Sunken Lands
Tor Elyr
Tor Anroc
Isle of the Dead
Tor Yvresse
Hoeth
Lothern
Ulthuan
The Broken Lands
Plain of Dogs
Isle of Great Beasts
Wraith Gate
The Bleak Coast
Petrified Forest
Boiling Sea
Straits of Fear
Viper Mountains
Ashen Coast
Rumbling Isle
Sulpheret Islands
Gulf of Lustria
Hexoatl
Pahuax (ruined)
Sea of Serpents
Pirate Coast of Araby
Copher
Al-Haikk
Zandri
Lashiek
Sorcerers Islands
Bel Aliad
Deserts of Araby
Araby
El-Kalabad
Elf Ruins
Gulf of Medes
Tlaqua
Scorpion Coast
Tarantula Coast
New World
The Far Sea
Tlanxla (ruined)
Tlaxtlan
Xahutec (ruined)
Tlax
The Vampire Coast
Chaqua (ruined)
Xlanhuapec
Huatl (ruined)
Spine of Sotek
Quetza (ruined)
Axlotl (ruined)
Volcanic Islands
Itza
Oyxl (ruined)
Mangrove Coast
The Turtle Isles
Xhotec (ruined)
Chupayotl (submerged)
Citadel of Dusk
Lustria
North
South

The Landes And Seas Of The Worlde

Wastes
The Lost hold of Karak Dum
The Northern hold of Karaka Drak
Kislev
Erengrad
Praag
Uzkulak
Kislev
Karak Vlag
Empire
Karak Ungor
Zharr Naggrund
Gash Kadrak
Vale of Woe
Ogre Kingdoms
Eastern Steppes
Karak Kadrin
Sylvania
The Moot
Zhufbar
The Dark Lands
The Gates of Zharr
Karak Varn
Karaz A Karak
Crookback Mountain
The Mountains of Mourn
Great Bastion
Nan-Gau
Wei-Jin
Ancient Giant Lands
Princes
Barak Varr
Karak Drazh
Mount Greyhag
The Tower of Gorgoth
Black Fortress
Karak Eight Peaks
Grand Cathay
Ash Ridge Mountains
Karak Azgal
Karak Azul
The Great Maw
Sour Sea
The Fortress of Vorag
Ruins
Dragon Isles
Numas
Straits of Nagash
Lahmia
The Sea of Dread
City of Spires
Nippon
Quatar
Mahrak
Lybaras
Serpents Coast
Kingdoms of Ind
Rasetra
Crater of the Dead
Hinterlands of Khuresh
Temple of Skulls
Worlds Edge Mountains
Shifting Mangrove Coastline
Golden Tower of the Gods
Teotiqua
Tower of Stars
Lost City of the Old Ones
Tower of The Rising Sun
Lands
Temple-Avenue of Gold
Tower of the Sun
The Lost Isles of Elithis
Tor Elasor
Gates of Calith
Tor Elithis
Fortress of Dawn

The Southern Wastes
Here Be Daemons

REALMS OF MEN

Though one of the shortest-lived races and particularly vulnerable to the lures and corruptions of Chaos, Men are also the pre-eminent race of the world. With the collapse of the great empires of the Elves and Dwarfs, the nations of Man have steadily grown in size and power.

Men are the most numerous and powerful race in the Old World and their cities are large and well fortified. Today only Men who live upon the steppes north of the Old World can rightly be called barbarians, the rest have multiplied and formed powerful nations. Some have built sprawling cities that have become centres of learning and prosperity, while fortified towns and farmsteads stake Man's claim to the wild areas of the world.

Of course, the Old World is still a wild and dangerous place, the nations of Men are more fragile than they seem and their cities are havens in a sea of dark terrors. These cities and the armies that protect them are the chief bulwark against invasion from the Chaos hordes to the far north, as well as from the Orc and Goblin tribes that infest the whole land. Constant dangers provide considerable incentive for the Old World nations to work together, but ancient rivalries and territorial ambitions run deep between them. War between the realms is common, if not the usual state of affairs, whilst rebellions and uprisings within can overturn nations and plunge them into long civil wars.

The Old World is an extremely violent and unpredictable place, where life is often short and death sudden and unexpected. Brought up amidst constant wars, dark forests full of Goblins and Beastmen, and the ever-present reality of plague and other incurable diseases, the people of the Old World are natural adventurers willing to risk all to win fabulous riches or fame in a world where their future is never certain.

Although the Old World may be the centre of Man's civilisation, it is by no means the only place in the world where they have prospered. In the Southlands and far to the east other nations have risen to claim dominance amongst the other races. Like the Old World, such races must battle for survival against many foes, and their future is uncertain, no matter how large and ancient their civilisation appears to be.

If Men are to be the true inheritors of the world, then it will be an inheritance protected with constant war and bloodshed.

Knight Panther

THE EMPIRE

The Empire is the largest and most powerful of all the realms of the Old World. It lies between the Worlds Edge Mountains and the sea, and encompasses all the lands north of the Grey Mountains and south of the nation of Kislev in the icy north. It is a land dominated by deep, dark forests and huge rivers. Its forests are infested with all kinds of monsters from the savage Chaos Beastmen to marauding Forest Goblins. These forests also hide the ruins of Elf cities destroyed in their wars against the Dwarfs, many containing as yet undiscovered treasures, but most have become the lairs of beasts or they are used as hideouts by bandits, Chaos warbands and evil creatures.

The southern and western lands of the Empire are more civilised with numerous cities built along the River Reik. This land, the Reikland, is now the heart of the Empire, ruled over by the Emperor from the largest city in the Old World, Altdorf. The north lands and the wilderness areas that rise into the foothills of the Worlds Edge Mountains are far more dangerous, where the power of the Empire's cities is distant and infrequently felt.

These wild and rough places breed tough Men, and it hardly surprising that the armies of the Empire are so successful. The backbone of the army is its well disciplined infantry, ably supported by effective cannons and the small but potent bodies of fully-armoured knights.

Praag
Erengrad
Laurelorn Forest
Salzenmund
Ferlangen
Bolgasgrad
River Lynsk
Forest of Shadows
The Wasteland
Midden Moors
Middle Mountains
Kislev
The Cursed Marshes
Middenheim
City of the White Wolf
Wolfenburg
River Urskoy
Kislev
The Empire
Worlds Edge Mountains
Marienburg
River Talabec
Bechafen
The Great Forest
Hergig
Carroburg
Karak Ungor
Red Eye Mountain
River Reik
Talabheim
Mordheim
(ruins)
Eerie Downs
Peak Pass
Gnashrak's Lair
Helmgart
Altdorf
Karak Kadrin
Slayer Keep
Axe Bite Pass
River Stir
Castle Drachenfels
Castle Reikguard
The Moot
Castle Drakenhof
The Desolation of Drakenmoor
Zhufbar
Nuln
Sylvania
Mount Gunbad
Blood Keep
River Sol
Black Water
Bugman's Brewery
Karak Varn
Cragmere
Black Fire Pass
Deadrock Gap
Karak Hirn
Horn Hold
Karaz-A-Karak
Everpeak
Border Princes
Mad Dog Pass
Skull River
Howling River
Barak Varr
Karag Dron
Thunder Mountain
100 Miles

The Warmaster Rides Forth

Of all the Old World nations, only the Empire has a professional standing army, each state raising and equipping its own regiments. Supporting the State Troops are the militia, formed from huntsmen of the forests, temporary Free Companies taken from the villages and towns, as well as mercenaries in many guises.

The Empire's capital city of Altdorf is the chief centre of magical learning in the Old World, and wizards come from all over to study at the Colleges of Magic. Thanks to the Emperor's careful patronage the Colleges provide the Empire with potent Battle Wizards. As well as College Battle Wizards, the armies of the Elector Counts are often accompanied by Warrior Priests of Sigmar, skilled in combat but more than this, able to steady the hearts of Men and instill in them abhorrence of the evil creatures of the world.

The Empire is also home to communities of Dwarfs whose forebears sought refuge there when their strongholds became untenable or fell to the Goblins. The Dwarfs have passed on a great deal of their technical knowledge, so that the Empire has many skilled metal workers and craftsmen who have created a bizarre arsenal of spectacular, if rather unreliable, weapons.

The Engineers School of Altdorf is the most famous of the institutions that teach and develop these skills, whereas the Gunnery School of Nuln is the foremost institute when it comes to creating great cannons and training the artillerists that man them. These are genuinely cosmopolitan places where people of many nations come together to study under some of the most learned Men in the Empire, perhaps the whole Old World.

Across the Empire can be found the keeps and houses of the Knightly Orders. There are many Orders of knights, foremost amongst them the Reiksguard – the Emperor's personal bodyguard. Amongst the most renowned of the other Knightly Orders are the Knights Panther, who trace their origins to the time of the Crusades, and the White Wolves of Middenheim – templars dedicated to Ulric, the god of battle, winter and wolves.

Together these warriors prosecute the wars of the Emperor and the Elector Counts, and defend the lands of the greatest realm of Men.

Back row, left to right: Halberdiers with Crossbowmen detachment, Greatswords, Helblaster Volley Gun, Mortar, Flagellants.

MORR - GOD OF THE DEAD

It is said that death is a soldier's companion. If this is the case, then as much as he gives veneration to the warrior gods Sigmar and Ulric, a soldier pays his due to Morr. Morr is the god of the dead and as such he is not openly worshipped. Those that take too much interest in the work of Morr are suspected of heinous deeds.

No matter what a person's most favoured god might be, it is Morr that rules over the dead – even a priest of Sigmar will eventually pass into the realm of Morr. To the people of the Old World Morr's underworld is a drab, numb place where souls flit about like bats, gradually forgetting their lives and losing their identities until they become mindless, twittering things. Remembrance of the dead feeds these souls and is seen as a duty for their descendants.

Cemeteries are called Gardens of Morr, where the dead are brought to the gates and handed over to the priests. After ritual preparation, the priests bury the corpses in one of the many mausoleums and tombs, which are built by the priests but paid for by the families of the dead. The Gardens are planted with the Black Roses of Morr. These are used in the funerary rites, while their petals are sometimes distilled by assassins into a sickly perfume that is said to cause death-like sleep. The priests of Morr form a bridge between this life and the next, and do not usually leave the Gardens of Morr. In the same way, the Gardens of Morr are not accessible to the living. Shrines in the walls of the Gardens of Morr face outwards and can be visited by the living so that they may offer up prayers for the dead and make donations to the priests.

Front row: Battle Wizard, Luthor Huss, Handgunners, Spearmen, Battle Standard Bearer, Emperor Karl Franz, Knights Panther, Pistoliers

BRETONNIA

Bretonnia lies to the south and west of the Empire between the Grey Mountains and the Middle Sea. To its south lies the vast Forest of Loren, home to the only permanent communities of Elves left in the Old World. The Bretonnians are ruled by a king whose castle rises high into the air in imitation of the ancient abandoned Elf towers along Bretonnia's northern coast, although it is in a constant state of repair and reconstruction like much of the country.

All Bretonnian knights are raised from childhood to practice their noble code of chivalry, which demands not only the highest standards of conduct, combat skills and horsemanship, but also states that knights fight to honour their lords and destroy the enemies of Bretonnia. The knights of Bretonnia are perhaps the most daring warriors in the Old World and they form the core of the Bretonnian army.

Compared to the large, wealthy and cosmopolitan cities of the Empire, the settlements of Bretonnia are parochial, run-down and impoverished. Though the king's court hall is hung with ancient, mouldering tapestries and decorated with fine golden carvings, the peasants live with large extended families in hovels gathered about the castle walls. So poor is the craft and trade of the land that the wealthiest knights will hire artisans from other parts of the Old World to build or maintain their keeps.

Bretonnian society is strictly feudal, where knights hold land on behalf of barons, whose duty is to their duke, and they in turn are the vassals of the king himself. This rigid hierarchy of responsibility extends right down to the lowest classes of society, the small farmers and peasantry. Few of these lowly individuals have any sort of military training because knights quite rightly regard the art of war as their exclusive province. The bulk of knights serving a duke will be young Knights Errant looking to prove themselves, and the Knights of the Realm who have already served in battle and earned their spurs.

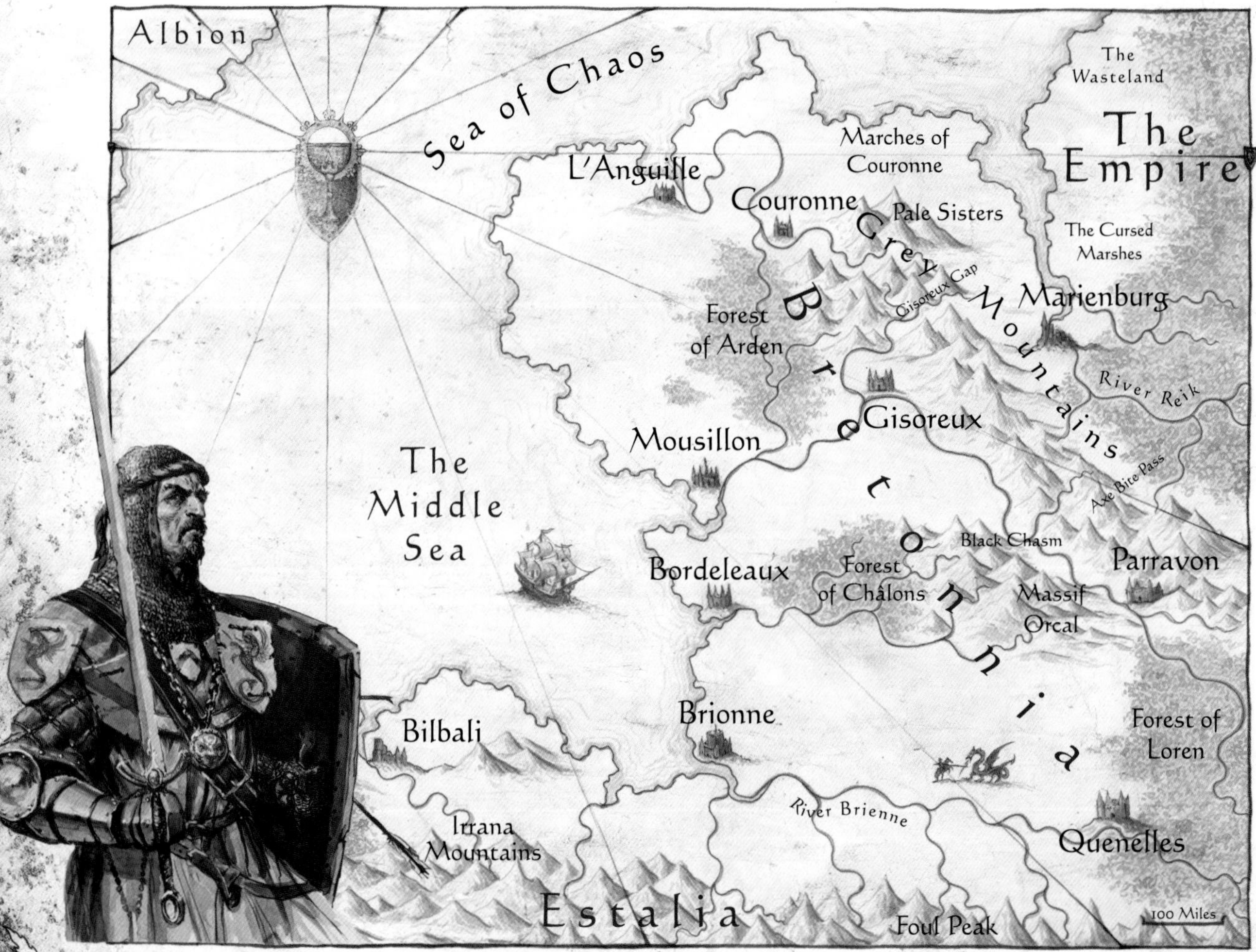

The Cleansing of Mousillon

Alongside the feudal hierarchy of the land there exists a spiritual one, stemming from the worship of the Lady of the Lake. The Lady is a mysterious goddess who is said to watch over the lands of Bretonnia and who aided the nation's founder, Gilles le Breton.

Every year a number of knights eschew their worldly possessions to seek out the favour of the Lady. They give up the trappings of whatever station they occupied and become Questing Knights. These knights travel all across the world seeking the Lady, to prove themselves pure and honourable. Few succeed in finding her, and those that do must sup from her fabled cup.

Possessed of magical powers, the grail of the Lady is the final test and those that survive become Grail Knights. These enigmatic warriors live a hermit existence, defending places sacred to the Lady, but in battle several Grail Knights may gather to lend their considerable strength of arms. Often a Grail Knight is followed by Battle Pilgrims – half-crazed peasants who wish to share in the Lady's favour,

Castle: Damsel of the Lady, King Leoncoeur, Bretonnian Lord. Far Rear: Pegasus Knights. Back row: Peasant Bowmen, Field Trebuchet. Middle row: Men-at-arms, Paladin,

often carrying into battle the relics of dead knights as a sign of their devotion.

While the loftiest ideals of personal bravery and strength can be found throughout the many knights of the land, there is a much grimmer existence for its vast peasant population. Generations of inbreeding mean that the peasants are, for the most part, ill-fed, downtrodden and physically deformed, and little use as soldiers. For their part, the knights are far superior in physique and ability, and often fail to see the woeful conditions the peasantry must endure.

In battle, the knights are supported by small bodies of men-at-arms crudely equipped by the knights; in effect their own private retinues of soldiers whose role is to protect their master's lands and guard his castle. In times of extreme danger the peasantry may be equipped and brought along to battle, but on the whole they make poor soldiers and the knights expect little of them. Most useful of this peasant militia are the bowmen, trained from an early age. These archers often protect their position with sharpened stakes to deter enemy charges.

Grail Reliquae with Battle Pilgrims. Front Row: Mounted Yeomen, Knights Errant, Questing Knights, Battle Standard Bearer, Grail Knights, Knights of the Realm.

KISLEV

Kislev is the most northern of the lands of the Old World proper and the closest to the Daemon-infested Chaos Wastes. It is a cold land bordered to the east by the Worlds Edge Mountains, and by the Sea of Claws to the west. In the northlands every town and village is heavily defended because the lands are infested with Chaos warbands and marauding monsters. The plains of the east are sparsely inhabited by nomad horse tribes; expert riders and archers born to the saddle. The western and southern tundra is more densely inhabited with many fortified settlements.

Kislev is ruled by great warrior-mages called Tzars and Tzarinas, who have potent magical powers rooted in their own elemental Ice Magic. The Kislevites are long-standing allies of the Empire. In times of great danger the two realms unite to overcome the perils of Chaos. This relationship has lasted for many centuries with only the occasional dispute that has set the two nations against each other.

The warriors of Kislev are amongst the finest cavalry in the Old World, with the resplendent Winged Lancers considered experts with horse and lance, aided by the Ungol Horse Archers from the eastern tribes. These are supported by Kossar infantry drawn from all across the lands of Kislev, trained to fight with bows and axes.

OTHER NATIONS

There are countless smaller realms of Men but none so powerful as the mighty kingdom of Bretonnia or the states of the Empire. The parched lands of Estalia to the far south comprise many tiny kingdoms, for example, few of which are known beyond the confines of Estalia itself. Similarly, the city states of Tilea are numerous and varied, but even all together they are not comparable to the nations of the north. Both Estalians and Tileans are traders and travellers, the Tileans in particular are renowned as mercenaries and adventurers. It is not unusual to find Estalian merchants in the north, and their mule caravans frequently tour the cities of the southern Empire.

The highlands where the Grey Mountains and Worlds Edge Mountains meet are known as the Vaults, and are inhabited by fierce mountain clans who guard the few passes and extort a heavy toll from merchants travelling between the Empire and the lands to the south. These mountain people sometimes travel down into the Reikland to join the Empire's armies. East of here is a large, wild area called the Border Land or the land of the Border Princes. This realm is extremely dangerous, full of marauding Orcs and wolf-riding Goblins as well as the worst kind of Men – bandits, brigands and

Back Row: Ungol Horse Archers, Kislev Kossars. Front Row: Gryphon Legion, Boris Ursus – the Red Tzar, Winged Lancers

Back Row: Braganza's Besiegers. Middle Row: Giant, Ruglud's Armoured Orcs. Front Row: Pirazzo's Lost Legion, Lorenzo Lupo, Long Drong's Slayer Pirates

outcasts from the rest of the Old World. These are new lands that adventurers and brave settlers are trying to civilise, and eventually where they will raise new cities and found new realms. Meanwhile it is a dangerous, but potentially profitable, place where honest Men live behind high wooden stockades under the protection of dispossessed nobles called Border Princes.

BEYOND THE OLD WORLD

There are other nations of Men outside of the Old World, though only the Grand Empire of Cathay in the East rivals its power and wealth. Cathay is a huge, sprawling land of different peoples and cultures, bound together by the rule of the supposedly immortal Celestial Dragon Emperor. It is a long and perilous journey to Cathay from the Old World, whether across the Dark Lands and the Mountains of Mourn, or by sea around the jungle-covered Southlands. Silks, ivory and other luxuries fetch high prices in the markets of the Old World, and so there are always those foolish or greedy enough to risk such journeys.

Even further east lies the nation of Ind, called the Land of a Thousand Gods. Exotic spices, jade and other treasures lure the adventurous to this sweltering realm, although few return. Some fall prey to bestial creatures on the route to Ind, others are captured and sacrificed by bloodthirsty cults. However, travellers that do return report that the rulers of Ind are wealthy and generous, living in opulent palaces surrounded by slaves and servants, and are great patrons of the arts and Ind's many golden temples.

South of the Old World, beyond the Border Princes and the Badlands, can be found the desert cities of Araby. Separated from the Undead-haunted ancient tombs of Nehekhara by a virtually impenetrable desert, the Arabyans' cities are clustered along the coastline and so Arabyans are merchants and corsairs for the most part.

Arabyans trade freely with others, including the Elves; they are also willing to set sail and take by piracy what they cannot buy. Arabyan merchants are not uncommon in the city of Marienburg and even further afield, and the sailors of Araby are acclaimed navigators, frequently to be found in the employ of shipmasters from other nations.

CHAOS

The people of the Old World live in constant fear of Chaos. To them it is an evil eating away at their society and creating armies on their borders; a destructive force subservient only to bizarre and cruel Dark Gods. To the far north of the Old World lie the Realms of Chaos, the breeding ground of mutated monsters and the refuge of roaming warbands.

Very few Old Worlders have ever been to the Realms of Chaos, but tales speak of a land of perpetual darkness lit only by monumental pillars of flame. Myths tells of days that run backwards and of a land where great champions from past times still fight on, trapped in a timeless world of eternal battle. Stories containing countless other perversions of time and space that change and mutate in an unpredictable way, can be heard n many Old World taverns.

From this nightmare region the armies of Chaos sweep down. As armies move south, the Realm of Chaos grows, fed by the slaughter of battle and wanton destruction, and the terror of the Chaos army's foes. The land itself is changed and twisted. It becomes absorbed into the horrific Chaos Wastes – the blasted lands surrounding the Realms of Chaos.

Several times in the history of the Old World the armies of Chaos have swept down through the northlands and overwhelmed everything in their path. These major invasions are rare, and though so far have been beaten back, it is always at terrible cost and the lands not wholly reclaimed. One day will come the last incursion, when the Realms of Chaos will expand so greatly that the entire world is engulfed. Known by many as The End Times, some Old Worlders believe that this apocalyptic battle has already begun.

The Chaos Wastes and Chaos armies are the playthings of the Chaos gods. There are many Chaos gods, with outlandish unpronounceable names, but the most important by far are the Great Powers, of which there are four: Khorne, the Blood God, is the most warlike and bloodthirsty; Slaanesh, the Lord of Pleasure, is seductive and enticing; Nurgle, the Lord of Decay, is the master of disease and physical corruption; and Tzeentch, the Changer of the Ways, is the architect of change whose chief tool is magic.

The Rising of the Chaos Beast

BEASTS OF CHAOS

The creatures of Chaos are not restricted solely to the Chaos Wastes by any means. The Old World is a vast and wild land, where cities and towns are little more than outposts of order amid a world of midnight horrors, where monsters prowl the sunless forests. The Beasts of Chaos live in warherds in the deep forests, from where they raid, fight with rival warbands and sometimes organise into armies to storm larger towns and castles.

Beastmen call themselves the Children of Chaos – many hundreds of years ago their forebears were ordinary humans and animals who became mutated by the coming of Chaos and turned into the half-man, half-beast forms.

All Beastmen are brutish in the extreme and much given to celebrating their victories with wild dancing, ritual head-butting and excesses of drunkenness. They care nothing for human life and often raid lone farmsteads in the dead of night, dragging their occupants from their beds and slaughtering them.

There are many other monsters beside Beastmen including bull-headed Minotaurs, horse-like Centigors and powerful Dragon Ogres, and those so misshapen and grotesque they are simply called Chaos Spawn.

All of these creatures are the creations of Chaos in some way or other. Not all of these creatures are intelligent, indeed many are ravening beasts and some are drooling, insane masses of pulsating flesh that must be goaded into battle if they are to be of any use.

Back row: Chaos Spawn, Dragon Ogres. Middle row: Beastmen Chariot, Chaos Trolls, Minotaurs, Chaos Hounds, Chaos Giant.

THE ENEMY WITHIN

Chaos champions and their warbands are forced to live in the forests and mountains. All normal Men fear and abhor Chaos, and no city in the Old World would tolerate the presence of a Chaos follower. However, not all followers of Chaos are so obviously marked that they are immediately recognised.

Men live in perpetual terror of the Enemy Within, the hidden followers of Chaos who they fear will mass together and destroy them one day. They are quite right to be afraid, as there are many agents of Chaos at work within the cities of Men, recruiting new followers, consulting their daemon masters by means of arcane ceremonies, and slowly but surely infiltrating the houses of the powerful. As the years pass, they build a network that extends from town to town and city to city.

These cults plot to overthrow the rule of civilised Men, summoning Daemons and casting spells with dark ceremonies. One day the End Times will come, and the followers of Chaos within the cities of Men will be ready to rise up and join the Chaos champions, Daemons, and Beastmen in the final battle for possession of the world.

Front row: Centigors, Khorngor, Bray-shaman, Khazrak the One-eye, Battle Standard Bearer, Gor and Ungor Beast Herd, Dragon Ogre Shaggoth.

CHAMPIONS OF CHAOS

The Chaos gods value their human followers far above their own minions, the Daemons that serve them and creatures of Chaos whose forebears they created, for Daemons and beasts of Chaos have little choice about their nature. The only way the Chaos gods can increase their power is by recruiting Men or other intelligent free-willed creatures to their cause.

The most important followers of Chaos are therefore Champions of Chaos – warriors chosen by the Chaos gods as their greatest servants.

Some of these souls are easily won; brigands, bandits and outcasts who would willingly follow any leader that brought them plunder and offered them protection. Such individuals are all too common in the Old World but there are few strong willed and powerful enough to turn into true Chaos Warriors.

The Chaos gods take great interest in their champions and will favour them with all manner of gifts including magical weapons, armour and talismans, arcane abilities and – strangest of all – physical mutations such as tentacles, bestial faces and razor-sharp talons. These gifts are borne with pride by the champion as a symbol of his complete allegiance to his master. The champions are representatives of the Chaos gods and as such they constantly strive to outdo each other. Sometimes their masters send them visions or direct them to band together and with other creatures of Chaos to destroy an army or sack a castle. On other occasions the champions will be deliberately set upon each other to determine who is fit to be rewarded with fresh gifts.

The ultimate reward for a successful champion is that he should be gifted with immortality as a Daemon Prince, so that he can live forever by his master's side and continue to fight on his behalf. It is this dream that drives the Chaos champions onwards, although only a very few will achieve immortality. Most champions will either die in combat or their masters will reward them with so many horrendous mutations that they become mindless slavering Spawn: monsters with malformed bodies and only the barest recollection of their former glory.

Engra Deathsword, Destroyer of Praag

HORDES OF CHAOS

The great bulk of the northern hordes of Chaos is made up of tribes of vicious, dedicated Marauders. These barbaric men live on the boundaries of the Realms of Chaos, upon the wide steppes and barren wilderness regions known as the Chaos Wastes. The nomadic tribes war with each other constantly for the pleasure of their gods, for slaves and for glory, and frequently raid the lands of other nations. From amongst the ranks of Marauders come some of the most deadly fighters in the world; the fearsomely armed and armoured Warriors and Knights of Chaos. Often gifted with unnatural strength and toughness by their gods, these fighters are feared the world over. The Marauder tribes are split into three main peoples, although in total there are scores of tribes, possibly even hundreds; no one knows truly how many Marauders live in the Chaos Wastes.

The Norse are barbarians whose wild drinking and fighting are legendary in the civilised lands to the south. They wear skins of animals and live in halls made from solid tree trunks. They hunt all kind of ferocious animals including wild wolves, bears and the monstrous mamut. All Norse are hairy with bristling beards and long hair that they often twist into plaits. They are big, hardy Men, with bulging muscles due to the constant exercise of rowing their Dragonships in search of fresh plunder. The Norse raid the shores of the Old World and waylay any ships they can find. Their warriors are feared and respected, and despite their ferocity and drunken habits they are also much in demand as mercenaries throughout the other realms of Men.

East of Norsca, across the High Pass of the northern Worlds Edge Mountains, is the land of the Kurgan. These dark-haired savages live even closer to the

Back row: Plaguebearers. Battle Standard Bearer, Horrors. Middle row: Marauders of Chaos, Aspiring Champion of Chaos, Daemonettes,

Realms of Chaos than the Norse, and are amongst the most bloodthirsty and vicious servants of the Chaos gods. They constantly raid each other for sacrifices to the Dark Powers, but on occasion one will rise from amongst their number to conquer or unite several tribes and set upon a whirlwind invasion of destruction and bloodshed. These invasions are often short-lived, as the tribes eventually fall out with one another, but the carnage left in their wake leaves scars for many generations. The Kurgan are great horsemen and hunters, and groups of fast-moving reivers armed with throwing axes and long spears are often the only heralds of the slaughter to come.

North of Cathay and the chill lands of Naggaroth can be found the Hung tribes. They are even more nomadic than the Kurgan, virtually living in the saddles of their sturdy steppe ponies. As well as assailing the watchtowers of the Dark Elves, the Hung are a constant threat to the lands of Cathay. They are kept at bay by the Great Bastion, a towering wall that stretches the entire breadth of Cathay's northern border. Garrisoned by thousands of warriors, even the Great Bastion is no defence against every Hung raid, and the northern provinces of Cathay live in constant terror of these barbaric marauders.

Those Marauders that become sufficiently proficient at their war craft will win better arms and armour and become Warriors and Knights of Chaos. Amongst the most fearsome fighters in the whole world, these behemoths of destruction often bear the Mark of their gods and show signs of mutation.

On the steppes east of the Worlds Edge Mountains, some tribes ride huge chariots into battle. Sporting banners proclaiming the riders' allegiances and with viciously scythed wheels, these chariots are pulled into battle by mutant beasts; sometimes powerfully strong horses but just as often strange lizard creatures or warped bears and wolves.

The most powerful Champions bind to their armies regiments of Daemonic warriors, but such bargains are rarely spoken of even in Marauder society.

Sorcerer of Chaos, Bloodthirster. Front Row: Chariot of Chaos, Knights of Chaos, Archaon, Bloodletters, Warriors of Chaos.

ELVES

Elves are one of the oldest of all the races, steeped in magic and held in awe by the people of the Old World. Though few Old Worlders realise it, their society, language and even some of their cities are all built upon the foundations laid down by the Elves when the world was young.

Elves are tall and very proud in their bearing and manner. Their bodies are slim but surprisingly strong for their size. Elves are pale skinned and their finely chiselled faces are slender and hairless, with disturbing, almond-shaped eyes that carry their ancient wisdom.

They can move exceptionally swiftly, and are dextrous and agile. Elven movements are performed with an efficient precision that a Man would be incapable of, allowing the Elves to achieve feats of weapons mastery and the mystical arts that is simply beyond lesser races.

All Elves are magical beings, in the sense that they can see the magical energy that permeates the world, and have at least a basic knowledge of its manipulation. This affinity means Elves learn spellcasting much more readily than other races, and they can achieve levels of wizardry beyond any race except the ancient Slann.

In general, Elves live for many centuries, but there are those amongst their number who may live longer, some of them for thousands of years. Though they are very long-lived, Elves are not immortal, and their numbers have slowly dwindled over the ages. They do not reproduce quickly and so are slow to replace their losses.

However, they are generally immune to the effects of old age until their death, showing none of the increasing physical frailties that Man has, and are resistant to disease and infirmity, and also the physical corruption of Chaos.

Their long lives allow the Elves to dedicate decades, even centuries, to learning their skills and crafts, and as such achieve a level of experience that none other than the Dwarfs can match.

Over time, the Elves have become a divided race, spread across the globe, split into distinct cultures. There are three major types of Elves: the High Elves of Ulthuan, the Dark Elves of Naggaroth, and the Wood Elves of Athel Loren. Regardless of their divisions from each other, all Elves still have many things in common.

They all retain their aesthetic sense, honed over many generations, and everything they make, even from the roughest materials, is well crafted. They are sophisticated, literate and intellectual, although the way they think is very different from that of a Man or Dwarf.

Athel Loren Awakens

WOOD ELVES

The Wood Elf realm of Athel Loren is all that remains of the once numerous Elven colonies of the Old World. Thousands of years ago when the Elves and Dwarfs fought their long and bitter war, most of these colonies were destroyed. The Elves left the Old World to face new troubles at home, in the land of Ulthuan where war was brewing between the High Elves and the Dark Elves. However, not all the Elven colonists abandoned the colonies, a few refused to do so, and retreated instead into the vastness of Loren Forest. These were to become the Asrai, the Wood Elves.

As they took to their new lives the Elves discovered places in the forest where magic was strongest, and there they set stones to fix the magic and contain it safely. As the Elves encroached upon its borders, the forest responded, primeval spirits emerging from trees and stones. Few Elves dared to enter the woods, and it took many years for the forest to trust the Elves that came to make it their home, whilst in far away lands the very name of Athel Loren is enough to conjure images of sorcerous deception and mysterious power.

The Wood Elves have relinquished all former ties with Ulthuan and its Phoenix Kings, and have chosen to tread their own path of wisdom and natural lore. Today the Wood Elves shun contact with other races and show no mercy to those who invade their woodland realm or who cause malicious damage to its ancient trees. The space around their realm is distorted by means of strange enchantments, so that it is almost impossible to enter Athel Loren without the leave of the Wood Elves themselves. Any that wander unwelcome into the greenwoods soon meet with an untimely end.

Back row, left to right: Wild Riders, Dryads, Treeman, Tree Kin. Middle row: Spellweaver, Drycha the Branchwraith, Eternal Guard,

The Queen, Ariel, and her consort, Orion, are not the only other-wordly beings to live alongside the Wood Elves. From before the coming of the Elves, Athel Loren was home to many spirits, formed from the power of the forest itself.

Most numerous are the spiteful, vindictive Dryads, who act as consorts to the more powerful Tree Kin and the mighty Treemen. The oldest Treemen are truly ancient and can remember the time before Men and Elves, and some perhaps were old even when Chaos came into the world.

Wood Elves are insular and often distrust even each other. They prefer to fight guerrilla wars against invaders of their forest home, but when a threat cannot be halted in this way, the Kindreds gather in larger numbers, putting aside their differences in the face of the common foe.

The bow is the Wood Elves' principle weapon, although they are not afraid of hand-to-hand fighting as they are very skilled warriors. They tend not to wear heavy armour, preferring to move as quickly as possible through the dense woods. Alongside the bow-armed Glade Guard fight the highly skilled warriors of the Eternal Guard, sworn to protect Ariel. They are aided by Scouts skilled in infiltration and disrupting the enemy army, although their skills pale in comparison to the deadly, secretive Waywatchers.

Even more outlandish are the Wardancers of Kurnous, whose skills and acrobatic abilities combine all the grace and elegance of dance with deadly weapon craft. When not fighting, they are lords of dancing and feasting, and they travel Athel Loren singing tales of ancient heroes and battles fought when Athel Loren was first found.

The mounted warriors of most Wood Elf Kindreds are the Glade Riders, but some have learned to ride upon the backs of giant Warhawks, or have befriended the Great Eagles that live in the Grey Mountains. Stranger still are the Wild Riders of Orion; Elves that have sworn their lives to the hunting lord of the Wood Elves and are no longer wholly mortal.

Wardancers, Warhawk Riders. Front row: Glade Riders, Waywatchers, Battle Standard Bearer, Highborn on Great Stag, Glade Guard

HIGH ELVES

Many thousands of years ago the High Elves of the kingdoms of Ulthuan, who call themselves the Asur, sailed across the Great Ocean to the Old World far to the east of their island continent. There they discovered the Dwarfs, and the fathers of Men, and built cities along the coasts for their ships to harbour. In those days, the swift ships of the Elves were busy indeed, carrying Dwarf gold and precious stones back to Ulthuan, returning with rare woods, silk and exotic wares from the far west. Whilst Dwarfs burrowed and mined beneath the mountains, the Elves raised tall towers amongst the forests, and both races prospered.

This state of harmony did not last as perhaps was inevitable given the very different natures of the two races. For whilst Dwarfs are quiet, serious, hardworking and materialistic with little time for frivolity, the Elves are a richly talented and expressive race, quick to laughter and song, but proud and haughty in their dealings with others.

The war between the Dwarfs and Elves lasted for many years and caused unending bitterness between the two races. Eventually the Elves abandoned the Old World and sailed back to their own realms in the far west. The High Elves have no permanent settlements of their own in the Old World any more, although trading ships still ply the seas between Ulthuan, the kingdom of Bretonnia, and the great trading port of Marienburg. This last city has a substantial Elven quarter inhabited by merchants and adventurers. Elves and Men trade and prosper, and on the whole relations between the two races are good. When the need of the Emperor or Bretonnian King is great, Elven armies sail to the lands of Men to support their struggle against the many great evils that beset the world.

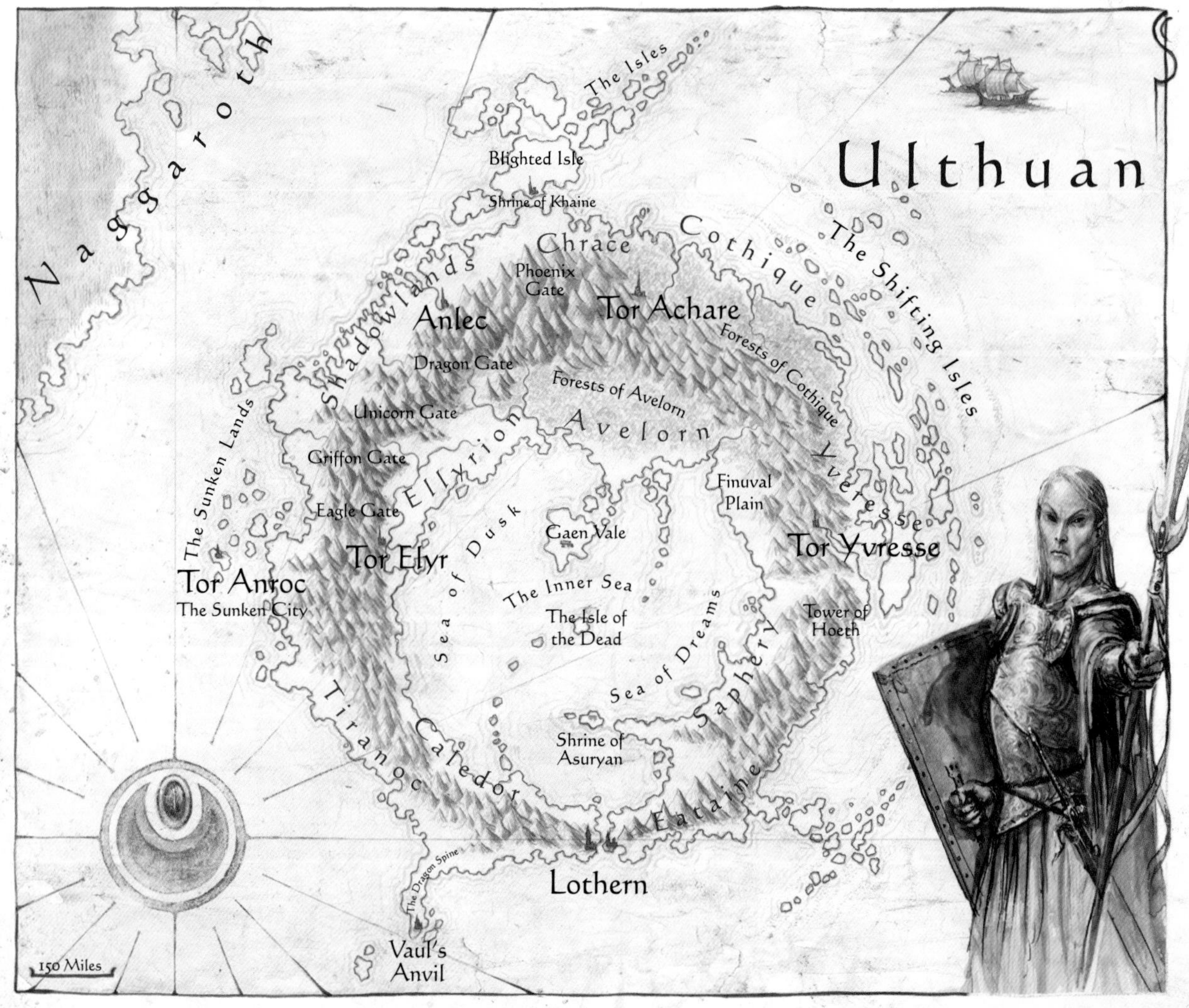

Teclis of Ulthuan

Although Elves are not wantonly aggressive, the people of Ulthuan are haughty and their lords are proud of their status. Wars between the kingdoms are often swift and bloody, for Elves are determined and mighty warriors.

From the time of Aenarion, the Elven armies have waged war in the interests of protecting Ulthuan and the wider world. The Dark Elves are the most hate-filled and implacable of foes, their raiders land upon the broken isles of the north and pour south destroying and slaying as they advance. Keeping them at bay is an eternal battle and one that has cost the lives of many brave Elves over the centuries.

Due to the constant Dark Elf raids, all High Elves must learn the art of war from an early age and become accomplished warriors with spears, swords and bows. Those of noble birth learn to ride with exceptional skill, and they are taught to bear the arms of the Silver Helms, as the High Elven knights are named. With tall lances, glittering armour, highbrowed helmets and long plumes, the Silver Helms are the proudest and most deadly amongst their own kingdoms.

Other Elves fight in tight phalanxes armed with glittering spears, protecting the ranks of deadly archers that form the rest of the army's core. These are supported by swift-firing Eagle's Claw bolt throwers that can launch a hail of spear-like bolts at the enemy.

The kingdoms of the outer coast of Ulthuan are more used to battle, for they are exposed to the raids of Dark Elves and fierce Norsemen. From here hail the Shadow Warriors; magnificent scouts whose hearts have become deadened to the horror of war through centuries of bitter fighting. The great Mists of Yvresse and swift ships from the Kingdom of Cothique protect the eastern approaches, and Elven fleets patrol the wide oceans.

To the north, the dour Elves of Chrace – foremost amongst them being the fierce White Lions who act as bodyguard to the Phoenix King – and the vengeful chariot-riding folk of Tiranoc guard the approaches from Naggaroth and the Shadowlands. These warriors have fought a long war against the legions of Naggaroth.

Rear left: Teclis. Back row: Archers, White Lions of Chrace, Repeater Bolt Thrower, Ellyrian Reavers, Spearmen.

From the lands of Caledor come the Dragon Princes, who once rode to battle atop the backs of mighty drakes. Now the Dragons rarely wake from their slumber and the Dragon Princes wage war from armoured Elven steeds. Though their power is much diminished from the time when the Elves were at their height, they are still a match for even the toughest foes.

The swift Reaver Knights of Ellyria are mounted archers and expert horsemen. They ride ahead of the Elven host to spy out the land and locate the foe. In battle their fast steeds take them around the flanks of the enemy, where the Reavers can harass the enemy line or attack into the rear, sowing confusion and disorder.

Just as accomplished are the silent Phoenix Guard. Guardians of the sacred flame of the god Asuryan, the Phoenix Guard are fearsome foes matching their skill with their halberds with an eerie silence that can unman even the most seasoned veteran.

Ulthuan is the most magical part of the whole world outside the Realms of Chaos, and the High Elves have developed their spells far beyond the accomplishments of even the other Elven societies. The forces of magic have been harnessed to protect the land of Ulthuan itself, for without the conjurations of the Elves the entire continent would sink beneath the waves forever.

In Hoeth, the slender pillar of the White Tower rises high into the azure skies. Here the greatest loremasters and mages of the Elves hone their magical arts. The High Elven mages are mighty and versatile spellcasters whose fiery blasts and protective enchantments have won many battles for the Phoenix King and his generals. It was the Elven Loremaster Teclis that, in years past, taught colour magic to Men, although the Elves far surpass the wizards of the Colleges of Magic in their power, skill and knowledge.

Protecting Hoeth from attack are the Swordmasters. Having dedicated their lives to mastering the skill of their long blades, they are swift and deadly beyond compare. Very few foes have opposed the Swordmasters in battle and survived to warn of their unsurpassed skill.

Front row: Swordmasters of Hoeth, Tiranoc Chariot, Dragon Princes of Caledor, Tyrion, Silver Helms, Phoenix Guard.

DARK ELVES

The Dark Elves were driven from the Elven land of Ulthuan many centuries ago and now live in the northern regions of Naggaroth: the bleak and unwelcoming Land of Chill. Dark Elves, or Druchii as they are called in Elvish, are close kin of the High Elves – although Dark Elves have extremely pallid skin in comparison to their old rivals.

Whereas the High Elves have always taken great care to protect themselves from dangerous magical energies, especially Chaos Daemons, the Dark Elves long ago embraced the gods of Chaos and make dark pacts with daemonic forces to unleash devastating spells upon their enemies and to gain magical power. The natural skill of the Elves and the unnatural vitality of Chaos are mated together in the Dark Elves, so that they have become the ultimate masters of dark sorcery.

Dark Elf armies set off from the harbour of Har Ganeth in huge Daemon-infested ships. When they reach their objectives, the Dark Elves rampage and destroy as much as they can, before retiring with their plunder back to Naggaroth. Many of their raids are undertaken for captives, which they take back to their sorcerous towers. Few have ever escaped from slavery at the hands of the Dark Elves, but such tales as are known speak of the Daemon-haunted dungeons of the Witch King, of living sacrifices to the God of Murder, and of souls seared to fuel the sorcery of Naggaroth.

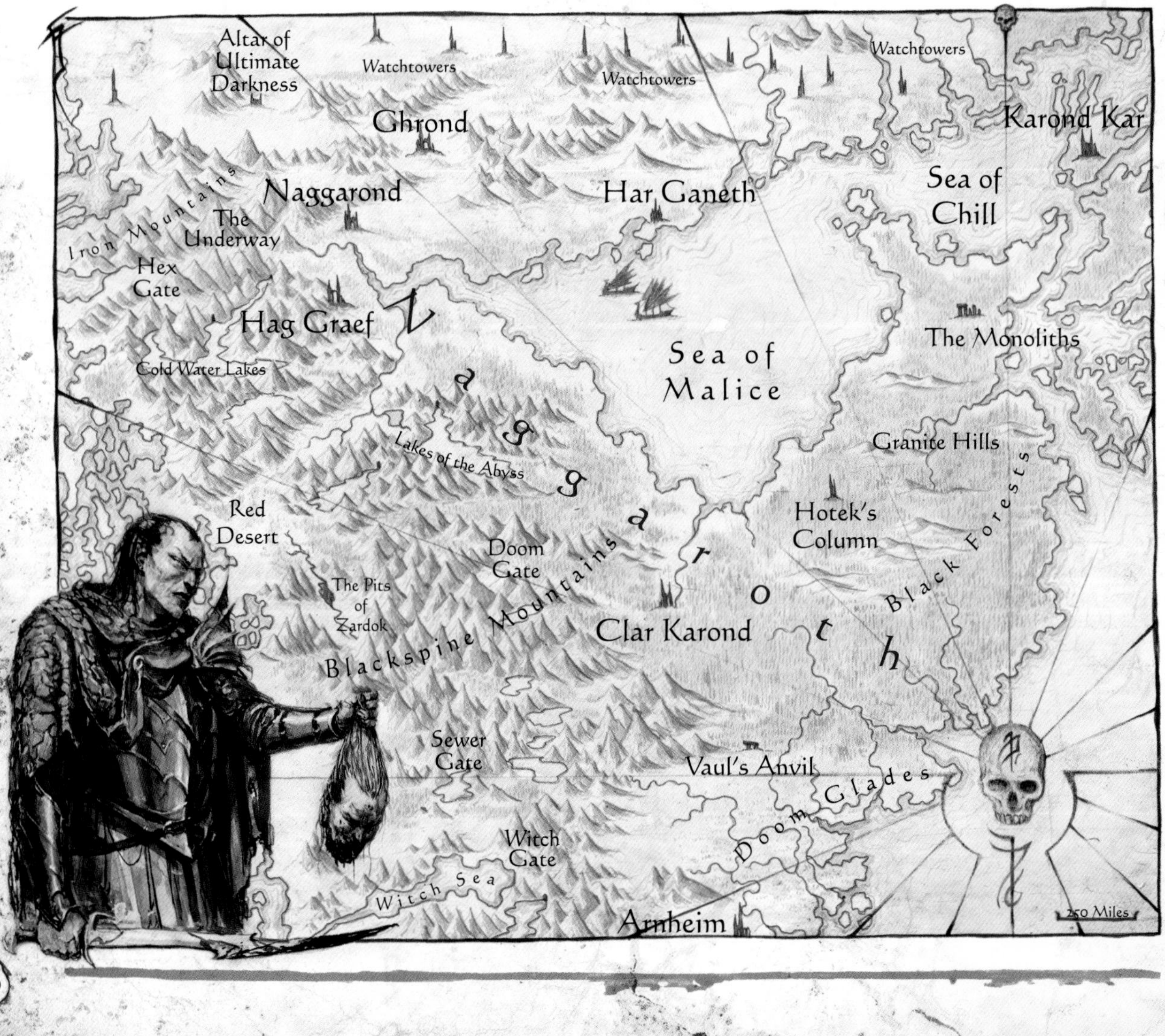

Altar of Ultimate Darkness
Watchtowers
Watchtowers
Watchtowers
Ghrond
Karond Kar
Naggarond
Har Ganeth
Sea of Chill
Iron Mountains
The Underway
Hex Gate
Hag Graef
Naggaroth
The Monoliths
Sea of Malice
Cold Water Lakes
Lakes of the Abyss
Granite Hills
Red Desert
Hotek's Column
Black Forests
Doom Gate
The Pits of Zardok
Blackspine Mountains
Clar Karond
Sewer Gate
Vaul's Anvil
Doom Glades
Witch Gate
Witch Sea
Arnheim
250 Miles

Malekith's Dark Vengeance

The backbone of the Witch King's armies are the City Guard, composed of vicious spearmen and warriors wielding repeater crossbows – a weapon capable of unleashing a hail of barbed bolts to tear through the enemy.

While these Dark Elf Warriors make up the bulk of Naggaroth's armies, it is the Corsairs of the Black Arks that are more likely to be encountered in the raiding parties that loot and pillage across the globe. Protected by cloaks made from the hides of sea dragons, the Corsairs lead the attack on the enemy.

Known simply as Dark Riders, the light cavalry of the army scouts out the foe, allowing the Dark Elves to spring their attack with perfect timing and surprise. When in Naggaroth, the Dark Riders make sport of chasing down escaped slaves, often giving them a head start of several days before setting off in pursuit. Few slaves have ever survived over the centuries to tell the ordeal of being hunted by these relentless pursuers.

The cities of the Dark Elves rise from the bleak land of Naggaroth like dark stalagmites, fortresses of pain and suffering for those captured on the raids. Amongst such dreaded places, the city of Har Ganeth has an even darker reputation, for it is home to the Executioners. Wielding double-handed blades called draich, the Executioners can decapitate a foe with a single sweep.

From Hag Graef hail the Beastmasters. Experts in controlling the creatures hunted in the caverns beneath the Blackspine Mountains and the depths of the Sea of Malice, the Beastmasters ride or goad their charges into battle. The most favoured mount is the Manticore, a hideous winged creature believed by the Dark Elves to be an aspect of Khaine. Apprentice Beastmasters drive fire-breathing Hydras into battle.

Smaller creatures are also captured and bred, foremost among them being the Cold Ones. These stinking, reptilian beasts are used as steeds by the Knights of Naggaroth, while the nobility of the Druchii often ride to battle in chariots pulled by these brutal but stupid creatures.

Perhaps most potent of all the Witch King's followers are the spellcasters of the Convents of Sorceresses. The Dark Arts of these hellmages are made possible by the power of infernal pacts with daemonic forces.

. Back row: Assassin, Warriors with repeater crossbows, Witch Elves, Dark Riders, Sorceress, Repeater Bolt Thrower. Rear left: Shades. Rear centre:

THE CULT OF KHAINE

Dark Elf women are just as deadly as their menfolk, and they are equally adept warriors, fighting alongside their males in battle. The wildest of all are the Witch Elves – a warrior sisterhood devoted to Khaine, Lord of Murder. They are the cruellest of all the Dark Elves and the most bloodthirsty. After a battle they choose victims to sacrifice to Khaine and fill cauldrons of blood in which they bathe – renewing their dark pact with the Lord of Murder.

Witch Elves eat only the flesh of sacrifices and they drink blood to which they add strong poisonous herbs, which cause nightmarish hallucinations and send them into frenzied dancing and obscene revelries. The Witch Elves live in the temples of Khaine under the glowering eyes of their Hag Queens. The Hag Queens are extremely ancient, and once a year they take part in the riotous celebrations of Death Night when the Witch Elves prowl the streets and steal away Dark Elves they find, sometimes breaking into houses to take petrified Elves away for sacrifice.

On Death Night the Hag Queens bathe in blood to restore themselves – at which time they are the most enchanting and voluptuous of all Elves, whose strangely cadaverous beauty is more powerful and captivating than any magic. Over the year they revert into the haggard crones that they really are, until Death Night comes round once more and Dark Elves hide in their homes, listening to evil laughter of the midnight celebrations of the Witch Elves. The Witch Elves steal away male children to raise in the temples to be assassins, and these are the most deadly and evil Dark Elves of all. They are masters of subtle and murderous magic, learned in poison lore and unparalleled in weapon craft.

War Hydra. Front row: Cold One Knights, Black Guard, Malus Darkblade, Executioners, Battle Standard Bearer, Spearmen, Cold One Chariot

ORCS & GOBLINS

Orcs are ferocious raiders and relentless warriors. Their constant attacks threaten to engulf the lands of the Old World and plunge the entire continent into a dark age of endless and unremitting warfare. Goblins are smarter than Orcs but nowhere near as warlike. They are cunning rather than strong, and rely a great deal on their Orcish cousins when it comes to the serious business of bashing heads.

Orcs and Goblins share a common ancestry with each other and with their smaller relatives, the Snotlings. They are all, to use a Human term, greenskins.

All Orcs and Goblins live in tribes some of which are huge with thousands of individuals, others are little more than warbands of a few hundred warriors. Tribes are led by a powerful chieftain called a Warboss or, if he is very strong, a Warlord. The more successful a Warboss is, the more Orcs or Goblins will flock to join his tribe. As the tribe gets bigger, the Warboss leads it to fight bigger battles, so he either becomes more famous still and his tribe gets even bigger or he is finally killed and his tribe breaks apart.

As Orcs enjoy fighting more than anything else, a successful Orc always tries to find bigger and more powerful opponents, until eventually he has to face a large Imperial or Bretonnian army, or a strong force of Dwarfs or Chaos Warriors. This is why Orcs are so dangerous, once a powerful Warboss starts to win battles, Orcs from all over the Old World will mass around him, anticipating fresh conquests and glorious victories. It is the fact that all Orcs live to fight that makes them so dangerous; it is also their greatest weakness as it means they expend much of their energy fighting each other. As tribes are constantly fighting amongst themselves and breaking up, there is never any shortage of Orcs and Goblins wandering about, ready to ally themselves under a powerful leader.

Orc and Goblin tribes live all over the Old World in areas that are sparsely inhabited or where Men cannot build their homes. They also found on the boundaries of the Old World in the lands to the south and east, and it is in these areas where they are most prolific. If there can be said to be an Orc homeland it is probably the area between the southern Worlds Edge Mountains and the Black Mountains known as the Badlands, and the foothills of the Worlds Edge Mountains between Blood River and Black Fire Pass. These areas are infested with Orc tribes, and the adjoining lands of the Border Princes are little better, although fortified settlements maintain the presence of Men on the very edge of civilisation. There are also many Orcs and Goblins inside the Old World, especially in the high mountain passes and deep forests that are virtually impenetrable to Men.

The Green Horde

ORCS

Orcs vary in height and physical appearance more than humans; some are no taller than a Man but many are substantially larger and the biggest Orcs stand well over seven feet tall. They are also much broader than Men, with massive shoulders and long, powerfully muscled arms. Orcs have large heads with huge jaws but tiny foreheads behind which lurks a thick skull and not very much brain.

Orcs are not the deepest thinkers in the world, but neither are they doubtful or divided – when an Orc wants to do something, he does it. This single-mindedness is their greatest strength, especially as Orcs enjoy fighting more than anything else. Orcs spend their whole lives fighting each other to establish their right to lead other Orcs.

A Warlord is an Orc who has either killed or driven away all of his rivals, and now leads several tribes in glorious conquest over other puny races such as Men, Elves and Dwarfs. The more battles and the more kills an Orc has under his belt the more respect he earns from other Orcs, the more his enemies fear him, and the happier he will be.

GOBLINS

Like their bigger relatives, Goblins vary in size a great deal although they are much smaller than a Man. All Goblins have quick, nimble fingers and small darting eyes, their teeth are tiny and very pointed. Their voices are high pitched, and they are extremely noisy and garrulous. Goblins are more intelligent than Orcs and love nothing more than bartering with, and stealing from, their slow-witted relatives.

Scouting parties mounted on huge slavering wolves patrol the area around the tribe, probing for enemies and scouting out small settlements that can be pillaged. Goblins can acquire a great variety of weaponry as they travel. Some Goblins become very wealthy by trading and raiding in this way and the tribe's king becomes the richest of all. A really successful Gobbo wears countless rings, ornamental daggers, swords, and the biggest helmet he can comfortably balance on his head. Others spend their ill-gotten gains on fast chariots that they race against each other, trying to outdo their rivals by having the flashiest machine.

Back row, left to right: Stone Trolls, Giant, Goblin Wolf Riders, Night Goblins, Rock Lobber, Goblin Arrer Boyz

 NIGHT GOBLINS

Thousands of years ago some Goblins took to living in the caves beneath the Worlds Edge Mountains. Over the centuries these became a distinct type and are known as Night Goblins. Night Goblins have become accustomed to darkness, so when they come out into the open they prefer to move around at night and hide away during the day. They wear long ragged cloaks, hooded coats, and dangling caps that cover their bodies and heads to protect them from the hated sunlight.

Night Goblins raise special subterranean fungus deep beneath the mountains in their cool damp caves. Some are food for themselves, others food for their strange animals, but many are grown because they have hallucinogenic or intoxicating properties or because they affect the Goblin metabolism in some other way.

These fungi are traded with other Goblins for weapons and many of the other items the Night Goblins need. The most amazing fungus brew is given to Night Goblins to turn them into whirling, uncontrollable Fanatics with incredible strength.

 GIANTS

Giants are exceptionally rare in settled parts of the Old World, having been hunted for many centuries by crazed Dwarf Giant Slayers and eager Bretonnian Questing Knights.

Giants are, as one might expect, exceptionally large and strong, but are slow-witted and clumsy. They mostly live solitary lives, content to raid farms for cows and sheep – and the odd herder – sometimes indulging their legendary thirst for strong ale by attacking breweries and roadside taverns. Some Giants do find company to keep, particularly amongst Orc and Goblin tribes, and will sometimes even join other armies if they are not driven away.

Giants are powerful but unpredictable allies, and most of the time they don't even know what they are going to do next, never mind what the enemy thinks they are up to. A Giant's fickle nature is not improved by the vast quantities of liquor and beer often consumed before battle, and their tendency to think of anything smaller than themselves as food has caused more than one mercenary arrangement to end messily for the Giant's employers.

Front row, left to right: Orc Boyz, Battle Standard Bearer, Boar Boyz, Warlord on Wyvern, Orc Shaman, Black Orcs, Boar Chariot

DWARFS

The Dwarfs have lived in the Old World for a very long time and have always made their homes deep beneath the mountains, in broad tunnels carved from solid rock. Today only a fraction of the Dwarfs' old empire remains. The Dwarfs themselves are few, and their wealth much reduced compared to former times. Still they remain a proud and defiant people, as grim as their mountains and as hard as the rock itself.

Like the mountains they were raised upon, Dwarfs are immensely strong and resilient, broad in the shoulder, wide in the girth. Above everything else they respect three things: age, wealth and honour.

Unless slain in battle Dwarfs live to a very great age. A Dwarf's age can be readily seen by the length and colour of his beard, with the oldest and wisest of all the silver-bearded ancients growing their beards to yards in length, so that they can be wrapped several times around the Dwarf's belly and yet still trail behind him like a cloak. This respect for age extends to all aspects of Dwarf culture, where ancient workmanship is held up as an example of achievement, and where weapons may be reforged time and time again so that their blades are the same steel that was wielded over a thousand years ago.

The second thing that Dwarfs respect is wealth. Hoarding wealth is a great passion amongst them; no Dwarf feels secure unless he has a substantial pile of treasure that he can pass on to his descendants. The hoards of some of the Dwarf Lords are of immense proportions and antiquity. Rumours of this wealth have driven ambitious armies to the gates of the Dwarf strongholds before now, where most of their bones still lie. Not all attackers have failed though, and some Dwarf holds have fallen to the Orcs and Goblins, their hoards lost or scattered across the world. Coupled with their love of gold, Dwarfs value skill and craftsmanship. All Dwarfs take pride in their work, whether it is making a tunnel, or carving some tiny gem. They are uncannily good at making small, intricate things, and everything they do is accomplished in a painstaking and thoughtful manner. Dwarfs hate to see rough or shoddy work, and everything they make is always built to last.

The last characteristic that Dwarfs admire is honour: they always keep their word. Dwarfs have a very rigid sense of pride and if a Dwarf makes a promise, he will remember it and keep it for the rest of his life. He will also honour a promise made by his ancestors no matter how far distant. To break faith is the worst possible dishonour to a Dwarf, a broken bond that will be bitterly remembered forever, leading to determined vendettas that last for centuries. These breeches of faith against the Dwarfs of a particular stronghold are recorded for posterity in a Book of Grudges, a huge tome carefully maintained by the hold's king and constantly updated. The Dammaz Kron, the Great Book of Grudges, is held by the High King in the capital, and contains every single grudge held by the Dwarf race.

The Defence of Karak Eight Peaks

With their kingdoms situated in the high mountains, the chief foes of the Dwarfs have always been Goblins. During the Goblin Wars, many holds fell to Goblin attacks and several are now the lairs of Night Goblins and other fell creatures. Though the Dwarfs have no love for any evil race, their true hatred is thus reserved for Goblins, and Goblins alone.

All Dwarfs are stout warriors, and their weapons and armour are well forged. Armed with axes and hammers, a regiment of Dwarfs is a foe few would wish to face, for they fight with the stubborn tenacity that characterises all of their culture. Dwarfs live for many years and veteran fighters, known as Longbeards, are easily marked out by their more ornate armour and white beards.

That is, of course, if the enemy can even approach close enough to fight. Most Dwarf armies will include rank upon rank of warriors armed with handguns and crossbows. Handgun-armed Dwarfs are often called Thunderers, from the noise of a rolling volley, and their lead shot can fell a Troll or take a fully armoured knight from his horse. Where range is more important, the crossbow-wielding Quarrellers come into their own, unleashing a hail of bolts against foes whose own weapons may well be out of range.

As if the withering fire from these troops were not deterrent enough, it is a rare Dwarf host that is not supported by several powerful war machines. Cannonballs roar through the air, while Grudge Throwers launch rune-inscribed rocks onto the heads of the enemy. Bolt Throwers glowing with runic magic hurl gleaming spears through the ranks of the foe. Even more outlandish engines, such as the fire-belching Flame Cannon and the multi-barrelled Organ Gun, sweep away whole regiments of the Dwarfs' foes at short range, guarded by their experienced crews.

These machines are the creations of the inventive minds of the Engineers Guild. Steeped in the knowledge of mechanics, these Engineers oversee the weapons and ensure their reliability and accuracy. Occasionally, a less-than-stable Engineer might take to the skies in a Gyrocopter – flying machines most often used to carry messages from

Rear right: Organ gun and Cannon. Back Row: Grudge Thrower, Anvil of Doom, Miners, Longbeards, Gyrocopter, battle standard bearer

hold to hold, but which are equally capable of reconnaissance or harrying the enemy rear.

Though the majority of Dwarfs live below ground in their great halls, there are some amongst them that ply their trade on the surface. Some are farmers, others are traders. Also, there are the Rangers, who act as the eyes and ears of a Dwarf king beyond his chambers and corridors. Veteran warriors and well equipped, Rangers are often the first Dwarfs an invading army will encounter.

In the deep tunnels, the first line of defence will be the Miners of the hold, and these will often be accompanied by solid blocks of Ironbreakers. Clad in armour made from gromril that can turn aside all but the strongest blow, the Ironbreakers can hold a tunnel or breach for hours on end.

Like the Ironbreakers, the Hammerers are well versed in battlecraft and form the bodyguard of the king himself. Armed with heavy warhammers, the Hammerers refuse to give ground to even the most overwhelming foe and crush the skulls of their enemies with relentless ferocity.

Most disturbed of all Dwarfkind are the Slayers – melancholic warriors instantly distinguished by their orange-dyed hair, stiffened into outrageous crests. Slayers are those Dwarfs that have suffered some loss or dishonour so terrible that they cannot live on. However, it would be cowardly for a Dwarf to take his own life, and so instead Slayers swear an oath to seek out the most terrible creatures and fight them, seeking an honourable death in battle.

Dwarfs have no innate magical ability, and in fact will have no truck with wizards, whom they suspect of being distinctly Elvish. Instead, the Dwarfs employ the ancient skills of the Runesmiths to forge magical weapons and armour, to craft finely sculpted talismans and adorn their banners with mystical runes.

The secrets of rune lore have been passed down from one generation to the next since the earliest days, and with the passing of time this wisdom slowly diminishes – only the greatest Runelords can wield the full power of rune magic, and in particular the devastating energies contained within the Anvils of Doom.

Front row, left to right: Ironbreakers, Warriors, Quarrellers, High King Thorgrim Grudgebearer, Slayers

THE UNDEAD

An Undead army is a horrific thing to behold; hordes of Skeletons and Zombies walk resolutely forward, bones rattling, dry flesh creaking, corroded wargear scraping and clanking. The smell of death hangs over the army like a cloud of contagion; the air is full of grave dust and the acrid stench of mummified flesh. Plucked from their stony tombs, angry Wights raise their ancient weapons. Spirits prowl like shadows amongst the ranks: powerful Wraiths and ethereal, wailing Banshees.

It is scarcely any wonder that the dead do not rest easily in their tombs. The Warhammer world is steeped in magic and everywhere there is magic, there is the power to change and undermine nature – even death. In places where sorcerous power is inexplicably strong, there are many Undead creatures that roam at night or gather in the cold comfort of their tombs. In the Southlands, such a place is the Land of the Dead, the ancient realm of Nehekhara where the Tomb Kings dwell.

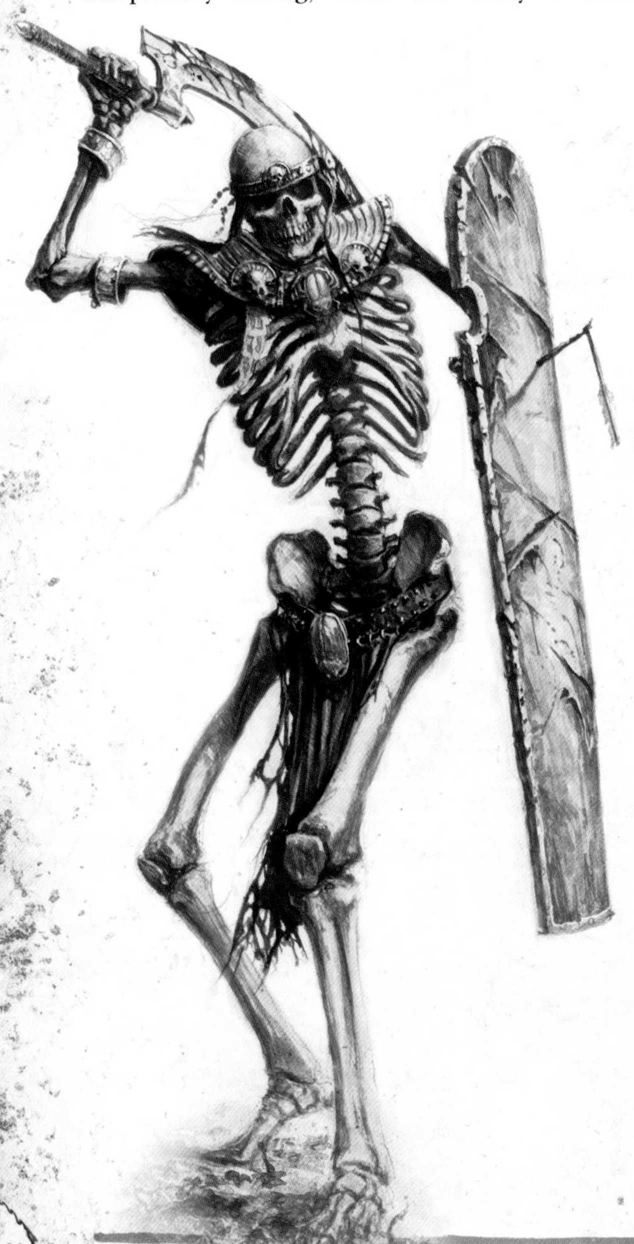

In the Empire, the province of Sylvania has an evil reputation and since ages past its Vampire Counts have waged war against the rest of the Empire. The name von Carstein is still whispered in hushed terror across the Old World.

Sylvania with its Undead Counts is not the only place of dread in the Old World. There is the cursed city of Mousillon in Bretonnia, the Zombie-haunted swamps of Skavenblight and the ancient tombs of the Grey Mountains. The Barrow Hills of the Border Princes is a land of fear that all living creatures avoid when possible.

Throughout Mankind's history there have been Necromancers, Vampires and Liches that have raised up great armies of Undead. There is none more powerful than Nagash, Supreme Lord of the Undead, the deadly master of an evil empire that stretches into the Old World and beyond, who rests today within his sarcophagus in Nagashizzar. It was Nagash whose great spell of awakening brought many foul creatures from their graves, including the dread Tomb Kings of Khemri. But there are others who have striven to overthrow the living world and make themselves its undisputed lord in death.

The Vampires created by Nagash's evil still hunt across the world, from Blood Keep to Silver Peak. Some are beautiful to look upon, others decayed and monstrous. All of them crave power over the lives of mortals.

Not only Vampires haunt the night. Lichemaster Heinrich Kemmler led a horde of Skeletons, Zombies, Ghouls and Wraiths down from the highlands of the Grey Mountains destroying all in his path. Arkhan the Black rose from his tomb to crush the enemies of his master Nagash, and for many long years harried the Southlands in the Wars of Death. These and other Lords of Undeath continue to plague the realms of the Old World.

The Legion of Blood Keep

THE VAMPIRE COUNTS

It is not only the von Carsteins that plague the lands of the living, for each of the seven Vampires that fled the Lands of the Dead with the victory of Alcadizaar went out into the world and founded bloodthirsty dynasties. Of these, some are secretive and shun the world of Men, others embrace their vampiric nature and prey upon the people of the Old World without mercy.

The Blood Dragons are a warrior sect of Vampires, dedicated to perfecting their fighting skills. Amongst Vampirekind they are unparalleled in battle and few foes can face them in single combat and survive. The Lahmian sisters of Silver Peak, on the other hand, are direct descendants of Neferata, the first Vampire, and it is through seduction and manipulation that they seek to gain power, only resorting to war when their other schemes are uncovered or foiled.

The degenerate, bestial Strigoi are all that is left of the Undead masters of the ancient city of Mourkain, now little more than mindless grave scavengers. The raw strength of the Strigoi is unfettered by any pretence of civilisation, making them abhorrent foes. Far from the eyes of Men dwell the Necrarchs. Wholly dedicated to the pursuit of the Necromantic arts, the Necrarchs are supreme sorcerers amongst the Vampires and though their bodies are rotted and withered, their magic can conjure entire armies from the dead of ancient battles.

The armies of the Vampire Counts are shambling hordes of Skeletons and Zombies, animated and driven forward by the powerful Necromantic magic of their undying masters. Bats gather in great clouds above the dead host, while supernatural wolves gather in the shadows, their spine-chilling howls tearing the dark sky. Wights are raised from thousand-year old barrows, marching forth as deadly Grave Guard; the merest touch of their weapons enough to slay a Man. Ancient mounted warriors ride from their graves as Black Knights, their deadly lances wreathed in unnatural energy.

All the while, unquiet spirits writhe and moan about the battlefield, while Banshees shriek the doom of the Vampires' enemies, their ear-piercing screams driving Men insane. Fell, ethereal Wraiths appear wielding scythes, sometimes riding atop Black Coaches pulled by red-eyed Undead steeds.

Back row, left to right: Black Coach, Necromancer, Skeleton Warriors, Fell Bats, Ghouls, Bat Swarms. Middle row: Dire Wolves

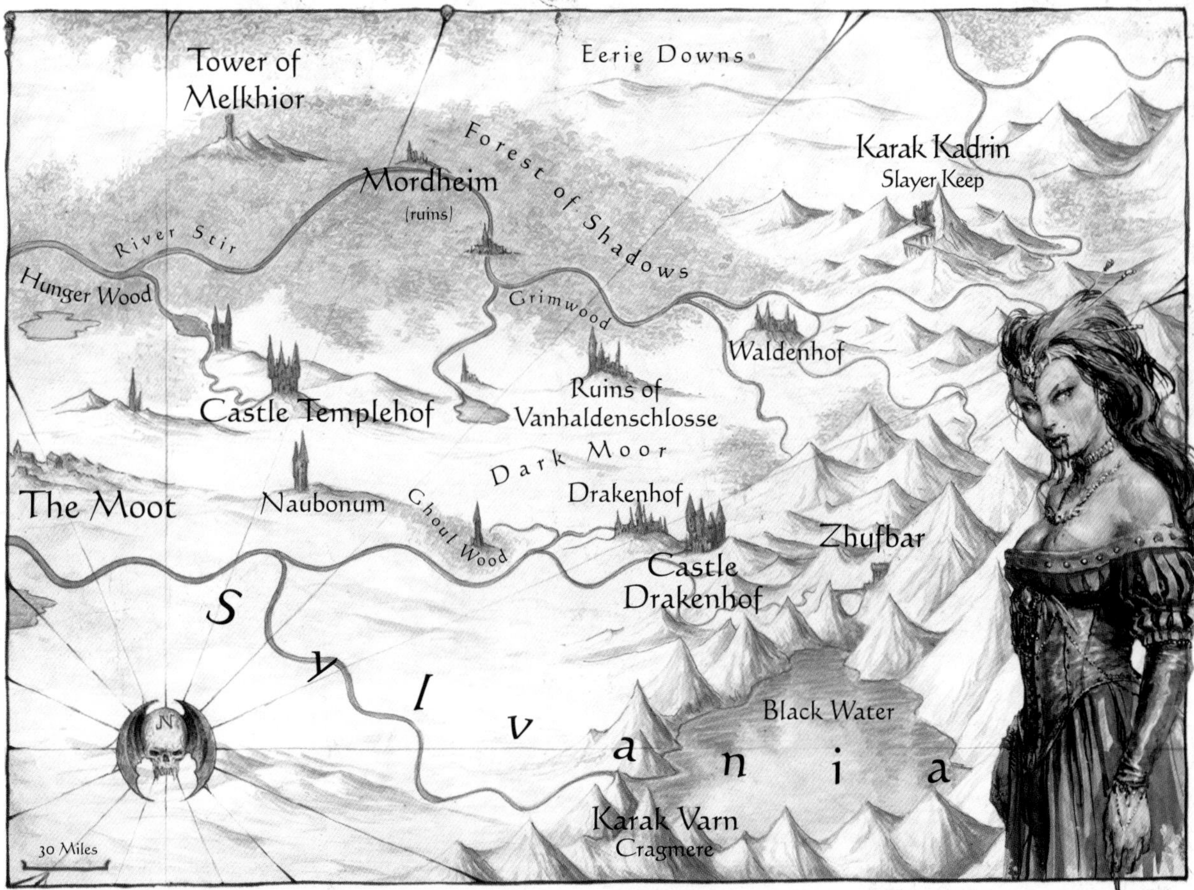

Spirit Host, Banshee. Front row: Skeleton Warriors, Zombies, Vampire Count, Battle Standard Bearer, Grave Guard, Black Knights.

THE TOMB KINGS

In ages past, the land of Nehekhara was fertile, populous and prosperous thanks to the waters of the Great River of Life whose annual floods irrigated the fields and guaranteed a bountiful harvest. Now it is a realm of desolated ruin, where not a living thing stirs. Razed by the enchantments of Nagash's Great Ritual, the Land of the Dead is now a ghost-haunted region, where unquiet spirits flit around the great mortuary temples and dark pyramids.

Largest of these dead cities is Khemri, seat of Settra the Imperishable and most powerful of all the cities of the Dead. In life, Settra ruled from here with an iron fist, his wealth beyond imagining. In death he hungers still for domination of his fellow Tomb Kings, and will suffer no rival to his rule.

Though smaller, the other cities are no less visions of decayed splendour. In the great harbours of Zandri, rotting hulks writhing with dark energy still float, while skeletal crews bend their backs relentlessly at the oars.

South lies Quatar, the gateway to the Valley of the Kings, ruled over by the Vizier Sehenesmet and guarded by an army of artificial beasts and giants.

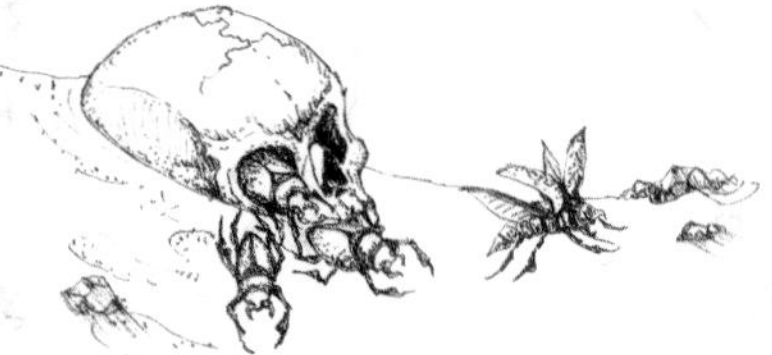

Far to the east can be found Lahmia, where the Vampires were first born. To the south of this cursed city lies Lybaras where, returned from the grave, Queen Khalida now rules over this realm. A sworn enemy of the Vampires that feasted upon her people after her death, Khalida shares Settra's hate for Nagash, though she stays fiercely independent of Khemri's distant rule.

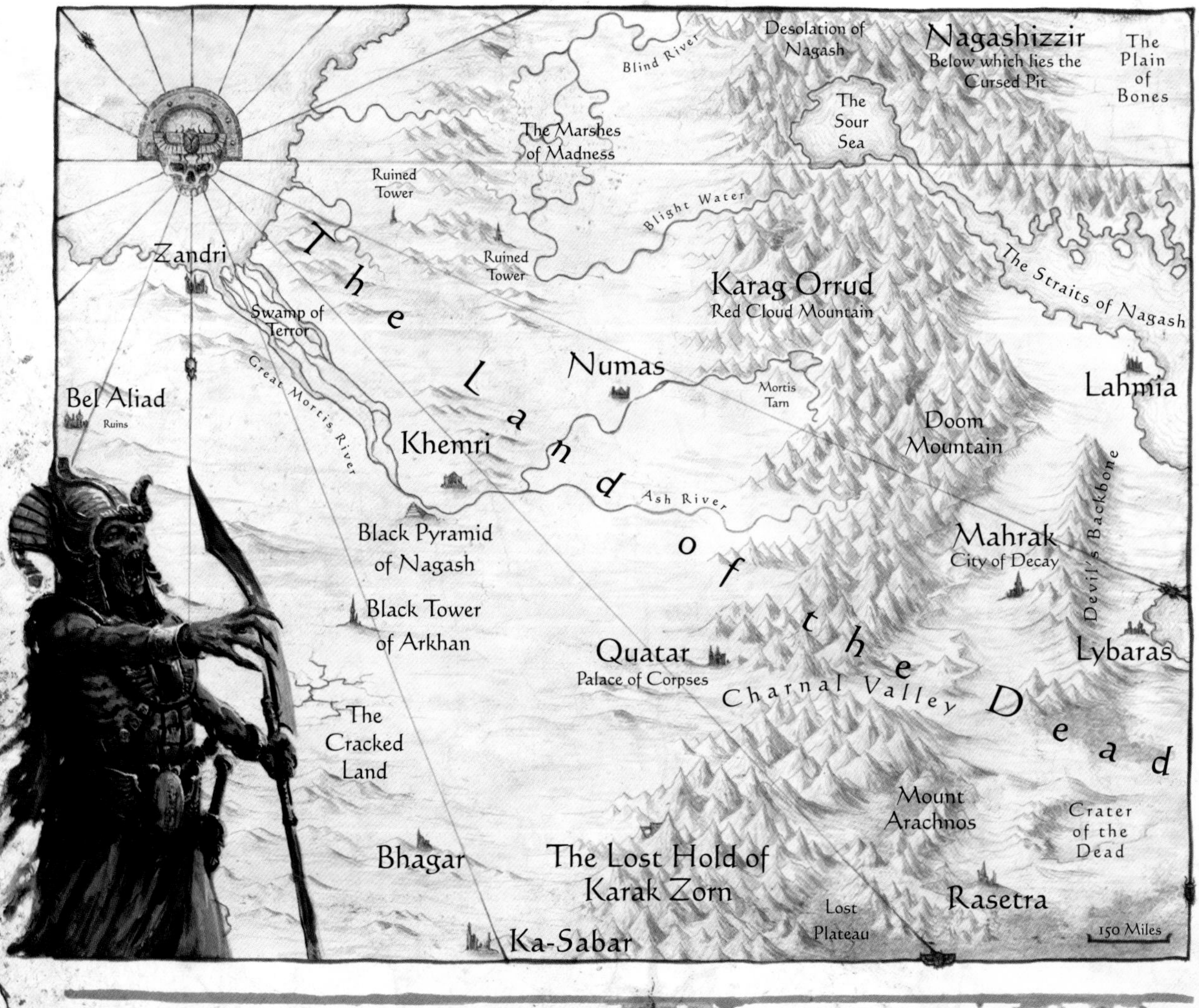

King Nekhesh of the First Dynasty Stands Victorious

The Tomb King is the leader of the army and all its troops are the slaves and servants that accompany him in undeath. His chief and most trusted ministers are his Liche Priests – wizards of great power whose sole job in life was to prepare the king's tomb and ensure his lasting immortality. When a king died, his Liche Priests would continue to perform rituals of immortality in his mortuary temple, and now they are responsible for the reawakening of his long-dead army.

Thousands upon thousands of troops were buried alive in the great pits of the kings of Nehekhara. In those days, it was considered the duty of a warrior to follow his king even in death. Troops were interred in serried ranks complete with all the weapons needed to protect their lord in the next life – spears, swords and shields. Many archers were also buried with their masters together with a great stash of ammunition. They live again to send their flint-, bronze- and iron-tipped arrows against the foe. Alongside the infantry gallop the Skeleton Cavalry, their spear tips glinting in the desert sun.

The giant birds of the mountains were revered as holy creatures by the Nehekharans. It was said that after a battle the Carrion would pluck the souls of the fallen from their bodies and carry them away to eternity. These birds were often mummified and placed in the tombs of the kings. Now they are bound by the spells cast upon them and serve the armies of the Tomb Kings.

When the Liche Priests built the tombs of the kings of Khemri they realised how much more effective it

Back row: Carrion, Casket of Souls, Screaming Skull Catapult, Tomb Scorpion. Middle row: Bone Giant, Ushabti, Icon Bearer,

would be to employ larger and stronger creatures to do all the heavy lifting. To this end they created Bone Giants from the bodies of gigantic animals – abominations that they filled with magical life of a simplistic and short-term kind. Once the tombs were complete, any giants that remained would be cast aside into the brimming charnel pits, their purpose complete. When Nagash cast his terrible spell of awakening, the giants crawled faithfully from their pits – bizarre amalgams of bone and sinew with awareness to do only the most rudimentary tasks.

To protect their masters throughout their journey to eternity, the Liche Priests wrought statues of guardian creatures such as the Tomb Scorpions, or the strange beings called Ushabti. These statues were fashioned from stone, wood, bones, flesh and certain magically potent organs. They were placed within the tombs of the kings to guard the sacred body, and the Liche Priests still rouse the magic within them and send them to war.

When the Tomb Kings awoke, they ordered the more obviously cognate of their Undead slaves to rebuild the cities of old and fill them with the carts, boats, markets and other things that they remembered from life. As no trees grow in the Land of the Dead all these things must be made from stone or bone. The same is true of the gigantic catapults constructed to bombard the armies and cities of the Tomb Kings' rivals. The heads of fallen foes make effective ammunition. The dry-screams of living skulls can be heard as they are propelled through the air spreading panic amongst the enemy ranks.

Skeleton Heavy Horsemen, Skeleton Bowmen. Front row: Liche Priest, Skeleton Spearmen, Settra the Imperishable, Tomb Guard. Light Chariots

SKAVEN

In the distant past, rats infesting some decaying ruin fed upon a mighty source of magic power. This power was a substance called warpstone – solidified fragments of raw sorcery formed during the coming of Chaos. Under its unwholesome influence the scuttling vermin mutated, growing in size and intelligence into the vile Skaven.

Over the centuries, the Chaos ratmen have spread across the world, establishing settlements in the sewers and catacombs beneath unsuspecting cities and invading underground strongholds from below. They have created a vast and intricate web of tunnels that spreads across the world. An equally complex network of spies and agents informs the Skaven of their enemies' plans. At the centre of this labyrinthine web lies the capital of the Under-Empire, the vast, sprawling city of decay called Skavenblight. This most secret and vile of places lies deep in the treacherous Zombie Marshes of northern Tilea.

With their heightened intellect and humanoid bodies, the Skaven have learned to use warpstone to fuel their corrupt sorceries and to create weapons of awesome power. Warpstone is vital to the Skaven, they depend on it to feed and drive their civilisation. It forms a vital part of their foul ceremonies and the worship of their pestilent god: the Horned Rat.

When the Horned Rat rouses, the Skaven erupt into an intense period of warfare and strife, laying waste to towns and cities in an orgy of destruction. In these times, not only do the Skaven wage war upon other races but among themselves as well: the slow, the weak and the foolish are set upon and torn apart. The Skaven race purges itself of its weaker members and makes slaves of the defeated.

The Skaven are divided into clans of which the Warlord clans are by far the most populous. Each Warlord clan has a fierce hierarchy ranging from the lowliest weakling slaves to the most powerful warriors, and ultimately to the Skaven Warlord, who is the cruel and cunning master of the entire clan.

The short lives of all Skaven are marked by constant squabbles and fights for supremacy. These individual clashes are fought with tooth and claw or knives, Nearly all Skaven are scarred in some way from these fights, many having lost an ear or eye. Skaven actually crippled in fights can expect only to be summarily despatched by the victor.

Skaven have many slaves, many of them other Skaven beaten in combat, but some are other races defeated in battle. Slaves occupy the most miserable position in Skaven society, often being used in dangerous experiments or as cannon fodder in battles. Their lives are brutish and painful but mercifully short.

Vermintide of the Horned Rat

Within the greater clan structure the story is the same; stronger clans dominate the weaker ones and any clan that becomes vulnerable is quickly enslaved. All of this is overseen by the Council of Thirteen – greatest of the warlords and dedicated servants of the Horned Rat. The four most powerful clans are Clan Moulder, Clan Eshin, Clan Skryre and Clan Pestilens. These Great Clans are the masters of the Skaven and the rulers of their Under-Empire, and have complete ascendancy over the struggling mass of the ordinary Warlord clans.

Each of the Great Clans has its own weird armaments and foul methods of waging war. Clan Moulder are powerful beastmasters and use warpstone to mutate breeds of ferocious fighting beasts. Clan Eshin are feared as assassins and stealthy murderers, active under and within the cities of Man. Wherever there is squalor, the adepts of Clan Eshin can be found, poisoning human food and water supplies and stirring up the rat packs. Clan Skryre are known as the Warlock Engineers, masters of the insane blend of magic and science that has produced, amongst other things, the dreaded warpfire throwers and the equally devastating poisoned wind. Clan Pestilens are also known as the Plague Monks; frenzied disciples, dedicated to spreading pestilence and plague.

The mysterious Skaven known as the Grey Seers are the servants of the Lords of Decay and carry their instructions to the clans. The Grey Seers occupy an elevated position amongst the Skaven, concerning themselves solely with the most important and devious of schemes. Grey Seers are sorcerers of great power, using warpstone to boost their magic abilities, and may be found leading hordes of Skaven clans into battle.

Skaven rely on weight of numbers and potent magic to overcome their foes. Regiments of Clanrat warriors wearing ragged clothing and scavenged armour swarm forward in a squeaking tide supported by the insanely dangerous warpstone weapons of Clan Skryre and the mutant beasts of Clan Moulder. Clan Eshin ambush unwary foes and the frenzied Plague Monks squeak their devotion to the Horned Rat as they hurl themselves into the enemy.

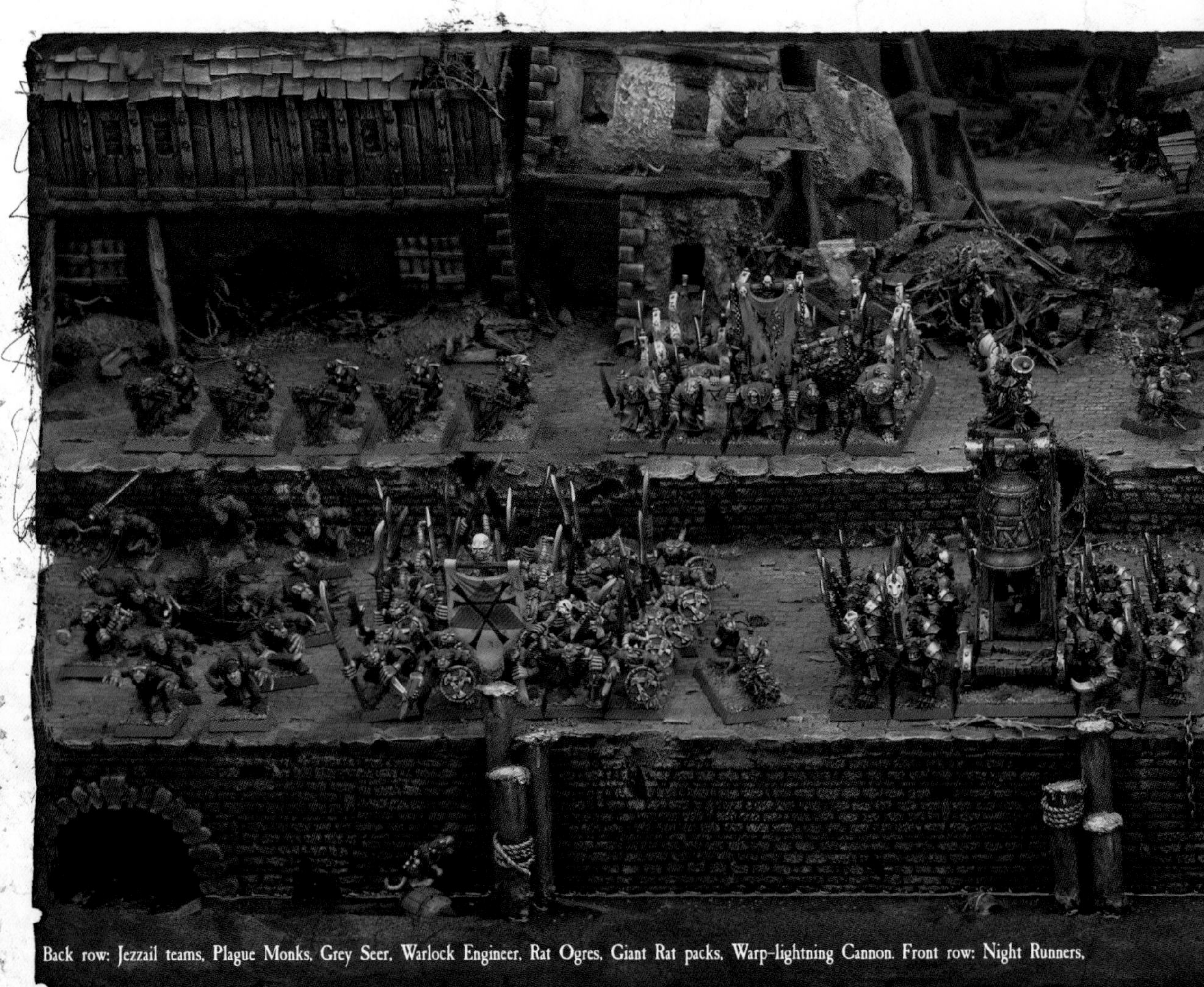

Back row: Jezzail teams, Plague Monks, Grey Seer, Warlock Engineer, Rat Ogres, Giant Rat packs, Warp-lightning Cannon. Front row: Night Runners,

WARPSTONE

Magic is the stuff of Chaos, and warpstone is magic in its physical form. When the gate of the Old Ones collapsed, warpstone was showered across the world, some of it as fine dust, much as larger chunks. Over the years, warpstone has been known by many races, and by many names – wyrdstone, thengduraz, mage gold amongst others – and those that crave magical power seek it out to help with their spells.

Over the history of the world, meteors of warpstone have crashed down from the heavens, creating areas of dense magical potential; warpstone is raw magic and its presence pollutes everything around it. It is such warpstone detonations that created the Sour Sea and the desert of Araby, levelled the Empire city of Mordheim and nearly wiped out the Ogres.

Skaven desire warpstone above all other things, for it created them in millennia past and their entire society is based upon it – their wealth, their magic and even their diet.

Clanrats with Ratling gun, Stormvermin with Screaming Bell, Battle Standard Bearer, Clanrats with Warpfire Thrower, Poisoned Wind Globadiers, Skavenslaves

LIZARDMEN

The Lizardmen are the inheritors of the Old Ones and the most ancient races of the world after Dragons. Through the sacred plaques that contain the pronouncements of the Old Ones from before the fall, the various types of Lizardmen strive to enact the plans of their cosmic masters, though now much knowledge is lost and their power is but a shadow of what it once was.

Many thousands of years ago, before the Time of Chaos, before the fathers of the Elves and Dwarfs knew of speech or song, the world was visited by a race of travellers.

Elven legends dimly recall them as the Old Ones. Silver craft brought the Old Ones to the world where they built a stellar gateway. The Old Ones created the ancestors of the Elves and Dwarfs and other races, nurtured them, taught them the arts of civilisation, though to what end remains a mystery.

Although the Old Ones have long since gone, the lands of Lustria and the Southlands where they dwelt have not been completely emptied of intelligent life, for the Old Ones did not come to the world entirely alone. They brought with them their slaves and servants, creatures whose minds or bodies the Old Ones found useful. Of these creatures the most intelligent were the Slann.

The bloated Slann were the organisers and architects – potent scientist-sorcerers whose endeavours built the cities of Lustria and moulded the Warhammer world into a shape commanded by their masters.

It was the Slann Mage-Lords who built the polar gateway and whose spells maintained its integrity. It was the Slann who moved the whole world closer to the sun to warm it, and who changed the shape of the lands. The Slann were second only in understanding to the godlike Old Ones themselves.

From the beginning, the Slann were few in number and their power dwindled with successive generations. Since those days they have all but died out but, even today, the Slann are the greatest wizards of the Warhammer world. Though they do not possess the power of their ancestors, they are more potent than the greatest of the Elven Mages.

Wrath of Hexoatl

The Old Ones relied upon the intelligence and sorcerous abilities of the Slann, but they never rated the creatures as warriors. Their bloated toad-like bodies left them sluggish and vulnerable, and lacked aggression if not cold-blooded malice. For their warriors the Old Ones chose another race, though whether they brought these soldiers to the world or whether they found and adapted them is not clear.

Perhaps the Saurus, as these reptilian warriors are called, were the first race cultivated by the Old Ones. Saurus are brutish creatures with slow minds that register little emotion except a crude, single-minded savagery. They can use simple weapons but are unable to master more complex devices, and their language is little more than growled commands. In terms of protecting the cities and temples of Lustria, however, they were just what the Old Ones needed.

The desire for a more physically adaptable, as well as mentally agile, workforce led the Old Ones to create a smaller race of Lizardmen called Skinks. These were weaker than the Saurus, but capable of far more involved and dextrous tasks. They formed the mass workforce of the Old Ones, as they do for the Slann today, and are capable of operating more complex weapons. In battle the Skinks form a skirmishing auxiliary to the ranks of the Saurus, harrying the foe with blowpipes and javelins.

In addition to the Slann, Saurus and Skinks, the Old Ones created or adapted many other creatures of reptilian origin. The gigantic Kroxigors were made as towering construction slaves, capable of carrying and placing massive boulders, though equally capable of crushing a foe in battle.

Creatures of the air with wide wings and sharp beaks were made that could ride the wind and carry the nimble Skinks as messengers and scouts, and the Old Ones also fashioned huge, lumbering monsters that were used to carry burdens over long distances. In battle, the massive Stegadons, Carnosaurs and other scaled beasts serve as mounts for warriors and war machines. They gore the foe with horns and tusks, or trample them under their immense bulk. Smaller but no less deadly are the Salamanders that belch gobbets of burning venom.

Back row: Saurus Cavalry, Temple Guard with Slann Mage-Priest, Stegadon, Terradon Riders, Skink Priest. Front row: Saurus Warriors,

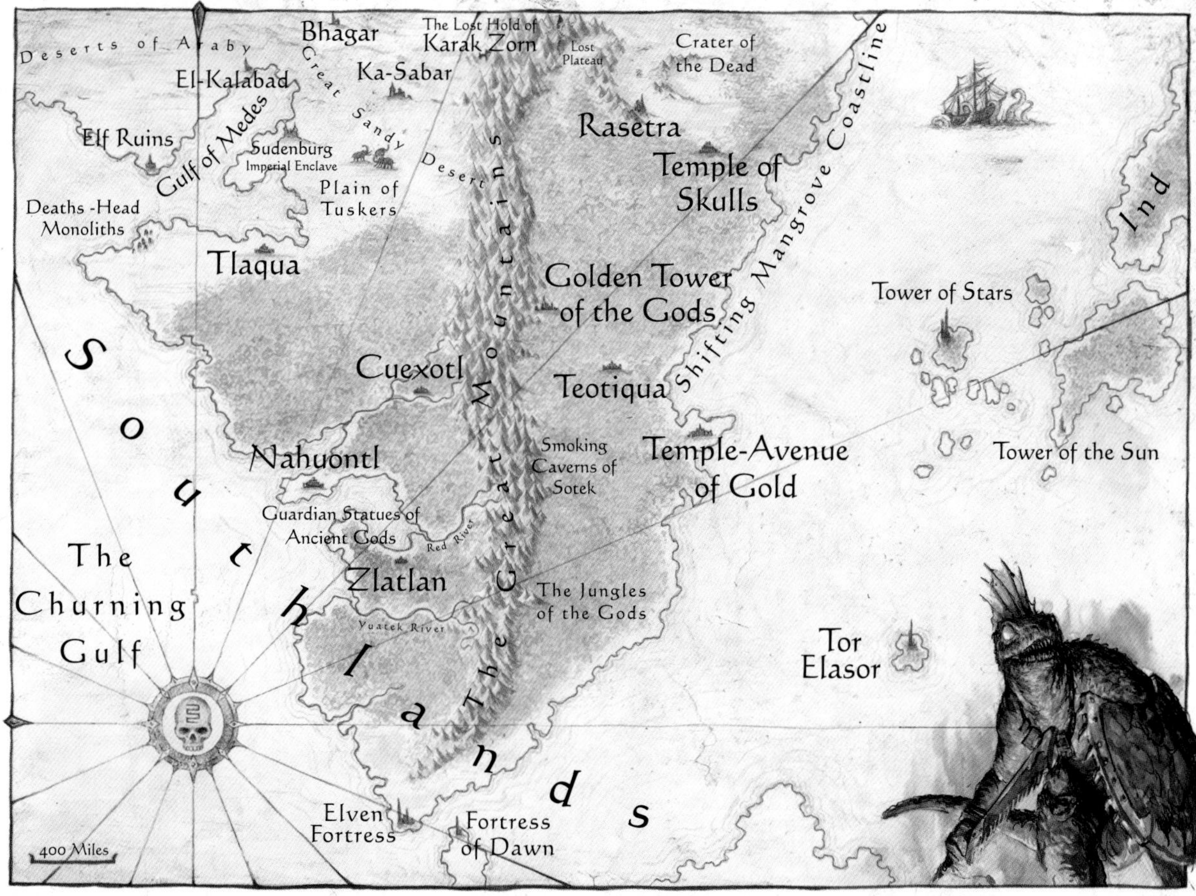

Salamander Hunting Packs, Kroxigor, Jungle Swarms, Scar-Leader Kroq-gar on Carnosaur, Skink Skirmishers, Battle Standard Bearer.

OGRES

Ogres are large, brutish creatures that can be found all across the Old World. However, they are not natives of these lands, but originate far to the east, across the Worlds Edge Mountains, past the Dark Lands, to the Mountains of Mourn. It is their natural wanderlust and mercenary tendencies that have taken them across the world from Araby to Norsca, from the Empire to Lustria.

There are few things Ogres need, but foremost amongst them is food. They are possessed of an insatiable hunger, and can eat just about everything. Driven by this unnatural appetite, Ogres are exceptional fighters with a natural desire for violence. In more modern times, the Ogres have combined these two traits to become sellswords without peer. As long as an Ogre can eat what he beats, he'll fight for any Man, Dwarf, Elf or Orc willing to put up with his presence.

The Ogres did not initially come from the Mountains of Mourn, but migrated there hundreds of years ago, driven from their ancestral lands further to the east by the most important moment in their history. A great comet crashed into the desert lands of the Ogres, and where it fell a great slavering mouth was born, devouring nearly the entire Ogre race. Those that survived were driven westwards in their search for food, now plagued by a never-ending feeling of starvation that drives them to feed constantly. Their god, the Great Maw, passed on its hunger to them and now feeding and worship are one and the same.

The Ogres live in a series of scattered kingdoms along the river valleys of the Mountains of Mourn. They spend much of their time fighting amongst themselves, but they also act as guides for the trade caravans that risk the perilous journey from the Old World to Cathay and Ind; perilous, in part, due to the fact that the Ogres sometimes also raid those same caravans. Exchanging services and loot for weapons and armour, as well as shiny trinkets that catch their attention, the Ogres exist from a thriving economy of war.

The Ogres have slowly learned that not only can they take what they need by force, they can also trade what they steal for food and other things less important to them. Thus the Mountains of Mourn have, in a twisted way, become a vital part of the trading missions between the Old World and the mysterious Orient. In the minds of the Ogres, trade and war are much the same thing, and they are renowned as aggressive bargainers, not least because of the Ogres' tendency to eat any merchant foolish enough to argue with them for too long.

The Gorging

Through their mercenary activities, trade and attacks on the caravans moving across the mountains, the Ogres have built up a considerable armoury. The Ogre Bulls, as most Ogre warriors are known, wield clubs and crude blades. At the other end of the scale, fine and balanced Cathayan longswords are wielded by veterans of many campaigns, called Maneaters by the Ogres.

From the Cathayans and Chaos Dwarfs the Ogres have also procured crude gunpowder weapons. These Leadbelcher cannons are carried into battle by the Ogres and fired at short range into the enemy, usually followed by a merciless charge by the Ogres wielding the cannons.

There are also other, stranger creatures dwelling in the peaks of the Ogre Kingdoms. The Yhetees are thought to be distant cousins of the Ogres, an offshoot of the race that moved to the highest peaks in an era past and have now grown long fur and vicious talons so that they might survive the extreme cold and scale the icy cliffs of their homes.

Gorgers, on the other hand, are from deep within the ground. Misshapen, feared monstrosities whose hunger drives them insane, Gorgers are mindless feeders that prowl the dark areas of the mountains as a shark hunts the seas. They are drawn to battle by the scent of blood, travelling many miles to feast upon the Ogres' enemies.

Ogres will naturally leave their tribe at a certain age and set off adventuring across the world, to make a name for themselves or just to see what is out there. This wanderlust owes its origins to the exodus that occurred when the Great Maw destroyed the Ogre homelands. As dogs of war, the Ogres ply their warcraft for anyone willing to pay or feed them, and when they return to their tribes, they will bring with them much plunder, experience and long stories. Ogres, unlike many mercenaries, are actually quite loyal to those they have struck a deal with, if only because they lack the wit to be truly duplicitous.

Rear, left to right: Tyrant, Butcher. Middle row: Gorger, Hunter with Sabretusks, Ironguts, Yhetees, Slavegiant, Scraplauncher.

GNOBLARS

As well as the Ogres, the Mountains of Mourn are home to the Hill Goblins, more commonly called Gnoblars. Fleeing from the slaving parties of the Chaos Dwarfs, the Gnoblars left their squalid villages in the foothills at the southern end of the mountains and moved further up towards the snow-capped peaks. Here they encountered the Ogres, who provided them with some means of protection, in return for the services the Gnoblars provide.

Gnoblars are now a vital part of Ogre society, fetching and carrying, trading and cooking for their large masters. Though it is a short, tough life they lead under the dominance of their brutish superiors, it is a better life than that offered by toil in the soul forges of Zharr-Naggrund.

Like all greenskins, Gnoblars are vicious and obsessed with hierarchy. However, they have managed to carve out their own subculture amongst the Ogre tribes, giving rise to such specialists as the Scrappers that loot the battlefields after the Ogres have finished fighting, and the Trappers that tag along with Ogre Hunters when they travel high into the mountain to slay mammoth, Rhinox and other creatures of the snowy heights.

Front row, left to right: Gnoblars, Leadbelchers, Gnoblar Trappers, Maneaters, Ogre Bulls.

OTHER RACES

CHAOS DWARFS

The great city of Zharr-Naggrund rises up out of the desolate plains of the Dark Lands, shrouded in an eternal pall of smoke. The ringing of infernal industry fills the sky as the millions of wretched slaves of the Chaos Dwarfs toil in the daemonic forges. Great ziggurat temples to the bull-headed god Hashut spill noxious fumes across the plain, tainted with the stench of hellfire. Amongst the diabolical furnaces, the Chaos Dwarfs labour to make great machineries of destruction. Iron and flesh are bound together with daemonic spirits to create great cannons and engines. In the dark smithies Chaos Dwarf artisans labour forging weapons and armour. These are traded with the Ogres of the east and the northern marauders in exchange for even more unfortunates for the Slavemasters.

DRAGONS

The oldest Dragons of the world, such as were befriended by the High Elf Caledor Dragon-tamer, can no longer be found, for they retired beneath the mountains and into the ocean depths. Their younger progeny can still be awakened from their slumber by powerful magic or the entreaty of a great hero, and though not as mighty as their sires, these younger drakes are still terrors capable of razing towns and sweeping aside armies. There are many types of Dragons: some of them breathe fire, while others exhale clouds of noxious gas or can cast spells of lightning from their fanged maws. Dragons are intelligent creatures, and like other beings can be disposed to good or ill deeds. Some are dire foes that prey upon villages, while others are of a more noble spirit and will fight alongside Men and Elves in the eternal war against the dark things of the world.

CATHAY

Of the East, little is known to the scholars of the Old World, and of that most is rumour and speculation. However, there is no doubt that the greatest power in the East is the Grand Empire of Cathay. The Celestial Dragon Emperor, believed by some to be an actual Dragon in the form of a Man, rules over the largest nation in the world, with untold millions of subjects.

The north of Cathay is protected from the attacks of the Hung tribes by the Great Bastion – a massive wall that stretches for hundreds of miles, and large enough to require a garrison tens of thousands strong. The armies of Cathay are said to be innumerable, and draw exotic warriors from all across the realm, including fierce hill people, strange warrior monks and well-disciplined armies supported by heavily armoured warriors and ornate cannons.

The opening of the recruiting station at Stichenfloch, Drakwald, offering 'The Soldier's Schilling'.

THE WARHAMMER HOBBY

Warhammer is much more than a game – it is a vast and vibrant hobby that encompasses collecting, painting, modelling, terrain making, and a limitless variety of challenges.

GETTING STARTED

This section of the book is about putting everything that has come before into practice. Here you will find advice, tips, and techniques for collecting, painting, modelling, and gaming, with practical advice for beginners right through to advanced ideas for gaming veterans to try out. Some players find they exclusively like one aspect of the hobby, but most discover that they enjoy at least dabbling in all the different facets. The most important step is the first one – getting started in the first place.

IT ALL TAKES PRACTICE

Becoming an expert in any aspect of Warhammer is not the kind of thing that happens overnight. Even the most famous Dwarf Runesmith started out as an apprentice. Don't be discouraged if your first results are not perfect or of award-winning quality – certainly none of ours were. Experiment, get creative, practice, and find out which elements you most enjoy.

The summaries on the following page give you an overview of each topic and how the information will follow.

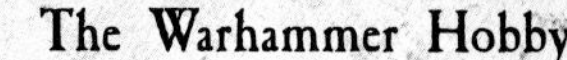

Eventually you may wish to play more diverse scenarios such as this example of a Wood Elf ambush on the outskirts of Athel Loren.

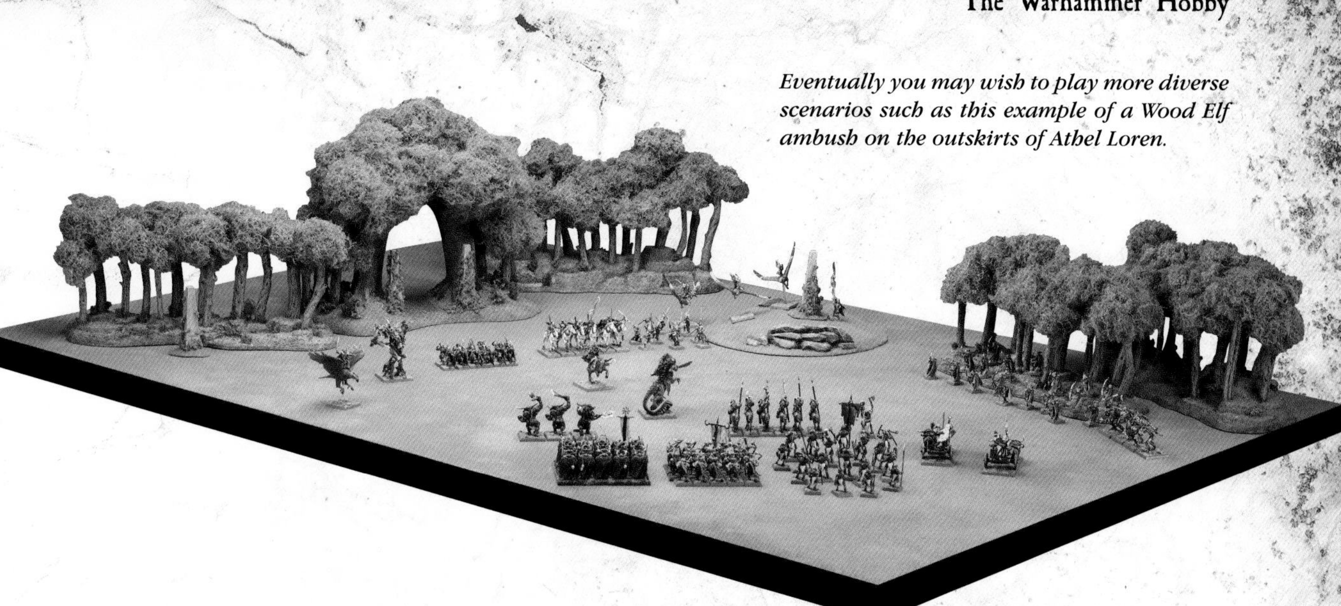

COLLECTING AN ARMY

In order to play Warhammer you will need an army. A useful guide to selecting an army is followed with key advice and the next steps towards building a force to be reckoned with. Sample armies are included as well, to give you ideas of what to collect first.

MODELLING

Covering practical tips on attaching models to bases as well as more advanced advice on assembling multi-part kits.

PAINTING

In this section you will find an introduction to the art and tools of miniatures painting and advice about painting a Warhammer army, with lots of examples provided.

TERRAIN

You will need a surface on which to play your battles and this section is all about how to make a battlefield and some key terrain features to go upon it.

GAMING

The culmination of all your hobby preparation is to deploy your forces and play a battle. This chapter is all about ways you can play a game, along with alternate set-up and deployment options to vary your battles.

GETTING MORE INVOLVED

The Warhammer hobby is a social activity with loads of ways to get more involved. The section ends on the myriad ways hobbyists can meet other like-minded individuals and dig deeper into the Warhammer world.

Core units, like this imposing block of plastic High Elf spearmen, form the bulk of most Warhammer armies. Games Workshop makes a wide range of plastic miniatures, which are ideal for building up your forces.

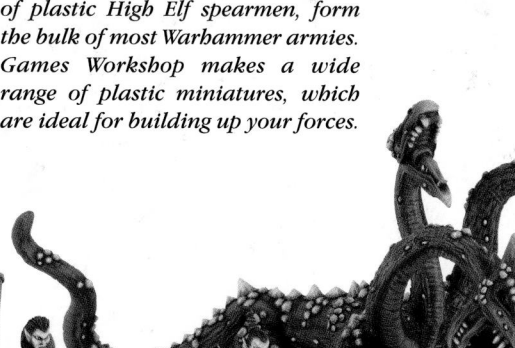

Assembling and painting a large multi-part model like this Hydra may take a bit of effort to complete but the finished product is a killing machine on the battlefield and the centrepiece of any gamer's collection.

COLLECTING AN ARMY

To play Warhammer you must first get your hands on an army. At first, amassing an army may seem daunting, but with a little forethought a battle-worthy force can be collected (and painted) in easy stages.

CHOOSING AN ARMY

There are over a dozen Warhammer armies, each with its own range of fantastic miniatures, background and style of play. Some players will choose their army because it fits their persona, matches with their preferred tactical style, or maybe just because they like the look of the models.

MINIATURES

Usually the biggest influence on choosing an army is the miniatures. After all, the more you like the models, the more likely you are to look forward to all the collecting, painting, and modelling. A player that favours collecting monsters would do well with a Dark Elf army with its Hydra, Dragon, Harpies, and more. Meanwhile, a gamer who enjoys painting bright colours and striking heraldry would suit the resplendent armoured knights of Bretonnia.

BACKGROUND

Each race in the Warhammer world has its own realm, history and goals. The Skaven, for example, live in tunnels and lairs, and have infiltrated into the sewers beneath human cities. Back-stabbing and deceit are common amongst the feuding Skaven clans and so a player looking for an honourable army should look elsewhere.

STYLE OF PLAY

Are you more interested in precise tactics, volleys of missile fire, or massed sledgehammer attacks? Each force has unique specialties. Wood Elves, for instance, excel at hit-and-run attacks punctuated with deadly bowfire. A player who prefers head-on close combats would do better with Orcs or Chaos.

The photographs, artwork and descriptions in this book will give you a good idea of how these three factors apply to the different armies. For more information, turn to the Armies books.

This Lizardmen force is a good example of a small, balanced starting army.

WARHAMMER ARMIES BOOKS

Every army has its own Armies book. Each one is the definitive guide to collecting and fielding that army, so it is an extremely useful purchase once you have chosen your force.

BACKGROUND AND RULES

The background information and characteristic profiles contained in this book will get you started, but the Armies books contain far more detail.

Each book contains an extensive account of the army's history, as well as descriptions and full rules for the individual regiments and characters that are available. Reading about the different units is bound to give you some inspiration as to which models you'd like to collect first.

THE ARMY LIST

Every book contains what is known as an 'army list'. This sets out exactly how many of each type of model you are allowed to field for a game. The army list allows you lots of choice, within certain parameters, and will turn your collection of models into a coherent, organised army.

ARMY COMPOSITION

To organise the process of collecting an army Warhammer Armies books classify each model type as Characters, Core, Special, or Rare. These categories are explained on page xiii.

Remember, the number of characters you are allowed depends on the overall size of your army, but you will always need at least one – your general.

Every army contains at least two Core choices, so it is sensible to collect those first – they will get a lot of use in your battles.

Special and Rare units are not nearly so common as Core troops and so the maximum number of selections of these categories are limited based on the overall size of the game you are playing.

POINTS COST

In order to allow players to fight evenly matched battles, the Armies books give each single model or troop type a points value.

The points value for each model represents its capabilities on the battlefield. The higher a model's points value, the better it will be in one or more respects: stronger, tougher, faster, gifted with better Leadership, or so on.

Knowing the points value of any chosen force allows players to fight out even battles or, conversely, set up and plan mismatched battles where one side is fighting against the odds.

COLLECTING UNITS

While purchasing a model or two is a fine way to see if you enjoy painting them, it will take you quite a while to build up a single unit, never mind an army. The fastest way to start an army is to purchase, assemble and paint a regiment. The plastic regiment boxed sets are an ideal way to jump-start an army – it's a good idea to choose one that is a Core choice, as you know it will always have a place in your force.

BUILDING IN BLOCKS

One of the best ways to build an army is to do it in stages. Blocks of about 500 points are ideal to collect, assemble, paint, and game with. Using this staged method you can get in some games once you have finished your first 500 points and at the same time you can begin planning, assembling, and painting your next batch of 500 points. In this way, you can learn about your army and what you might need next while you go.

Wise collectors will try to even out their model selections. For instance, a Core choice or two can be balanced out with the higher points cost of a Special or Rare selection. This will also add more variety to your painting and gaming. After assembling a big block of infantry it can be quite rewarding to put together a more specialised or unique character model, war machine, or monster!

It may be tempting to purchase an entire army in a single burst of enthusiasm, but this can easily lead to discouragement as you try to assemble every model at once or look up at a seemingly endless mountain of painting projects. An army cannot be mustered overnight, and slow and steady progress is often the best approach.

HOW LARGE AN ARMY TO COLLECT

There really is no set size for a finished army – it depends on the collector and how the army is being used. The rules and the army lists are designed for battles between armies of between 500 and 3,000 points. Small armies of 500 to 1,000 points will

Building an army isn't as daunting as it first appears. This Dwarf army has been split into easily managed 500 point blocks.

Building an army is all about making small but important decisions – should a Dwarf commander select troops armed with handguns or crossbows, or some of both?

Thunderers are a Core troop choice for a Dwarf army. These Dwarfs are equipped with handguns. The shots from this deadly weapon inflict a -2 modifier to any armour saves. Additionally, due to the superior design, all handgun shots gain a +1 to hit modifier.

Quarrellers are a Core troop choice for a Dwarf army. These Dwarfs are armed with crossbows that have a range of 30" – longer than a Dwarf handgun. Quarrellers also cost fewer points than a Thunderer.

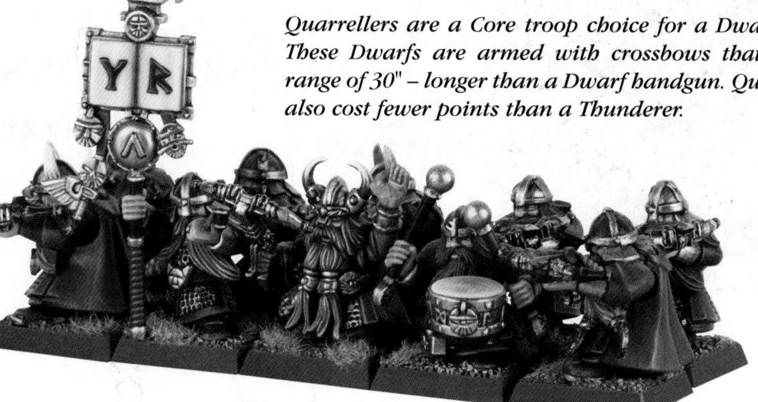

There is no 'correct' choice, but the right unit at the right time can make all the difference.

work perfectly well, but may miss out on some of the complexities of a bigger game. However, this makes them ideal when you're learning the ropes with a new force. Huge battles between armies of more than 3,000 points each are also possible but will require longer to set up and to play. On occasion it is well worth dedicating an entire weekend to Warhammer, as there is nothing quite like the grand spectacle of a really massive game!

ENDLESS VARIETY

One of the best things about Warhammer armies are the countless ways in which you can construct each force; within the same army you can fashion dozens of different configurations to suit tactics, battlefield conditions, army themes, or merely the models you own. Just when you think you've seen it all, a new army, strategy, or paint scheme will turn up.

Not only can this ability to customise your army give players great scope for collecting and painting, but force variation can open up new tactical horizons as well. A cunning commander, even playing an opponent that he has faced dozens of times, will always leave the foe guessing exactly what forces and tactics are up his sleeve until the game begins.

BUILDING THE ULTIMATE ARMY

For really dedicated players, one of the best luxuries is to have more models in their collection than they usually field in a single battle. This will allow flexibility and afford you the advantage of switching your army around, perhaps tailoring the force to fight a certain opponent, give a tactical edge, or maybe just to throw a new challenge at a familiar adversary.

By way of example, imagine a High Elf player about to face a Bretonnian army. Sensible choices might be Eagle Claw Repeater Bolt Throwers and troop types like Swordmasters and White Lions. These potent selections offer High Elves their best chances to overcome the impressive armour saving throws of the well-protected knights that are bound to be a part of any Bretonnian army. When facing the Undead hordes of a Vampire Count, the High Elf commander might prepare deep protective ranks of Spearmen to ensure winning combats against the Fear-causing creatures that will make up the bulk of the walking dead host. Any army can beat any other force, but taking the right mix of troops for the right situations will certainly help your cause.

BRETONNIAN ARMY

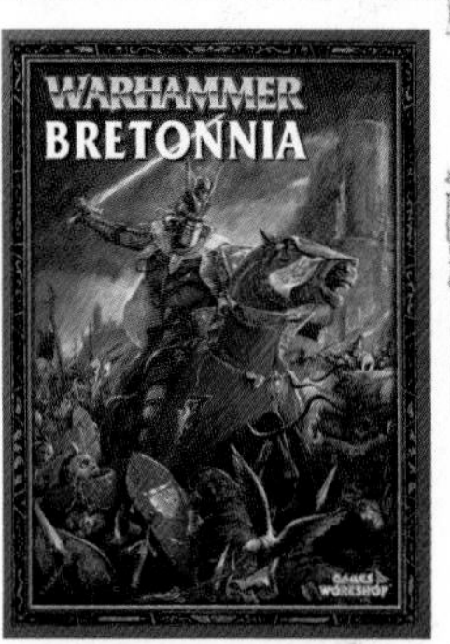

This army shows the type of units available to the Bretonnian player. Each of the main reasons to collect an army – miniatures, background and style of play – are shown to good effect. The amazing miniatures feature a mix of mighty knights, their deadly lances raised, and lowly peasants complete with defensive stakes and scruffy equipment. The background presents a nation of noble heroes and mystical enchantresses, determined to uphold the purity of the beloved Lady of the Lake and to defeat the foul enemies of Bretonnia. On the tabletop, the army is one of the hardest hitting there is, favouring heavy armour, stout mounts, sharp lances and dedicated prayers to the Lady.

Field Trebuchet

Peasant Bowmen

Pegasus Knights

Men-at-arms

Mounted Yeomen

Knights of the Realm

Knights Errant

Grail Knights

Questing Knights

Damsel of the Lady

Bretonnian Lord

Paladin with army battle standard

ASSEMBLING MODELS

Modelling refers to both the process of assembling and gluing your models as well as the more involved art of posing and converting miniatures.

When building an army, it's quicker to assemble entire units in one go. This Ogre regiment demonstrates the process.

PREPARING YOUR MODELS

Before you can paint any models you must first assemble them. Warhammer miniatures are made of plastic or metal (a high quality tin alloy) or sometimes both in combination. Some models are cast as single pieces and will just need to be fixed to their plastic base, while other figures are multi-piece and must be assembled.

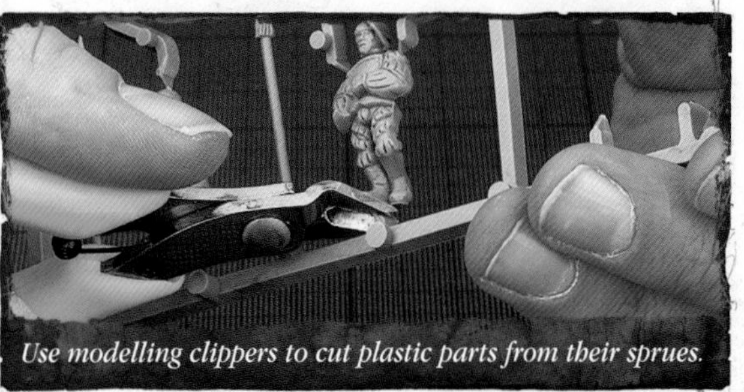

Use modelling clippers to cut plastic parts from their sprues.

CLIPPING OFF PLASTIC MODELS

Plastic mouldings are produced on a frame (often called a sprue) and it will be necessary to clip out the models or pieces. The best way to remove models from the sprue without damaging them is with a pair of clippers. Pulling and twisting the models off by hand can bend or break the delicate extremities.

CLEANING YOUR MODELS

The casting process can leave miniatures with tiny imperfections, but with a little time and patience these can be quickly remedied. On plastic models you might notice mould lines. After you have clipped the pieces off the sprue, you can gently pare away these lines with files or a craft knife.

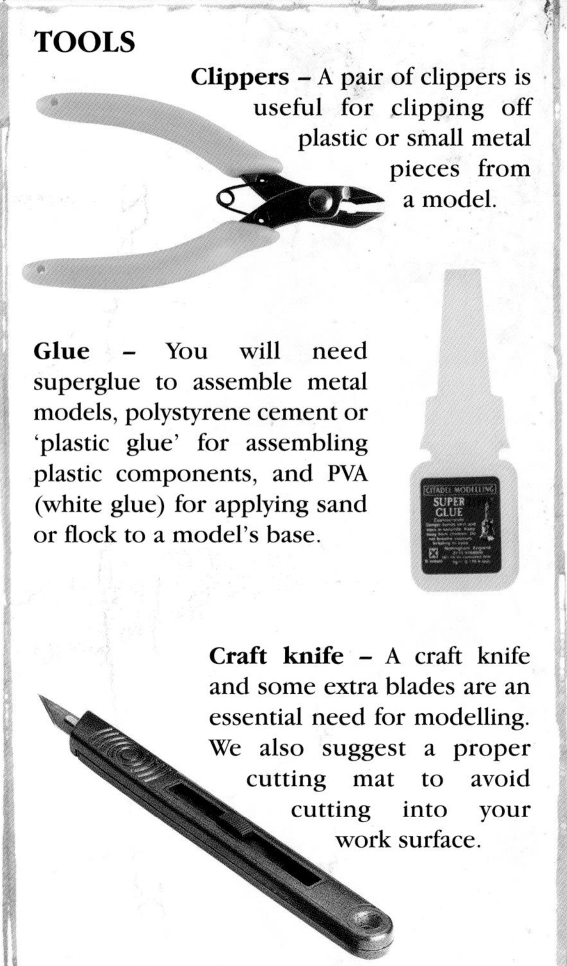

TOOLS

Clippers – A pair of clippers is useful for clipping off plastic or small metal pieces from a model.

Glue – You will need superglue to assemble metal models, polystyrene cement or 'plastic glue' for assembling plastic components, and PVA (white glue) for applying sand or flock to a model's base.

Craft knife – A craft knife and some extra blades are an essential need for modelling. We also suggest a proper cutting mat to avoid cutting into your work surface.

PLASTIC MODELS

Plastic regiments form the mainstay of many armies and a few key points will aid you when assembling such models.

USE THE RIGHT GLUE

Polystyrene cement, or plastic glue, is best for sticking plastic models together. It doesn't dry instantly, so you have a few moments to make certain each piece is in just the right place.

ENSURE MODELS FIT INTO A UNIT

When gluing your models together it is essential to ensure that the final model will fit into a unit once it is assembled. It is no use creating a striking and dynamic pose if that means the model cannot fit inside its intended unit. Assembling an entire unit at a time will give you an opportunity to test poses to see if the configuration will fit with the unit before gluing. Champions, musicians, and standard bearers are especially important models that you will want to fit neatly into the front rank of your unit.

SAFETY FIRST

Modelling tools, especially craft knives, can be dangerous and should not be used carelessly by adults or at all by children. Cut on a firm surface and always away from yourself. If you find yourself applying real pressure with a craft knife you are using the wrong tool. One slip can result in a nasty cut so pay strict attention to safety at all times.

BITS BOX

This is simply a box to keep all the spare pieces that are left over once you've finished assembly. Most kits have alternative weapons and heads to give you plenty of variety. Don't throw away these spare bits, keep them handy in a suitable container. Later on, they can be used to add detail to bases, or even to combine with other pieces to create your own unique models. Both these uses are covered in later pages.

SPEEDING UP YOUR ASSEMBLY TIME

An assembly line can help you quickly clean up and put together an entire plastic unit in one go. Try clipping out all the pieces and sorting them into piles (left arms holding spears, torsos, heads, etc). Use a hobby knife to trim up each piece you are using – you'll quickly learn where to look for mould lines – then you can begin gluing. Work each step down the line, for example, starting off by gluing all legs to their bases, then all torsos to legs, and so on.

These High Elf spearmen have been assembled so they fit together as a unit.

METAL MODELS

There are several points to remember when working with metal miniatures.

CLEANING YOUR MODELS

Cleaning metal models is a bit trickier than plastic ones. Mould lines can be smoothed down with a file, while venting (a thin extra spur of metal from the casting process) can be removed with some clippers before being filed.

USE THE RIGHT GLUE

Superglue is the only practical way to stick metal pieces together or to glue a plastic piece to a metal one. Use extra caution with superglue as it will stick to anything, including your fingers. For the best results always use just a dab of glue as too much actually makes the job of sticking together harder.

Sometimes a model's tab will need to be twisted to ensure it fits securely into its base.

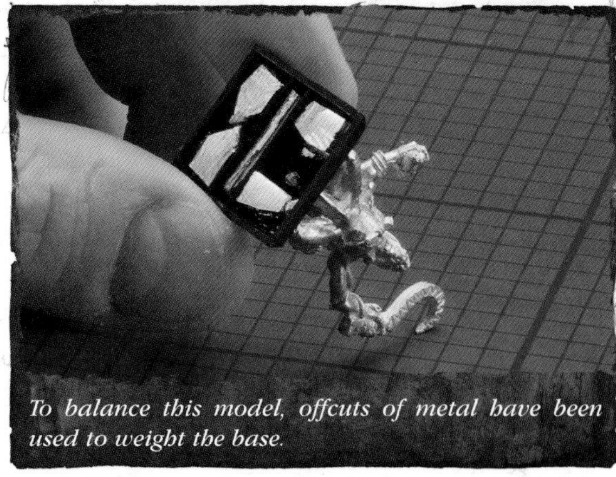

To balance this model, offcuts of metal have been used to weight the base.

TWISTING TABS

Many metal models come with a tab or a peg on their feet that fits into the base and helps to keep them together. It is quite common for a metal model to sit too loosely in its base to be effectively glued – it will simply keep falling over! By using a pair of pliers to bend a small kink into the model's base tab, a metal figure can be more easily glued into its plastic 'slottabase'.

WEIGHTING BASES

Sometimes models – particularly tall models such as standard bearers, or hybrid models made of both metal and plastic – have a tendency to overbalance. A good tip for countering this is to pack the empty space underneath the base with something heavy. Bits of waste metal left over from cleaning up your models, washers, or even old coins are ideal to glue into place to add weight.

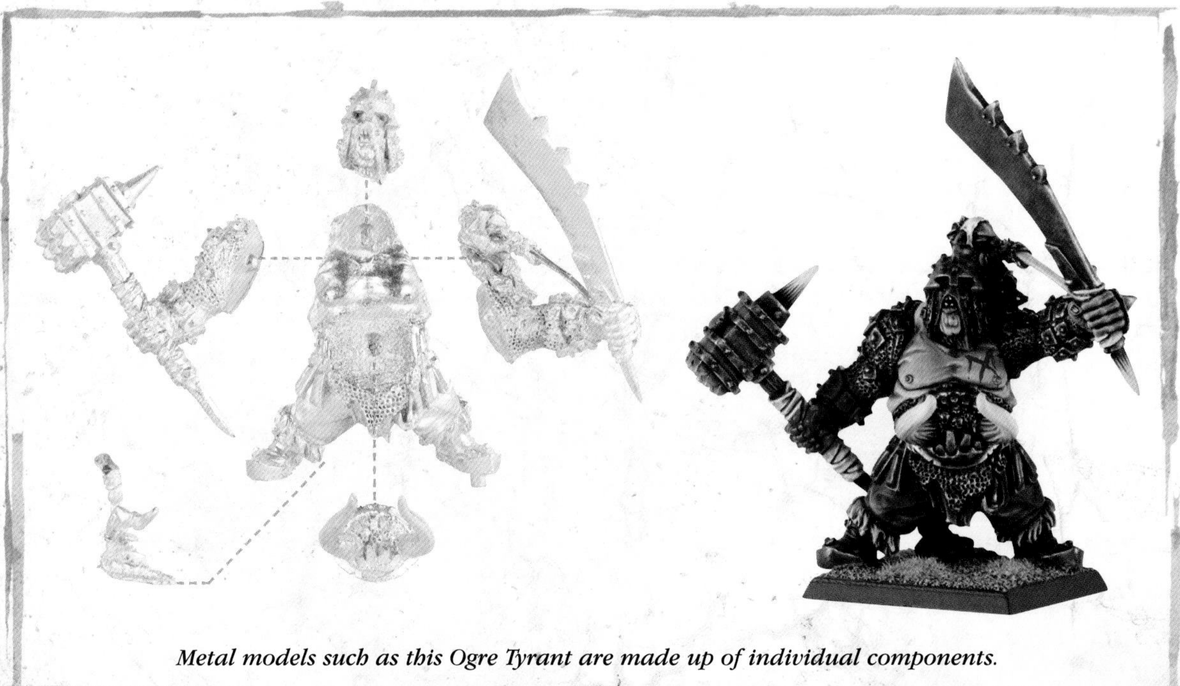

Metal models such as this Ogre Tyrant are made up of individual components.

LARGER MODELS

There are a number of large metal multi-piece Citadel models available in boxed sets. Often these are highly desirable units like powerful war machines, enormous monsters, or heroes of legend. These models take a degree more patience and skill to assemble and may also require a few specialised tools.

Once you have accounted for all the pieces, as well as where they go, it is time to 'dry-fit' the model. This is simply holding the pieces in place to see how they will fit together. Due to the nature of rubber moulds, the larger the metal piece the less exact the fit will be. Some filing may be required, so it is important to check before you start applying the glue!

With large, multi-part models, such as this Lizardmen Carnosaur, it may be necessary to pin certain pieces together.

GLUING LARGER PIECES

Particularly large pieces or metal parts that stick out at an odd angle may give you some difficulty even when using superglue. There are two excellent solutions to aid you: modelling putty and a pin vice.

For less troublesome spots, sometimes all that is needed is a small blob of putty wedged in at the join. More on how to use putty can be found in the Converting section (page 228).

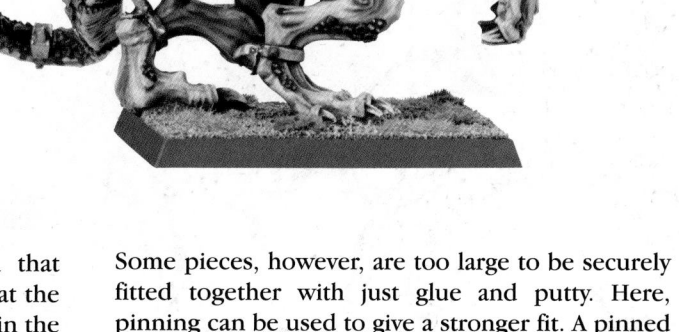

Some pieces, however, are too large to be securely fitted together with just glue and putty. Here, pinning can be used to give a stronger fit. A pinned model is less likely to break during the rigours of wargaming, so pinning especially large multi-piece miniatures is always a good idea.

PIN VICE

A pin vice is a useful tool when two large pieces of a model being joined could use some extra support. Use the pin vice to drill a tiny hole in each piece and then use a pin, perhaps a small rod or straightened piece of paper clip, to help strengthen the join.

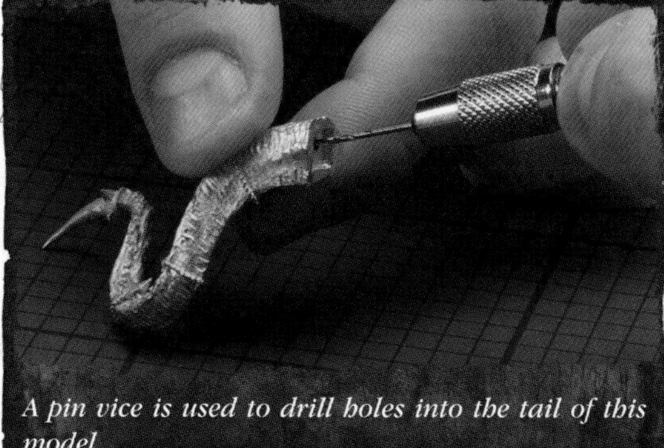

A pin vice is used to drill holes into the tail of this model.

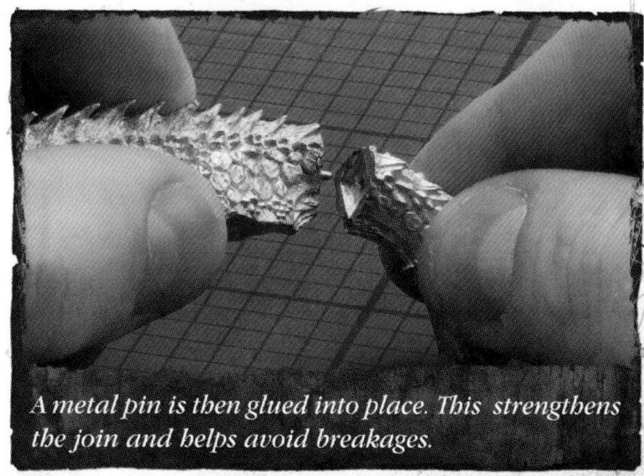

A metal pin is then glued into place. This strengthens the join and helps avoid breakages.

BASING

Most Warhammer models are mounted on square bases and are packaged with the correct base. However, when building large armies it makes sense to take advantage of multi-basing techniques.

MULTI-BASING

Games Workshop make a selection of bases that can make moving a particularly large unit easier. For some armies, like Skaven or Goblins, this sort of basing makes perfect sense, as units are large and casualties tend to come off in handfuls. Other forces, like Chaos Warriors or High Elves, are less likely to need such basing techniques. Always ensure you have the right ratio of single models compared to those on multi-bases, after all, you don't want to have to remove a group of four models if you've just lost one figure.

These examples show models that have been based together. Moving units becomes easier as there are less individual models.

MOVEMENT TRAYS

Movement trays are ubiquitous plastic or card sheets that are placed under large blocks of models and allow a player to move a single tray as opposed to picking up and manoeuvring each model separately. It is not necessary to use these time-saving devices in games but they can greatly speed things up, especially when it comes to units of twenty models or more.

Some players like to texture and paint their movement trays to match the bases of their models. In this way, the movement tray serves its function of making the unit easier to move, but doesn't take anything away from the look of the models.

This unit of Chaos Marauders is ranked up on a twenty man movement tray.

Apply PVA to base

Dip base in sand

Allow to dry before undercoating

ADDING TEXTURE TO BASES

To improve a model's finished look you can add a textured material to its base. Sand is ideal as it is both widely available and is very cheap.

Games Workshop supplies conveniently sized pots of sand for basing miniatures. These contain grains of different sizes, affording a varied, naturalistic look to the finished model.

Examples and tips on painting sand bases can be found in the Painting section on page 223.

ADDING MORE DETAIL TO BASES

Adding extra modelling touches to your miniatures' bases is a great way to help further theme your army. Picture an Empire Militia force with cobblestone bases, a unit of Skeletons raising themselves out of a graveyard, or even the undergrowth-covered bases that could adorn a Wood Elf force.

A few simple details work best as you don't want the base to overshadow the model itself. The easiest approach is to stick on one or two of the spare pieces you have saved in your bits box – abandoned weapons and shields look great or you could even use the occasional severed limb!

The most elaborate details are best saved for your characters, war machines or monster bases, as these provide focal points in your army.

All these models have had extra details added to their bases.

PAINTING

Painting your models is an enjoyable part of the Warhammer hobby. There is nothing quite like the glorious sight of two painted armies squaring off for a tabletop battle.

Superbly painted miniatures, such as the ones shown here, can be the centrepieces of any force. However, a fully painted army doesn't have to be this detailed to look good on the tabletop.

LEARNING TO PAINT

If you can write with a pen then you can paint Warhammer miniatures. Simply applying neat coats of paint is fine for beginners wanting quick, pleasing results. More ambitious painters can master further techniques for highlighting and shading. For in-depth advice and practical help for beginners and experts alike, refer to the *How to Paint Citadel Miniatures* book or ask your local shop if they run painting lessons.

PAINTING VERSUS PLAYING

You do not need to paint in order to enjoy a game of Warhammer and the temptation of getting to battle quickly often overwhelms new warlords. It is quite common for armies to be fielded unpainted for their first few games and only gradually reach a painted stage. Most experienced gamers take great pride in the appearance of their armies and doubtless, after a few battles, the urge to paint your models will at least match your zeal for tabletop bloodshed and conquest. Many players who were exclusively interested in Warhammer's tactical aspects have grown into enthusiastic painters. Those that gave their brushwork a chance discovered that painting can be a rewarding and satisfying hobby in its own right. Some hobbyists even forsake gaming and spend long hours painting individual models for their collection. For the rest of us, however, it is important to learn how to paint quickly and effectively, perhaps saving our best efforts for our generals and favourite figures.

PAINTING AN ARMY

When you are first learning, painting a single model at a time is best. For players trying to paint an entire army, however, it is a good idea to speed the process up once you've mastered the basics.

Even if you are fortunate enough to buy and assemble an entire army in one go, it probably isn't a great idea to attempt painting the whole thing at once. The prospect of so many unpainted models will overwhelm almost anyone and often the best solution is to break the project down into more achievable chunks. By working on a reasonable group of figures at a time you will go faster than painting models individually (see Assembly Line Painting on page 223) and you will not burn yourself out by overreaching.

PAINTING EQUIPMENT

Before starting to paint your warriors, you will need some essential tools. The most obvious things required are some paints and a paintbrush, but there are a few others as shown here.

1. Brushes

Good quality brushes are essential for painting. Most dedicated hobbyists find having a few different brush sizes works best, using a larger brush for broad surfaces and a smaller brush for intricate details. Even if it is looked after carefully, a brush will eventually fray. Rather than discarding these old warhorses, keep your ragged brushes for applying glue or painting bases.

2. Paints

Citadel Colour paints are non-toxic and water-based acrylics. They are formulated for painting plastic and metal miniatures and come in a variety of hues configured especially for use on Citadel miniatures (for example, Goblin Green).

3. Paint Palette

A paint palette can be any large flat piece of plastic or even a white tile. Cardboard and paper make poor paint palettes as the paint dries out faster. It's a good idea to clean your palette between painting sessions.

4. Tools

For preparing and assembling your model warriors you will need superglue and a pair of modelling clippers. A craft knife and some needle files may also be handy, while tweezers can be used for applying transfers.

5. Water Pot

When using acrylic paints, your brushes can be cleaned in cold, clean water. It is a good idea to have a separate pot for cleaning your brush after using metallic paint – this helps prevent the silvery flecks from contaminating your other paints.

6. Light

When painting, try to sit as close to a window as you can to get the best light possible. An alternative is to use a spot lamp with a daylight bulb. Good lighting allows you to see clearly what you're painting.

7. Tissues

Having a roll of kitchen towels or tissues handy can be very helpful, especially if you accidentally spill some water or paint.

8. Newspaper

It is a good idea to spread newspaper down over your painting area as even the most careful of painters will spill a paint pot over the course of time.

THE CITADEL COLOUR RANGE

The paint range includes metallic colours that are ideal for armour and weapons, as well as inks that are used for shading. Paints can be used straight from the pot or mixed together to form variant colours and unique shades.

Scab Red	Red Gore	Blood Red	Blazing Orange	Fiery Orange	Golden Yellow	Sunburst Yellow	Bad Moon Yellow	Scorched Brown	Graveyard Earth	Bestial Brown	Snakebite Leather	Desert Yellow
Bubonic Brown	Vomit Brown	Bleached Bone	Dark Flesh	Terracotta	Vermin Brown	Tanned Flesh	Dwarf Flesh	Bronzed Flesh	Elf Flesh	Liche Purple	Warlock Purple	Tentacle Pink
Midnight Blue	Regal Blue	Ultramarines Blue	Enchanted Blue	Ice Blue	Hawk Turquoise	Catachan Green	Dark Angels Green	Snot Green	Scorpion Green	Scaly Green	Goblin Green	Camo Green
Kommando Khaki	Rotting Flesh	Chaos Black	Codex Grey	Fortress Grey	Skull White	Shadow Grey	Space Wolves Grey	Boltgun Metal	Chainmail	Mithril Silver	Tin Bitz	Brazen Brass
Shining Gold	Burnished Gold	Dwarf Bronze	Yellow Ink	Flesh Ink	Red Ink	Purple Ink	Brown Ink	Chestnut Ink	Magenta Ink	Blue Ink	Dark Green Ink	Black Ink

PRIMING YOUR MODELS

It is highly recommended that models are primed before painting. This is simply a matter of applying an undercoat over the entire model. We do this because an undercoat is a better surface for the paint to 'stick' to, as opposed to bare metal or plastic. Paint will go on more easily with an undercoat and will also be more resistant to flaking off.

To speed up the painting process, undercoat entire units in one go. Double sided sticky tape can be used to stick models to an upturned box.

There are two methods for undercoating your models. The easiest is to use a spray can of Citadel primer, which provides easy coverage of models and can do a group of figures at a time. The downside is that spray primers need ventilation (using them outside is best) and can leave a mess so put newspaper down first.

The second method is priming by hand, either using paint or Citadel Smelly Primer. This is nothing more than painting on an even coat over the entire model. Hand priming is a good way to get a few models done, but a very hard way to prime an army.

There is a wide difference of opinion amongst painters as to whether models are easier to paint with white or black undercoat. It is easier to paint bright colours over a model with a white undercoat. On the other hand, a model with a lot of armour that is going to be painted in metallics may be easier with a black undercoat. There is no right or wrong, only personal preference.

When spraying miniatures cover as much of the model as possible. Otherwise you'll end up having to paint it all in by hand, as on this model.

PAINT SCHEMES

When choosing colour schemes for their own models, some players like to match the painted examples found in published Games Workshop material while others prefer to invent their own unique choices. Definitive painting information can always be found in the corresponding Warhammer Armies book.

The majority of models benefit from having a few distinct colours rather than trying to use your entire palette of colour choices on each figure. On this page you will find classic examples of paint schemes from some of the key armies in the Warhammer world.

Beastman Gor of Khazrak's warband

Dark Elf Spearman of Naggarond

High Elf Spearman of Tor Yvresse

Tomb Kings Skeleton Warrior of Khemri

Ogre Bull of the Gutripper tribe

Skaven Clanrat of Clan Mors

Undead Zombie of Sylvania

Dwarf Warrior of Karaz-a-Karak

Night Goblin of the Crooked Moon tribe

Empire Halberdier of Middenheim

Lizardmen Saurus of the Itza Spawnings

Warrior of Chaos, follower of Archaon

Bretonnian Man-at-arms sworn to King Leoncoeur

Orc Boy of Waaagh! Grimgor

Wood Elf Glade Guard of the Kindred of Lakoys

PAINTING A WOOD ELF WARRIOR

A fully painted army looks impressive and helps to evoke the feel of a Warhammer battle. However, each player will paint his army in a slightly different way and to a different standard. This page demonstrates some different approaches to painting which can be used on any models.

WHITE UNDERCOAT

1

To start the model, a coat of Skull White spray paint has been applied. This a good undercoat to use when painting predominantly light models.

2

The applied colours are instantly brighter. However, you will require a couple of coats of paint to achieve a non streaky finish.

3

Once finished with flat coats of paint, the model is of a good enough standard to grace your regiment.

BLACK UNDERCOAT

1

Undercoat the model with Chaos Black spray paint. This is suitable for most miniatures, especially those with dark colour schemes or lots of armour.

2

Working over a black undercoat means the colours will appear darker, so a couple of coats may be needed.

3

The finished model shows how, by leaving the black undercoat in the recesses, natural shading can be achieved.

SHADED MODEL

Using the flat coloured model, a series of ink washes have been applied. Inks are a great way to add greater depth and shade to a miniature.

HIGHLIGHTED MODEL

Once the ink washes have dried, the edges of the model are given a simple highlight with a lighter shade. This creates a more natural finish.

'EAVY METAL STANDARD

Achieving a standard such as this requires practise, patience and hard work. It can be a time-consuming process so is best saved for your heroes or elite regiments.

FINISHING THE BASES

Using simple techniques, you can achieve a wide variety of looks for your miniature's bases. It is best to use the same technique for an entire army to maintain a cohesive appearance.

1. Simple Painted Bases

The easiest way to finish your bases is to paint them an appropriate colour. Goblin Green and Graveyard Earth are common choices.

2. Sanded Bases

Sand can also be glued to your bases to provide texture. This is easier (but not essential) to do after assembling your models, but before painting (see page 217). After the rest of the model is finished, you can paint the sand the colours of your choice.

3. Flocked Bases

There are a number of modelling products available that provide a realistic texture for your bases, including flock and static grass. They are applied in the same way as sand, described on page 217.

4. Combining Techniques

Some people combine these approaches, adding small patches of flock to the top of the sand. Some of the sand is left showing to represent the bare earth between the tufts of grass.

ASSEMBLY LINE PAINTING

An assembly line process (also known as batch painting) will allow you to paint the same area on each of your models in turn and, by doing so, you can finish a unit more quickly. For instance, if you were working on the armour of your Chaos Warriors you would work down the line, painting that part of each model in turn. By the time you've finished, the first model should be dry and ready for the next step.

These Chaos Warriors have been painted as a batch of four models. By painting the same colour on every model, it's possible to race through a unit.

When painting a unit using the assembly line method, it will speed things up even more if you mount each rank on a strip of rigid card using double-sided adhesive tape. Of course, if you have mounted your miniatures on a multi base, you won't even need to do this.

PAINTING SHIELDS

Many Warhammer models bear shields and when painted with special attention they can really make a unit stand out. What follows is advice for making your shields more than just a 6+ saving throw!

PAINT SHIELDS SEPARATELY

The best way to paint shields is to do them before attaching them to your model. Some painters prefer to leave the shields on their plastic sprue while painting, although when using this method you will have to go back and touch-up the areas where you have clipped the shield off the frame.

The shields on this Bretonnian Men-at-arms regiment unifies them by use of both colour and shield iconography.

Examples of moulded shield designs.

PAINTING YOUR OWN DESIGNS

Some ambitious painters apply their own creative designs onto their shields freehand. This can make the unit look even more special, but remember, a complicated design may be hard or time consuming to duplicate on a large regiment.

1
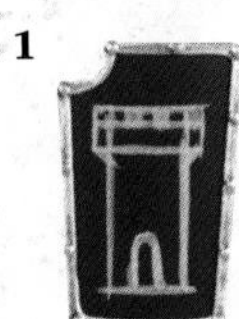
2
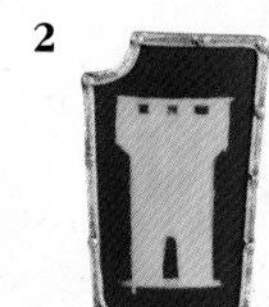
3

The outline is painted first before being filled in. Finally, the design is tidied up, and extra details added, using the background colour of the shield.

PAINTING MOULDED SHIELD DESIGNS

Many miniatures, especially the plastic regiment boxes, come with a two-part shield: the basic shield shape itself and a moulded design or icon to fit in the centre. There are often several different designs that a player may choose from or all may be used in the same unit to create a varied and more ragtag appearance – whichever look you feel is more appropriate for your regiment. It is best to glue these pieces together before priming and painting. Some shading and bright highlighting can quickly make these shields the centre of attention for your unit.

APPLYING TRANSFERS

Transfers provide a quick, easy way of applying details such as shield designs to your miniatures. Some Warhammer regiment box sets come complete with appropriate transfer sheets, providing a wide range of symbols and designs to choose from.

PAINTING BANNERS

One of the most majestic looking aspects of many Warhammer armies are the unit standards. These bold banners or totems give painters a chance to add character and theme to their armies, and provided below are some great tips to make your banners rise proudly above the rest...

MOULDED BANNERS

Many Warhammer regiments come with moulded banners that look very realistic when painted. It is best to assemble and prime the entire model before painting the banner.

MAKING BANNERS OUT OF PAPER

It is also possible to affix a paper banner to a pole to make a standard bearer. Some Armies books include banner designs that you can photocopy, while other painters prefer to make their own banners or pennants to fit in with their army's theme. Regular drawing paper works best, but over the years painters have experimented with parchment, vellum, and even thin foil.

A banner template can be photocopied, and painted using Citadel Colour paints. It can be attached to a banner pole by folding it around and applying a dab of PVA glue to the inner surface of the paper.

PAINTING AN ORC BANNER

1

First paint the outline of the skull motif. Next, fill this in with a couple of thinned down coats of Codex Grey mixed with Blood Red.

2

Paint a couple of layers of watered down Blood Red over the basecoat. This will provide a bright, flat colour.

3

Finally, use a Fine Detail brush to tidy up any edges. The broken tusk has been achieved by painting a thin crooked line with Chaos Black.

A FINISHED UNIT

The colour scheme chosen for this unit consists of Shining Gold, Red Gore and Hawk Turquoise, plus Bleached Bone for the Skeletons themselves. The models were painted using the assembly line method, painting all the bone first, then the metal, etc.

This banner comes as part of the plastic regiment kit, and has been painted to match the rest of the unit. It has been embellished with a few simple freehand markings.

These miniatures were primed with Chaos Black spray. The undercoat has been left showing in the deepest recesses of the model to provide dark shading.

The command group, (the champion, standard bearer and musician), are the focus of the unit, dominating the front rank. For this reason, many painters finish the rank-and-file troops as fast as possible, but take more care on these three key models.

The bases, as well as the movement tray, have been dipped in sand and painted to represent the desert.

The shields have moulded designs, while a few have been given additional iconography, painted freehand with white paint.

A FINISHED ARMY

Here you can see the same unit as part of a complete army. The models all use a limited palette of colours and the bases match the desert environment.

The same limited palette has been used to paint the bone of all of the Skeletons in the army, as well as their undead mounts. Red appears as an accent colour in all of the units, but is used as a main colour in the elite Tomb Guard, marking them out as special whilst maintaining the army's overall colour scheme. The general too uses the entire palette, but stands out as far more time has been spent in painting this important miniature.

For a wealth of useful techniques and ideas about painting your models:

CONVERTING

Some gamers like to make their models more special and show off their modelling skills by creating new poses and substituting or adding parts from other models. This practice is known as converting. It is not an essential part of playing Warhammer, but it is very satisfying to know that your army includes a completely unique model.

Converting can be as simple as sticking on a few extra pieces, or as challenging as scratch-building new parts.

There are many reasons for converting a model. Giving a hero another hand weapon, flail, or great weapon is common, as is trying to better represent a particular magic item. Just make sure you can get the upgrade in your army list before you do the conversion. Other good reasons for converting a model are to add variety to a unit, or simply because it looks cool!

As it can take quite a bit of time, many players reserve conversions solely for their army commander or other characters.

The arm joints of this Chaos Warrior were cut away, so the arms could be repositioned at a different angle.

This High Elf has been given an interesting new pose, as well as a cloak from the Empire Knights kit.

This Orc has been given a mighty club taken from an Ogres kit.

MIXING KITS

The simplest conversion is to combine plastic parts from different kits. For example, you might have a few spare pieces from your lord kit that will look great on the champion of a regiment. You can even take parts from other armies, if you think it looks right. A great tip is to use Blu-tack (adhesive putty) to hold the part in place, so you can see how it looks before gluing.

CHANGING POSES

A slightly trickier conversion is to change the pose of a model. Citadel plastic kits provide a lot of variation, but you might want your model to brandish its weapon in a particularly dynamic way, or to stand in a characterful position that the basic kit does not allow. You will need to cut some of the plastic parts (commonly at the elbow or shoulder) and glue them back together in a different way.

MODELLING PUTTY

Two-part modelling putty, often known as Green Stuff, is commonly used when converting, because joining parts that weren't designed to fit together often leaves gaps to fill. With practice, it is even possible to sculpt new features instead of taking parts from other models.

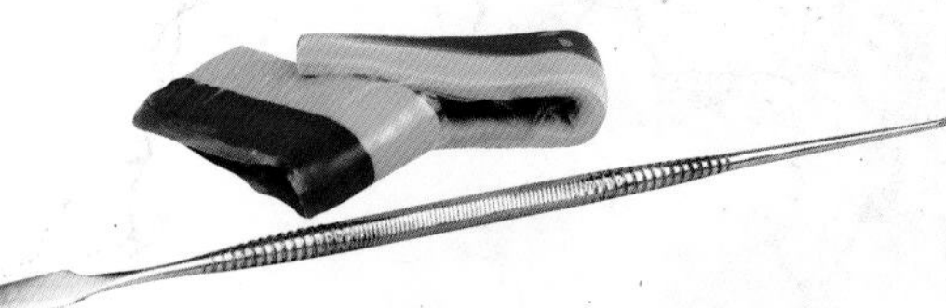

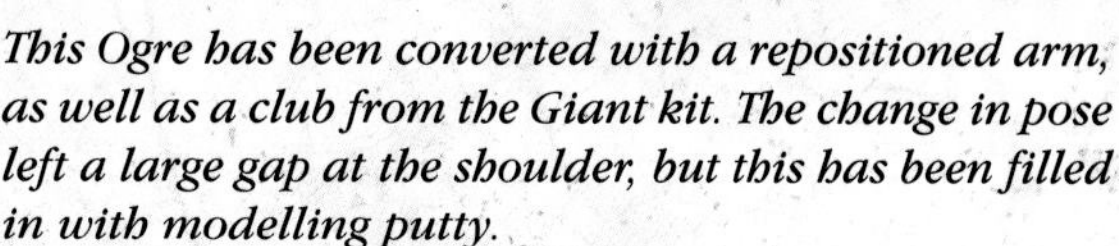

This Ogre has been converted with a repositioned arm, as well as a club from the Giant kit. The change in pose left a large gap at the shoulder, but this has been filled in with modelling putty.

The blue and yellow parts are mixed together to form a green putty that will slowly set hard.

CONVERTING METAL MODELS

Converting is relatively easy with plastic models but with metal ones it can be a lot trickier. Some small extremities can be snipped off with clippers but in order to cut through a more substantial metal piece you will need a saw. For such serious conversion work there are two types: the craft saw (or junior hacksaw) and the more delicate jeweller's saw.

These models have all been lovingly converted, using components from other miniatures as well as extensive use of modelling putty.

WOOD ELF ARMY

This striking Wood Elf army belongs to gamer Joe Sturge. Instead of choosing the traditional green of the Wood Elves, Joe has opted for a winter colour scheme that ties the entire army together. The force uses as few colours as possible: a strong primary colour, a narrow range of complimentary colours to provide a backdrop, and a couple of sharp contrasting colours to provide overall definition. By choosing such a focussed colour scheme, the Wood Elf and Spirit elements tie together to provide a finished army that clearly belongs in its environment.

DARK ELF ARMY

Stuart McCorquodale has been collecting Dark Elves for many years and this army reflects just a small portion of his collection. His diverse force includes many models from previous editions of Warhammer alongside current favourites, and it's this mix that provides such a rich assortment of miniatures. The force focusses on a strong centre of infantry that is ably supported on the flanks by cavalry. Units of Dark Riders harass the enemy while the hard-hitting Cold One Knights offer a fast and powerful counter-attacking option. As with many Dark Elf armies ranged weaponry is well represented with particular attention paid to Repeater Bolt Throwers.

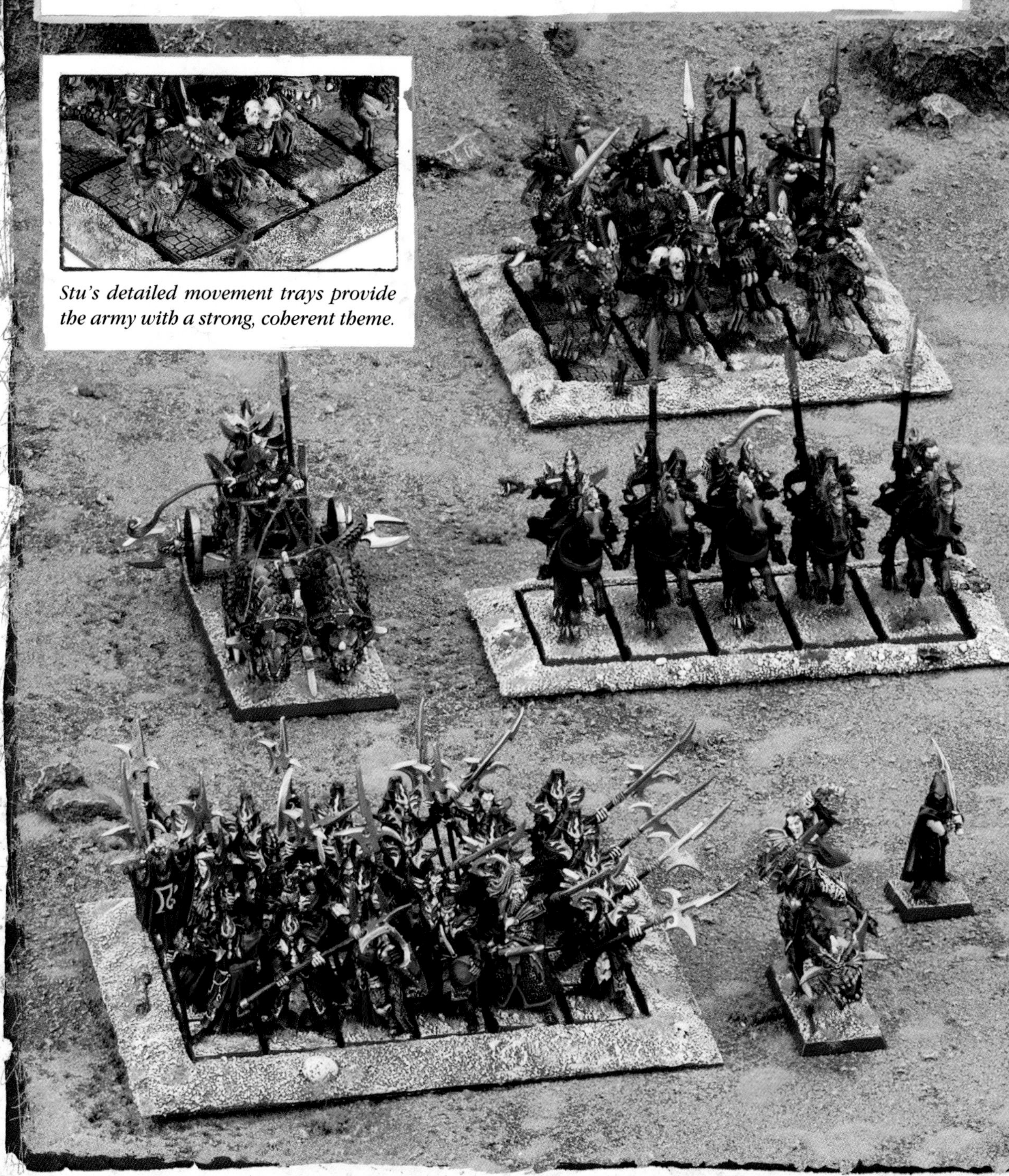

Stu's detailed movement trays provide the army with a strong, coherent theme.

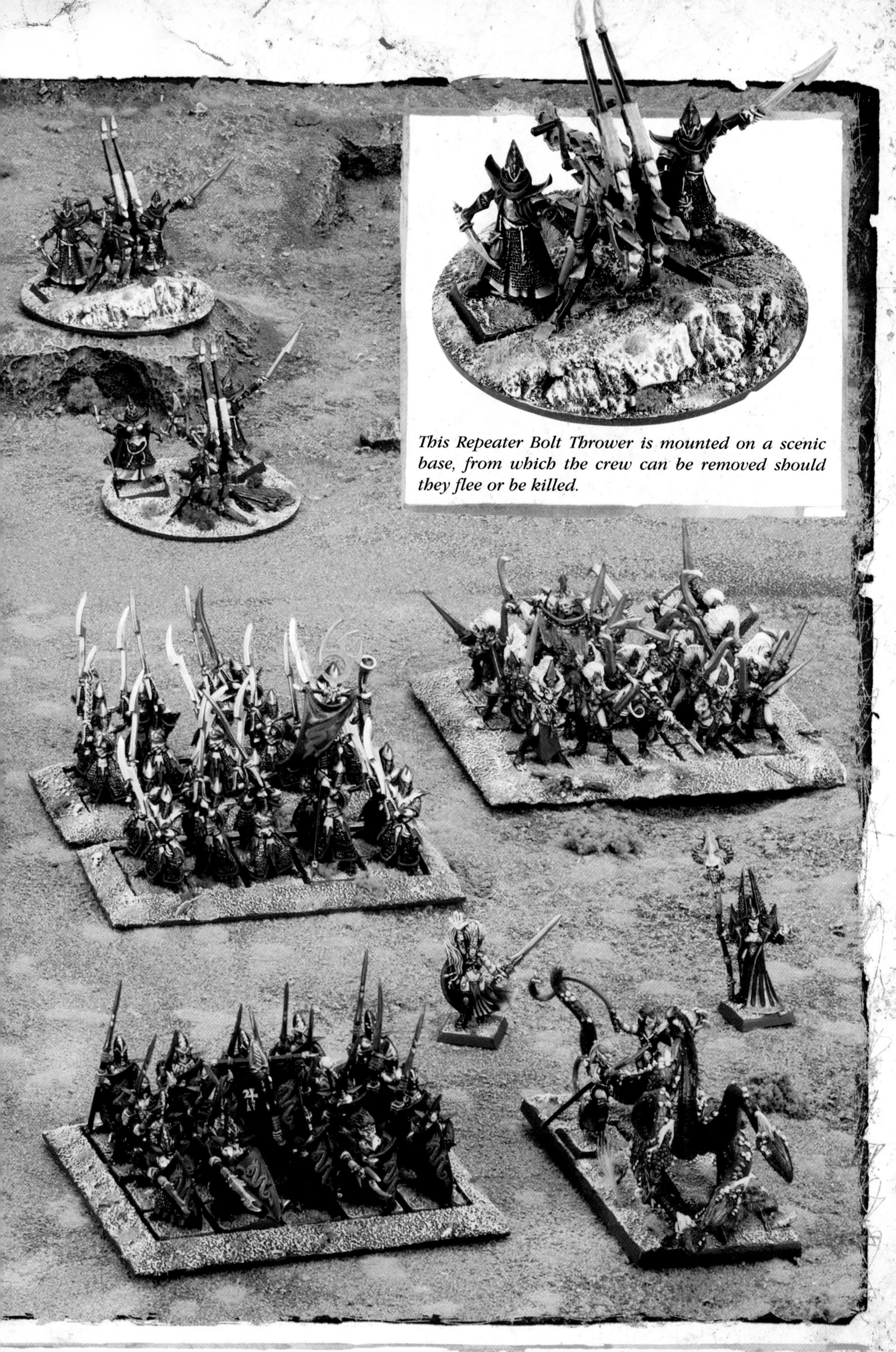

This Repeater Bolt Thrower is mounted on a scenic base, from which the crew can be removed should they flee or be killed.

TERRAIN

It is quite possible to play on an unadorned table and to have many enjoyable games. However, even the most basic scenery, like woods and hills, will add infinitely to both the look of the battle and the gaming possibilities.

When a tabletop wargamer talks about terrain, he is referring to the gaming table and the lay of the battlefield. Is there high ground that offers line of sight to rain missile weapons upon the foe? Are there defensible areas or avenues of advance where flanks will be protected by streams or cliffs? Terrain does more than offer tactical options, it sets the story of the battle and can help transport players further into the Warhammer world.

THE GAMING TABLE

The most basic piece of wargames terrain is the table itself. You can make do with the kitchen table or even wage a battle on the floor, but a dedicated gaming board looks better and, unlike the floor, is virtually immune from anyone accidentally stepping on your general. But if you've never made a wargames table, where should you start?

SIZE

The best place to start is to determine the size of the gaming board you can fit in your available space and still easily store when the fighting is done.

Getting as large a gaming board as you can reasonably manage is always the best answer – after all, you can mark off and play on a smaller area of a large board, but you cannot easily add extra space to a small gaming table. 6'x4' is generally considered the standard size, although smaller battles work quite nicely on 4'x4'. If you have the space, 8'x4' or larger will allow for huge games.

Terrain features like this hill can be moved about on the battlefield between matches. This provides a wide variety of gaming set-ups.

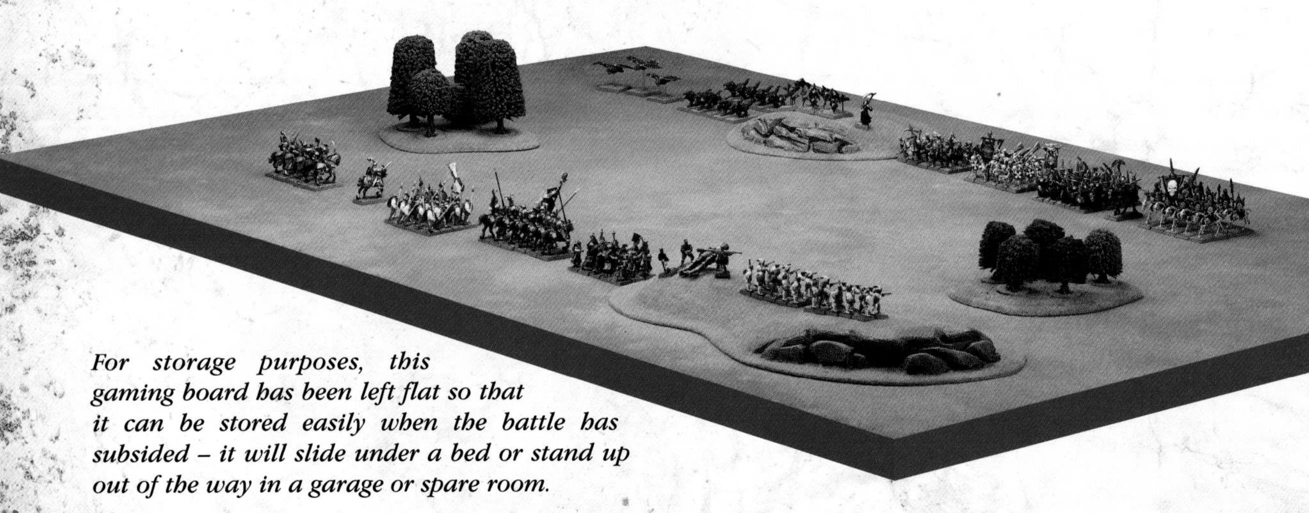

For storage purposes, this gaming board has been left flat so that it can be stored easily when the battle has subsided – it will slide under a bed or stand up out of the way in a garage or spare room.

One of the great appeals of gathering together at a club or attending a large gaming event is that you can join in immense battles spread across massive tables (see page 258 for more about clubs and events).

MAKING A GAMING TABLE

There are dozens of different ways to make a great gaming table and each has its own advantages when it comes to such factors as durability, storage, ease of construction, looks, cost, and availability of certain materials. Here are some examples made from materials found at any good home supply or DIY (do-it-yourself) store. Whatever material you choose, it will need to be painted to look like a battlefield, or for a more realistic look, apply glue and sand to the surface just as you would a miniatures base.

This modular board is made out of a 2'x2' square of polystyrene with duct tape reinforced sides. The polystyrene has been carved and textured to look more realistic.

Here is a modular board section made with a sturdy plywood base. Features like roads or streams can be used with modular boards, allowing a variety of set-ups.

This gaming table is made from hardboard and is very durable (and heavy). Some DIY stores will even cut wood to your exact specifications.

WOODS

The Warhammer world is full of forests, such as the enchanted Athel Loren, the Empire's foreboding Drakwald, or the scraggy pines high up in the Worlds Edge Mountains. Unless you want to set your battles in the desert, trees are incredibly common and useful additions to any gaming table.

Why are woods useful? In game terms, they block line of sight, hinder movement, and provide cover to troops on the edge of the woods – all elements that a tabletop commander can use tactically to his advantage! The easiest way to make a wood is to take some commercially available trees and affix them to a base, as per our example below. A base of hardboard or card can be cut into an irregular shape to serve as the forest floor.

MAKING A MORE FLEXIBLE FOREST

During the course of a game, it is possible that units will want to enter the woods, perhaps to flush out enemy skirmishers or to come at the foe unexpectedly. To make their forests more flexible and more model-movement friendly, some players prefer a more modular approach to woods. With this approach, you put the trees on individual bases and position them on a larger base to represent the edge of the woods.

The trees can be easily removed to allow troops to move through them.

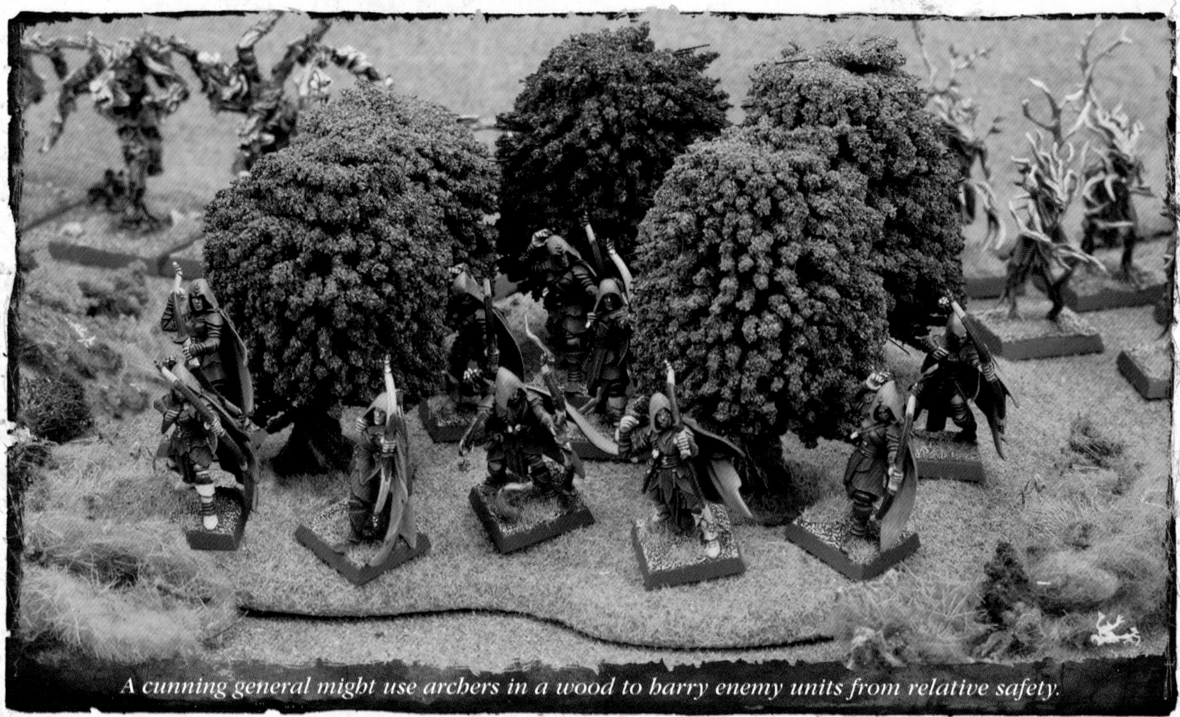

A cunning general might use archers in a wood to harry enemy units from relative safety.

HILLS

Whether you are talking about the rolling green mounds of Bretonnia or the shifting sand dunes of the haunted Khemri desert, hills are common, but important, battlefield terrain.

In close combat, high ground gives an advantage, but the biggest benefit of a hill is the line of sight it provides. When placed atop a hill, a war machine has clear line of sight over friendly troops and often commands a view over great swathes of the battlefield. Troops with missile weapons on top of hills are allowed to fire with an additional rank – all of which means well-placed war machines or archers can greatly affect a battle's outcome. Conversely, a cunning warlord can sometimes use the cover of hills to block line of sight and so manoeuvre his troops close to the foe without being subjected to enemy missile fire.

STYLISED STEPPED HILLS

To make it easier for a unit of models to move over or stand on top of a hill, it is often best to make a slightly stylised stepped hill. This offers both a visually pleasing representation of a hill as well as clear flat places for models and units to stand. Slopes that are too steep will interfere with model placement and make it nearly impossible to game upon.

A simple low hill can be made from polystyrene and flocked to match your gaming table.

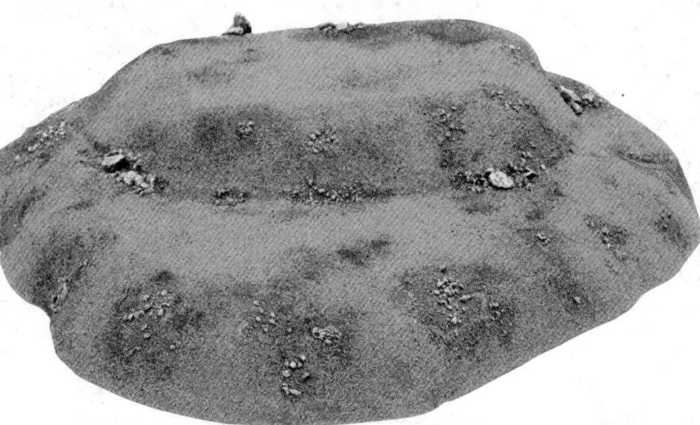

By adding a second tier, a hill becomes a great vantage point for your missile troops.

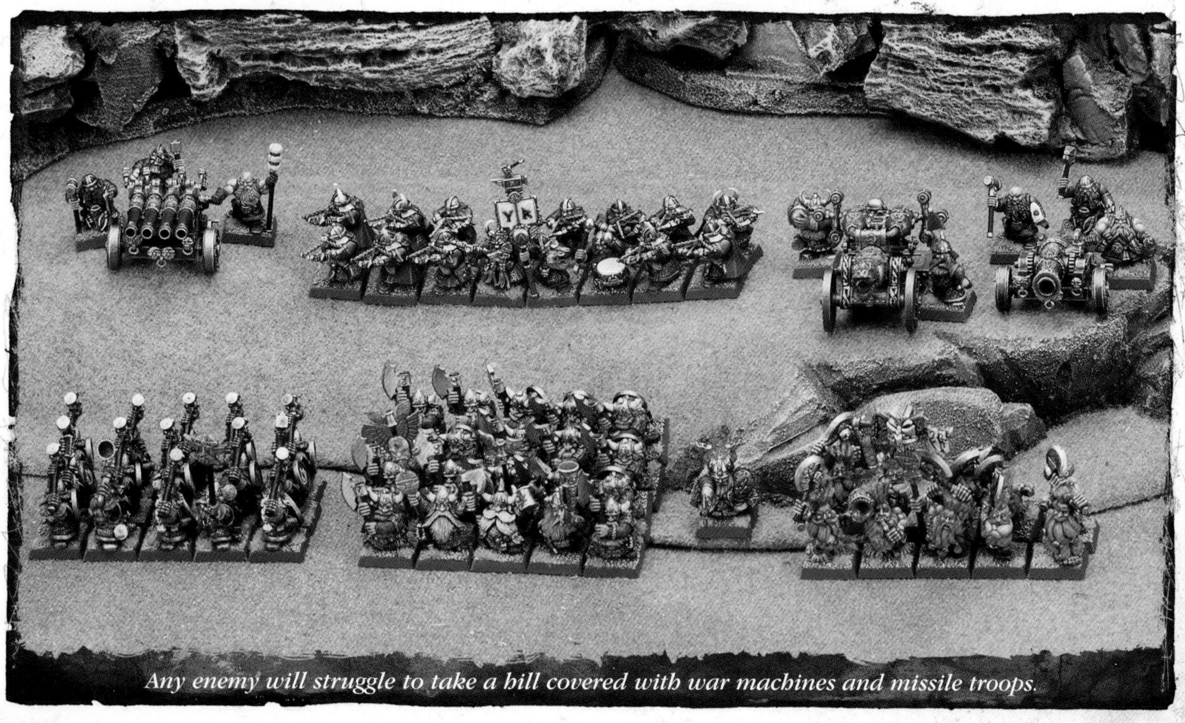

Any enemy will struggle to take a hill covered with war machines and missile troops.

TERRAIN FEATURES

While hills and trees are the most common terrain features found in many wargamer's collections, they are only a fraction of the many terrain possibilities of the Warhammer world.

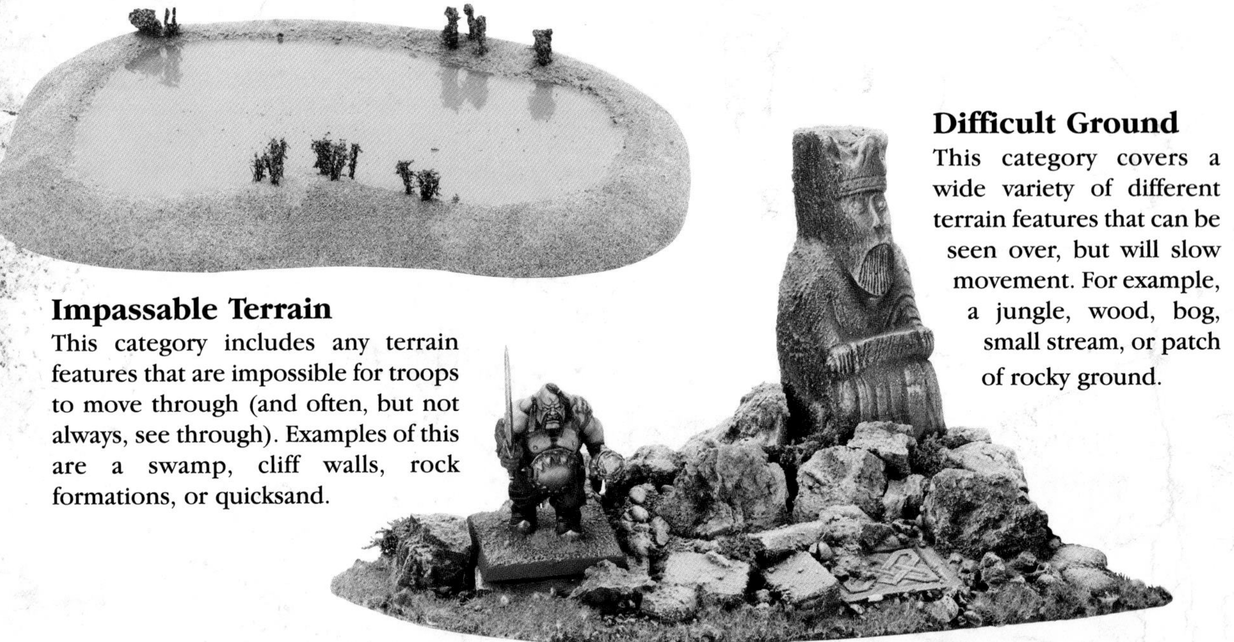

Difficult Ground

This category covers a wide variety of different terrain features that can be seen over, but will slow movement. For example, a jungle, wood, bog, small stream, or patch of rocky ground.

Impassable Terrain

This category includes any terrain features that are impossible for troops to move through (and often, but not always, see through). Examples of this are a swamp, cliff walls, rock formations, or quicksand.

These Dwarfs have their backs to the wall – literally, as the cliff and building are impassable terrain.

Buildings

These structures can form important defensive positions in a game and could be represented by heavily shuttered inns of the Empire, Bretonnian hovels, the enormous tents of the Ogres or more.

Obstacles

An obstacle is any linear terrain feature, such as a wall, hedge, fence, or hastily constructed barricade. Troops gain defensive advantages by staying behind such obstacles and they can become strategic items on a battlefield.

Rivers

A river counts as a single terrain feature and should run from one edge of the battlefield to another. To keep things simple, players should agree ahead of games which sections of a river are fordable, and which will count as either difficult ground or impassable.

SPECIAL FEATURES

Special features is an exciting and open-ended class of terrain that can add some fantastic elements to a game of Warhammer for ambitious gamers and terrain builders.

While it is possible to nominate any particular terrain as a special feature – such as a strategically located hill or building – a custom-made special feature will add character to a game.

On these pages you will find some examples of special features and how you might want to use them in your battles.

Warpstone meteorites are lumps of pure chaos that crash down onto the Warhammer world. Armies will fight desperately to possess such a powerful magical substance.

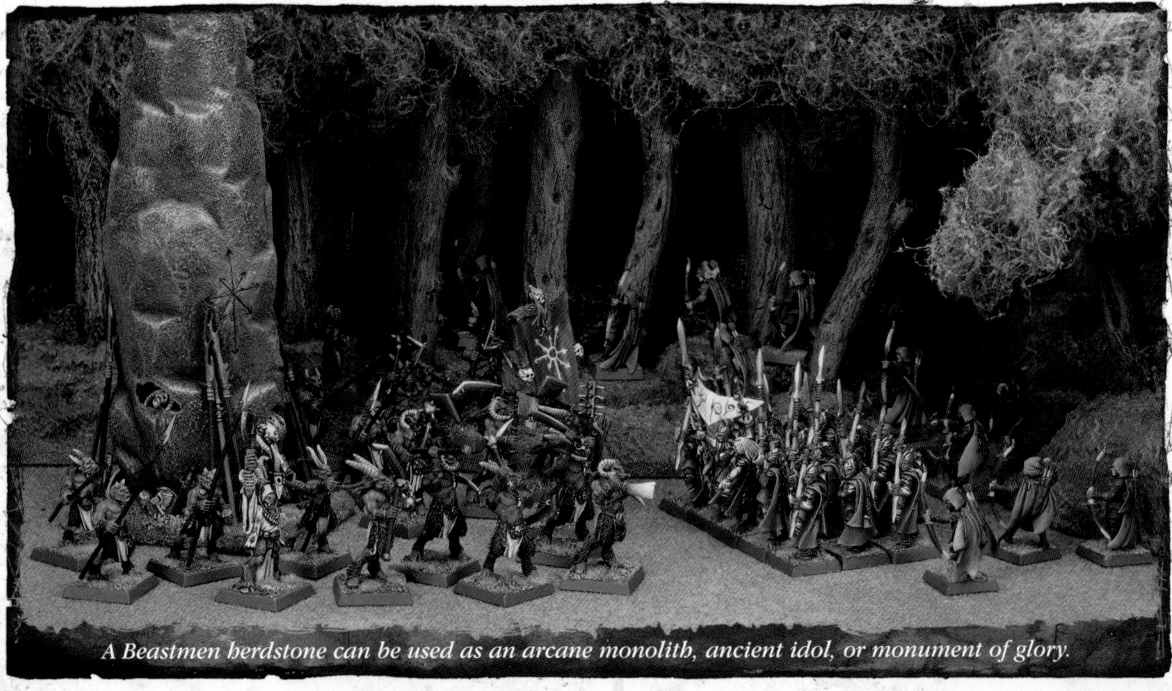

A Beastmen herdstone can be used as an arcane monolith, ancient idol, or monument of glory.

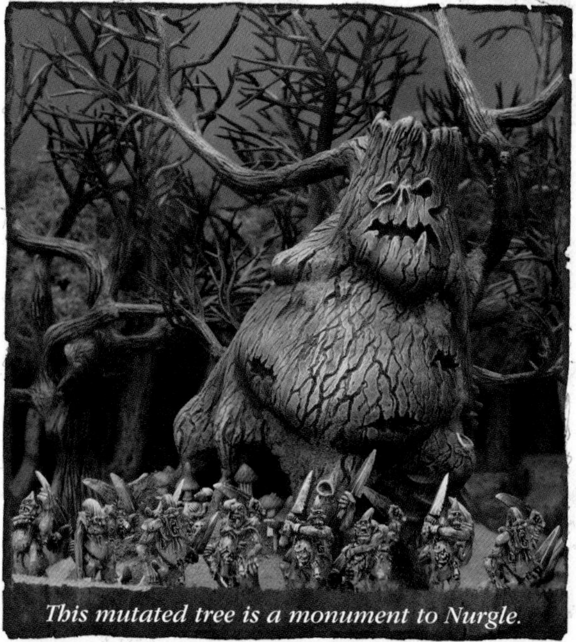

This mutated tree is a monument to Nurgle.

Ancient standing stones such as this one are easy to make and represent arcane monoliths.

An Undead force lurches forth from an ancient burial mound.

THEMED BATTLEFIELDS

Warhammer battlefields can be as varied and interesting as you can imagine and build. Shown here are some expertly built and heavily themed tables that just cry out to be played upon.

KHEMRI

It is a goal of nearly every tabletop commander to play a game on a spectacularly set up battlefield. This themed terrain perfectly captures the spirit of an ancient Tomb Kings setting and still leaves plenty of room for units to manoeuvre and fight.

Obelisk

Over the years this monument has begun to shift in the sands, adding to the ancient, ruined look of the battlefield.

Skull Tomb

In a standard battle, the burial tomb centrepiece could be declared as either a hill or as impassable terrain. In a specially devised scenario it is easy to imagine endless reinforcements of Skeletons emerging from the dark tomb entrance.

Sphynx

Worn down by centuries of sandstorms, this edifice can act as a piece of impassable terrain or could perhaps be used as a special feature.

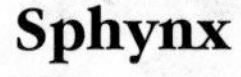

LUSTRIA

This enormous table shows off a temple-city deep in the steaming jungles of Lustria. Originally produced in France as a display piece for a Games Day (a fantastic Games Workshop event), this is a truly inspirational table to battle on. Covered with loads of elaborate modelling, the more you look at this board the more details you can pick out.

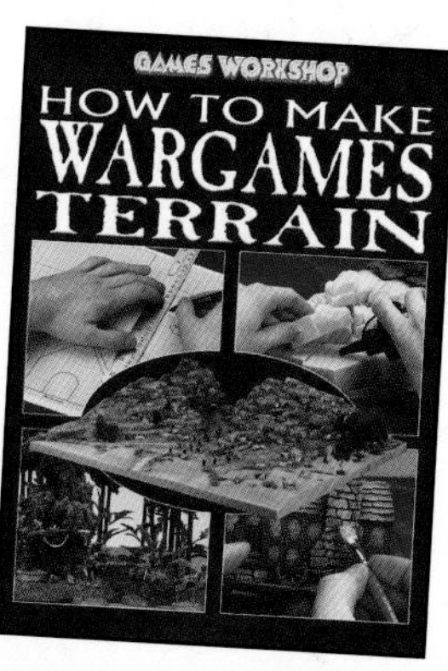

Those interested in building great wargaming terrain should check out this book. It includes loads of tips, techniques, how-to's, and inspiration for making your own terrain.

The vine-encrusted architecture and worn paint scheme work together to build up the impression of an ancient and powerful Lizardmen city.

GAMING

Gaming is the heart of the Warhammer hobby and this is true whether you are playing a battle on beautiful terrain or on your dining room floor; whether you are trying to beat your best friend or re-enact an exciting story.

SETTING UP A GAME

As there are so many ways to play Warhammer, and so many styles of gaming, it pays to discuss the following subjects with your opponent before the match begins:

- How many points?
- How many players?
- How to set up your battlefield?
- Will you be playing a standard game or scenarios?

HOW MANY POINTS?

When deciding how many points to play there are two overriding factors – how many models you have to choose from, and secondly, how much time you can dedicate to the battle?

The number of models in your collection will, of course, limit the maximum number of points you can muster for a battle.

The time it takes to fight a battle depends on how many models are being used and how familiar the players are with the rules.

The Dwarfs and greenskins fight a bitter battle high in a mountain pass.

Multi-player games with allied commanders provide new challenges and opportunities.

Generally speaking, in a small game of Warhammer each player has an army of between 500 and 1,000 points – the battle will probably take an hour or so to play out. Medium games are between 1,000 and 3,000 points, usually taking an evening to play. Anything over 3,000 points is a large game that may take all day!

Very experienced and ambitious gamers will even play matches that last over a weekend or longer, but of course this kind of game will need a lot of models and a gaming table that can be left standing in mid-battle.

TEAM GAMES

While the majority of the examples in this book have assumed that battles are fought between two opposing players, there is nothing to stop Warhammer being enjoyed by three, four or more players at once.

It can be a lot of fun to join forces with some friends for a team game. Also, if you fancy playing a bigger battle but don't have enough models yet, then this is a good solution. Any number of players can join together to form a single side, just as long as the overall points total is roughly the same as the opposing team's. These sides are often, but not always, split amongst good and evil forces. For example, a High Elf and Bretonnian army can team up to fight an enormous Chaos horde. Most often, each player commands his own army and the allied warlords consult each other and coordinate their plans. This adds camaraderie to a match and can take away the sting of bad luck or losing as you have someone to commiserate with (or, being less scrupulous, someone to blame it on!).

No matter how many players join in, a team game is played out in very much the same way as a one-against-one Warhammer battle. Perhaps the only exception is that the gaming takes a little more time due to the added tactical conversations amongst players as they try to decide a course of action. Many gaming stores, clubs or conventions host large multi-player games where a participant has an opportunity to get involved in a spectacular battle involving dozens of players or more.

ALTERNATIVE SET-UPS

As described at the beginning of the book, there is a specific system for setting up terrain and deploying armies for a battle. This can be considered the standard method, but there are alternatives that you can try out if both players agree. Players are free to use more terrain, or to theme a battle in any way they see fit. If you can't agree what to do, simply revert to the standard game.

COMMON SENSE

It is difficult to come up with hard and fast 'fair' rules for terrain without making all battles occur on the same ground, or even worse, trying to standardise everyone's terrain collection (such as saying all hills must be 5" by 5"). Varied and imaginative terrain set-ups are one of the pleasures of the Warhammer world, and the best advice is to use your common sense and talk to your opponent about which approach you want to use.

ONE PLAYER SETS UP, OTHER CHOOSES

• One player (determined by agreement or high dice roll) sets up all the terrain for the battlefield.

• When the set-up is done the other player may choose which side of the table to deploy from.

From then on, deployment and which side goes first is decided as per standard.

Advantages: This method allows for a cohesive themed battlefield to be set up in a way that alternating terrain placement does not.

Themes, like a small crossroads settlement or a mountain pass, can easily be laid out. Also, this can speed up the game as the host can set up the terrain before an opponent arrives so army deployment and battle can be entered into even more swiftly.

Disadvantages: It is possible that the battlefield will not be set up in a 100% equitable manner and one side may get a slight advantage. Conversely, in a player's fervour to strike a perfectly balanced set-up, a symmetrical gaming table is set up (a hill for me, a hill for you and so on). The problem with this fairness is that the battles are always set up in pretty much the same way.

A themed battle over an Empire settlement is the kind of evocative battlefield that can arise from an alternate game set-up.

IMPARTIAL THIRD PARTY

• An impartial third party or games master sets up the entire gaming board.

After this, choosing table side, deployment and which side goes first is decided as standard.

Advantages: An impartial party can set up a cohesive and aesthetically pleasing layout and still maintain perfect fairness.

Disadvantages: You have to find a third party who understands Warhammer and is unbiased towards the outcome.

HIDDEN SET-UP

• Both players set up terrain in an alternating fashion as normal.

• When the set-up is complete, both sides roll and the highest scorer chooses the table side.

• Armies are then deployed in a hidden fashion – this can either be achieved by placing a barrier (such as empty boxes) down the middle of the table or by each player making a map of his deployment zone and marking which units go where.

After both sides have finished their secret deployment, the barrier is removed or the maps are revealed. Once all models are placed on the table then which side goes first is decided as per standard.

Advantages: There is great shock and surprise value in not seeing any of your foe's set-up while doing your own. More emphasis must be placed on your own overall strategy as opposed to countering a foe's deployment plan.

Disadvantages: Hidden set-up requires a bit more effort and you must be prepared for barriers that wobble or displace terrain features or opponent's who forget to write down key units on their deployment map.

WHICH SET-UP METHOD?

Each set-up method has its own advantages, and finding the most agreeable method can lead to some enjoyable battles along the way.

Indeed, there are times when an equitable set-up is more desired than a themed battle or vice versa. It is as easy to imagine scouts going ahead of a main force and selecting terrain to a warlord's liking – say hills in a deployment zone for war machines to sit upon, or forests on a tableside to discourage outflanking manoeuvres. On the other hand, having to deal with the landscape as it stands in the heat of battle can be a particularly satisfying challenge to a commander.

This is the kind of map an Orcs & Goblins player might draw up to show the initial deployment of his units in a hidden set-up battle.

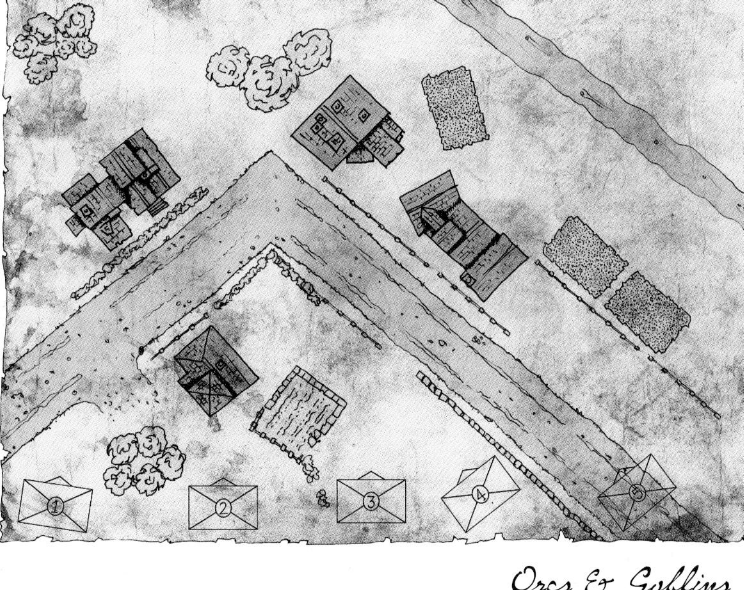

Orcs & Goblins hidden set-up

1. Unit of 12 Orc Boyz
2. Unit of 20 Savage Orcs
3. Unit of 25 Black Orcs
4. Unit of 25 Orc Boyz
5. Unit of 25 Orc Boyz

SCENARIOS

Warhammer scenarios are used when you want your battle to be something a bit different. Changing the 'story' of the battle affects where models are set up or even what the players must achieve to win.

The standard game of Warhammer, also known as a Pitched Battle, is described at the beginning of this rule book. Two players line up their armies opposite each other across the wargames table, then they begin the battle, playing out six turns. The army that has done the most damage to the enemy is deemed to be the winner.

You can imagine that both armies have approached the battlefield head on, made camp for the night and formed up their battle lines at dawn, steadily marching in battle array towards each other until they clash. The only strategy in the minds of the Generals is to smash the opposing army. In reality, this only represents one sort of battle. There are many others.

In the course of a war or a campaign, many battles will not be pitched battles, since a general will try to outwit his opponent with his strategy, leading his army by devious routes or luring his foe into a trap, for example. This can lead to one of many possible battle scenarios, such as an ambush, flank attack, encirclement or even a siege.

HOW SCENARIOS WORK

Scenarios are available from sources such as White Dwarf and the web, and three are given here. Essentially each scenario changes one, some or all of the aspects of the standard pitched battle.

Many scenarios change the terrain set-up. For example, if you mark out (or model) a river running between the two armies with a bridge in the middle, your game will become a battle to control this key crossing point. Equally, you can try games with lots more woods, hills or buildings than usual. These changes can have dramatic effects.

Some scenarios alter the deployment positions, perhaps starting with one army marching down a road while the other launches an ambush from the side. You could play down the length of the table instead of across it, or you could even start with one army completely surrounded.

Scenarios can also add special rules to better recreate a particular situation. For instance, part of one army may not deploy on the board – instead it arrives part way through the game, moving on from the side table edge to launch a flanking attack.

OUTNUMBERED BATTLES

The standard pitched battle and the points system are designed to pit two equal forces against each other in a fair fight. However, in the Warhammer world, army commanders seek any advantage over a foe and would eagerly bring a larger force to smash a weaker one. Some scenarios recreate this situation by matching a larger force against a smaller one.

When the points totals aren't matched, it stands to reason that the victory conditions must likewise be altered so both sides have a balanced chance to claim victory. There are any number of ways to turn mismatched games into entertaining and nail-biting battles where only the last moves of the last turn can reveal the ultimate victor. The smaller force may have to hold out until a relief force arrives to achieve victory, breakout from an encirclement, or destroy a certain proportion of the attacker's force.

INVENTING YOUR OWN SCENARIOS

You might also like to invent your own scenarios. We have suggested a lot of ideas here, and you'll find it's not hard to come up with more. The best place to start is to come up with a situation or story, then work out what changes to the pitched battle will fit your idea. Bear in mind that simple ideas are often the best – one or two changes may be all you need for a great game.

The hardest part is working out the victory conditions to ensure both sides have an equal chance of winning. It is also a good idea to play the scenario from both sides, so you can experience both attacking and defending, for example. This way you can try to outdo your opponent in the same situation.

THE LAST STAND

In this battle, a vastly outnumbered defender must sell the lives of his troops as dearly as possible.

Armies

Both armies are chosen to an agreed total, using the Warhammer army lists. The defender has half the points of the attacker. For example, 2,500 points of attackers would face 1,250 points of defenders.

Battlefield

Use the standard battlefield set-up (page 2) or any mutually agreeable manner.

Deployment

1) The defender must set up his army first, in an 18" square centred on the middle of the table. All of the units must face towards the same table edge. Scouts must be set up with the rest of the army.

2) The attacker then deploys his army. This may be set up anywhere at least 18" from a defending unit. Scouts may be set up at least 18" from the enemy.

Who goes first?

The defender goes first.

Length of Game

The battle lasts six game turns or until one player surrenders.

Special Rules

The defenders are expecting to die and so are immune to panic.

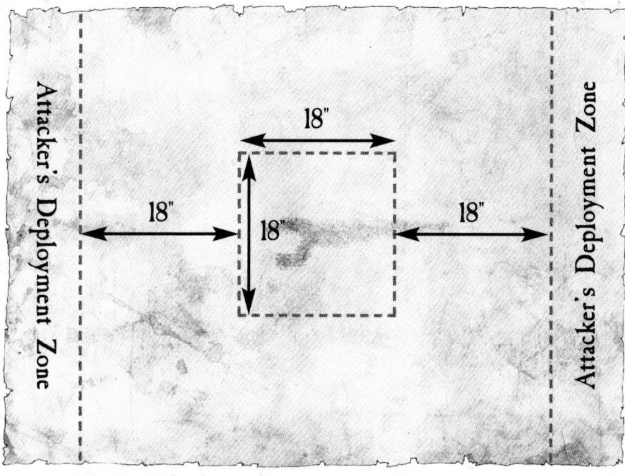

Victory Conditions

The battle is mismatched in points and so the victory conditions are also altered to fit. To determine which side may claim victory, calculate the defender's victory points as normal (see page 102).

If the defender's victory point total is more than their starting points value, it is a victory for the defenders. This is true even if the defenders are wiped out as they have slain enough of the enemy or held them up long enough to achieve glorious victory.

If the defender's victory points total is less than half of its starting points value then the attackers win.

Any other result is a draw.

A surge of Orcs threatens to overwhelm the last few Dwarven defenders.

BATTLEFIELD SUPREMACY

Two armies clash intending to wrest total control of the battlefield from the foe. Claiming the battlefield is more important than casualties.

Armies
Both armies are chosen to an agreed total, using the Warhammer army lists.

Battlefield
Use the standard battlefield set-up (page 2) or any mutually agreeable manner.

Deployment
Use the standard deployment (as described on page 2).

Who goes first?
Both players roll a dice and the player who rolls highest may choose to go first or second.

Length of Game
The battle lasts six game turns or until one side surrenders.

Victory Conditions
Normal victory points are NOT used in this scenario but instead the victor is determined as the army that claims more table quarters (as per the rule under victory points on page 102).

Alternatives
Territorial battles are a classic and challenging type of scenario. There are numerous simple but characterful options that can be used to refine your games – for example, replacing the board quarters with specific terrain items from your collection, such as hold the high ground (hills), claim a key road, or take the village. A special feature, if players choose to include one, could be treated as a tie-breaker in case of an equal number of claimed table quarters.

Skaven attempt to take control of a Lizardmen temple.

FLANK ATTACK

Thanks to superior tactics, scouting, or luck, one army begins the game in the advantageous position of outflanking its foe.

Armies

Both armies are chosen to an agreed total, using the Warhammer army lists. After armies have been chosen, players should agree or dice off to decide which side should be the attacker and which the defender.

Battlefield

Use the standard battlefield set-up (page 2) or any mutually agreeable manner.

Deployment

1) The defender may choose on which table side he will set up his forces and then deploys his entire army.

2) The attacker can then survey the battlefield and decide which (if any) of his units and/or characters will serve as his flanking force.

3) The attacker then sets up his entire non-flanking army on the opposite table edge from the defender.

4) Scouts may then be placed. If both sides have Scouts then the defender always places his first.

Who goes first

Both players roll a dice and the player who rolls highest may choose to go first or second.

Length of Game

The battle lasts six game turns or until one player surrenders.

Special Rules

At the start of the attacker's second turn he may roll to determine if the flanking force has arrived. On a roll of 4+ the flanking force turns up. If it does not turn up, roll again at the start of each subsequent turn, adding +1 to the dice roll for each roll after the first (so the flanking force will turn up on a roll of 3+ on the third turn, and so on).

Once the attacker has made a successful arrival roll, some or all of the units in the flanking force may be moved onto the table along any appropriate board space (see Flanking Zones on map).

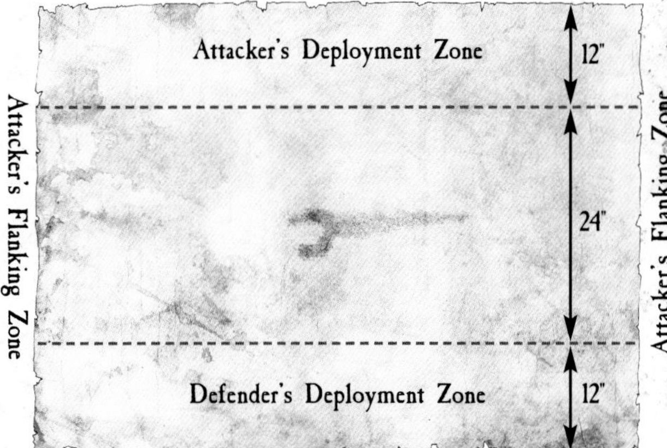

Units that turn up act exactly as units returning from pursuit off table (see page 43). Different units in a flanking force do not have to arrive at the same time or on the same flanking zone. Units that are not brought immediately onto the table after a successful arrival roll may be brought on board from either flanking zone in any of the attacker's remaining turns; there is no need for further rolls.

Victory Conditions

Victory points are determined as normal (see page 102) with the lone exception that the defender gains double the victory points for any units of the attacker's flanking force that are destroyed. Note that to count as destroyed, units must be wiped out completely, be fleeing at the end of the game or have fled the table. All other victory points are as normal, so for instance, the defender will not gain double points for each enemy unit from the flanking force that is reduced to half strength.

CAMPAIGNS

A campaign is a series of battles, linked by a story, a map or some other method. Many players enjoy inventing extra rules for spies, court intrigues, plagues, and logistics of all kinds.

There are countless types and configurations for campaigns such as map-based, narrative, or tree campaigns. They can involve just two players or dozens. In fact Games Workshop periodically runs worldwide campaigns in which thousands of gamers enter their battle results onto a website to determine the army that has done best overall!

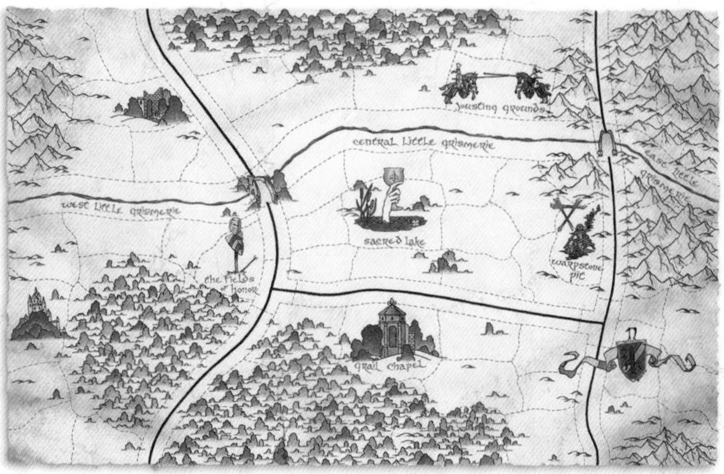

A campaign map set in the lands of Bretonnia.

MODELLING INSPIRATION

How to play campaigns could easily fill an entire supplement, and perhaps one day such an endeavour will be brought to light. In the meantime, it's suffice to say that campaigns are a way to interweave battles so that each game has some knock-on effect to the next.

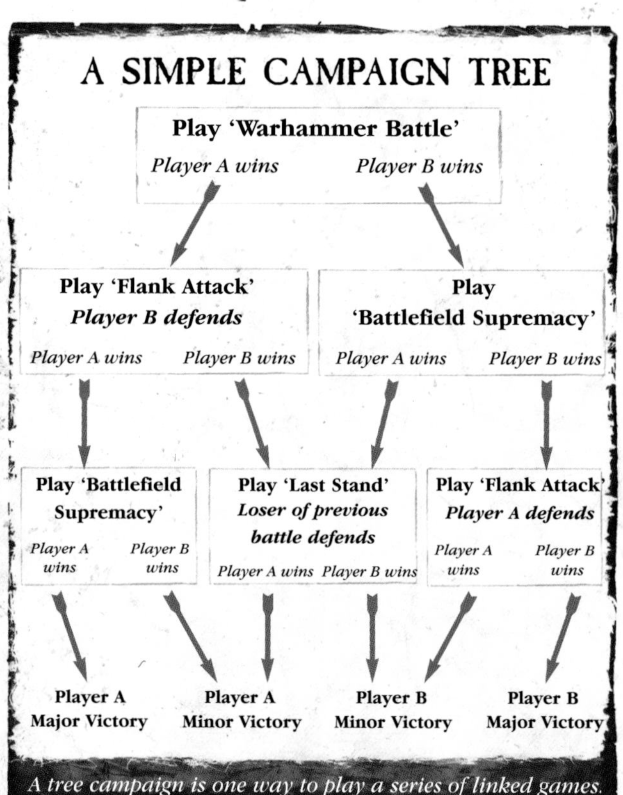

A tree campaign is one way to play a series of linked games.

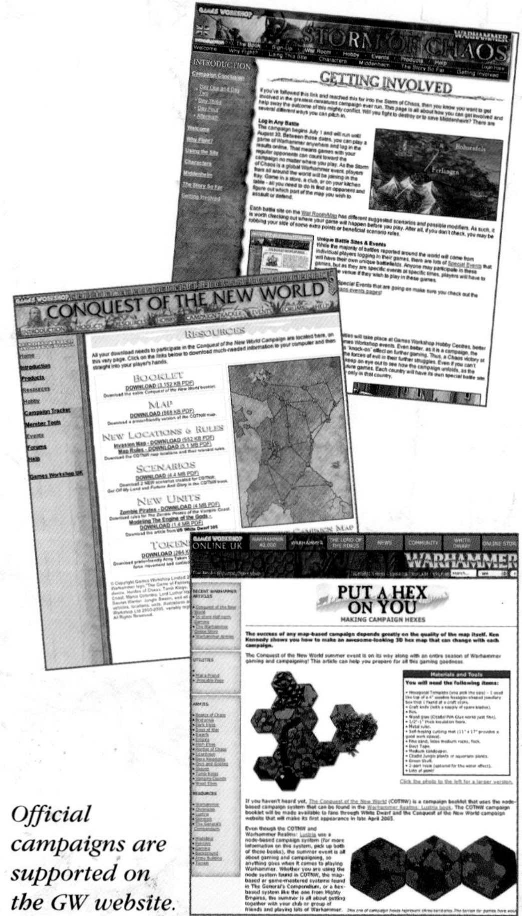

Official campaigns are supported on the GW website.

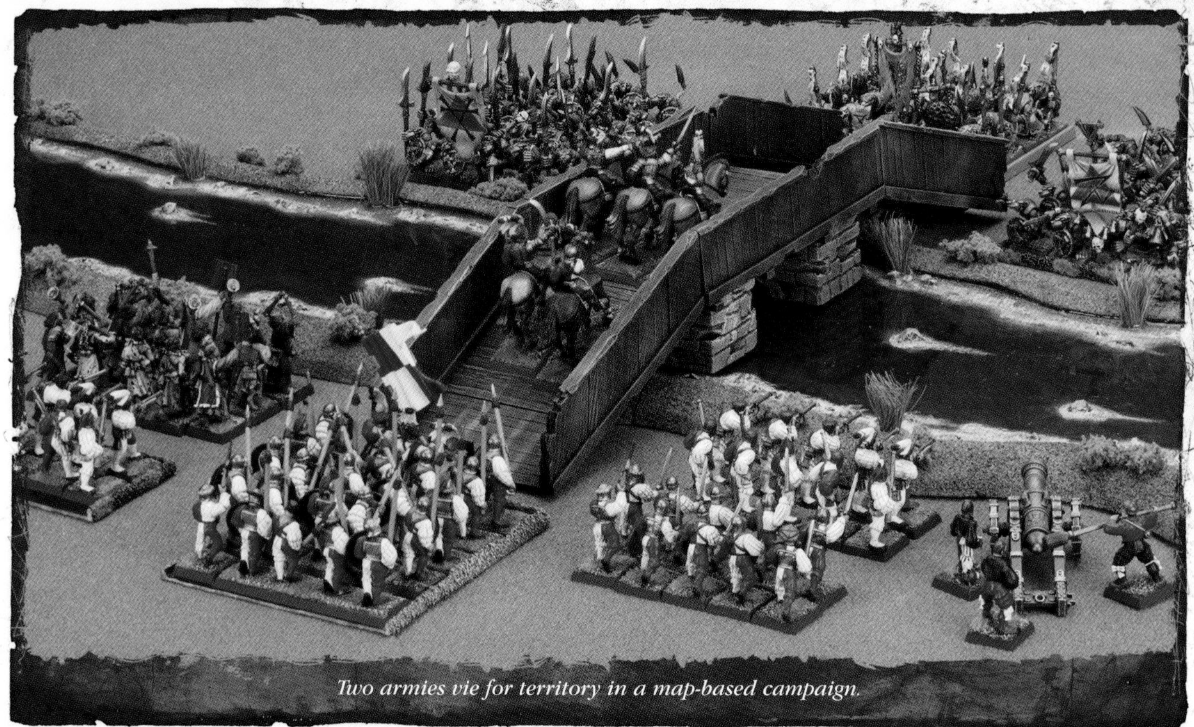

Two armies vie for territory in a map-based campaign.

This can be as simple as two linked scenarios played in a row, or as complex as a sprawling map campaign that plots out grand scale troop movement and supply chains long before the action ever gets to the tabletop.

As campaigns help to create more of a story than a single battle, they often inspire players to customise their armies or their terrain in some way. For instance, if your Black Orcs decimate a unit of Bretonnian knights, you might model Bretonnian shields and helmets adorning your Orc models as trophies taken from the battle. This will remind your opponent of his crushing defeat in every subsequent campaign game. This page shows some examples of models inspired by in-game events…

Over the course of a campaign, this Beastmen Champion has achieved so many mighty (and foul) deeds that the player has converted the model with a daemonic mutation.

The severed heads of your enemies make excellent totems, reminding you of past victories and grudges.

In a story-driven campaign you can make models or conversions of such things as loot or even unique magic items.

THIS WAY LIES MADNESS

The Warhammer world is vast, full of war and battles, sieges, raids and ambushes, invading hordes and lone adventurers, pirates and traps, dark rituals, plots, and insane inventions. All of this is yours to explore.

This brief section will offer inspiration for further possibilities. But beware, to tread further down these paths is to enter further into the Warhammer world itself, and, as the saying goes... here be dragons.

There is a vast world of gaming out there for you to experiment and try. Conversely, there is nothing wrong with having a favourite and sticking with it if that's what you enjoy. It's your world, conquer it as you see fit!

A converted steam-powered Dwarf battering ram, ready to pound down reinforced gates and enemy castle walls!

The desperate defenders of an Empire town attempt to fend off a Bloodthirster of Khorne.

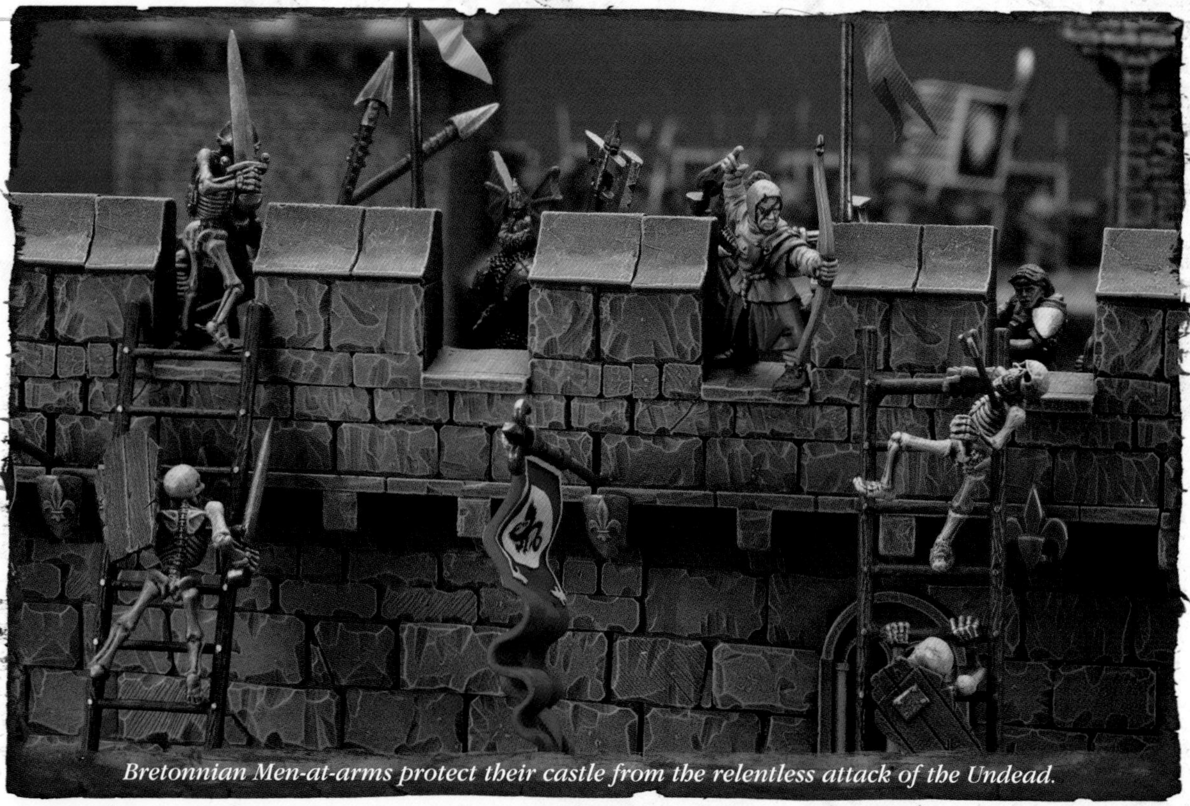

Bretonnian Men-at-arms protect their castle from the relentless attack of the Undead.

Night Goblins ambush Dwarf Miners in an underground tunnel fight.

A baggage train is too tempting a target for this Orcs & Goblins warband to pass up.

Blood on the high seas – merciless undead corsairs ply the waters off the Vampire Coast.

In a skirmish battle, a small band of Skaven Gutter Runners ambushes some Empire Militia.

Skaven and Empire armies clash over a recently landed warpstone meteorite.

GETTING MORE INVOLVED

One of the best things about Warhammer is the community that has sprung up around the hobby. There are a host of events, activities, and more where like-minded enthusiasts can meet to game, or just talk about the hobby.

Warhammer can be a very involved hobby and over the years the popularity of the game has soared. Indeed, it can be reliably said that Warhammer enthusiasts are everywhere and come from all walks of life, including students, real-life soldiers, university professors, professional business people and many others. Games have sprung up in schools after classes or during meal breaks, in officers' mess halls, in fire station houses, and nearly every corner of the world.

Whether you are just getting involved or are a long-time hobbyist, it's always fun to meet, game and talk with other enthusiasts. Here are some great ways to get more involved.

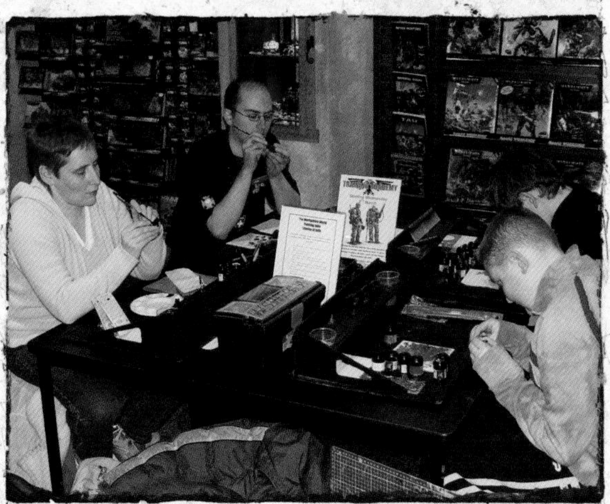

LOCAL GAMES SHOPS

Many Warhammer players are lucky enough to live near a Games Workshop store or independent retailer or hobby shop. In addition to being places to stock up on miniatures, paints and supplies, you can find out about upcoming gaming or hobby activities. Whether you are looking for a basic painting lesson, searching out veteran gamers to battle against, or seeking a nearby club to join, your local shop is an ideal starting point and can either help you directly or point you in the right direction.

GAMING CLUBS

Gaming is a social hobby and many like-minded enthusiasts gather together to form clubs. Clubs meet regularly to game, paint, build terrain or perhaps plan some future endeavor. By harnessing the passion and enthusiasm of many hobbyists together, clubs can achieve what no lone hobbyist could do – such as exceptionally large battles, vast campaigns, or spectacularly involved scenarios. Clubs come in all shapes and sizes and can range from very large and formal proceedings to small and casual get-togethers. A club can be three or more hobbyists who meet regularly at one player's house to game, or a large group that meets at a rented hall or gathers at gaming conventions to put on demonstration or display games. If there isn't a club in your area that fits your needs, why not consider starting one yourself? Even the largest club had to start with someone!

EVENTS & ACTIVITIES

Gaming shows or conventions are a great way to see a whole spectrum of hobby activities and meet a variety of fellow players. There are many different shows across the globe, some hosted by Games Workshop, but many by clubs and independent retailers. Many Warhammer fans enthusiastically await these events and mark them as highlights on their hobby calendars.

TOURNAMENTS

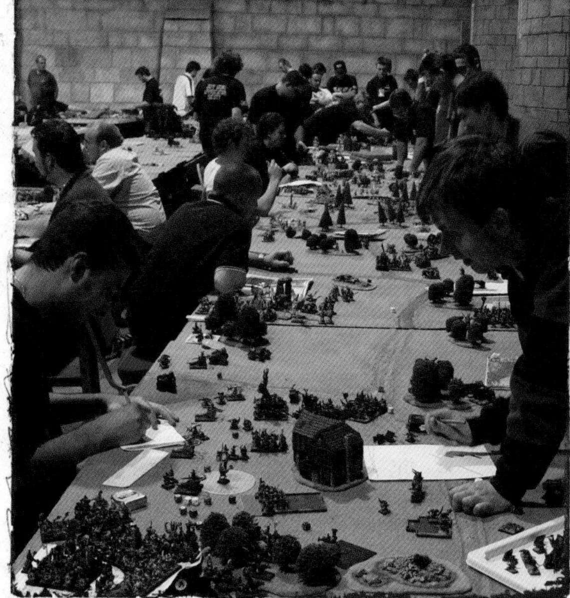

Many Warhammer players enjoy tournament play more than anything else. A tournament is a series of games where players test their tabletop mettle against other competitive players. In addition to finding the best of the best Warhammer Generals, a tournament is a great chance to show off fantastic paint jobs and cleverly themed armies.

There are numerous Warhammer tournaments across the globe. Many of these gaming events are put on by clubs, independent shops, or even as the main event at a large gaming convention. In many countries Games Workshop runs a particularly glorious event known as the Grand Tournament. These massive spectacles guarantee a high level of competition and camaraderie as hundreds of different Warhammer armies converge and compete to be the ultimate conquering commander.

GAMES DAYS

A Games Day is the pinnacle Games Workshop event where Warhammer and all our other games, figures, and the hobby in general are celebrated. Throughout the world there are many Games Days unique to the countries that host them. Currently you can find a Games Day in England, the United States, Canada, France, Germany and Spain.

Each Games Day will present a variety of activities to explore from special scenarios, massive games, awesome model displays, and the highly prestigious Golden Demon painting competition.

Left to right: Games Day 2000 limited edition model, admittance ticket, Golden Demon statuette, winning entry and painter.

FIND OUT MORE

 WHITE DWARF MAGAZINE

Each month White Dwarf magazine is jam-packed with the latest and greatest from Games Workshop. If you are a dedicated Warhammer fanatic you won't want to miss out on this full-colour assault on the broad spectrum of the hobby. Each issue brings a variety of articles on gaming, painting and a host of other hobby information, from tactics to terrain! You'll also find new release information and pictures of all the newest models painted by the world famous 'Eavy Metal team, as well as in-depth battle reports of real games.

News – All the latest on releases, upcoming events, and more.

Featured armies – Infamous Warhammer warlords and their beautifully painted armies.

Concept art – Sketches and background for your favourite armies and models.

By AXE & GUN

The Refused Flank

Volgrim's Steelfists

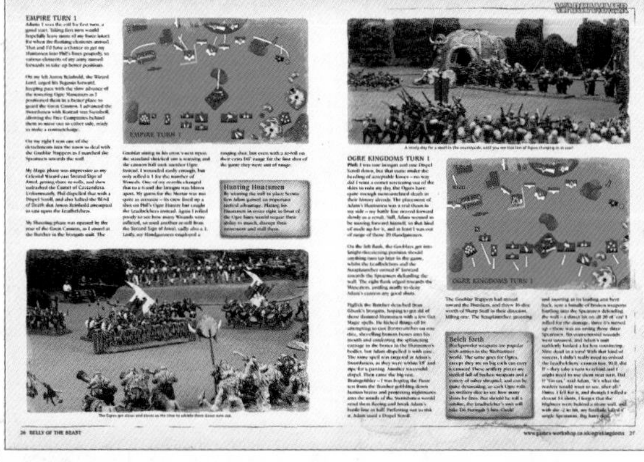
EMPIRE TURN 1

OGRE KINGDOMS TURN 1

Bretonnia, Land of Heroes

PAINTING BRETONNIAN HORSES

500 Points

ON TO 1,000 POINTS

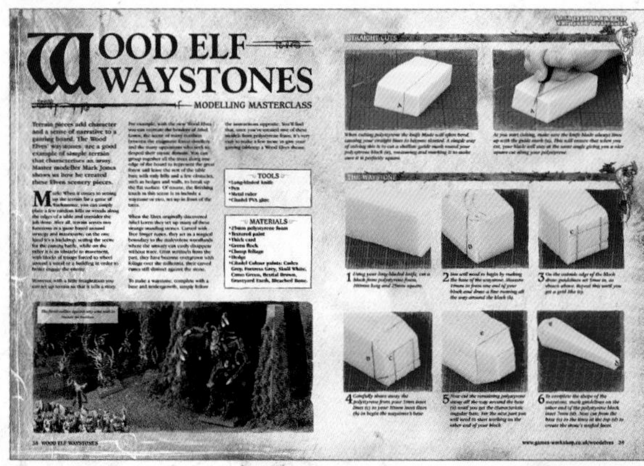
WOOD ELF WAYSTONES

MODELLING MASTERCLASS

BATTLE REPORTS

For well over a decade, one of the most popular White Dwarf article types has been the battle report. These articles offer blow-by-blow accounts of battles or games. The action in question could be an important historic battle from the world of Warhammer or perhaps a competitive match between two masterful tabletop Generals.

Battle reports offer tactical insight, a view into a commander's head during a fight and action-packed reading about the Warhammer world.

DON'T MISS:

Tactica articles – Hone your strategies to razor-fine perfection.

Painting tips – Great advice for everyone, from beginner to expert.

Modelling workshops – Turn your next project into a work of art!

Also – Terrain how-to articles, new fiction, scenarios, special rules, events coverage, interviews.

WARHAMMER ON THE WEB

Perhaps one of the best ways to find out more about Warhammer is to access the Games Workshop website. This vast reservoir of information has pictures of every Warhammer miniature currently available, painting guides, sample army lists, getting started information and lots more. You can also find additional articles, assembly guides, scenarios, previews of upcoming new releases and a library of fantastic hobby projects you can build yourself.

The Games Workshop website also has a store locator so players can find the Games Workshop store or independent retailer that is nearest to their home or travel destination. If no shops are nearby you can find the full range of products available on our safe and secure online store.

WWW.GAMES-WORKSHOP.COM

The above web address will take you to the global Games Workshop site. Once there you can select your home country and from then on that homepage will become your default setting. If you are travelling or want to brush up on your foreign language skills you can access any country's Games Workshop page by re-accessing the global site link.

EVENTS & DISCUSSION FORUMS

Other great aspects of the Games Workshop website are the Events listing and Community section. The Events listing posts dates and details for upcoming major events like Games Day or Grand Tournaments. The Community section has moderated public forums where players can meet online to discuss tactics, ask questions, or search for nearby foes.

DON'T MISS:

Getting Started sections for each army – Perfect for players seeking guidance on which force to collect.

Banners – To download, print out and paint yourself!

Step-by-step guides – For a host of Warhammer painting, converting and terrain-making projects.

New scenarios – Loads of new battles to try out.

Sample army lists – Read other gamer's army lists and see how they compose their forces.

BASIC CHARACTERISTICS

The characteristics given in the following lists allow you to start playing games of Warhammer straight away with your collection of Citadel miniatures. Once you have chosen which army you would like to collect, the next step is normally to buy the appropriate Armies book.

The Warhammer Armies books provide you with the points value of each of the models, allowing you to plan and build your army to a specific total points value. The points values are not given here, as they reflect many special rules that apply to each model and have not been included for the sake of simplicity.

In the Armies books you will also find powerful new units, such as Lord-level characters and Special Characters, mighty monsters such as Giants, and baroque war machines like the Empire Helblaster Volley Gun. Players can, of course, already field these models using the characteristics of a similar model from the following lists, until they buy the relevant Armies book (for example, you could use the model of the Emperor Karl Franz to represent an Empire Captain on a Griffon, or use the model of a Dwarf Flame Cannon with the characteristics and rules of a Dwarf Cannon).

To decide what weapons and armour each model has, take a good look at the miniature and then agree with your opponent what each model is equipped with.

Character models and their characteristics are in italics. If the model is a Wizard, it has a (W) next to its name (agree with your opponent which level it is and which Lore of Magic it is going to use).

Models marked with an asterisk (*) can fly.

EMPIRE

	M	WS	BS	S	T	W	I	A	Ld
Grand Master	*4*	*6*	*3*	*4*	*4*	*3*	*6*	*4*	*9*
Captain	*4*	*5*	*5*	*4*	*4*	*2*	*5*	*3*	*8*
Warrior Priest	*4*	*4*	*3*	*4*	*4*	*2*	*4*	*2*	*8*
Master Engineer	*4*	*3*	*4*	*3*	*3*	*2*	*3*	*1*	*7*
Battle Wizard (W)	*4*	*3*	*3*	*3*	*3*	*2*	*3*	*1*	*7*
Warhorse	8	3	0	3	3	1	3	1	5
Pegasus*	8	3	0	4	4	3	4	2	6
Griffon*	6	5	0	5	5	4	5	4	7
Halberdier	4	3	3	3	3	1	3	1	7
Spearman	4	3	3	3	3	1	3	1	7
Swordsman	4	4	3	3	3	1	4	1	7
Handgunner	4	3	3	3	3	1	3	1	7
Crossbowman	4	3	3	3	3	1	3	1	7
Free Company	4	3	3	3	3	1	3	1	7
Archer	4	3	3	3	3	1	3	1	7
Knight	4	4	3	3	3	1	3	1	8
Greatsword	4	4	3	3	3	1	3	1	8
Pistolier	4	3	3	3	3	1	3	1	7
Great Cannon	–	–	–	–	7	3	–	–	–
Mortar (stone thrower)	–	–	–	–	7	3	–	–	-
Flagellant	4	2	2	3	4	1	3	2	10

WOOD ELVES

	M	WS	BS	S	T	W	I	A	Ld
Noble	*5*	*6*	*6*	*4*	*3*	*2*	*7*	*3*	*9*
Branchwraith (W)	*5*	*6*	*0*	*4*	*4*	*2*	*8*	*3*	*8*
Spellsinger (W)	*5*	*4*	*4*	*3*	*3*	*2*	*5*	*1*	*8*
Elven Steed	9	3	0	3	3	1	4	1	5
Warhawk*	1	4	0	4	3	–	5	1	5
Unicorn	10	5	0	4	4	3	5	2	8
Great Stag	9	5	0	5	4	3	4	2	7
Great Eagle*	2	5	0	4	4	3	4	2	8
Forest Dragon*	6	6	0	6	6	6	3	5	8
Glade Guard	5	4	4	3	3	1	5	1	8
Glade Rider	5	4	4	3	3	1	5	1	8
Warhawk Rider	5	4	4	3	3	1	5	1	8
Eternal Guard	5	5	4	3	3	1	5	1	9
Dryad	5	4	3	4	4	1	6	2	8
Wardancer	5	6	4	3	3	1	6	1	8
Wild Rider	5	5	4	4	3	1	5	1	9
Tree Kin	5	4	0	5	5	3	3	3	8
Treeman	5	5	0	6	6	6	2	5	9
Waywatcher	5	4	5	3	3	1	5	1	8

DWARFS

	M	WS	BS	S	T	W	I	A	Ld
Thane	*3*	*6*	*4*	*4*	*5*	*2*	*3*	*3*	*9*
Dragon Slayer	*3*	*6*	*3*	*4*	*5*	*2*	*4*	*3*	*10*
Runesmith	*3*	*5*	*4*	*4*	*4*	*2*	*3*	*2*	*9*
Master Engineer	*3*	*4*	*5*	*4*	*4*	*2*	*2*	*2*	*9*
Warrior/Ranger	3	4	3	3	4	1	2	1	9
Quarreller	3	4	3	3	4	1	2	1	9
Thunderer	3	4	3	3	4	1	2	1	9
Miner	3	4	3	3	4	1	2	1	9
Troll Slayer	3	4	3	4	4	1	2	1	10
Longbeard	3	5	3	4	4	1	2	1	9
Hammerer	3	5	3	4	4	1	2	1	9
Ironbreaker	3	5	3	4	4	1	2	1	9
Cannon	–	–	–	–	7	3	–	–	–
Bolt Thrower	–	–	–	–	7	3	–	–	–
Grudge Thrower (stone thrower)	–	–	–	–	7	3	–	–	–
Gyrocopter*	0	4	0	4	5	3	2	2	9

WARRIORS OF CHAOS

	M	WS	BS	S	T	W	I	A	Ld
Lord of Chaos	*4*	*8*	*3*	*5*	*5*	*3*	*8*	*5*	*9*
Sorcerer (W)	*4*	*5*	*3*	*4*	*4*	*2*	*5*	*1*	*8*
Chaos Steed	8	3	0	4	3	1	3	1	5
Daemonic Mount	8	4	0	5	5	3	5	2	8
Dragon of Chaos*	6	6	0	6	6	6	3	6	8
Warrior of Chaos	4	5	3	4	4	1	5	1	8
Marauder	4	4	3	3	3	1	4	1	7
Marauder Horseman	4	4	3	3	3	1	4	1	7
Knight of Chaos	4	5	3	5	4	1	5	1	8
Warhound of Chaos	7	4	0	3	3	1	3	1	5
Chariot of Chaos	–	–	–	5	5	4	–	–	–
Chaos Warrior	–	5	–	4	–	–	5	1	8
Chaos Steed	8	3	–	4	–	–	3	1	–

BRETONNIANS

	M	WS	BS	S	T	W	I	A	Ld
Paladin	*4*	*5*	*3*	*4*	*4*	*2*	*5*	*3*	*8*
Damsel (W)	*4*	*3*	*3*	*3*	*3*	*2*	*3*	*1*	*7*
Warhorse	8	3	0	3	3	1	3	1	5
Pegasus*	8	3	0	4	4	3	4	2	7
Hippogryph*	8	4	0	5	5	4	4	4	8
Knight Errant	4	3	3	3	3	1	3	1	7
Knight of the Realm	4	4	3	3	3	1	3	1	8
Pegasus Knight	4	4	3	3	3	1	4	1	8
Questing Knight	4	4	3	4	3	1	4	1	8
Grail Knight	4	5	3	4	3	1	5	2	9
Man-at-arms	4	2	2	3	3	1	3	1	5
Peasant Bowman	4	2	3	3	3	1	3	1	5
Battle Pilgrim	4	2	2	3	3	1	3	1	8
Mounted Yeoman	4	3	3	3	3	1	3	1	6
Field Trebuchet (stone thrower)	–	–	–	–	7	4	–	–	–

DARK ELVES

	M	WS	BS	S	T	W	I	A	Ld
Noble	*5*	*6*	*6*	*4*	*3*	*2*	*7*	*3*	*9*
Beastmaster	*5*	*4*	*4*	*3*	*3*	*2*	*6*	*2*	*8*
Assassin	*6*	*9*	*9*	*4*	*3*	*2*	*10*	*3*	*10*
Sorcerer (W)	*5*	*4*	*4*	*3*	*3*	*2*	*5*	*1*	*8*
Dark Steed	*9*	*3*	*0*	*3*	*3*	*1*	*4*	*1*	*5*
Cold One	7	3	0	4	4	1	3	1	3
Dark Pegasus*	8	3	0	4	4	3	4	2	7
Manticore*	6	5	0	6	5	4	3	4	7
Black Dragon*	6	6	0	6	6	6	3	5	8
Warrior	5	4	4	3	3	1	5	1	8
Crossbowman	5	4	4	3	3	1	5	1	8
Warrior	5	4	4	3	3	1	5	1	8
Shade	5	4	4	3	3	1	5	1	8
Witch Elf	5	5	4	3	3	1	6	1	8
Harpy*	4	3	0	3	3	1	4	1	6
Executioner	5	5	4	3	3	1	5	1	8
Black Guard	5	5	4	3	3	1	6	1	9
Dark Rider	5	4	4	3	3	1	5	1	8
Cold One Knight	5	5	4	3	3	1	6	1	8
Cold One Chariot	–	–	–	5	5	4	–	–	–
Dark Elf	–	4	4	3	–	–	5	1	8
Cold One	7	3	–	4	–	–	3	1	–
War Hydra	6	4	0	5	5	6	2	5	6
Beastmaster Apprentice	5	4	4	3	3	1	5	1	8
Bolt Thrower	–	–	–	–	7	3	–	–	–

HIGH ELVES

	M	WS	BS	S	T	W	I	A	Ld
Commander	*5*	*6*	*6*	*4*	*3*	*2*	*7*	*3*	*9*
Mage (W)	*5*	*4*	*4*	*3*	*3*	*2*	*5*	*1*	*8*
Elven Steed	9	3	0	3	3	1	4	1	5
Griffon*	6	5	0	5	5	4	5	4	7
Great Eagle*	2	5	0	4	4	3	4	2	8
Dragon*	6	6	0	6	6	6	3	5	8
Spearman	5	4	4	3	3	1	5	1	8
Archer	5	4	4	3	3	1	5	1	8
Seaguard	5	4	4	3	3	1	5	1	8
Phoenix Guard	5	5	4	3	3	1	6	1	9
Swordmaster	5	6	4	3	3	1	5	1	8
White Lion	5	5	4	4	3	1	5	1	8
Shadow Warrior	5	4	4	3	3	1	5	1	8
Ellyrian Reaver	5	4	4	3	3	1	5	1	8
Silver Helm	5	4	4	3	3	1	5	1	8
Dragon Prince	5	5	4	3	3	1	6	1	9
Bolt Thrower	–	–	–	–	7	3	–	–	–
Tiranoc Chariot	–	–	–	5	4	4	–	–	–
High Elf	–	4	4	3	–	–	5	1	8
Steed	9	3	–	3	–	–	4	1	–

VAMPIRE COUNTS

	M	WS	BS	S	T	W	I	A	Ld
Vampire Count (W)	*6*	*7*	*5*	*5*	*5*	*3*	*7*	*4*	*9*
Wight Lord	*4*	*4*	*3*	*4*	*4*	*2*	*4*	*3*	*9*
Wraith	*4*	*3*	*0*	*3*	*7*	*2*	*2*	*2*	*7*
Necromancer (W)	*4*	*3*	*3*	*3*	*3*	*2*	*3*	*1*	*7*
Nightmare (horse)	8	2	0	3	3	1	2	1	5
Zombie Dragon*	6	3	0	6	6	6	1	4	4
Winged Nightmare*	6	4	0	5	5	4	2	3	5
Skeleton	4	2	2	3	3	1	2	1	3
Zombie	4	2	2	3	3	1	1	1	2
Ghoul	4	2	2	3	4	1	3	2	6
Bat Swarms*	1	3	0	2	2	5	1	5	10
Dire Wolf	9	3	0	3	3	1	3	1	6
Grave Guard	4	3	3	4	4	1	3	1	8
Black Knight	4	3	3	4	4	1	3	1	8
Fell Bat*	1	3	0	3	3	2	3	2	6
Spirit Host	6	2	0	3	7	4	1	4	6
Banshee	6	3	0	3	7	2	4	2	8
Black Coach	–	–	–	5	6	5	–	–	9
Wraith	–	3	0	3	–	–	2	2	–
Nightmare	8	2	–	3	–	–	2	1	–

OGRE KINGDOMS

	M	WS	BS	S	T	W	I	A	Ld
Tyrant	*6*	*5*	*3*	*5*	*5*	*4*	*3*	*4*	*8*
Butcher (W)	*6*	*3*	*2*	*4*	*5*	*4*	*2*	*3*	*7*
Ogre Bull	6	3	2	4	4	3	2	3	7
Leadbelcher	6	3	2	4	4	3	2	3	7
Irongut	6	3	2	4	4	3	2	3	8
Gnoblar	4	2	3	2	3	1	3	1	5
Hunter	6	5	4	5	5	4	3	4	8
Sabretusk	6	4	0	4	4	2	4	3	4
Gnoblar Trapper	4	2	3	2	3	1	3	1	5
Scraplauncher	–	–	–	5	5	4	–	–	–
Gnoblar	–	2	–	2	–	–	3	1	5
Rhinox	6	3	–	5	–	–	2	3	–
Yhetee	7	3	0	5	4	3	4	3	7
Gorger	6	3	0	5	5	4	2	4	10
Maneater	6	4	4	5	4	3	3	4	9

BEASTS OF CHAOS

	M	WS	BS	S	T	W	I	A	Ld
Doombull	*6*	*6*	*3*	*5*	*5*	*4*	*5*	*5*	*9*
Wargor	*5*	*5*	*3*	*4*	*4*	*2*	*5*	*3*	*7*
Bray-shaman (W)	*5*	*4*	*3*	*3*	*4*	*2*	*4*	*2*	*6*
Gor	5	4	3	3	4	1	3	1	6
Ungor	5	3	3	3	3	1	3	1	6
Bestigor	5	5	3	4	4	1	3	1	7
Minotaur	6	4	3	4	4	3	4	3	8
Tuskgor Chariot	–	–	–	5	4	4	–	–	–
Bestigor	–	4	–	4	–	–	3	1	7
Ungor	–	3	–	3	–	–	3	1	–
Tuskgor	7	3	–	3	–	–	2	1	–
Warhound of Chaos	7	4	0	3	3	1	3	1	5
Dragon Ogre	7	4	0	5	4	4	2	3	8
Shaggoth	7	6	0	5	5	6	4	5	9
Chaos Troll	6	3	1	5	4	3	1	4	4

SKAVEN

	M	WS	BS	S	T	W	I	A	Ld
Grey Seer (W)	*5*	*3*	*3*	*3*	*4*	*3*	*5*	*1*	*6*
Assassin	*6*	*6*	*5*	*4*	*4*	*2*	*8*	*3*	*8*
Chieftain	*5*	*5*	*5*	*4*	*4*	*2*	*6*	*3*	*6*
Master Moulder	*6*	*5*	*5*	*4*	*4*	*2*	*6*	*3*	*6*
Warlock Engineer (W)	*5*	*3*	*3*	*3*	*3*	*2*	*4*	*1*	*5*
Plague Priest	*5*	*5*	*3*	*4*	*5*	*2*	*5*	*3*	*5*
Clanrat	5	3	3	3	3	1	4	1	5
Stormvermin	5	4	3	3	3	1	5	1	5
Night Runner	6	3	3	3	3	1	5	1	6
Globadier	5	3	3	3	3	1	4	1	5
Packmaster	6	3	3	3	3	1	4	1	5
Giant Rat	6	3	0	3	3	1	4	1	3
Rat Swarm	6	3	0	2	2	5	1	5	10
Plague Monk	5	3	3	3	4	1	3	1	5
Clanrat Slave	5	2	2	3	3	1	4	1	2
Jezzail	5	3	3	3	3	1	4	1	5
Gutter Runner	6	4	4	3	3	1	5	1	7
Rat Ogre	6	3	0	5	4	3	3	3	5
Censer Bearer	5	3	3	3	4	1	3	1	5

ORCS & GOBLINS

	M	WS	BS	S	T	W	I	A	Ld
Black Orc Big Boss	4	6	3	5	5	2	3	3	8
Orc Big Boss	4	5	3	5	5	2	3	3	8
Savage Orc Big Boss	4	5	3	5	5	2	3	3	8
Orc Shaman (W)	4	3	3	3	4	2	2	1	7
Sv Orc Shaman (W)	4	3	3	3	4	2	2	1	7
Goblin Big Boss	4	4	3	4	4	2	3	3	7
Night Gob Big Boss	4	4	3	4	4	2	4	3	6
Gob Shaman (W)	4	2	3	3	3	2	2	1	6
Nt Gob Shaman (W)	4	2	3	3	3	2	3	1	5
Boar	7	3	0	3	4	1	3	1	3
Wolf	9	3	0	3	3	1	3	1	3
Giant Spider	7	3	0	3	3	1	4	1	2
Wyvern*	4	5	0	6	5	5	3	3	6
Orc Boy	4	3	3	3	4	1	2	1	7
Savage Boy	4	3	3	3	4	1	2	1	7
Arrer Boy (archer)	4	3	3	3	4	1	2	1	7
Goblin	4	2	3	3	3	1	2	1	6
Wolf Rider	4	2	3	3	3	1	2	1	6
Spider Rider	4	2	3	3	3	1	2	1	4
Night Goblin	4	2	3	3	3	1	3	1	5
Snotlings	4	2	0	2	2	3	2	3	10
Black Orc	4	4	3	4	4	1	2	1	8
Boar Boy	4	3	3	3	4	1	2	1	7
Savage Boar Boy	4	3	3	3	4	1	2	1	7
Squig	4	4	0	5	3	1	3	2	3
Boar Chariot	–	–	–	5	5	4	–	–	–
Orc	–	3	–	3	–	–	2	1	7
Boar	7	3	–	3	–	–	3	1	–
Wolf Chariot	–	–	–	5	4	3	–	–	–
Goblin	–	2	3	3	–	–	2	1	6
Wolf	9	3	–	3	–	–	4	1	–
Spear Chukka (bolt thrower)	–	–	–	–	7	3	–	–	–
Rock Lobber (stone thrower)	–	–	–	–	7	3	–	–	–
Troll	6	3	1	5	4	3	3	3	5

TOMB KINGS

	M	WS	BS	S	T	W	I	A	Ld
Tomb Prince (W)	4	5	4	4	5	3	3	3	9
Icon Bearer	4	4	3	4	4	2	3	2	8
Liche Priest (W)	4	3	3	3	3	2	2	1	8
Skeletal Steed	8	2	0	3	3	1	2	1	5
Skeleton	4	2	2	3	3	1	2	1	3
Skeleton Archer	4	2	2	3	3	1	2	1	3
Skeleton Horseman	4	2	2	3	3	1	2	1	5
Tomb Swarms	4	3	0	2	2	5	1	5	10
Chariot	–	–	–	4	4	3	–	–	–
Charioteer	–	3	0	3	–	–	2	1	7
Steed	8	2	–	3	–	–	2	1	–
Tomb Guard	4	3	3	4	4	1	3	1	8
Ushabti	5	4	0	6	4	3	3	3	10
Tomb Scorpion	7	4	0	6	5	4	3	4	8
Carrion*	2	3	0	3	4	2	3	2	4
Bone Giant	6	3	0	6	5	6	1	4	8
Screaming Skull Catapult (stone thrower)	–	–	–	–	7	3	–	–	–

LIZARDMEN

	M	WS	BS	S	T	W	I	A	Ld
Slann Mage-Priest (W)	4	4	3	3	6	6	2	1	9
Saurus Scar-veteran	4	5	0	5	4	2	3	4	8
Skink Chief	6	4	4	4	3	2	5	3	6
Skink Shaman (W)	6	2	3	3	2	2	4	1	5
Cold One	7	3	0	4	4	1	2	1	3
Saurus Warrior	4	3	0	4	4	1	1	2	8
Cold One Rider	4	4	0	4	4	1	1	2	8
Temple Guard	4	4	0	4	4	1	2	2	8
Jungle Swarm	5	3	0	2	2	5	1	5	10
Skink	6	2	3	3	2	1	4	1	5
Kroxigor	6	3	0	5	4	3	1	3	7
Chameleon Skink	6	2	4	3	2	1	4	1	6
Salamander	6	3	3	5	4	3	4	2	5
Skink Handler	6	2	3	3	2	1	4	1	5

DAEMONS OF CHAOS

	M	WS	BS	S	T	W	I	A	Ld
*Daemon Prince (W)**	6	8	0	5	5	4	8	5	9
*Bloodthirster**	6	10	0	7	6	7	10	7	9
*Lord of Change (W)**	6	6	0	6	6	6	10	5	9
Keeper of Secrets (W)	8	9	0	6	6	6	10	6	9
Great Unclean One (W)	4	8	0	6	6	10	4	6	9
Bloodletter	4	5	0	5	3	1	4	2	8
Plaguebearer	4	4	0	4	4	1	4	1	8
Daemonette	5	4	0	4	3	1	5	2	8
Horrors	4	2	0	3	3	1	3	1	8
Flesh Hound	7	5	0	4	3	1	4	2	8
Nurglings	4	3	0	3	3	4	2	4	8
Flamer	6	2	0	4	4	1	4	2	8
Screamer*	1	3	0	4	4	2	4	2	8
Fury*	4	4	0	4	3	1	4	1	6

CHAOS DWARFS

	M	WS	BS	S	T	W	I	A	Ld
Hero	3	6	4	4	4	2	3	3	10
Sorcerer (W)	3	4	3	3	4	2	2	1	9
Bull Centaur Hero	8	5	3	4	5	2	4	4	9
Hobgoblin Hero	4	5	3	4	4	2	3	3	7
Wolf	9	3	0	3	3	1	3	1	3
Warrior	3	4	3	3	4	1	2	1	9
Blunderbuss	3	4	3	3	4	1	2	1	9
Hobgoblin	4	3	3	3	3	1	2	1	6
Sneaky Git	4	3	3	3	3	1	2	1	6
Hobgoblin Wolf Rider	4	3	3	3	3	1	2	1	6
Orc Boy	4	3	3	3	4	1	2	1	7
Goblin	4	2	3	3	3	1	2	1	6
Earthshaker (stone thrower)	–	–	–	–	7	3	–	–	–
Bolt Thrower	–	–	–	–	7	3	–	–	–
Bull Centaur	8	4	3	4	4	1	3	2	9
Black Orc	4	4	3	4	4	1	2	1	8

Note: The Chaos Dwarfs do not have an Armies book in print at the time of writing. See the Games Workshop website for more information.

REFERENCE

THE TURN

1. **START OF THE TURN PHASE**
2. **MOVEMENT PHASE**
3. **MAGIC PHASE**
4. **SHOOTING PHASE**
5. **CLOSE COMBAT PHASE**

MOVEMENT PHASE

1. DECLARE CHARGES
If you want any of your troops to charge, you must declare this at the very start of the movement phase.

2. RALLY FLEEING TROOPS
If any of your troops are fleeing, you can attempt to rally them after declaring charges.

3. COMPULSORY MOVES
Move troops that are subject to a compulsory movement rule.

4. MOVE CHARGERS
Move charging troops and resolve other movement resulting from the charge.

5. REMAINING MOVES
Move the rest of your troops.

SHOOTING PHASE

- Declare the ranges at which all guess-range weapons are firing.
- Resolve the firing of all guess-range weapons, in any order you wish.
- Resolve the firing of all units equipped with missile weapons that do not require you to guess the range, in any order you wish.
- The opposing player makes any Panic tests required (as explained in the Psychology section on page 48).

Ballistic Skill	**1**	**2**	**3**	**4**	**5**	**6**	**7**	**8**	**9**	**10**
To Hit score	6	5	4	3	2	1	0	-1	-2	-3

To Hit Modifiers
+1 Shooting at large target
-1 Shooting while moving
-1 Stand & shoot
-1 Shooting at long range
-1 Shooting at a single model or skirmishers
-1 Target is behind soft cover
-2 Target is behind hard cover

7+ To Hit

Score needed to hit	**Dice rolls needed**
7	6 then 4, 5 or 6
8	6 then 5 or 6
9	6 then 6
10	Impossible!

CLOSE COMBAT PHASE

- Pick any one of the combats on the table and resolve it, following the sequence given below.
- Pick another combat and resolve it.
- Continue like this until all combats are resolved.

HOW TO RESOLVE COMBATS

1. Fight Combat
Models in base contact with the enemy will fight, as explained in the rules that follow.

2. Combat Result
Work out which side has won the combat and by how much. If the fight is not a draw, the losing side will have lost by 1, 2 or more 'points'.

3. Break Test
Each unit on the losing side must take a Break test.

Any units failing their Break test are deemed 'broken' and will run away.

4. Flee & Pursue
Units that have broken must flee away from their enemy.

Units whose enemies have broken and fled that turn are allowed to pursue them and might possibly catch and destroy them.

5. Redress Ranks
Units are tidied up, ready to continue the battle.

COMBAT RESULT BONUS

Situation	Bonus
Extra rank	+1 per rank after the first (maximum+3)
Outnumber enemy	+1
Battle standard	+1
Standard	+1
High ground	+1
Flank attack	+1
Rear attack	+2
Overkill	+1 per excess wound (maximum+5)

ARMOUR

Unarmoured	No Save
Light armour	6+
Heavy armour	5+
Shield	+1
Barding	+1
Mounted	+1

Armour Save Modifiers

Strength of hit	Save modifier
3 or less	None
4	-1
5	-2
6	-3
7	-4
8	-5
9	-6
10	-7

MAGIC PHASE

1. Generate Power Dice & Dispel Dice
2. Cast
3. Dispel
4. Spell Fails or Spell Succeeds
5. Repeat Steps 2 to 4
6. Dispel Spells in Play

MAXIMUM CASTING DICE CHART

Wizard Level	Maximum Number of Dice
Level 1	2
Level 2	3
Level 3	4
Level 4	5

POWER DICE

The player whose turn it is generates power dice as follows:

Power dice pool:	2 dice
Each Level 1 Wizard:	1 dice
Ech Level 2 Wizard:	2 dice
Each Level 3 Wizard:	3 dice
Each Level 4 Wizard:	4 dice

DISPEL DICE

The player whose turn it is generates dispel dice as follows:

Dispel dice pool:	2 dice
Dwarf army:	+2 dice
Each Runesmith:	+1 dice
Each Runelord:	+1 dice
For each Level 1 Wizard:	+1 dice
For each Level 2 Wizard:	+1 dice
For each Level 3 Wizard:	+2 dice
For each Level 4 Wizard:	+2 dice

MISCAST TABLE

2D6	Result
2	The Wizard is annihilated and immediately removed as a casualty, regardless of any protective magic item or special rule he might have. Models in base contact, friend or foe (including the Wizard's monster or chariot mount), suffer one Strength 10 hit (no armour saves allowed) as their flesh mutates and their soul is sucked away.
3-4	The Wizard and all models in base contact with him (including his monstrous mount or chariot) suffer a Strength 6 hit, with no armour saves allowed.
5-6	The opposing player may immediately cast any one of his own spells. No casting roll is required – the spell is automatically cast – but it can be dispelled by the player whose turn it is as normal (by using power dice in the same way as dispel dice). He needs to beat the basic casting value of the spell to dispel it.
7	The caster suffers one Strength 2 hit (no armour saves allowed), loses all his remaining power dice and cannot do anything else during this magic phase.
8-9	The caster suffers one Strength 4 hit (no armour saves allowed). In addition, all spells currently in play on the entire battlefield are automatically dispelled and the magic phase ends. All power and dispel dice stored in magic items are also lost.
10-11	The caster suffers one Strength 8 hit (no armour saves allowed) and loses a Wizard level (the spell lost must be the one he just attempted to cast). If the caster reaches Level 0, he stops counting as a Wizard and therefore will not be able to use any arcane magic items he is carrying (see the Magic Items section) and will generate no power/dispel dice.
12	The spell the caster attempted is successful and counts as having been cast with irresistible force, but after this the caster forgets how to cast the spell and will not be able to cast it again during this battle.

TO HIT CHART

Opponent's Weapon Skill

Attacker's Weapon Skill	1	2	3	4	5	6	7	8	9	10
1	4	4	5	5	5	5	5	5	5	5
2	3	4	4	4	5	5	5	5	5	5
3	3	3	4	4	4	4	5	5	5	5
4	3	3	3	4	4	4	4	4	5	5
5	3	3	3	3	4	4	4	4	4	4
6	3	3	3	3	3	4	4	4	4	4
7	3	3	3	3	3	3	4	4	4	4
8	3	3	3	3	3	3	3	4	4	4
9	3	3	3	3	3	3	3	3	4	4
10	3	3	3	3	3	3	3	3	3	4

TO WOUND CHART

Opponent's Toughness

Attacker's Strength	1	2	3	4	5	6	7	8	9	10
1	4	5	6	6	N	N	N	N	N	N
2	3	4	5	6	6	N	N	N	N	N
3	2	3	4	5	6	6	N	N	N	N
4	2	2	3	4	5	6	6	N	N	N
5	2	2	2	3	4	5	6	6	N	N
6	2	2	2	2	3	4	5	6	6	N
7	2	2	2	2	2	3	4	5	6	6
8	2	2	2	2	2	2	3	4	5	6
9	2	2	2	2	2	2	2	3	4	5
10	2	2	2	2	2	2	2	2	3	4

SINGLE MODELS

The following chart summarises the many subtle ways in which different single models relate to the Movement rules when they are moving on their own. Where models are ranked into units, they follow the normal rules for unit movement, except for skirmishers, flyers and fast cavalry, which follow the rules detailed in their own sections.

Basically, single models move in two different ways, depending on their type (see chart below):

As Monsters: No need to turn or wheel – can pivot on the spot with no penalty but behave like units in all other respects (90° arc of sight, pay penalties for difficult terrain/obstacles and have clear flanks and rear).

As Skirmishers: No need to turn or wheel, can pivot on the spot with no penalty, 360° arc of sight for charges, etc, no penalties for difficult terrain/obstacles, will line up to formed units charging them and not vice versa, and do not have front/flanks/rear until engaged in close combat.

SINGLE MODEL MOVEMENT CHART

Model Type	Movement
Roughly Man-sized Square 20/25 mm base On foot	As skirmishers
Up to and including Ogre-sized* Square 40/50 mm base On foot	As monsters
Monster (larger than Ogre-sized)** Any base/no base	As monsters
Cavalry*** 25 x 50 mm base	As monsters
Chariots	As monsters (may not march)
Ridden monsters/chariots	As monsters/ chariots

** Includes Swarms, Chaos Spawn, etc.*
*** Includes Great Eagles, Stegadons, Giants, etc.*
**** Includes Chaos Hounds, Dire Wolves etc.*

FLYERS

Units of flyers and flying cavalry move as skirmishers. They cannot fly inside woods even if they move as skirmishers.

Single flying models follow the rules for their type on the chart (eg, skirmishers, monsters, etc), except they have a 20" flying move, as described in the Flyers section.

WAR MACHINES

Move as skirmishers, with the exceptions noted in their rules.

LAST MAN STANDING

The last surviving model of a unit of infantry with a unit strength of 1 is treated in all respects like a skirmisher.

The last surviving model of a unit of infantry with a unit strength of more than 1 or of a unit of cavalry is treated in all respects like a monster (except that characters may still join it to form a unit).

INDEX

CHARTS AND TABLES

CREDITS

Writers
Alessio Cavatore, Gav Thorpe,
Jeremy Vetock, Dominic Murray & Graham Davey

Original Material
Rick Priestley

Illustrations
John Blanche, Alex Boyd, Paul Dainton,
David Gallagher, Nuala Kinrade,
Karl Kopinski, Adrian Smith & Geoff Taylor

Graphics
Alun Davies

Maps
Nuala Kinrade

Hobby Material
Dave Andrews, Andy Hoare, Neil Hodgson,
Mark Jones, Chad Mierzwa,
Dominic Murray & Adrian Wood

Citadel Miniatures Designers
Tim Adcock, Mike Anderson, Juan Diaz,
Martin Footitt, Jes Goodwin, Mark Harrison,
Alex Hedström, Gary Morley, Aly Morrison,
Trish Morrison, Brian Nelson, Alan Perry,
Michael Perry, Steve Saleh & Dave Thomas

'Eavy Metal Painters
Fil Dunn, Pete Foley, Neil Green, Neil Langdown,
Darren Latham, Keith Robertson, Anja Wettergren
& Kirsten Williams

Production
Michelle Barson, Simon Burton, Jon Cave, Chris Eggar,
Marc Elliott, Talima Fox, Kris Jaggers, John Michelbach,
Dylan Owen, Mark Owen, Adam Shaw,
Kris Shield, Ian Strickland & Nathan Winter

Thanks to...
John Blanche, Alan Merrett,
Jervis Johnson & The Geeks

UK	US	Australia	Canada	Northern Europe
Games Workshop,	Games Workshop,	Games Workshop,	2679 Bristol Circle,	Games Workshop,
Willow Rd,	6711 Baymeadow Drive,	23 Liverpool Street,	Unit 3,	Willow Rd,
Lenton,	Glen Burnie,	Ingleburn	Oakville,	Lenton,
Nottingham,	MD	NSW 2565	Ontario	Nottingham,
NG7 2WS	21060-6401		L6H 6Z8	NG7 2WS

Product Code: 60 04 02 99 026 **Games Workshop world wide web-site:** www.games-workshop.com ISBN: 1 84154 759 X

TEMPLATES

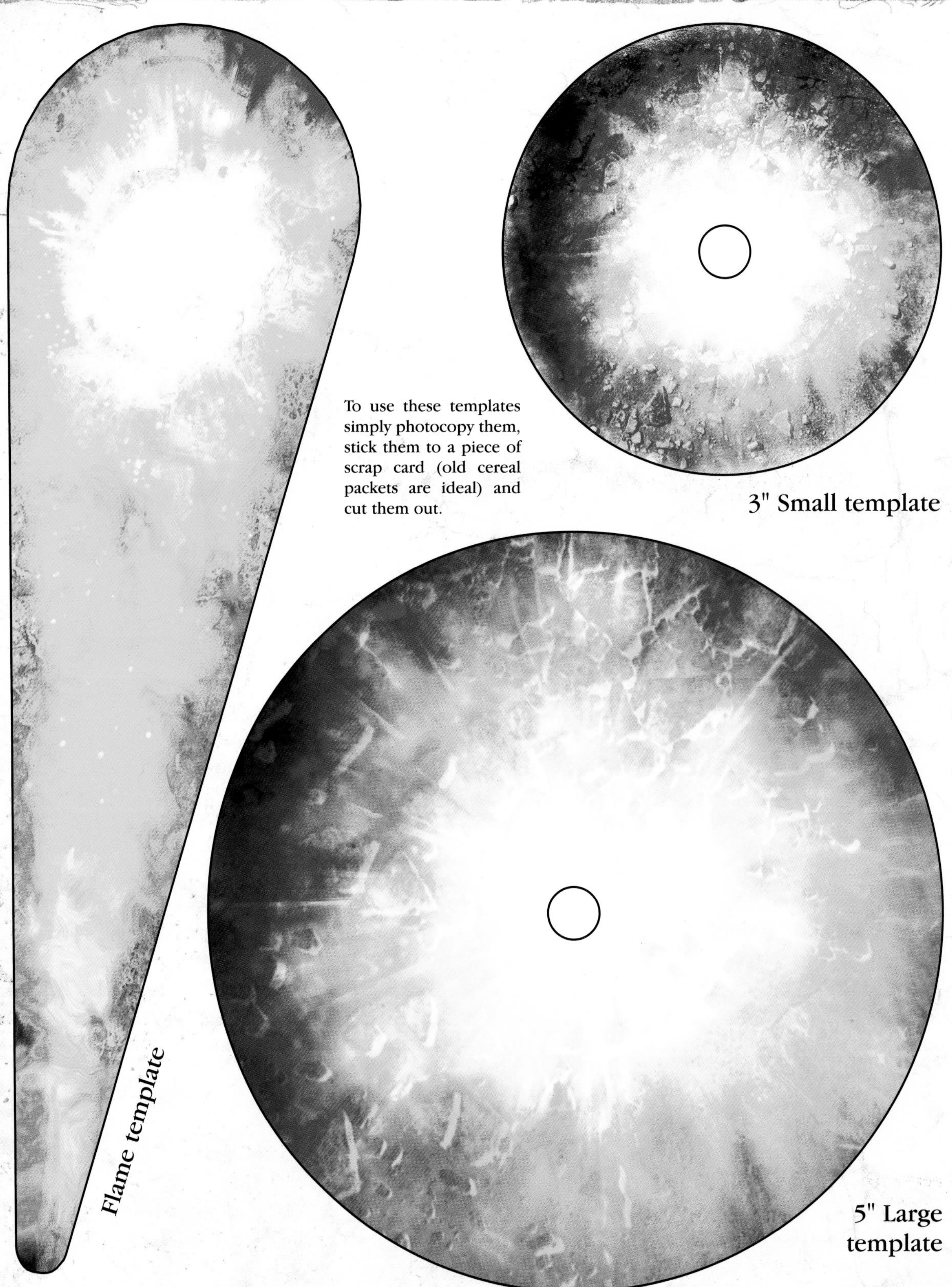

To use these templates simply photocopy them, stick them to a piece of scrap card (old cereal packets are ideal) and cut them out.